THE
SURVIVAL
FACTOR

Also by Stanley A. Blumberg and Gwinn Owens:

ENERGY AND CONFLICT:
THE LIFE AND TIMES OF EDWARD TELLER

THE
SURVIVAL
FACTOR

ISRAELI
INTELLIGENCE
FROM
WORLD WAR I
TO THE
PRESENT

STANLEY A. BLUMBERG
AND GWINN OWENS

G.P. Putnam's Sons, New York

To Herbert B. Cahan,
who introduced us,
and Bradford Jacobs,
who published our first joint article.

Library of Congress Cataloging in Publication Data

Blumberg, Stanley A.
  The survival factor.

  Bibliography: p.
  Includes index.
  1. Intelligence service—Israel. 2. Spies—
Israel. 3. Zionism—History. I. Owens, Gwinn.
II. Title.
UB251.I78B56 1981   327.1'2'095694   81-8618
ISBN 0-399-12646-5

AACR2

PRINTED IN THE UNITED STATES OF AMERICA

ACKNOWLEDGMENTS

A book with the broad scope of this one must of necessity draw upon the generosity of hundreds of people. We cannot hope to thank adequately, or even name them all, but some are deserving of special mention.

Our Putnam editor, Elisabeth Jakab, skillfully combined enthusiasm with exacting standards, to bring us through to completion of the manuscript. She was preceded by Edward T. Chase, editor of our first book and originator of the concept for this one, whose talents were such that he was lured away to become head of another major publishing house. We were briefly the beneficiaries of the kind counsel of Judy Wederholt before Ms. Jakab took over.

Of the contributors to the substance of the book, our first debt is to Boris Guriel, a veteran secret agent and first chief of political intelligence in Israel. Mr. Guriel submitted to many hours of interviews and then contributed thousands of words of written recollections. Isser Harel, the most famous of Israeli intelligence chiefs, also made a large contribution in a lengthy interview. Nachum Bernstein, a "teacher" of spies, provided some of this book's most amazing and amusing anecdotes. The late Ruth Klüger recounted in detail her rescue of Jews from Europe before World War II, as did William Perl, who was involved in a similar enterprise. Mose Speert contributed many details of the gathering of arms for Israel in Baltimore and elsewhere. Other adventures of the immediate postwar period were related by Joshua Palmon, Yaacov Meridor, Shlomo Hillel, Yehuda Tagger, and the late Amihi Paglin.

Dr. Bernard Reich of George Washington University helped us acquire the necessary historical background on Middle East intelligence. Dr. Joseph Baumgarten of Baltimore Hebrew College supplied much of the biblical

underpinning of the Jewish quest for survival, and Dr. Robert Freedman of the same institution brought us up to date on relations between Israel and the Soviet Union.

Sources connected with United States defense or intelligence services who helped us include Major General George Keegan, former chief of Air Force Intelligence; Joseph Churba, former Middle East specialist with Air Force Intelligence; Lieutenant Colonel Ray Hamilton of Air Force Intelligence; and Ray Cline, former deputy director of the Central Intelligence Agency.

We are also grateful to Simcha Dinitz, former Israeli ambassador to the United States; Abba Eban, former Israeli ambassador to the United Nations and foreign minister; Chaim Herzog, another former UN ambassador; Admiral Moshe Tabak; Navy Captain Mila Brenner; Admiral Shlomo Erell; Arie Eliav; Major General Avraham Adan; William Braiterman; Rivka Gur-Arie; Shimon Peres, former defense minister; Norbert Grunwald, who translated documents from the German for us; Dr. Daniel Bass; Dr. Yuval Ne'eman; Mohammed Haki, information officer of the Egyptian embassy in Washington; Mordechai Hacohen; Pinhas Zusman, former Israeli director-general of defense; Yaakov Caroz; Eugene Blum; Shlomo Gur; Shula Lasnitski; Edward Teller; Jerold C. Hoffberger, who arranged an introduction to Chaim Vinitisky of the Jewish Agency in Jerusalem, who, in turn, arranged several key interviews; Harry Steinberg of the American Zionist Federation; and last but not least, Bernard Kiewe, director of the Baltimore chapter of the Jewish National Fund.

Institutions from which we obtained valuable information include the Library of Congress, the Jabotinsky Institute of Tel Aviv, the Baltimore Hebrew College library, and the Enoch Pratt Free Library of Baltimore.

Acknowledgments to wives are often pro forma. In this case, however, they are well earned. Berty Blumberg reviewed and typed most of the early drafts of this book; she was, in a word, indispensable. Joan Owens, applying her craft as an English teacher, called our attention to misplaced commas and run-on sentences. Both are gifted with the patient disposition that makes it possible for husbands to be writers. The four Owens children likewise lent their encouragement and seldom interrupted.

To those mentioned and unmentioned who made this book possible go our sincerest thanks. For the use we made of their contributions, however, we accept full responsibility.

Stanley A. Blumberg
Gwinn Owens
Baltimore, May 1981

Contents

Introduction

THIS IS A story of the survival of a people, as ensured thus far by the desperately innovative intelligence services of Israel. We have purposely not written about some of the most reported tales of Israeli intelligence, such as the capture of Adolf Eichmann or the rescue of the hostages at Entebbe, which have been well reported in previous books and articles. Instead, we have chosen to focus on unusual and thus-far unreported events for the new light they shed on the survival motive behind the Israeli secret services.

The struggle is only beginning. As this book goes to press, Israeli intelligence faces its greatest challenge—the threat from enemies who are acquiring, or seeking to acquire, the means to produce nuclear weapons. For tiny Israel, the prospect of such a threat is not unthinkable, for the very reason that its intelligence services must constantly think about it. And obviously, for the rest of the world, more than Israel's survival is at stake. A Middle East nuclear war could bring the world to the brink of annihilation.

Consider what is happening as we write. American intelligence sources believe Pakistan will have a nuclear weapon by 1982, and Iraq, by 1983. The great threat to Israel—and Egypt—will come when the intractable Colonel Muammar Qaddafi of Libya receives his first nuclear weapon from Pakistan. The strong man of Tripoli has financed and provided the raw material for Pakistan's nuclear development program, and Pakistan will be expected to pay for Qaddafi's help.

Uranium oxide is mined in Niger and transported by truck across the border to Libya. From there it is transshipped to Pakistan. President Anwar el-Sadat of Egypt is concerned that when the bomb is delivered to Qaddafi, Cairo, rather than Jerusalem, will be the first target. His fears are well grounded. On several occasions Qaddafi has conspired to have Sadat assas-

13

sinated and, at least once, the plan failed because Israeli intelligence warned Sadat of his danger. Sadat can expect no respite. Ever since the president of Egypt agreed to the Camp David peace accords with Israel, Qaddafi has considered him a traitor who deserves to die.

The other reason why Cairo may be the preferred target for annihilation is that Israel almost certainly has the capacity to retaliate in kind. Qaddafi's actions, however, have seldom been predictable or even rational, and he may yet regard Jerusalem as the better target.

This common threat to the survival of Israel and Egypt has led to an uneasy cooperation between their intelligence services. The twin objectives of their services are, first, to monitor the development of the Pakistani bomb and, second, when it is created, to destroy it before it can be used. This would involve intercepting the weapon while it is being delivered, or destroying it after its arrival in Libya.

Late in November 1980 the Egyptian ambassador to Washington was asked, "What will your country do when Qaddafi takes delivery of the bomb?" His response: "Let me ask you a question. What will your government do? It is also your problem. If Washington does not act, the oil fields of the Middle East could go up in flames."

The Reagan administration is already cooperating with Israel and Egypt in the gathering of intelligence about the progress of nuclear-bomb development in the Middle East but is not involved in the execution of the plan to destroy the nuclear weapon. This would be left to the exquisite talents of the Israeli intelligence services, possibly with help from the Egyptians. In any event, American-supplied intelligence may contribute to the thwarting of Qaddafi's ambitions.

The alternative to destruction of a bomb after it has been developed would be for Egypt to eliminate Qaddafi and possibly even invade and annex the Libyan state. Obviously the thought has crossed the mind of the Egyptian leadership, regarding both short-term protection from the dangerous designs of Qaddafi and Egypt's long-term economic security. Libya's oil is coveted by Egypt as a source of wealth to gird up its fragile economy and help feed its 40 million people (there are only 3 million Libyans). Further, conquest of Libya would eliminate one of the Palestine Liberation Organization's main paymasters and reduce Soviet influence in North Africa. The prospect of such a move by Egypt is by no means unlikely. As this book goes to press, Sadat's armies have made feinting moves toward Egypt's neighbor to the west. Whether Israel is, or would be, involved is an unanswered question.

An equally serious, and in many ways more dangerous, threat to Israel comes from the growing regional power of Iraq. President Saddam Hussein, Iraq's aggressive leader, is trying to extend his sphere of influence, especially in the Persian Gulf region. With the assistance of France, Iraq is engaged in a sophisticated nuclear-arms development program. Paris has delivered to Baghdad its most advanced research reactor and a supply of enriched (92-percent fissionable) uranium that can easily be converted to 97-percent-fissionable, or weapons-grade, uranium. The French reactor can also be used to

produce plutonium for nuclear weapons. There is no doubt that Saddam Hussein expects to build a bomb.

Nor is France his only friend in the West. Italy, which imports one-fifth of its oil from Iraq, has sold this volatile state a radiochemistry laboratory that can reprocess fuel elements and, in so doing, extract plutonium. Brazil has also agreed to barter oil for nuclear technology. A $10 billion contract with Iraq provides for the construction of nuclear power plants, technical expertise, and slightly enriched uranium that can be converted to weapons-grade uranium.

Israeli intelligence sources interpret Iraq's striving for the ultimate weapon as part of that country's strategy aimed at the total obliteration of the Jewish state. It is accompanied by other ominous developments, such as the building of highways that run to the Syrian and Jordanian borders and an increasing concentration of MIG-23 fighter planes on Iraq's western frontier.

Hence, despite all of the ingeniousness and courage described in this book, we send it off to the printer with a sense of foreboding; for although Israel's intelligence has been successful—astoundingly so—in ensuring the Jewish state's survival thus far, we know that its achievements in the past must be surpassed. For Israel there is no other way.

Editor's note: The above was written before the destruction by the Israeli Air Force of the Iraqi nuclear reactor in June 1981.

"And Moses sent them to spy out the land of Canaan, and said unto them, Get you up this way southward, and go up into the mountain:

"And see the land, what it is; and the people that dwelleth therein, whether they be strong or weak, few or many;

"And what the land is that they dwell in, whether it be good or bad; and what cities they be that they dwell in, whether in tents or in strong holds;

"And what the land is, whether it be fat or lean, whether there be wood therein, or not. And be ye of good courage, and bring of the fruit of the land."

Numbers 13:17–20

1

The Survival Factor

Zionism was fathered by a vision, mothered by necessity, and nurtured by political and military intelligence. The vision is almost as old as Judaism, the necessity was made acute by Adolf Hitler, and the intelligence explains to a great degree why the State of Israel exists today.

At one particular moment in August 1938, in Vienna, William Perl was aware in the most personal sense of the Zionist necessity. Perl was feeling the barrel of a pistol pressed against his stomach.

"Tell me who it is," said Perl's adversary, "or I'll give you a second belly button."

The finger on the trigger belonged to Adolf Eichmann. Perl sensed correctly that the future agent of Hitler's "final solution" was not, at this point, ready to commit a solitary murder. Only a few months had passed since the *Anschluss*, the Nazi annexation of Austria. Perl, the Jewish lawyer, and Eichmann, the still-minor Nazi functionary, were cooperating; they needed each other. As chief of the Austrian branch of the Office of Jewish Emigration, Eichmann wanted to get the Jews out of Austria. For different reasons, so did Perl: he knew that escape was necessary to avoid persecution, although he was not yet aware that the persecution would eventually be supplanted by annihilation.

But Eichmann, in his pretentious S.S. uniform, was trying to extract a price for his cooperation. Austrian Jews, even before the *Anschluss*, had been boycotting German goods. To the Nazi mind, such an outrage could not be spontaneous. As a condition of the expatriation negotiations, Eichmann demanded the names of the boycott's instigators.

Perl, even with a pistol against his stomach, could not answer, because he

17

did not know. He could only pit his courage and his sense of logic against the possibility of instant death.

"Put away your gun. You and I have more important things to do."

Eichmann laughed heartily at his own joke about the second belly button and put the gun back in his desk drawer.

The gun was, in truth, an instrument of humiliation. Eichmann could use it as a toy in threatening Perl, and a Jew was in no position to protest. In this instance, the Nazi was the host. His office was in one of the sumptuous halls of the Rothschild Palace, the commandeered and looted home of the wealthy Jewish banking family. Eichmann was willing to see Perl, because Perl could serve his purposes. The Jewish lawyer had organized a system for transporting his beleaguered compatriots away from the Nazi menace. With Eichmann's passive support he was herding frightened families onto Danube riverboats. At the Danube's mouth in the Black Sea the huddled refugees were transferred to ships that ran the British blockade of Palestine, defying His Britannic Majesty's decree against Jewish immigration into the Promised Land.

In 1938 Eichmann's talent for genocide was still untapped. Before long, his pathological anti-Semitism would so endear him to the Führer that he would become chief of the Jewish Department of the Gestapo. In that role he would perpetrate horrors so appalling as to block the mind's ability to accept them; he was the mad scientist of a Niagara of nightmares come true. Even though by 1939 Perl had supervised the escape of some forty thousand Jews and even though other, similarly dedicated people would guide perhaps one hundred thousand more out of danger, their best efforts still left 6 million or more at Eichmann's mercy. Next to Hitler, Eichmann was, to Jews, the most odious of Nazis. Hitler, however, died in the holocaust he had created. Eichmann, that giant among history's butchers, escaped.

Fifteen years after the end of World War II a pitiable figure lay blindfolded on a bed in a suburban house near Buenos Aires. He was a prisoner in a hideout, the captive of the State of Israel. An efficient and dedicated corps of secret intelligence agents had ended one of the great manhunts of all time by tracking him down, ending his routine, middle-class existence in Argentina, ten thousand miles from Germany.

The helpless prisoner accepted his fate. His concern was for his family. "How will my wife and sons live?"

His guard was not without compassion. "No harm will come to them. They'll manage all right without you. But tell me, please, you who worry so much about *your* children, how could you and your colleagues murder little children in the tens and hundreds of thousands?"

The prisoner was willing to respond. "Today I don't understand how we could have done such things. I was always on the side of the Jews. I was striving to find a satisfactory solution to their problem. I did what everybody else was doing—I wanted to get on in life."

Thus did Eichmann explain away 6 million murders. The conversation is reported by Isser Harel in his book, *The House on Garibaldi Street*. Harel, the

most celebrated of Israeli intelligence agents, was Chief Executive of the Secret Services. He had masterminded the tracking-down, identification, capture, and secret removal from Argentina of Eichmann. It was a massive operation, involving dozens of agents, two years, and millions of dollars. Eichmann was tried and convicted in an Israeli court and executed in accordance with Israeli law.

Psychologists are still debating whether Eichmann possessed a grossly demented personality or whether he was a cowering bureaucrat deferring to the demented Nazis above him. For historical purposes the argument is academic. What is significant is the symbolism of his capture, trial, and death. Ordered by Hitler to expunge all Jews from the earth, he was brought to justice by the authorities of an organized parliamentary democracy, the Jews of the world coalesced into a thriving nation. In spite of the overwhelming Nazi power turned against the Jews and even though one out of every two of them in Europe died, the Jewish people had survived. The Nazis, who had boasted of their Thousand-Year Reich, had not.

Survival—it is a word that seems to define the Jews more than any other ethnic group on the face of the earth. Thirty-five hundred years ago the Jews were one small tribe eking out a mean existence in a hostile climate on the eastern shore of the Mediterranean. There were, in equal or greater numbers, Assyrians, Babylonians, Phoenicians, Philistines, Samaritans, Canaanites, Sumerians, and Hittites, just to name a few. Each was conquered or exiled and eventually assimilated or obliterated. The Jews, too, have been repeatedly conquered and exiled, but they have never been more than partially assimilated and, obviously, never obliterated. From all of those ancient tribes, they alone survive as a definable ethnic unit.

Why? For the Jews, what has been the survival factor? What special quality set them apart so as to assure their continuity? Presumably they have no special inborn characteristics or acquired will. At best, the reasons for Jewish survival are a matter for speculation and are probably based on a coincidental combination of factors. Most historians put a strong emphasis on the concept of monotheism—belief in the single, transcendent, omnipotent God, devoid of the human passions of the pagan gods. He is a god whose presence requires no idols and no temples. He is a "portable" deity, as historian Max Dimont describes Him, always present in the consciousness of every believer, and whose word—the Bible—verifies His existence. Hence, the worldwide dispersal of the Jews did not destroy their religious structure nor the cultural heritage that is an intrinsic part of it.

That cultural heritage has been especially viable because the nature of the Jewish faith is such that it has imposed a minimum of strictures on freedom of thought and will. For many Christians, as indeed for adherents of most major religions, every human act is ordained by God as part of His plan. Allowing for a degree of theological oversimplification, it may be said that a Jew is, within certain limits, free to act as he pleases but is strictly accountable to God.

This kind of freedom provides an immense stimulus to intellectual inquiry, resulting in a strong emphasis on education and cultural growth. Per-

haps the best example of the effect of this came with the clash of Greek culture with the Hebraic tradition in the late fourth century B.C. Alexander the Great had conquered most of the peoples of the Eastern Mediterranean world, including the Jews. He was a disseminator of the Greek ideas that had flowered under Pericles a century earlier. Greek culture was heavy with philosophical insight but also with a sensuality that was anathema to the ascetic moral code of the Jews. To Dimont, "The Greeks regarded Jews as barbarians without manners, and the Jews viewed the Greeks as heathens without morals."

While the Jews generally eschewed Greek hedonism, they enthusiastically explored the sophisticated ideas on government, philosophy, science, and aesthetics that were spread by the Greek conquerors. The Jews were able to partake of this intellectual splendor without poisoning their fundamental moral and religious nature. This is but one early example of a process that has continued throughout Jewish history.

The refusal of most Jews to walk the last mile into a surrounding culture has provided them with internal strength but has provoked external hostility. Even as they emerged as thinkers and scholars, adherence to their religious tradition has made them victims of the characteristic human suspicion of a neighbor who is different. Suspicion begets resentment and resentment begets hostility. Hostility means danger, which has been a living presence for most Jews. Since their first dispersal from their native soil, they have been subject to laws that restrict their rights. Such restrictions have been capricious: no Jew has ever known what to expect from his host society. Hence, a Jew's intellectual achievements have been applied not only to the general good but also to protecting himself and his family from oppression and often from violence. He has had to outthink, outguess, outwork, and, if possible, outwit his oppressors. Usually his numbers were too small for physical defense. His defense was his intelligence.

In choosing the word *intelligence*, the authors are purposely employing a term that has both broad and narrow meanings. Intelligence is the sum total of intellectual attainments. *Intelligence*, usually preceded by an adjective such as *military, political*, or *secret*, describes the information gathered in order to assess the capability or intent of one's enemies or potential enemies.

The important point is that to gather intelligence in the narrow sense demands intelligence in the broad sense. Jewish intellectual vitality therefore provides a sound basis from which to build an effective military and political intelligence system—hence the acclaim given to the modern Israeli intelligence system, often described as the best in the world. Perhaps for Israel, intelligence (combining both meanings) truly is the survival factor.

After the astounding defeat of three enemies on three fronts in the Six-Day War in June 1967, an embittered editor of the Arab paper *El Sabua el Araby* wrote of Israel, "Intelligence preceded the state, and in order to understand one, we must learn the other."

To follow the Arab's advice, the student of intelligence must go all the way back to the Bible. In assessing the relationship of the Jews to the Scrip-

tures, Christians often fall into the error of equating it with their own reverence for the Bible. As important as the Scriptures are to Christian teaching, the identification by Christians with biblical events is far less intimate and direct than it is among the Jews. It is not unusual to hear a rabbi refer to Old Testament figures as "our ancestors." He means this in the same sense that twentieth-century Americans refer to their great-grandparents. The connection is unbroken and personal, somehow transcending the passage of millennia.

The Book of Numbers describes how Moses sent agents of the Israelites into the Promised Land of Canaan to "see what the land is like, and whether the people who live there are strong or weak . . . and whether the cities in which they live are weakly defended or well fortified." These "spies" (the Bible does not use that word), one man from each of the Twelve Tribes of Israel, returned to their base in the Sinai to report that "the land . . . floweth with milk and honey . . . the people be strong . . . and the cities are walled and very great."

Caleb, from the tribe of Judah, wanted to risk attempting to seize the land anyway. Joshua agreed with Caleb, but the other ten leaders were afraid: "We will not be able to go up against the people; for they are stronger than we."

There are theological overtones to the failure of the Israelites to attack; perhaps they were of insufficient faith. In any case, having missed this opportunity, they spent forty years in the desert, awaiting the chance to try again. When Moses was near death, the Israelites moved northward to the lowlands of Moab, directly across the Jordan River from the city of Jericho. Moses died in sight of the Promised Land, and God called upon Joshua to assume the leadership. By divine order, Joshua was to cross the Jordan and reclaim the land stretching from Lebanon on the north to the Sinai desert on the south and from the Mediterranean on the west to the Euphrates on the east.

Once again the Israelites hesitated until Joshua could obtain sufficient military and political intelligence. In this instance the Bible does use a word that is logically translated as *spies*, to describe the two tribesmen selected by Joshua to slip into the city of Jericho. Their mission proved to be successful, although highly unconventional.

Pretending to be Canaanites, the two agents visited the house of a sympathetic prostitute, Rahab. Even as they entered her house, however, a few local citizens suspected that they were strangers and reported the incident to the king of Jericho. Two soldiers of the king were shortly knocking on Rahab's door. They demanded to know if she had admitted strangers into her dwelling. Rahab had, in fact, hidden them in her attic, but she lied to the soldiers and misdirected them down the road toward the Jordan.

Amazingly, the king's agents believed her and set off in futile pursuit. When they were out of sight, Rahab climbed up into the attic to speak with the hiding Israelites. She gave them the information they had hoped to hear: The Canaanites, and especially the residents of Jericho, were alarmed by reports of divine intervention on behalf of the tribes of Israel. It seemed as if

Joshua's armies were predestined to be victorious. Consequently, Rahab's people were in a panic; they had lost the will to fight.

In return for this intelligence she asked only that when the Israelites invaded the city, they spare her and her family. The spies were agreeable as long as she would not betray them.

With Rahab's information the two Israelites stole safely back to their camp across the Jordan and brought the news to Joshua. In due course Jericho and the Canaanites were besieged, defeated, and—in Jericho, at least—slaughtered, all but Rahab and her family. Eventually Joshua's army conquered all of the Promised Land. Like the victories of Israel thirty centuries later, it was achieved in large measure by skillful use of intelligence.

The grasp of the Jews on the Promised Land was never secure. Continuous wars and internecine quarrels resulted in a succession of victories and defeats and ultimate exile. The Diaspora (literally, "scattering") gradually drove the Jews across the earth, but in greatest numbers to Syria, North Africa and Europe.

And yet the Diaspora, on its first impact a tragic and wanton displacement of an evicted people, may be one of the most important factors in the perseverance of the Jewish people, a perseverance that brought them back home after two thousand years of exile. During their years as the uneasy guests of other cultures, two traditions prevailed. One determined that Jews remained Jews and never abandoned hope of a return to their homeland. At times this hope was reduced to an annual ritual—the prayer at the seder table that invokes the hope "Next year in Jerusalem." This has been intoned by every Jewish family during the Passover holiday for almost two millennia. The second tradition was that while holding to the bedrock of their religion and culture, the Jews continued that uncanny ability, first confirmed in their brush with Hellenism, to absorb and even become preeminent in the cultural life of their host countries. One need only look at the disproportionate number of Jews who have won the Nobel Prize.

And despite the strictures against intermarriage with gentiles (a resistance more religious than cultural), Jews did intermarry. Less fortunate Jewish women were raped. In either case, they acquired the genes of non-Semitic peoples, mainly Europeans. Thus, Jews, while predominantly dark and brown-eyed, are not infrequently blond and blue-eyed and generally display some of the ethnic characteristics of the spectrum between the extremes.

The Zionist fervor waxed and waned in direct proportion to the pressure on Jews. When the restrictions were imposed on their freedom, the seder prayer for a home in Jerusalem became an ever more active desire.

By the nineteenth century the vision of a world without oppression was alternately as vivid and as blurred as the aurora borealis. In Germany, for example, the Jews played an active role in the revolutionary uprisings of 1848. In gratitude, German liberals championed the cause of Jewish emancipation. One German state after another removed restrictions against Jews from its laws. In 1871 a major victory was achieved on paper when the

newly created German Empire produced a constitution that abolished all restrictions based on religious beliefs. Shortly afterward the parliaments of Austria and Hungary passed similar legislation.

The more enlightened attitudes toward Jews were a part of the liberal-national waves of revolution that had been set in motion by the defeat of Napoleon in 1815. In the beginning, liberalism, with its attendant commitment to religious liberty, advanced hand in hand with nationalism. By the last third of the century, however, nationalism had taken the lead. Feelings began to turn against the "alien" Jews despite their contribution to the replacement of the pre-Napoleonic dynastic state with the modern national state.

Thus, the Germany of Count Otto von Bismarck was created with liberal Jewish support, but having forged the disparate German states into a single empire, Bismarck held the new federation together by stirring up a nationalistic fervor that glorified the ethnic character of the new German. This was the dawn of the Aryan-superman concept that would form the core of Hitler's nationalism sixty years later.

In 1873 a financial panic overtook Germany, stemming partly from the wild speculation following the German victory in the Franco-Prussian War. Bismarck had used the war as a vehicle to weld the German peoples into one. The business panic, coinciding with the birth of the new Aryan supremacy, triggered the need for a scapegoat. At about the same time, Germans had been exposed to some new pseudoscientific theory proving that Jews had smaller cranial cavities than their Teutonic or Nordic brothers. Therefore, Jews were held to be inferior, despite their relative success in business and the professions. Germans were convinced they were superior to Jews but simultaneously felt the deadly pangs of jealousy. In the Jews, they found the scapegoat that could assuage their psyches.

Bismarck, the Iron Chancellor, bent to the winds of popular discontent. Ignoring his Jewish support and bowing to the new racial theories, he bypassed the constitution to suppress the rights of the Jews. By decree he barred them from the chair of any university, from army commissions, and from important state offices.

As if the chancellor's actions were a signal, anti-Jewish riots broke out in a dozen cities in the new Germany. Once under way, the new wave of anti-Semitism spread to Austria and Hungary. The latter country had been a welcome haven for Jews since the so-called dual monarchy gave it limited independence from Austria. Overt anti-Semitism was still several decades in the future, but the danger signs were building all over central Europe.

On the continent of Europe, France was looked upon as the cradle of modern Jewish emancipation. Optimists reasoned that however prevalent the sickness might be in Germany and the other central states, it would never spread to France. The optimists were wrong, and the surfacing of latent anti-Semitism in liberal France, personified in the Dreyfus affair, literally changed the course of Jewish history.

In 1894 French army intelligence officers found, purportedly in a wastebasket, a document listing military information that had been turned over to

the German embassy. The document was the work of a debauched aristocrat, Major Ferdinand Walsin Esterhazy. A philanderer and spendthrift, he had run through several fortunes and finally, in desperation, augmented his income by selling secrets to the Germans. If there was any suspicion that Esterhazy was the culprit, his exalted status precluded an open accusation. And yet the French General Staff, highly conservative and yearning for the glorious days of the Second Empire, felt honor-bound to clear up the case of obvious treason. Suspecting that the traitor was within their own ranks, the sleuthing included a handwriting analysis. This led to Captain Alfred Dreyfus, the only Jew on the General Staff. Dreyfus was as conservative, proud, and arrogant as his fellow officers; only his Jewishness separated him. He was duly charged, court-martialed, convicted, and sentenced to life in prison on the infamous Devil's Island. The case sparked an anti-Semitic orgy in the conservative French press and among a segment of the French people.

The novelist Emile Zola suspected that Dreyfus was the scapegoat because he was a Jew. With the cooperation of a courageous newspaper publisher, Georges Clemenceau (later premier), Zola counterattacked with his famous manifesto "J'Accuse!" He presented evidence to show that Dreyfus had been framed. He charged the military, with the connivance of the government, of fanning the passions of anti-Semitism and falsifying evidence. Zola contended that the army was concerned only with its "honor" and that to salvage that honor the treason was blamed on the General Staff's only Jewish officer. The army supplied more information to bolster its case, but Zola and his colleagues immediately furnished counterevidence to prove that the charges against Dreyfus were pure fabrication.

Five years passed before the political pendulum had swung sufficiently far for a new president, Emile Loubet, to order Dreyfus retried. Again he was convicted. Loubet then sought to pardon him, but with Zola's backing, Dreyfus rejected the pardon on the grounds that he had committed no crime. Dreyfus appealed, and the French Court of Appeals, coincidental with the turn of the tide of public opinion, vindicated him. He was promoted and awarded the Legion of Honor.

The irony in the case is that Dreyfus himself was a shallow and doctrinaire military zealot who barely understood the significance of his own situation except in personal terms. He never quite grasped the principle that motivated Zola's fight for an individual against the power of the state. Many observers believe that if Dreyfus had been the accuser instead of the accused, his sense of the honor of the army would have made him as obstinate as his fellow officers.

He was, however, a Jew, and for this reason the Dreyfus case marks a turning point not only in French history but in the effort of Jews to survive. This turning point rests not on any of the Dreyfus case participants but on a mere observer, a journalist whose brooding on the fate of Dreyfus was to give birth to an organized movement.

The journalist was a Jew, Theodor Herzl, Paris correspondent for the prestigious Viennese newspaper *Neue Freie Presse*. Herzl had undergone some private agonies in trying to assess the degree of accommodation a Jew might

find in Europe's non-Jewish society. A handsome, bearded intellectual, Herzl had first thought in terms of assimilation through which a Jew would simply cease to be a Jew. This trend in his thinking was all the more remarkable in that Herzl's parents were apparently orthodox, which is to say that they represented those most deeply instilled with the traditions and permanence of Judaism.

Herzl seems to have been distressed by the fact that whatever his achievements in life, he was still regarded first as a Jew. His own diary, quoted by M. Hirsh Goldberg in *The Jewish Connection*, reveals his troubled state: "About two years ago I wanted to solve the Jewish Question, at least in Austria, with the help of the Catholic Church. I wished to gain access to the Pope and say to him: Help us against the anti-Semites and I will start a great movement for the free and honorable conversion of Jews to Christianity."

Amazingly, in the light of his eventual role in history, Herzl offered himself as the leader of this massive, systematic conversion movement. However well intentioned, it exposed his own ignorance of the nature of his faith as well as the nature of human psychology.

Herzl was still in the midst of this troubled period when he was assigned to his newspaper's Paris bureau. By this time he had come to expect anti-Jewish feeling in Austria, but France, after all, was the birthplace of the Declaration of the Rights of Man. Herzl arrived in Paris with high expectations. Instead he ran headlong into the virulent anti-Semitism brought on by the Dreyfus affair.

His convictions turned 180 degrees. He abandoned his ideas on Jewish assimilation and began to think of collective efforts to survive. If mobs could call for Jewish blood in the streets of Paris, there was only one solution—a Jewish state.

Der Judenstaat (The Jewish State) was the title of the small book that Herzl wrote in 1896. In it he despairingly concludes that Jews, even when their religion is tolerated, will still be rejected as an alien race. Survival depends on their having a state of their own. Only in this way can they escape the daily humiliation and the physical danger attendant on being Jewish. To live in dignity, Jews must control their destiny.

Such control implies that Jews must acquire the same accommodation—a space on the earth—that other national groups enjoyed. Instead of depending on the whims of a host country, the persecuted people must have their own police force and their own army. This Jewish entity would be established on the holy soil of the biblical *Eretz Yisroel* ("the Land of Israel"), which was then Turkish-occupied Palestine.

Herzl was not the first Zionist; the return to the homeland is implicit in the Jewish faith and is voiced in the annual benediction "Next year in Jerusalem." Only three decades before *Der Judenstaat*, a German, Moses Hess, had proposed a Jewish home in Palestine. Hess's proposal, however, was a mere academic treatise. Herzl had written a call to action.

Having proposed the movement, Herzl proceeded to take charge of it. He immediately contacted Jews all over Europe to lay the groundwork for an international Zionist organization. In 1897 he convened the first Zionist Con-

gress in Basel, Switzerland. Now driven by his dream, he called for a mass migration of Jews to Palestine.

Although the first Zionist Congress marks the formal beginning of the steps that were to lead to the creation of the State of Israel, Jews, especially in western Europe, did not immediately rally to the banner of Zionism. Despite the Dreyfus affair and other outcroppings of prejudice, they were relatively comfortable.

In eastern Europe it was a different story. There the Jews lived under active oppression in ghettoized poverty. The hope of *Der Judenstaat* found fertile ground. In Russia, especially, the Herzl book was the literary matrix for the spreading hope of a new life in the Promised Land. Sporadic emigration had started in the late 1870s and was given added momentum by a series of pogroms in 1881. The sufferings of that year gave birth to the Lovers of Zion, an organization that eventually yielded up some seven thousand Russians to the Promised Land, including the famous Aaronsohn family, whose intelligence exploits will be discussed in the next chapter.

By 1903 the message of Herzl had been heard among Russian Jews and had its first encounter with violence. In a small community called Gomel, between White Russia and the Ukraine, the young people were growing increasingly resentful and hostile under the systematic persecutions of the czar. Many had joined a new Zion Socialist party. That year a particularly vicious pogrom was inflicted on the tiny Jewish *shtetl* ("small town") of Kishinev in Bessarabia. The young militants of Gomel vowed to shed their passivity in the face of such outrages. They knew that more pogroms would sooner or later come to Gomel. Obviously they could not defeat the czar's army, but they swore that they would make the authorities realize how high a price had to be paid for harassing, beating, and killing Jews.

In *The Shield of David*, Yigal Allon describes their preparations:

> It seemed unlikely that any self-defense could be effective but the young Zionists of Gomel made careful plans. Defense in depth was impossible, but nevertheless they bought weapons; they did their best, sometimes ludicrously disguised as Russian peasants, to set up an intelligence-gathering organization so that they would not be taken by surprise; they amassed and assessed information about the rioters' mood and preparations, and they divided the Jewish streets of Gomel into small defendable blocks.

Like their ancestor Joshua and all the Jews who would come after them, the residents of Gomel leaned heavily on intelligence. Consequently, when their predictions based on this intelligence were borne out and the pogroms started, the Jews were ready to defend themselves. The first assault came not from the army but from a mob of drunken, marauding hooligans. When they met an orderly battle line of gun-bearing villagers, the hooligans were dumbfounded. They fled in terror after one or two shots had been fired. Since when had Jews dared to defend themselves with arms?

The victory, as expected, was short-lived. Within hours, units of the imperial army were marching on Gomel to teach the Jews a lesson. The defend-

ers, however, did not flinch and, from behind their hillocks and hedgerows, opened fire. The czar's troops were startled, but they were professionals. They returned every shot in double measure. Screams of wounded Jews sounded over the noise of battle, but the villagers did not retreat. For three days the battle raged. The casualties in the little village were enormous, but the czar's units were also badly shattered. Eventually the town's defense crumbled and the soldiers overran Gomel. But the czar had learned a lesson: a high price in Russian lives would have to be paid for the killing of Jews.

The Hebrew word that denotes the return of Jews to the Promised Land is *aliyah*, which literally means "ascent." The wave of immigrants in the 1880s, often described as "the first *aliyah*," had a philosophy and life-style markedly different from the larger "second *aliyah*," which took place mainly after 1904, stimulated largely by Herzl's Zionist movement.

The earlier settlers had an essentially colonial approach to living on their new land, which, in most cases, they had purchased from Arabs. They usually hired Arab labor to carry out their chores and saw themselves as managers dealing with a laboring class. In contrast, the second *aliyah* was dominated by settlers imbued with a sense of social justice. Strongly influenced by Karl Marx and nineteenth-century socialism, they formed labor cooperatives known as *kibbutzim* and believed in maintaining their own defense force.

These conflicting traditions have persisted into modern times and to some extent affect the politics of present-day Israel. The colonial settlers, with their essentially mercantilist-capitalist philosophy, represent one of the several threads leading to the modern Likud Coalition and Menachem Begin. The Labor Zionists represent a different thread, one that extends directly to the present Labor party and such leaders as David Ben-Gurion, Golda Meir, and Shimon Peres.

Typical of the labor group were the residents of beleaguered Gomel who, after their clash with Russian troops, emigrated in great numbers to Palestine. They were both socialistic and militant. Just as they had defended their village in the old country, so they were prepared to defend their new homes against Arab or Ottoman marauders.

The older settlers, many of them from the first *aliyah*, did not always see eye to eye with the Labor Zionists. They had achieved, at least temporarily, a *modus vivendi* with their Arab neighbors. Their guards were often Arabs, paid to protect Jews.

The newer immigrants felt, as a matter of principle, that Jews should defend Jews. Their major problem was to convince the established settlers that a formal Jewish defense force was a realistic alternative to Arab hired guns and, in the long run, safer.

The schism had its nonmilitary aspect as well. There were few jobs for the new arrivals. In the main the Arabs were the workers and traders, while the Jews were managers and employers. The socialistically inclined newcomers reasoned that without Jewish labor there could be no Jewish homeland.

New zealots came along to press the idea of a Palestine sustained by Jews

and defended by Jews. Israel Shochat, a Russian socialist, typified the new idea. He believed that the survival of the Jewish settlements depended on an organized military force. For months in 1907 he traveled about the country trying to convince the settlers that they needed the means to defend themselves.

Shochat's example for reluctant Jews was the Circassians. They were Moslems, but Caucasians, not Arabs, who had migrated to Palestine in the nineteenth century. They were a small group, probably less than a thousand, but they were proud and tough. As horsemen and marksmen they were held in such awe by the Arabs that, for the most part, the Arabs left them alone. If the Circassians could defend themselves in such hostile surroundings, Shochat reasoned, so could the Jews.

Shochat made little progress with the older settlers. Their dependence on Arabs as laborers and guards was a system that they could live with—a kind of pragmatic symbiosis. Why change it and antagonize the Arabs? And why should veteran farmers of Palestine entrust their lives and property to new arrivals who had so little knowledge of the territory and its customs?

Even while Shochat's debate with the colonists continued, ten members of the Gomel group, not to be deterred, met in Jaffa and formed a secret defense organization. Shochat threw his lot in with them. They called the new group Bar Giora, after a famous Hebrew fighter against the Romans in A.D. 70. Their banner was a blue and white flag embroidered with Bar Giora's motto: "By blood and fire Judea fell; by blood and fire Judea shall rise again." Shochat was elected leader.

This small, seemingly insignificant force was, in a sense, the ancestor of all the Jewish fighting units that followed, up to and including the modern Israel Defense Force, victor in five wars with its Arab neighbors. Prophetically, this nucleus called Bar Giora included Yitzhak Ben-Zvi, who, four decades later, would be the second president of Israel.

Bar Giora's insight into future leadership was not flawless. Another settler applied for membership but was turned down. His name was David Green or, in his native Polish, Grin. This short, rugged pioneer possessed a combination of seemingly contrasting qualities, which was not uncommon among Zionist patriots. He was a tough soldier and manual worker and, in his tranquil hours, an ardent scholar. One can almost imagine him with a shovel in one hand and a book in the other.

Grin was born in a small wooden house on the dirt Street of the Goats in Płońsk, Poland, on October 16, 1886. David's father, Victor Grin, was, for his day and his environment, an emancipated Jew. He eschewed the traditional long, black robe that identified him as Hebraic. He was a lawyer, a profession that brought him into frequent contact with the gentile community. He was deeply interested in Western culture.

Victor Grin was, nonetheless, conscious of his religious and cultural roots. He spoke Hebrew fluently. He taught his young son that of necessity the Jews must return to their ancestral homeland. He took the seder ritual seriously: it was a pledge as well as a prayer. To his son, David, the mere pledge was not enough. In 1906, when he was twenty, the pledge seemed possible of fulfillment. He said farewell to his family and emigrated from Poland to

Palestine. There he adopted a Hebrew name, David Ben-Gurion, which means "David, son of the Lion."

In addition to his father, another strong influence shaped young David's life. From someone as unlikely as Harriet Beecher Stowe and her melodramatic *Uncle Tom's Cabin* came a concern with social justice that was to lead Ben-Gurion along the path to socialism and, in so doing, influence the political coloration of the future state of Israel.

On January 29, 1967, from his retirement home in Sde Boker, Ben-Gurion sent the authors a handwritten note: "*Uncle Tom's Cabin* was one of the first books I read in my youth when I was nine or ten. I read it then in Hebrew translation and it made a very deep impression." A few months later, when we interviewed him at Sde Boker, he elaborated on this theme: "*Uncle Tom's Cabin* made me a socialist. I was determined not only to help build the Jewish state, but a Jewish state with social justice."

Ben-Gurion's concern with social justice was melded into his synthesis of cultural and religious force as the motivation for the creation of a new state. As he said more than once, "The Jews are not God's chosen people, but rather they chose God." From this he extrapolates his belief that a Jewish state without the Bible and the Mosaic code could not fulfill its historic destiny.

In 1908, at the time of the embryonic Bar Giora, skirmishes between Jews and Arabs occasionally erupted in the farmlands among the cool and fertile hills of Galilee in northern Palestine. It was in these northern settlements that the Labor Zionist ideology was strongest. The skirmishes were directly related to the Jews' decision to defend themselves, in accordance with the Labor Zionists' conviction.

In this area, in the foothills of Mount Tabor, was a farm community known as Sejera, which had been established as the site of a future agricultural school. Because of the school's potential importance, the Bar Giora decided to put its ideas into action, to assume the responsibility of defending Jewish lives and property. It was a brave but brash decision, since the Bar Giora still consisted of just ten men. A certain amount of courage was also displayed by the farmers, who put their trust in such a small, inexperienced handful of guards.

Taking on the Bar Giora as defenders meant discharging the Arab and Circassian guards who had been paid to protect the Jews. Predictably, the now unemployed non-Jews were angry. Peaceful relations with their Jewish employers had been dependent only on the frail thread of a business arrangement. Now that the thread was broken, they threatened physical retaliation. When the farmers were unmoved, the former guards made good their threat and staged a raid on Sejera.

The members of the Bar Giora were ready for them. Verbal threats were shouted across the field, and eventually there was some shooting. The Arabs and Circassians retreated. There were no casualties.

As a military exercise, this was almost comic opera. And yet the successful defense of Sejera, although a brief, seemingly unimportant event, nonetheless became a legendary inspiration for the Jewish settlers. A Jewish community with its own fighting force had survived an attack. If Jews were

capable of self-defense, then the concept of a Jewish state had validity. If ten Jews could defend a small farm, then a larger Jewish armed force could conceivably protect the entire Jewish community in the Holy Land. The vision, however, was slow to become reality.

In the spring of 1908 the Labor party honored Sejera by selecting it as the site of its convention. Ben-Gurion, then a farm laborer, was one of the delegates; he wrote of the meeting:

> We gathered in the upper Klan, the old Arab staging inn, in the farm compound. The large hall, which was once a cow shed and afterwards became the workers' dormitory, was decorated in "Galilee style." The two long walls were draped with eucalyptus and pepper branches and looked like an avenue of trees. On the inner wall hung farm tools and weapons—plows, spades, harrows and hoes were wreathed in bright spring flowers, and rifles, pistols, swords and daggers were hung above the windows. The faces of the young men who sat and sang around the table testified that this arsenal was more than a decoration.

The members of the Bar Giora, flush with their success at Sejera, acquired another client. In that same year of 1908 the Jewish village of Mes'cha (now Kfar Tabor) called upon these Jewish guardsmen to provide for their defense. In this case Bar Giora needed to expand its ranks beyond the ten-man nucleus. The original members of Bar Giora became teachers of self-defense to settlers not only in Mes'cha but in other settlements throughout Galilee. Weapons were collected, and a headquarters was set up in a local schoolhouse. The young amateur soldiers drilled under the blazing sun and went on forced marches to toughen up. By the time their training was completed, they were proud professionals.

This training of new defenders by the original Bar Giora began a geometric expansion of defense forces as the indoctrinated recruits returned to their villages to pass along their newly acquired knowledge to their local comrades. Meanwhile, Mes'cha entered into a formal contract with Bar Giora. The terms provided that the soldiers of Bar Giora would fulfill their defense obligation so long as the colony employed Jews only, observing one of the fundamental precepts of the Labor Zionists. Mes'cha, for its part, agreed to pay the guards for their services and furnish each with basic arms. These included a Martene rifle, 162 bullets, and four cartridge belts.

The growing need for defense forces was persuasive evidence to the members of the original Bar Giora that the time was ripe for creating a unified organization that could evolve into a national defense force. In the spring of 1909 a clandestine meeting was held at Mes'cha. It was obvious to the members of Bar Giora and its offshoots that their small, secret organization would not long be adequate to meet the needs of the proliferating Jewish settlements in Palestine.

In April 1909, two years after the founding of Bar Giora, its members decided to expand into a national force and to abandon their secrecy. They

created the Hashomer (meaning "the watchmen") and greatly enlarged their recruiting efforts. Within less than a year, the Hashomer numbered in the hundreds and assumed the responsibility for guarding all Jewish settlements, replacing once and for all the mercenary Arab guards. Even though Hashomer was conceived as a nonideological defender of Jews, its members tended to adhere to the socialistic beliefs of the Labor Zionists.

The soldiers of the new Hashomer acquired arms and learned to use them. Of equal importance, however, was their inbred sense of the need to assess the intentions and the capabilities of their Arab neighbors; in short, they became experts in gathering intelligence. When visiting an Arab village, they seldom missed an opportunity to pick up the drift of Arab attitudes. In the transition from Arab to Jewish guards, the Hashomer soldiers, many of them fluent in Arabic, often shared their sentry duties with Arabs. Here, too, the Jews sought to assess the long-term intentions of the Arabs. There was no overt effort to alienate the Arab villagers; it was to the advantage of both to maintain friendly relations.

The Hashomer leadership preached the necessity of both military preparedness and hard physical labor. The young recruits were imbued with the broad concept of building viable Jewish settlements. The wilderness had to be conquered; the swamps had to be drained. Although the organization sought to expand its ranks as much as was practical, it maintained high standards, and consequently most applicants were turned down. Those accepted had to possess great physical stamina, the ability to improvise under Spartan living conditions, and an adaptability to changing situations. This was no army for docile military robots. Even after meeting all the basic requirements for acceptance and enduring the rigors of basic training, the recruits had to serve a one-year probationary period before they were granted full standing as members of the Hashomer.

Within a few years the Hashomer, as the only tightly organized Jewish unit in Palestine, was called on to provide more than farmers and soldiers. Men and women were needed who could meet the intellectual needs of the growing society. There were constant conflicts with the Turks, often requiring legal representation for Jews in corrupt Turkish courts. The Hashomer, going beyond its original responsibilities, raised money and sent several of its members, including Ben-Zvi and Ben-Gurion (who was eventually admitted despite his earlier rejection by Bar Giora), to Constantinople to study law. Other students were dispatched to Turkish universities to study medicine, engineering, and economics.

By the spring of 1914, on the eve of World War I, eighty thousand Jews lived in Palestine, most of them in small towns and more than fifty agricultural settlements. Their children would be the revered sabras, native-born citizens of the future Israel. They were so called after a ubiquitous variety of cactus that is hard on the outside and soft and sweet on the inside. Presumably the typical Israeli, toughened by his hostile climate and his implacable enemies but forever involved in cultural, humane, and even sentimental diversions, is aptly named for the sabra.

The populace that was accumulating in Palestine was not only dedicated to survival but intrinsically suited to ensuring it. Somewhat like the pioneers who settled the New World in the seventeenth and eighteenth centuries, the Jews in Palestine, especially the leaders, possessed an ability to reconcile the pragmatic needs of survival with the intellectual and philosophical outlook necessary to secure it.

As both the active founders and the philosophical fathers of Israel, Ben-Gurion and Chaim Weizmann were not unlike George Washington and Thomas Jefferson, applying Western cultural ideas to survival on the frontier. Ben-Gurion, making life-and-death decisions in the War for Independence in 1948, always remained an amazing combination of warrior and scholar. Weizmann was a world-famous chemist before he became the first president of Israel. Yigal Yadin, a fighter in the preindependence Haganah forces and later chief of operations in the Israel Defense Force, eventually became a renowned archaeologist. Then, in 1977, without surrendering his archaeological career, he jumped back into public life as founder of a new political party, the Democratic Movement for Change. In coalition with Menachem Begin's Likud party, he became deputy prime minister.

The authors became particularly aware of this soldier-scholar quality in our interviews with the older generation of intelligence agents, many of whom had known little but danger and hardship for most of their lives. To hear a hard-bitten old warrior discuss his adventures in literary allusions borrowed from several languages was a revelation.

Consistent with this tradition is the fact that the first great intelligence agent of modern Jewish history was a man who, had he not decided to fight for his country, would have had a secure reputation as a scientist. His story, told in the next chapter, begins in World War I when there were deep divisions in the international Zionist leadership. Jewish loyalties were torn between the Allies and the Central Powers. Czarist Russia, the proven enemy of the Jews, was allied with Britain and France. Weizmann and other prominent Zionists argued that this alliance was but a temporary marriage of necessity and that when the war was over a victorious Great Britain would support Jewish claims for a national homeland.

Others, including many Palestinian Jews, felt that the best hope lay in support of Turkey, an ally of the Central Powers, on the grounds that in time the Turkish government, assured of the loyalty of the *yishuv* (the Jewish settlers in Palestine), would temper its hostility toward them. Hence, many future Zionist patriots, such as Moshe Shertok (later Sharett) served as officers in the Turkish army.

In general, the attitudes of the Jews of Palestine depended mainly on that which governs the attitudes of all human beings, the weighing of the best chance for survival. There was no doubt in the mind of Aaron Aaronsohn that his support, even at the risk of his life, belonged with the British. He became a legendary spy in the pre-Israel Promised Land. Many more spies were to follow.

2

The Spies on the Distant Shore

ON SEPTEMBER 3, 1918, near the ancient Roman fortress of Caesarea, some twenty miles south of Haifa, the Turkish *moudir* (local chief of police) was scattering grain for his pigeons. This functionary of the disintegrating Ottoman Empire was not concerned that the grain had tempted a passing pigeon from the course dictated by his homing instincts; even a carrier pigeon might get hungry en route. The Turk's attention was only aroused when he noticed that the uninvited guest had a small metal cylinder attached to its leg. Quickly grasping the flapping bird, he removed the cylinder, snapped off its cap, and extracted a coiled bit of paper. On it was a message, obviously in code. The *moudir* had accidentally come upon evidence of the first organized Jewish spy ring in modern Palestine.

The errant pigeon had been released by Sarah Aaronsohn. A handsome, forceful woman, just twenty-eight, she was the sister of Aaron Aaronsohn, a self-taught agronomist whose work had already gained him worldwide attention. The soil he nursed was in a God-forsaken wasteland at Athlit, on the coastal plain of Sharon. Sarah and Aaron were the children of Romanian immigrants who had taken advantage of the waning influence of the Ottoman Empire to settle in the village of Zichron in 1882. They were members of the first *aliyah*.

The Ottoman Empire at its height had controlled the Middle East, North Africa, and eastern Europe. Its beginnings went back to the late thirteenth century to Osman I, prince of Anatolia. Over the next two centuries, the Ottomans, as the followers of Osman were known, extended their conquests, taking Constantinople, the capital of the Byzantine Empire, in 1453. By the end of the sixteenth century the empire extended from Baghdad on the east to most of present-day Hungary on the west. In the seventeenth century the

33

growing power of the national states, especially Austria and Russia, impeded Ottoman expansion, and little by little the edges of its territory were nibbled away.

By the nineteenth century the empire was suffering from administrative deterioration. Greece and the Balkan countries freed themselves from the Ottoman yoke, and in the Middle East provincial rulers were challenging the imperial authority. This was especially true in Palestine, where local pashas, while nominally under Ottoman control, were actually controlling local fiefdoms.

This was the situation in the late nineteenth century when families such as the Aaronsohns immigrated to Palestine. For the most part the land was purchased from local owners, and the Ottoman sultan could do little to interfere with the transaction. To further weaken the Ottoman position, the settlers, backed by their former governments, began to demand nullification of Turkish law in favor of the law of their countries of origin. In the case of the Aaronsohns' group, the sultan managed to block the landing of their ship for forty days, but in the end the local leaders prevailed; the sultan was not strong enough to enforce his edict.

However, once the various contingents of Jewish immigrants had settled in Palestine, the Ottoman authorities, as well as the local pashas and the surrounding Arabs, left them relatively free so long as they did not try to usurp more territory. In the early years of the twentieth century many—perhaps a majority—of the Jewish settlers were in favor of peaceful coexistence with their Arab neighbors. But the Zionist dream had captured the imagination of many members of the *yishuv* (Jewish settlements), and with the outbreak of World War I, they saw the chance of making this dream a reality by trying to acquire more territory.

Aaron Aaronsohn was somewhat of a hybrid in his thinking. With the earlier, more conservative *aliyah*, he saw nothing wrong in hiring Arab labor at minimal wages, although he was often chastised by the Labor Zionists, who, with their socialistic outlook, advocated the kibbutz concept of self-contained, work-sharing communes. But Aaronsohn believed fiercely in the ideal of the Zionist state, and in World War I the most direct path to his goal was, he believed, to help the British oust the Ottoman Turks from Palestine. His active involvement with the British was not popular with the *yishuv*; the settlers feared retaliation from the Turks.

The recovery of the coded note from the carrier pigeon sparked the very investigation that Aaronsohn's neighbors feared. He had started his spying in the spring of 1915. Aaronsohn hoped that his intelligence activities would hasten the Turks' defeat. He was not sure the British wanted his help or trusted him because, he admitted, "we do it for our own cause."

The first step in commencing secret activities against the Turks was to contact the British, to persuade them that Aaronsohn and his associates were ready and willing to help. The most feasible contact point appeared to be Port Said. The logical person to carry out the assignment was Aaronsohn's first important disciple, Absolom Feinberg, the son of Russian intellectuals who, like Aaronsohn's parents, had immigrated to Palestine with

that wave of pioneers in 1882. As a child he had been taught both the Koran and the Bible. He could read, speak, and write Arabic as well as any educated Arab. His intellectual horizons had been broadened by four years of study, from his fifteenth to his nineteenth year, in France. To make his passage legally acceptable, Feinberg had acquired a forged Russian passport. With this and an address in Port Said, he sailed on the French passenger ship *Des Moines* on August 30, 1915.

The address that Feinberg carried was that of an Arab Christian, Charles Boutagy, whose father, a friend of Feinberg, had been assistant British consul at Haifa. Charles was now serving as an interpreter with British naval intelligence at Port Said. The prospective Jewish agent was received warmly by the younger Boutagy, and a meeting was arranged between Feinberg and Lieutenant Charles Leonard Woolley, a capable young officer whose service was later to win him a knighthood.

Feinberg presented two proposals to Woolley. One was to begin an armed rebellion by the Jews against the Turks; the other was to supply British authorities with intelligence information. The lieutenant brushed aside any consideration of open revolt. He apparently felt that there was little chance of success, or perhaps he considered the question to be beyond his authority.

Spying was a different matter. The British were certainly in need of information from Palestine. Woolley's position was that while he realized that such an undertaking would be dangerous for the Jews involved, His Majesty's Government would be grateful for their cooperation.

Formal arrangements commenced immediately. There was a pressing need for a means of contacting a French warship that regularly sailed between Port Said and Tyre on the Lebanese coast. Woolley called in a British captain named Weldon, who was a passenger on each voyage, representing naval intelligence. He and Feinberg arranged a system of signals for the Jews to contact the ship as it passed Athlit. Later Feinberg wrote of this meeting: "The die is cast. Our fate becomes more and more linked with the Allied cause."

This inherently dangerous coupling of British and Jewish war aims showed bravery on the part of Aaronsohn and his colleagues, but arrogance as well. They never thought to ask the consent of the Jewish community or its leaders in Palestine before embarking on this endeavor. The Jews were surrounded by Turks and totally vulnerable. If the Aaronsohn operation were to be discovered, all would pay the price of Turkish vengeance.

Feinberg returned to Athlit in high spirits and spelled out the arrangements with Woolley to Aaronsohn. The small band of spies immediately began to collect all manner of information about the Turks—military, economic, political. This meticulously gathered information was recorded, placed in a leather pouch, and buried in a tin box in the basement of the agricultural experimental station at Athlit.

On the night of the first scheduled passage of the spy ship, Feinberg, Aaronsohn, and a few others gathered on the beach to notify the British agent that they had intelligence material available. A lamp on the beach was lighted. It was flashed on and off in accordance with a code that Fein-

berg had brought back from Port Said. The ship maintained full speed and ignored them. Obviously, something had gone wrong.

A long time later they were to learn that Arab spies for the Allies in Lebanon had been asked to notify the band at Athlit that the signals had been changed. The Jews could only speculate why they had not been advised. One theory was that the Arabs, who accepted money for their espionage, were resentful of the Jews who carried out an equally dangerous mission without pay. The Jews were, in effect, unfair competition.

At the time of the failure, however, Aaronson and Feinberg did not know what had caused the breakdown. They were alarmed and desperate. Their carefully gathered information was wasted.

Was it possible, they wondered, that Lieutenant Woolley had second thoughts about the integrity of the Athlit group? They were also concerned about their moral obligation. Woolley had taken a serious responsibility on his own shoulders in acceding to the Aaronsohn mission, and so, they did not want to let him down. Feinberg wrote: "I don't want the commander to think that the first Jew in his service betrayed him."

Aaronsohn and Feinberg felt deeply the need for an immediate reestablishment of contact with British authorities, both to reassure them of the Jews' cooperation and to assist in measures against the Turks. This time Feinberg could not gamble on another voyage by ship to Port Said. The Turks might already be suspicious. The only alternative, an overland trek with new and different perils, was probably the best hope.

Taking the trail from Athlit southward to Port Said meant evading the suspicious Turks and the pillaging bands of Bedouins, coping with a scarcity of water, and battling the *chamsin*, the dry desert wind that choked and burned and sometimes buried an unwary traveler. The war augmented the problems. The Turks were alert for British spies and, when in doubt, often assumed the worst of any suspicious traveler. The Bedouins' reputation for hospitality was not dependable in these disruptive times, for they had been known to rob and even murder non-Arab strangers.

Aaronsohn was familiar with these dangers and tried to discourage Feinberg from making the trip. Feinberg was insistent. To protect his friend, Aaronsohn made a unique suggestion. One of the Jews' few cooperative projects with the Turks was a so-called Locust Brigade, conceived by the agronomist as a semimilitary corps to battle the frequent plagues of locusts. The Locust Brigade uniform was known to the Turks. Absolom Feinberg would wear it on the first leg of his journey. Farther south, when he approached Bedouin country, he would change into Bedouin clothing in an attempt to pass as one of them.

With Aaronsohn's good wishes, Feinberg departed Athlit in the uniform of the Locust Brigade. For a time the disguises worked perfectly. He passed through the patrols of unsuspecting Turks in central Palestine and then, in bedouin disguise, through the Negev. As he approached the Suez Canal, the Turkish forces again were predominant, so that the wary spy had to switch back again to the garb of the Locust Brigade.

He was only a few kilometers from the canal when he was intercepted by

a Turkish patrol, augmented by a small contingent of German soldiers and officers. The Turks refused to believe that Feinberg had wandered alone into the desert seeking locust swarms. The Germans were more dogmatic. They believed he was a spy and insisted that he be hanged immediately.

Fortunately, the Germans did not prevail. The Turks chose instead to convey their captive all the way north to the Negev desert city of Beersheba, the biblical community whose name means "seven wells." There were several Jewish settlements in the vicinity, and the word spread rapidly that Feinberg, an associate of the well-known Aaronsohn, was imprisoned in Beersheba. In the settlement of Ramala, Yosef Lishansky, a member of the Hashomer, the embryonic defense unit, knew that Aaronsohn should be informed of Feinberg's predicament. He was able to send a message to the agronomist; meanwhile, because he enjoyed considerable freedom of movement in Beersheba, he was allowed to visit Feinberg in jail.

It was not unusual for prisoners of the Turks to be allowed to purchase food to supplement their meager prison fare. Consequently, there was no particular concern that Feinberg was buying loaves of bread from Lishansky. These loaves, however, included in their core a succession of notes from Aaronsohn. Aaronsohn was desperately seeking a means of heading off Feinberg's almost certain execution as a spy. Meanwhile, Lishansky was liberally distributing *baksheesh* (Arab for "gratuity" or "tip") in further hopes of postponing the death of the prisoner.

The key to Feinberg's fate (as well as to his cell) was in the hands of an enigmatic personality, General Djemal Pasha, the alternately ruthless and reasonable commander of the Turkish Fourth Army. Unpleasant in appearance—he was so short and stooped as to appear hunchbacked—he had, coincidentally, an overriding interest in agricultural reform. For this reason he knew and respected Aaronsohn not only for his skill in argonomy but for Aaronsohn's outspoken courage. On many occasions the agronomist had challenged the general's policies, and surprisingly, Djemal seemed to be impressed. On many occasions he was almost casual about whom he sent to the gallows.

Djemal Pasha had another engaging attribute that Aaronsohn turned to his advantage. The general hated his allies, the Germans. Their overbearing efficiency and military discipline contrasted sharply with the ragged, corruption-ridden Turkish army. Djemal resented the implied odious comparisons.

To free Feinberg, Aaronsohn would have to outthink and outwit General Djemal. He arranged to maneuver a local agriculture committee into requesting of Djemal that they seek Aaronsohn's advice. The general took the bait and immediately asked his favorite agronomist to prepare a report for him on the particular agricultural problem. Aaronsohn was cordial and cooperative. He was anxious to help, but there was one nearly insurmountable handicap. It would be difficult, nearly impossible, to prepare the report on time without the help of his capable secretary, Absolom Feinberg. And where was Feinberg? In jail, Aaronsohn told Djemal, where the "stupid" Germans wanted to hang him.

The general agreed the Germans were indeed stupid. He told Aaronsohn he would request an immediate trial for Feinberg by a military tribunal in Jerusalem. Since the Turks lacked any solid evidence against their prisoner and since their leader seemed concerned about him, Feinberg was acquitted and released.

Although Feinberg's desperate effort to reach Woolley had failed, what the Athlit spies did not realize was that the British officer was equally concerned about the breakdown in communications. He was desperately in need of the intelligence information about the Turks that Aaronsohn and Feinberg had promised him.

The specific cause of Woolley's unrest was the alarming report that the Central European powers were massing large concentrations of troops in the Sinai desert. Perhaps the reports were exaggerated, but if the enemy was planning an attack on the Suez Canal, British intelligence had to know his strength.

Woolley and other intelligence officers pondered some means of reestablishing contact with Athlit. They found their hope in Zvi Rabin, a wounded Jewish soldier convalescing in a Cairo hospital. Rabin had been a member of the famous Zion Mule Corps, adjunct fighters of the British army. In April 1915, just 650 strong, they had fought valiantly against the Turks in the disastrous Gallipoli campaign.

In his hospital ward, Rabin received a surprise visit from a British intelligence officer. The officer had done some research on the wounded soldier's background. Before the war Rabin had been a coachman in the coastal region between Haifa and Acre. He not only knew Aaronsohn but also had an intimate knowledge of the terrain in the vicinity of the experimental station. This background, plus his military experience, made Rabin a prime candidate for a dangerous journey to reestablish contact with Athlit.

Rabin agreed to the journey and was given a letter to deliver to Aaronsohn. He was to board the spy ship on its regular run to Lebanon and disembark on the wild coastline near Athlit.

The night was dark and cloudy when Rabin was put over the side in a small boat. The roar of the Mediterranean surf provided a protective cover for any sound he might make, and the sand dunes and low vegetation shielded him as he crawled from the beach to the main coastal road. On the far side of the highway was his destination, the Athlit agricultural experimental station.

For two days and two nights he lay in the brush on the beach side of the highway, not daring to cross. In the daytime he was fearful of being discovered. At night the road was jammed with troops moving south for the attack on the Suez Canal. The delay had disrupted his schedule and left him in danger of being trapped, since he was to reboard the ship on its return trip, scheduled for three days later.

Finally, on the third night, there was a sufficient lull in the troop movement for him to make the dash across the road and into the bushes close to the station. Just as he made his decision to cross, however, he caught sight of the distant lights of the British ship returning. This left him with only

minutes to complete his mission. The station was dark. A barking dog in the courtyard added to his fear of discovery. He did not dare approach the house, but somehow the letter had to be delivered. In the darkness he detected a plow in the adjacent yard. He placed the envelope under the crossbar, prayed silently that it would not fall into the wrong hands, and returned to the shore to meet the approaching ship. His prayers were answered. In the morning one of Aaronsohn's farm workers found the letter and delivered it to the master spy. Aaronsohn, his sister, and Feinberg rejoiced—contact with the British had been reestablished. The message from Lieutenant Woolley gave elaborate new instructions for the exchange of signals. In three weeks, he told them, the ship would pass again, and Athlit would become a major point for the transmission of intelligence to the British forces.

The rejoicing was premature. At the appointed time, the ship did not appear. Only later would Aaronsohn learn that it had been torpedoed and sunk en route. This time Lieutenant Woolley himself was a passenger. He escaped into a lifeboat, only to be picked up and taken prisoner by the Turks.

It was a dismal time. Despite the efforts of Feinberg and the daring of Rabin, the desperate attempt to communicate with the British had come to naught. Then Aaronsohn faced disaster in his main vocation—a plague of locusts. It was so totally destructive as to be reminiscent of the biblical eighth plague that God had visited on the Jews' ancient Egyptian captors. The locusts swarmed northward from their breeding ground in the south, and by October 1916 it was evident that the food supply of the entire country would be wiped out. To the disruption of war was added the specter of starvation.

For the Jews the prospect of competing with the Turks for the meager stores of food was an ugly one. Aaronsohn knew what had happened to the Armenians, and he was determined to do what he could to spare Jews the same fate. The Armenians, anxious to throw off the Turkish yoke, had supported the British, in spirit if not in deed. The Turks, who had always considered the Armenians to be an inferior race, turned their resentment into a policy of genocide. Families were driven from their villages into the desert, without food or water. Women were raped, and the crawling, stumbling refugees were rifle-butted into near-extinction. Fifteen million Armenians were killed.

Aaronsohn was now more determined than ever to reestablish contact with the British. This time he was motivated not only by the desire to provide intelligence but to send out an alarm that food was desperately needed in the Jewish settlements. If London was aware of the Jewish plight, he reasoned, the British would find a way to feed his brethren. Without food, the Jews might very well share the fate of the Armenians.

New tactics were needed if Aaronsohn was to carry out his mission. Contact with the passing ship thus far had failed. It could be tried again, but Aaronsohn now felt he would have to go to London and secondarily to Cairo. There was no hope of his leaving the country secretly, for he was too well known. His only hope was to concoct a reason acceptable to the Turks. This

proved to be relatively easy. Once again he played on Djemal Pasha's interest in agriculture. Aaronsohn was granted permission to travel to Europe in
connection with his research on an oil-rich variety of sesame seeds.

There was one important task to perform before his departure. When he
had completed his mission in London, Aaronsohn intended to travel to Cairo
to make yet another attempt to establish an intelligence link with the British ships passing Athlit. This time he, Sarah, and Feinberg drew up a complex system of signals for the ships. Aaronsohn would explain the signals to
the British intelligence agents. This time he wanted to make sure that nothing would go wrong. In July 1916, with his secretary, Liova Schneersohn,
Aaron sailed for Constantinople.

Although his means of accomplishing the trip are not certain, the agron-
omist-spy, now a self-styled organizer of a pro-British rebellion among the
Palestinian Jews, reached London in early November. In the bleak fall days
in England, this stocky, sunburned Jew presented a sharp contrast to the
pale dignitary he had sought out in a London office. Aaronsohn had managed an appointment with Sir Basil Thompson, the head of British intelligence.

The Palestinian made no secret of his own goal. As a Zionist, he wanted to
build a Jewish homeland, but he thought it could best be achieved by cooperating with Great Britain, which, with Jewish help, could be victorious.
Now there was an immediate problem. The locust plague had destroyed
much of the grain in Palestine. British success was essential, if only to
facilitate the import of food. Aaronsohn, his friends, and Jewish soldiers
would do their share.

Aaronsohn pledged, "I offer what I am able to give—my knowledge of the
country, the character of the inhabitants, and useful information on the
military situation of the enemy now occupying it." To back up his pledge the
agronomist offered an immediate suggestion to solve a problem that he knew
was bothering British forces in Palestine—the daily burden of supplying
thirsty desert soldiers with sufficient drinking water. At that time the water
was provided by means of a long, dangerous overland haul from Egypt.
Aaronsohn had an alternative suggestion, born of his years of work in agron-
omy.

"Why do you bring water for the army from Egypt? It slows your progress. There is water right there in the desert, three hundred feet down. All
you have to do is drill for it."

Sir Basil reacted almost as if he thought Aaronsohn were joking. "How do
you know that?" he asked.

Aaronsohn responded by recalling the writing of the Jewish historian
Flavius Josephus, who reported walking for a full day south of Caesarea,
through fertile, flowering fields. "Today," Aaronsohn continued, "the desert
sands reach to the walls of Caesarea. Where there were gardens there must
have been water. Where is the water now?"

The agronomist answered his own question. "I had the chance to explore
the geology of Palestine, and from the rock strata I learned that there is
sufficient water there at a depth of three hundred feet." Aaronsohn now

became caught up in his own enthusiasm. "Even the whole of the Sinai peninsula could be turned into flourishing fields of wheat by means of irrigation. There is water there, only waiting for pipes to bring it to the surface."*

Aaronsohn's suggestion reflected not only his immediate concern for the welfare of the British army but his long-term aspirations for the survival of the Jewish settlements in an arid land. Despite some skepticism, the British army did drill and, as the agronomist had predicted, found water three hundred feet below the desert.

The question of the immediate need for food was still to be answered. Aaronsohn saw military conquest by the British as the best means of rescuing the hungry Jews. To this end, Sir Basil Thompson arranged a meeting at the war office with Lieutenant G. M. MacDonough, chief of Military Intelligence, and his assistant, Colonel W. H. Gribbon. Aaronsohn's proposal that immediate contact be reestablished between his Athlit spies and the British intelligence was warmly received. The stalemated trench warfare in Europe was producing a ghastly number of casualties. The British War Office reasoned that, with the aid of Jewish intelligence, an expanded Near Eastern campaign might create a way to break the stalemate. With high hopes and what he considered to be a mandate to carry out his plan, the agronomist arrived in Cairo on December 12, 1916, to make arrangements with British authorities there.

To his dismay, he was received with cold reserve and suspicion. There was no Lieutenant Woolley to support his plan. The Cairo command was not impressed with his credentials from London nor his previous exploits. He was treated as a foreigner, a Jew and an alien, someone not to be trusted. Aaronsohn was offended almost as much by their failure to take him seriously as by their lack of interest in opening a Palestinian offensive.

Aaronsohn spent more than a month in Cairo in angry frustration. He expressed his fury in a letter to Feinberg: "Until the moment I started conversations with *them*, I have never allowed any man to behave to me with such indifference and lack of respect as I allowed them, because their ideas and their behavior are so different from ours."

Eventually the aspiring intelligence agent was given his opportunity—so long as he acted in accordance with the rule book. He was invited to submit a formal application for service in British intelligence. He might have wondered at that point how many regulations a Jew had to follow in order to risk his life in His Majesty's service. He was interviewed by Norman Bentwich, a British officer.

After a full day of discussion Bentwich decided that Aaron Aaronsohn, the dedicated agronomist, was equally sincere in his devotion to the Allied cause and could supply potentially important intelligence information. Bentwich passed his conclusions along to the senior officer in British intel-

---

*Modern geologists refer to underground water-bearing rock layers as aquifers. In some cases their origins probably date back nearly ten thousand years to the end of the last Ice Age.

ligence in Cairo, General Sir Gilbert Clayton, and the general's aide, Major Wyndham Deedes. Aaron's hazardous journey was, in the end, not in vain.

Specifically, Major Deedes ordered that the contact with Athlit be reestablished. Once again, the contact required the dropping of a courier from a passing ship to collect the information gathered at Athlit. In this case it was expected that the courier would swim from the ship to shore and back, limiting the choice to a man who was an excellent swimmer.

Again, as in the case of Zvi Rabin, the ranks of the Palestinian Jewish refugees in Egypt were searched. Again, another former member of the Zion Mule Corps was offered the assignment. He was Leibel Bornstein, a native of the village of Petach Tikvah. Bornstein had earned his living as a driver in Palestine. There he had known Aaronsohn and considered it a high honor to be able to work for him.

Even before the preparations were under way for Bornstein's departure, Aaron Aaronsohn had begun to worry about his sister, Sarah, and Absolom Feinberg. He had been out of touch with them for six months.

As it turned out, there was reason for alarm. In anticipation of Aaron's arrangements with British intelligence, Absolom and Sarah continued to prepare reports on Turkish activities, expecting any day that a courier would be dispatched from a passing ship. The sons of a few trusted neighbors were also enlisted in these acts of Jewish patriotism and Turkish treason.

Absolom was understandably impatient. Why didn't Aaron write? Nearly five months passed before there was at last a cable. It advised them that Aaron was sailing for America—his coded way of saying that he was en route to England. Apparently the cable was garbled, leading Absolom Feinberg to take it literally: Aaron Aaronsohn, their trusted leader, had deserted them! Feinberg's mistake was to cost him his life.

With so much information compiled, no contact with the British, and Aaron apparently out of the picture, Absolom decided once again to go to Cairo to meet with British intelligence officers. Sarah tried to persuade him not to give up hope for her brother, but Feinberg could not bring himself to wait any longer. This time he did not set off alone but chose as his companion Yosef Lishansky, a brash young man with a yen for high adventure, brave to the point of being foolhardy.

The departure of Absolom and Yosef left Sarah in full charge of the station at Athlit. The gathering of intelligence continued in expectation of that still-elusive time when the Jewish spies would be met by a messenger from the command in Egypt.

While Sarah worked and waited, Feinberg and Lishansky pursued their carefully planned trek across the desert. They had started out disguised as Bedouins, riding camels. They had even recruited a Bedouin guide from a small settlement north of Beersheba. The journey was going well. During the night they would pass through the Turkish lines; by day they would hide out or move only where they felt certain they would not be detected.

After about a week they ran into trouble. The skies clouded over. The stars, which had served as navigational aids, were not visible. They were

attempting to find a British encampment near Al-'Arīsh on the Mediterranean coast of the Sinai. The guide claimed he was lost. There was no choice but to wait until sunrise when, Feinberg hoped, the encampment would be in sight. They tethered their camels and waited. It was not yet dawn when the cold silence of the desert night was shattered by the shouts of a band of Bedouins.

At precisely this time, Aaron Aaronsohn was in Cairo, concluding his drawn-out arrangement for clearance as an intelligence agent. On the evening of January 25, 1917, as he was returning to his hotel in Cairo, he was met at the entrance by a British intelligence officer, a Captain Edmunds. Edmunds delivered a cryptic message: "Your presence is required immediately at Port Said. One of your men has reached there through the desert." Edmunds could not identify the man or his condition.

Within the hour, Aaronsohn was on a train to Port Said. There, in a hotel, he found Lishansky seriously wounded and distraught. Haltingly, under Aaron's patient questioning, he related the story of their disaster in the desert.

The most demoralizing fact was that Absolom Feinberg was dead. According to Yosef's account, they were attacked by thirty or forty Bedouins who demanded that the Bedouin guide be turned over to them. They claimed that a blood feud existed between their tribe and that of the guide. The demand was apparently part of a plot, because suddenly, in the midst of the argument, as Feinberg refused to comply, the guide suddenly ran over and joined the surrounding tribesmen. The two Jews, convinced they would be killed, attempted to run for cover. A gun battle ensued. Absolom and Yosef held off the Bedouins until their ammunition was exhausted. Absolom was shot dead; Yosef was wounded and lost consciousness. He regained consciousness in the hot desert sun of the next morning. He was alone. Despite his pain, he crawled across the sands for several hours until he encountered a British patrol.

A bitter Aaronsohn blamed the British for his friend's death. The agronomist had been in Cairo for more than a month. If he had not had to waste so much time persuading the authorities to accept his mission, if they had sent a messenger to Athlit sooner, Feinberg would never have undertaken his fatal journey.

The tragedy of Feinberg's death did not, however, divert British intelligence or Aaronsohn from concluding their plans. The spy ship *Monegam* was fitted out at Port Said and was ready to sail. On this trip, Aaronsohn would be a passenger. At the pier he met Leibel Bornstein, the intrepid young man who was to swim from the ship to Athlit and back again. Aaronsohn was joined by a friend, the Christian Arab Charles Boutagy. The British intelligence officer present was Captain Smith, who was accompanied by an Arab agent for naval intelligence, Abdullah, and Abdullah's two sons.

Aaron was on the bridge as the ship passed Athlit. Through binoculars he watched two figures hanging out a white sheet from the station. This meant that they had seen the ship and that it was safe to send a courier ashore. Before sundown, Aaron pointed out to Leibel some familiar landmarks on

the shore. Then he instructed Bornstein specifically: "From the highway you'll take the road that leads to the gate of my experimental station, and you'll go to the nearby two-story house. There you are to call out the name of Rabb—that's the man who works at the station. When he opens the door, go in and give him what you are to receive from me. Take whatever he gives you. Tell Haim Cohen he's to come back with us to Egypt. Tell Reuven Schwartz that I want to see him. When you get back to the shore, signal the ship, and the Arabs will meet you and swim back with you. That's all."

At midnight the ship's engines were shut off. It rested in tomblike silence about a mile offshore. The wintry night was moonless. A small boat was lowered into the choppy sea to convey Bornstein as close as possible. When the little craft reached a point where it was in danger of being capsized by the breakers, it was time for Bornstein to plunge into the icy water. Abdullah had volunteered to go with him, and the two men stripped and dove overboard.

Strapped to Bornstein's back was a waterproof leather pouch. It contained papers, a flashlight, a bottle of whiskey, dry clothes, and a loaded revolver. When they reached the shore, Abdullah wished Bornstein good luck and swam back to the boat.

His body processes nearly halted by the cold water, Bornstein staggered ashore, opened the pouch, removed the dry clothes, and struggled into them. He took a long slug of whiskey to restart his metabolism. The cold and the alcohol rendered him almost incoherent, but he groped his way through a wadi leading from the beach, crossed the highway, stumbled along the road to the gate of the experimental station, and collapsed. Two members of the station found him there. He was able to mumble his instructions to the extent that he was recognized as the awaited courier.

At last, the Jews had established a workable arrangement with British intelligence. It would continue productively for twenty months under Aaron's direction from Cairo and Sarah's in Palestine. It seemed that all the organization lacked was a name.

On the way back to Cairo from the successful mission to Athlit, Aaron and his secretary, Liova Schneersohn, were sitting on the deck of the *Monegam*. Liova was reading his Bible. A young British intelligence officer approached Aaron and asked, "Does your organization have a password?"

It did not, but Aaron turned to Liova, who thumbed through his Bible until he found a ringing sentence. In Hebrew, he read *Netzach Israel lo ishakare* ("The Eternal Israel will not die").

"Our password," proclaimed Liova, "should be NILI" (the acronym of the Hebrew sentence, pronounced *nee-lee*).

Thus, on the day after its first truly successful mission, the espionage group founded by Aaron Aaronsohn found its name. The NILI spies became a famous and familiar chapter in Jewish history.

The recruits that Sarah gathered into the dangerous work of the NILI were mainly young people in their early twenties. There were never more than two score, all united by family ties, friendship, and a zeal to work and risk their lives, if necessary, to serve the Jews of Palestine.

Unfortunately, the *yishuv* had not been consulted about the spying activ-

ities of the NILI group, and this led to serious problems. The very nature of espionage precludes any widespread discussion, even among those who might endorse the activities in question. But the *yishuv* was close-knit, and it was inevitable that some information about the mission of the NILI spies would leak into the general community. The community, for the most part, resented the spies because their discovery could potentially mean Turkish revenge against all members of the *yishuv*.

So frightened did most Jews become of the NILI threat that Hashomer, their own self-defense organization, considered measures to put an end to the espionage. Yigal Allon, in *The Shield of David*, summarizes the line of thought of the Hashomer's leaders: "Perhaps it would be possible for Hashomer itself to hold the NILI in protective custody until the end of the war. Perhaps, all sentiment aside, it was the duty of Hashomer to do away with NILI's leaders before the entire *yishuv* paid the penalty for their irresponsibility."

The community was in this state of alarm when, in September 1918, the Turkish *moudir* captured Sarah's carrier pigeon. Immediately the Turkish authorities began to make inquiries among the Jews of Zichron. Before any actual spies had been pinpointed by the Turks, the village committee summoned Sarah before them and ordered her to cease her spying activities. They warned her, "We don't want you to endanger the whole *yishuv*." Even worse for Sarah, they repudiated the whole NILI effort: "Our leaders and our people do not want this imaginary treasure that you are getting for us. We don't want to endanger the small property that we have. We don't want the Turks to slaughter us and drive us out. We don't want to be hanged for a few people who want to endanger themselves."

Sarah left the meeting deeply shaken. She knew that they were not entirely wrong, that her responsibility was awesome, that the work of the NILI spies was endangering the total Jewish community. But she was now so deeply involved in espionage that any question of stopping work was academic.

Her problems quickly mounted. The captured carrier pigeon had put the Turks on guard. They began to search actively for evidence of Jewish treason. Their suspicions were confirmed when a NILI spy was captured near Beersheba. He was a brash young man named Naaman Belkind. The Turks, cleverly, did not mistreat him—at first. He was offered every kindness and was even promised his freedom. He was plied with wine, which he accepted, unaware that it was laced with hashish. This reduced him to a placid, nonrational state. Naaman began to boast of his exploits. After this charade had run its course, the kindness was terminated. He was tortured to extract more information and then hanged.

Sarah, in the face of this disaster, knew that her days of freedom were numbered. Yet, despite the closing in of the Turks, she was reluctant to try to escape from the experimental station. One of her proclaimed reasons was that she would not leave her father alone on Rosh Hashanah, the Jewish New Year. But the Turks did not come. Nine days later was Yom Kippur, the Day of Atonement, and still there was an eerie stillness as Sarah fasted and prayed.

The desperate wait ended on the eve of Sukkoth, the holiday that marks

the fall harvest. Sarah heard the clatter of marching Turkish troops surrounding the house at Zichron. An officer pounded on the door and demanded the surrender, not of Sarah, but of Yosef Lishansky, who, the Turks had decided, was the resident leader of the NILI. Yosef, however, had escaped. When Sarah refused to reveal his whereabouts (she did not know), she, her brother Zvi, and her father, Ephraim, were arrested. The old man was tied up and ordered to provide information on Lishansky. When he was silent, they beat him on the soles of his feet. Between his cries of agony, Ephraim intoned, "Sh'ma," the beginning of the ancient prayer identifying man with his God—"Sh'ma Yisroel, Adanoi Elohenu, Adanoi Echud" ("Hear, O Israel, the Lord thy God, the Lord is One").

Then it was Sarah's turn. Her hands were tied to a gatepost, and she was savagely beaten until she lost consciousness. When she was revived, unspeakable vulgarities were inflicted on her body. Her hair was torn out by the roots. Hot bricks were placed under her armpits. Her fingernails were ripped out with pliers. She was unmercifully flogged.

They could not break her. Throughout the ordeal she remained defiant and taunted her captors.

Anita Engle, in *The NILI Spies*, records Sarah's defiance: "Beat me as much as you want, you won't get anything out of me. You think because I am a woman I'll be weak. I despise you. No one but I did anything. Only I knew. I despise you and death. Hit, torture, I will be avenged. Your death is coming."

For three days and nights the horror continued. The soldiers would take turns torturing her. Not only Sarah, her brother, and her father were subjected to the Turkish wrath but other members of the village community of Zichron as well.

After the third day, Sarah persuaded her captors to let her go alone into the bathroom. They did not know she had hidden a pistol there. She shot herself through the mouth. Three days later her agony ended in death.

Shortly afterward Yosef Lishansky was captured. In contrast to Sarah's tenacity, Yosef gave the Turkish inquisitors the names of all the members of the Hashomer that he could remember. Whether or not the information was given freely or under flogging is in dispute. The end result, however, was the same. The Turks rounded up nearly everyone associated with the Hashomer. Scores were jailed, and many were exiled from Palestine.

After the chance capture of the carrier pigeon in September, all the subsequent events confirmed the worst fears of the members of the *yishuv*. The NILI spies had done their dangerous work bravely and successfully, but at terrible cost to the *yishuv*. By winter the food shortage brought on by the locust plague had been compounded by Turkish vengeance. Executions, jailings, and starvation reduced the leaderless Jewish population in Palestine to about fifty-six thousand.

Was the venture worth the suffering it caused? Such a judgment depends partly on whether the work of the NILI spies is measured against the immediate and drastic hardship it brought to the Jews of Palestine or, in the larger, historical sense, the advantages the espionage provided the British in their eventual elimination of the Turks from the Holy Land.

Aaronsohn, through the NILI network of spies, had provided Field Marshal E. H. Allenby with crucial intelligence that made possible a successful assault on Beersheba. A year and a half later, William Ormsby-Gore acknowledged the contribution: "They were the most valuable nucleus of our intelligence service in Palestine during the war. . . . The British government owes a very deep debt of gratitude to the Aaronsohn family for all they did for us."

The deputy military secretary to Allenby, Captain Raymond Savage, added to the accolades. In discussing the British success at Beersheba, he said, "It was very largely the daring work of young spies, most of them natives of Palestine, which enabled the brilliant Field Marshal to accomplish his undertaking so effectively. The leader of the spy system was a young Jewess, a Miss Sarah Aaronsohn."

In fact, of course, the leader was her brother Aaron, although his long absence had shifted much of the burden and danger to Sarah. Aaron never returned to Palestine. In directing the NILI operations he had shuttled between Cairo and London. When the war ended, Aaronsohn intended to make his voice heard at the Paris Peace Conference in May 1919. He never arrived; his plane, en route from London to Paris, crashed in the English Channel.

Before the war ended, however, when the Turks were still attempting to stem the British military advances and the Jews in Palestine were trying to stay alive, events in Europe were shaping the future of *Eretz Yisroel* (the land of Israel).

3

World War I: The Zion Mule Corps and the Jewish Legion

AS THE SETTLERS of their first or second *aliyah* and their children were sinking their roots deeper into the soil of Palestine, the necessities of survival were creating a unique society. A successful defense system rendered the farmer and the soldier interchangeable, and in either role, the defenders had to outthink their foes and develop the art of innovative resistance, to compensate for the overwhelming numerical superiority of potential attackers. It is not surprising that Aaron Aaronsohn and his sister were farmers first, but—in their own way—innovative fighters as well.

There were, of course, to be many intermediate steps between the makeshift defense of a humble village and the superb Israeli military and intelligence organization of today. The progression was replete with heroic, tragic, triumphant, and sometimes even comic incidents. Through it all can be seen the remarkable transition of the Jew from Europe—most often eastern Europe—where he was allowed to be neither farmer nor soldier, to a new land where, in a generation, he became a stalwart example of both.

Among the giants of the era of World War I was a fiery orator, Vladimir Jabotinsky, who later adopted the Hebrew first name Zeev. In 1914 he was sent to the western front as a correspondent for the liberal Russian newspaper *Russkiye Vyedomosti*. His dispatches dealt primarily with, in his own words, "the moods and sentiments produced by the war." Jabotinsky was even more persuasive as a speaker than as a correspondent. In this respect, he was often compared with the great Bolshevik Leon Trotsky. Jabotinsky's cause, however, was Zionism.

In 1914 Jabotinsky, then thirty-six, read a news placard in Bordeaux announcing the entry of Turkey into the war on the side of the Central Powers. He came to a series of conclusions. As an informed correspondent, he

was well aware of the chaotic internal instability of Turkey, and that its government was weak and ineffectual. He was convinced that the "sick man of Europe" would be defeated and dismembered. Jabotinsky's hopes soared: there was an opportunity for the establishment of a Jewish state—on the ruins of the Turkish empire. Hence, it was the moral obligation of Jews to join the British in the battle to crush the Turks. Jabotinsky was impelled to find Jews motivated to join his crusade.

Not every Jew in Palestine had felt moved to make such a commitment, but the Turks unintentionally forced the hand of the Jewish settlers. In the summer of 1915 Turkish authorities learned of secret stores of arms that the Hashomer had accumulated. Ironically, the arms were not intended for use against the Turks but for protection during raids against the *yishuv* by the Arabs. Nevertheless, the Turks considered the arms a potential threat against Ottoman rule. The weapons and ammunition were commandeered, and hundreds of Jews were arrested and expelled from their villages. Active Zionists were the first to be rounded up, including Ben-Gurion and Ben-Zvi. Both protested, insisting they were comporting themselves as loyal Turkish citizens. The Turks were not impressed. More than a thousand Jews were exiled, among them Ben-Gurion, who proclaimed, "I will be back some day."

Most of the exiles went to Egypt, a disrupting experience that nonetheless proved to be in their long-term interests. There they were given shelter by the British in the crowded Egyptian barracks at Gabbari and Mafrusa. They were fed and clothed by the bounty of the Jewish community in Egypt, but their existence was strained by idleness into a persistent discontent. Who would be the contemporary Moses to lead them out of Egypt, back to the land of Israel?

Two dissimilar men came remarkably close to a second fulfilling of the biblical promise. One was Jabotinsky, by then actively trying to create a Jewish military force. Joseph Trumpeldor was the other. Like Jabotinsky, he was a Russian, but the resemblance ended there. Trumpeldor was a professional soldier with the unique distinction of being one of the few Jews (perhaps the only one) to hold a commission in the czar's army. He fought in the Russo-Japanese War of 1905. In the Battle of Port Arthur, his left arm was ripped off by a burst of shrapnel. In this state of mutilation he was captured and imprisoned by the Japanese, and somehow survived to be released when the war ended. The czar decorated him for valor and allowed him to retain his commission on a reserve status.

With Jabotinsky, Trumpeldor shared the Zionist passion and in 1912 immigrated to Palestine. There he adhered to the socialist tradition of the second *aliyah* and advocated armed struggle against the Turks. He was working in a collective settlement on the shores of the Sea of Galilee when the Turks drove the Zionists into Egypt.

Trumpeldor was sulking in the Egyptian camp at Gabbari when Jabotinsky arrived to seek recruits for a Jewish military unit. The two men soon found that they held identical views. Before they could approach the British army, however, they had to test the range of support among the other exiles.

A meeting made it clear that the support was there. They framed a resolution: "It is resolved to form a Jewish Legion and propose to England to make use of it in Palestine." One hundred Jews signed the petition.

As the acknowledged leaders, Jabotinsky and Trumpeldor were elected to present the petition to British authorities in Cairo. Trumpeldor was dressed in his full Russian officer's regalia, including four St. George crosses for heroism—a calculated effort to impress the British. But Jabotinsky did the talking.

For all his eloquence, he might have saved his breath. The British had no plans at that time for an offensive in Palestine, nor did they seem to have much confidence in the band of ragged refugees, despite the Palestinians' eagerness to risk their lives in His Majesty's service.

The lack of faith in the Jews as fighters must have been the key factor, because the British officers had a counterproposal that could only be described as humiliating. They needed someone to care for the army mules, probably on the Turkish front. Would this Jewish contingent accept such an assignment? Jabotinsky was insulted; so were most of the prospective fighting men. This was an affront to their manhood, an example of British arrogance. Were these dedicated Jews to march into the Holy Land leading mules instead of carrying rifles?

Surprisingly, it was Trumpeldor, the decorated hero, who argued in favor of the mule assignment. The important thing, in his view, was for the Jews to get involved in the fight against the Turks. If, for the present, their role was a menial one, accept it. After some bitter arguments, with Trumpeldor pitted against Jabotinsky, the former won the day. Some 650 Palestinian Jews signed up for mule duty, forming a unit that was soon to be known as the Zion Mule Corps.

The corps was fortunate in the assignment of a devout, Bible-quoting Christian as its commanding officer. Colonel John Henry Patterson was one of several Protestants whose Christian fundamentalism engendered an emotional belief in the Zionist cause. In the Bible, God gave the Holy Land to Abraham, father of the Jews; hence, a Christian who believes in the Bible must also believe in Zionism. Patterson was a slender Irish aristocrat, so fervent in his conviction that to him the greatest mystery was why all Jews, especially those in England, were not Zionists.

"Why any Jew should be anti-Zionist passes my comprehension," he wrote in his own account, *With the Judeans in the Palestine Campaign*, "for the Zionist ideal in no way interferes with the rights and privileges of those fortunate Jews who have found many homes in friendly countries, but aims at establishing a national home for those less happy ones who, against their will, are forced to live in exile and who never ceased to yearn for the land promised to their forefather Abraham and his seed forever."

Trumpeldor was honored with the appointment as Patterson's second in command. These two professionals created from the bedraggled and inexperienced refugees a disciplined transport battalion. The members created their own Hebrew lexicon of military terms and carried the blue and white Zionist flag into battle.

Unfortunately, their baptism of fire was in the disastrous Gallipoli campaign, one of the greatest military fiascos in British history. This assault on the Gallipoli Peninsula, undertaken in the hope of capturing Constantinople from the Turks, lasted nine months and cost the forces of Great Britain two hundred and fifty thousand casualties before its ignominious end. Repeated assaults on a fortified shoreline were beaten back under appallingly destructive Turkish fire.

The soldiers of the Zion Mule Corps, however, acquitted themselves well. Under heavy Turkish fire, they guided their supply-laden mules to the front. Some were killed, many were wounded, and a few displayed such bravery that they were later decorated. Those who died were later buried in the British military cemetery on Mount Scopus in Jerusalem, with the Star of David carved on their tombstones. The Mule Corps, whatever it may have lacked in surface dignity, marked a significant event—the first time in modern history that Jews had participated as a unit in a full-scale war.

When the Gallipoli campaign came to an inglorious end, with the British in full retreat, the Zion Mule Corps received a new and unwelcome assignment. The unit was called on to assist in a peace-keeping mission in Ireland, where anti-British riots had broken out. Whereas the Jewish soldiers were willing to continue the fight against the Central Powers, they were not in the least anxious to be thrust into quelling a civil rebellion.

Their spokesman politely requested to be excused from the assignment. The British military authorities did not press the issue but, as a kind of retaliation, disbanded the Zion Mule Corps in May 1916. One hundred and twenty of the Jews then signed up in other units. Their greatest contribution to the British army was still in the future.

If Herzl's pamphlet, *Der Judenstaat*, provided the stimulus for the active Zionist movement, the Balfour Declaration of November 2, 1917, bestowed on Zionism a degree of international legitimacy. The declaration gave official British approval to the Zionist cause. Specifically, the declaration was a somewhat guarded statement of policy by the British cabinet, officially expressed in a letter signed by Foreign Secretary Arthur James Balfour, to the Lord Lionel Rothschild, president of the British Zionist Federation. The letter said, in part:

> His Majesty's Government view with favor the establishment in Palestine of a national home for the Jewish people, and will use their best endeavors to facilitate the achievement of this object, it being clearly understood that nothing shall be done which may prejudice the civil and religious rights of existing non-Jewish communities in Palestine, or the rights and political status enjoyed by Jews in any other country. I should be grateful to you if you would bring this declaration to the knowledge of the Zionist Federation.

The landmark political document, contrary to a well-established story, did not constitute a reward to Chaim Weizmann, the renowned chemist, for his

major contribution to the chemistry of explosives for the British War Office.* Actually it was engendered mainly by Britain's political interests, leavened to some degree with idealism and compassion.

At the time, many national groups were caught up in the zeal for self-determination, the chance to control their own destiny. In every case, with one exception, these national communities comprised the majority in the territories they wished to control. The Jews were the exception: they did not constitute a majority in Palestine. The Zionist claim for recognition was unique. It was based on a sovereignty conferred by the Holy Scriptures but not exercised for nearly two thousand years. It was true, however, that in spite of mass expulsions and purges, some Jews had lived in Palestine continuously since biblical times. This continuity of the Jewish presence was a consideration in the decision to draft the Balfour Declaration.

The declaration was issued in spite of opposition from some of the most powerful members of the Anglo-Jewish community. They were concerned that their own status as loyal British subjects would be jeopardized. But it was the well-organized Zionists who could claim a following among a majority of British Jews and so commanded the attention of the British government. The Zionists' prestige was greatly enhanced by their leaders, notably Weizmann.

Weizmann had been born in 1874 in the small hamlet of Motol, near Pinsk, Russia. He was one of fifteen children in the poverty-ridden household of a small timber merchant, where, despite the hardships, education was almost an obsession. Weizmann's exceptional intellectual gifts enabled him to acquire an education in Germany and Switzerland. In 1904 he won a chemistry instructorship at the University of Geneva.

At that time Geneva was a haven for Russian revolutionaries, including Leon Trotsky. Weizmann was soon disturbed over the influence that the fiery Russian exerted over Jewish students on behalf of international socialism. In an attempt to counter the socialist fervor, Weizmann tried to organize a Zionist club to promote Jewish nationalism. The idea died aborning when the Jewish group could not reconcile its conflicting national and international outlooks.

Not long after, Weizmann was offered, and accepted, a teaching position at the University of Manchester. In England the young chemist found the intellectual climate much more to his liking. A tall, slender man of ascetic habits, he was a powerful debater and a person of unusual charm. These qualities were to prove useful, for Weizmann's value to the Zionist movement, in England especially, lay in his talent to acquire influential friends and to convert them to the necessity of establishing a Jewish state. Among his most important converts were the editor of the influential *Manchester Guardian* and Arthur James Balfour, the future Lord Balfour.

---

*Weizmann developed a process for synthesizing acetone, an essential ingredient in the explosive, cordite. His major achievement, however, was the extraction of pectin from apples, making possible the compounding of kaopectate, now used worldwide in the treatment of diarrhea.

Weizmann shared the Zionist leadership with Lord Rothschild, the 2nd Baron, head of the English branch of the most prestigious Jewish family in Europe. The influence of a Rothschild opened even the most reluctant doors to pleadings for the Jewish cause. His father, Lord Rothschild, the 1st Baron, had, in 1874, loaned Prime Minister Benjamin Disraeli $20 million to buy for the British government the controlling interest in the Suez Canal Company. Neither the English people nor the Crown had forgotten this act of patriotism, for control of the Suez proved to be pivotal in World War I.

From the moment the Turkish government entered the war, the Allies anticipated that the shaky Ottoman Empire would be defeated and that its dominions in the Middle East would be severed from Turkish control and distributed as spoils to the victors. The Jews were among the claimants. As early as 1914, the Zionists had asserted their right to "reconstitute a national home in Palestine." For the British and French, however, a more important issue in the Middle East was to reconcile their own territorial disputes.

The British were already entrenched in Egypt and professed to have no further claims, but the French Foreign Office on the Quai d'Orsay had grander visions. The immodest claim of France was for political control of all the Turkish provinces from Syria southward to the Egyptian border. In the spring of 1915, when the French first asserted this ambition, Great Britain was in a delicate position. His Majesty's Government did not want to risk antagonizing an ally in the midst of a taxing war, but the French claim was a bit excessive: it would bring a powerful force close to the Suez Canal, Britain's lifeline to India.

The difficulty of Great Britain's position suggests that the Foreign Office saw a possible solution in a third force—a Jewish presence in Palestine under a British mandate. Such a concept seemed to make the Balfour Declaration a logical next step. Actually the situation was far more complex than that.

For one thing, Britain coveted the support of the seven hundred thousand Zionists who were a powerful moral force in the Western world. Officially the Zionists were neutral, but it was clear to the warring powers that they were an influence that could not be ignored. For another thing, the British were alarmed by—and anxious to head off—a proposal of Henry Morganthau, United States ambassador to Turkey, for a Jewish state in Palestine with internal autonomy but under the sovereignty of Turkey. And finally there were press reports from Germany that the Germans were weighing a Jewish Palestinian state under German protection. This was an unlikely prospect, but one that could not be completely dismissed.

The combined impact of all these possibilities brought forth the Balfour Declaration, which in turn paved the way for the British mandate. The government's emphasis, however, was a moral one. Balfour himself stated that Britain had been moved "by the desire to give the Jews their rightful place in the world; a great nation without a home is not right."

While the political maneuvering and infighting leading to the Balfour Declaration were taking place, the war was going badly for the Allies. Great

masses of men were being chewed up on the western front, and Colonel Patterson wrote that "England was in deadly peril." He cited the appalling shipping losses from U-boat torpedoes; the military subjugation of Belgium, Serbia, Romania, and a large part of France; Italy stalemated; and Russia, in the throes of revolution, a now useless ally.

Jabotinsky had arrived in England shortly after the Gallipoli defeat to persuade the Foreign Office to muster an all-Jewish army. For two frustrating years he stalked the corridors of the military without success. The British image of Jews, it seemed, was of tradesmen and tailors. No one appeared to take Jabotinsky seriously. Even when Trumpeldor joined his old comrade, their pleas, carried to the point of harassment, were unsuccessful. Not the least of their problems was the opposition of some of the powerful Anglo-Jewish leaders, who also listened to the importunings of the two Jewish warriors.

In the end, it was the desperate military situation that made people listen to them. In the late spring of 1917 Prime Minister Lloyd George, through his secretary, Leopold Amery, asked Jabotinsky and Trumpeldor to submit a proposal for a Jewish legion. The two Jewish leaders then waited impatiently for several months before Lloyd George instructed the war secretary, Lord Derby, to implement the plan. The pair of self-appointed Jewish spokesmen were summoned to the War Office, where Lord Derby listened with some skepticism to their plans for a Jewish military force. Then he asked the crucial question: "Could we count on a large number of volunteers?"

Trumpeldor, in his thick Russian accent, responded with a series of conditional answers: "Your Lordship, if it is to be just a regiment of Jews, perhaps. If it is to be a formation for the Palestine front, certainly. If together with this formation, there will be a government pronouncement in favor of Zionism, the response will be overwhelming."

Lord Derby was convinced. The formation of the "Jewish Regiment" was officially announced in the *London Gazette* of August 23, 1917. Its first commanding officer was to be none other than Colonel John Henry Patterson, then in Ireland in command of a battalion of the Royal Dublin Fusiliers. Jabotinsky was assigned to help in the organization and recruitment.

Among the Jews of England, the new military unit was not a popular idea. With the exception of Weizmann and Lord Rothschild, most influential Jews objected to the unique identification of the regiment. On August 30 an angry delegation met with Lord Derby to protest the whole concept. The War Office bowed to the pressure from these influential citizens. The name Jewish Regiment was dropped, as was the use of a special insignia. The battalions were to be called simply the Royal Fusiliers.

This concession to the anti-Zionists turned out to be effective only on paper. For the new recruits, proud of the Jewishness of their organization, there was no question of identification. As Patterson later wrote, "Our worthy friends might have saved themselves all the trouble they took . . . because from the moment that the battalions were formed, although they were

known officially as Royal Fusiliers, unofficially, everywhere, and by every person, they were known solely as the Jewish Battalions."

The recruiting for the legion started in London, mainly among the Jewish immigrants from Russia. Most of them lived in Whitechapel and conversed primarily in Yiddish. As aliens they were exempt from conscription and hence felt no strong compulsion to join up. However, the vision of a liberated Holy Land had a deep religious and emotional appeal. Jabotinsky was a master salesman; he spoke on street corners and in neighborhood halls. He reminded them of their heritage, of their duty to fulfill God's command to return to Zion. In a matter of weeks the indifference and mild hostility of the crowds melted under Jabotinsky's passionate oratory. First in a trickle and then a stream, the volunteers signed up. Their training began at the Crown Hill barracks near Plymouth.

The nucleus of the new legion was none other than those 120 veterans of the Zion Mule Corps who were still in the British army. At Patterson's request they were transferred to Plymouth to assist in training. As the recruits arrived in batches of twenty or thirty, Patterson personally interviewed each one. He inquired into the man's family and background and "gave every man some advice on how to conduct himself as a good soldier and a good Jew." One of the most promising recruits, later recommended for a commission, was Jacob Epstein, one day to become England's most famous sculptor.

The Jewish battalion was unusual in many ways. As Patterson reported, "we had no crime to stain our record . . . there was not a single case of civil offense being recorded against us all the time we were at Plymouth." But perhaps the most amusing difference between Patterson's Jews and other military units had nothing to do with fighting ability. The "wet canteen," where beer and ale are sold, is an honored fixture of the British, but the canteen set up to serve the Jewish battalion had to be shut down: it did not have a single customer.

If the Jews tended to be light drinkers or even nondrinkers, a more serious problem arose through a conflict between Jewish dietary law and military custom. A religious Jew is required to eat only certain types of food, prepared in a ritually prescribed way to make it proper, or "kosher." In many ways Muslims observe similar dietary restrictions. For example, neither Jew nor Muslim is permitted to eat pork. Although special food was provided to meet the religious needs of Muslim troops under British command, the army refused to furnish kosher meals for Patterson's troops. The problem was compounded by the refusal of the authorities to recognize Saturday as the Hebrew Sabbath. Not until Patterson threatened to resign did the War Office reverse itself and make concessions to Jewish tradition.

In the late fall of 1917 the picture began to change dramatically in the Middle East. The decimated and discouraged Jewish community in Palestine learned of the Balfour Declaration at almost the same time that British troops were driving the Turks out of the southern half of the country. Thousands of Jewish men and women signed petitions urging the formation of a

volunteer Jewish legion, convinced they would now be allowed to fight for
Eretz Yisroel. Six weeks after Balfour, British troops, with General Allenby
at the head, marched into the holy city of Jerusalem.

The momentum for Jewish participation was building rapidly. Before
Patterson left England, he received welcome news. General Macready announced that he was recommending to Allenby the formation of a complete
Jewish brigade "as soon as two complete Jewish battalions arrive in Europe."

The first contingent of Palestinian Jews were organized into the Fortieth
Royal Fusiliers and were sent to Egypt for training. There was a memorable
leave-taking ceremony in front of a small synagogue on the main street of
Tel Aviv. As hundreds watched, the flag of the Hashomer was transferred
to these new, officially sanctioned Jewish warriors. Chaim Weizmann,
choked with emotion, reminded them of their historic mission as the advance guard for the establishment of a Jewish homeland. Once again the
scarlet and white banner was waived aloft—"In blood and fire Judea shall
arise." The recruits marched to nearby Jaffa, where they boarded freight
cars on the narrow-gauge railroad that then rumbled off toward Cairo.

Meanwhile, additional volunteers were emerging in the United States,
protected by one of history's most unusual military contracts. It had been
prepared by a lawyer who, by the time most Americans were enlisting, was
sitting on the Supreme Court. Louis Dembitz Brandeis, elevated to the Court
by Woodrow Wilson, was one of the eminent leaders of the American Zionist
movement. It was his task, when recruits were sought in America for the
Jewish legion, to protect the rights of his clients, the Jewish volunteers.

Brandeis drafted the agreement with great skill and understanding of his
clients' needs. The British army was to provide kosher food and permit the
observance of Jewish holidays. It was understood that the enlistees would be
sent to fight only in Palestine and at the termination of the war could not be
reassigned to any other country. Jews not subject to military service for the
United States were eligible for the legion.

Brandeis, however, for all his legal brilliance, missed one point, and thereby caused a minor incident. He had neglected to specify that recruits must
be male. Consequently, an intrepid young woman from Milwaukee decided
to enlist, pointing out correctly that nowhere did the contract specify the sex
of those eligible: it simply limited recruits to those of the Jewish faith. "I
can fight as well as any man," she insisted. Perhaps she was right, but
nonetheless, her application was rejected, an experience that, she later
claimed, almost crushed her spirit. Almost, but not quite. Years later when
she became a member of Ben-Gurion's cabinet, he paid her a genuine, if
male-chauvinist, compliment: "She is the only member of my cabinet with
batesem [balls]."

The woman from Milwaukee was Golda Meir. Perhaps if she had been
allowed to join the Jewish legion, she might have become a general instead
of the first woman prime minister of Israel.

When recruiting started, Ben-Zvi and Ben-Gurion were in New York seeking volunteers for the legion. They found the entire American Zionist com-

munity involved. William Braiterman, a young man caught in the spell of this romantic adventure, described the scene for us some sixty years later: "There were soapbox orators who would set themselves up on a street corner. Those of us who came to listen were led on by the singing of Hebrew songs. When a crowd had gathered someone would get on the soapbox and make an appeal for volunteers. It was something like the Salvation Army."

But the recruiting went to unorthodox places, as Braiterman remembered. "In New York there was the famous Yiddish theater on Second Avenue. Boris Thomashefsky, a talented Yiddish actor, was one of the most widely acclaimed members of the profession. When his handsome figure strode the boards, the audience applauded wildly. This deeply respected actor would stop the play at its most dramatic moment and make an appeal for volunteers for the Jewish legion.

"This type of appeal not only attracted recruits, but had an effect on the theater's audience. The concept of Zionism was stimulated. We didn't have our own country, and yet we were going to go out and fight for a flag and country that wasn't even established."

Braiterman's experience was a typical example of the lengths to which some Jews would go to fight for the dream of Zion. When he decided to enlist, he was seventeen. The minimum age for recruits was eighteen. By coincidence, Braiterman's family physician was Dr. Herman Seidel, not only a renowned pediatrician but an ideological dean of the Labor Zionists and known throughout the movement. He had been appointed by the British authorities as examining physician for recruits in the Baltimore area, where both he and Braiterman lived. The Baltimore recruiting office was in a shabby neighborhood just east of downtown. On a cold, cloudy day in January 1918, the slight and slender Braiterman marched into Dr. Seidel's office and announced that he was going to enlist and wanted a physical examination.

The doctor quite properly refused to examine Braiterman, knowing full well that the youth was but seventeen. Braiterman insisted he was eighteen. Seidel was angry. "Don't tell me you are eighteen. I'll tell you when you are eighteen."

Recalling the incident as an elderly man, Braiterman was philosophical. "He refused to commit perjury to help me enlist in the legion."

That was not the end of the story, however. Braiterman went to Philadelphia, where he was not known, called himself William Cohen, and was promptly sworn in.

Braiterman's adventure was not unique. All over the United States the prospect of a return to the Promised Land was a compelling force. To be sure, not everyone was moved by patriotic fervor. As Braiterman recalls, "The 150 volunteers recruited from the Baltimore-Washington region consisted of all kinds of people. Some joined out of idealism, some to escape personal responsibility, married men to get away from their wives, and some who even were criminals out on bail. But we could not accept as volunteers anyone subject to the U.S. draft. Foreigners could join, and the majority were Labor Zionists."

In Egypt, American enlistees joined their religious brethren from all over the world. The Jews from Palestine were in the vanguard sent to Al-'Arīsh in the Sinai. Most of the Palestinian Jews had grown strong and tough from a generation or more in the rocky, sparsely vegetated land of their new country. Long used to making do with scarce resources, the Palestinian Jews amazed the British with their frugal nature. After practice-firing their Lewis guns, they would carefully gather up the brass cartridge cases so as not to waste any metal.* One of their prize recruits was Private L. Shkolnik, later to be known as Levi Eshkol, prime minister in 1967 during the Six-Day War.

The recruits, whether sturdy Palestinians or small and spindly city-dwellers from London, New York, and elsewhere, bore the rigors of training in good spirits—except when they faced occasional anti-Semitism among some of the British officers and noncoms. Epithets such as "heathen" and "nigger" were occasionally muttered and were more difficult to bear if an officer compounded the insult by referring overtly to Arab soldiers as "white men."

On occasion Jewish resentment came close to mutiny. One such incident is reported by Colonel Richard Meinerzhagen in his *Middle East Diary*. The first Jewish battalion was being inspected by an unnamed brigadier. Scrutinizing the ranks of soldiers, he came upon one with unpolished buttons. The brigadier reprimanded the soldier and called him "a dirty little Jew." The reaction to this was such that Colonel Patterson ordered his men to fix bayonets and form a threatening square around the officer until he apologized. Under the circumstances, the brigadier had no choice. He apologized—and Patterson got away with his insubordinate tactics.

The sardonic humor of war was present even during training. Braiterman recalls a battle-hardened British sergeant introducing Ben-Zvi to the bayonet. "Aim at the enemy's heart," said the sergeant, "but stick the blade into the bloke's stomach, twist it, and withdraw it before it rusts—otherwise the Turk might die of blood poisoning." Ben-Zvi, essentially a pacifist, was revolted by such remarks; Braiterman still recalls the shock on his face.

In June the first two battalions left Egypt for the Holy Land to join the great British offensive of 1918, moving across the Sinai by train. In a slightly romantic vein, Colonel Patterson described the journey: "All through the night, as we sped across the Sinai desert, they could see the funnel of the engine belching forth a pillar of flame, and we were greatly reminded of the wanderings of the forefathers of these men in this very desert who, in their night journeys, were always guided by a pillar of fire."

At first their main enemy was heat. The first encampment, in the Jordan River valley north of the Dead Sea, the lowest spot on earth, was a hell. The legion headquarters was in the Wadi el-Mellahah, a salient surrounded on

---

*Nor have the Jews of Israel given up this kind of frugality. In late October 1973 we watched Israeli soldiers on the west side of the Suez Canal tidying up the battlefield. A caravan of trucks picked up abandoned Russian-made armor, and beside the road were neat piles of brass artillery shells awaiting salvage.

three sides by the Turks. Militarily it would have proved indefensible if the Turks had chosen to attack. Fortunately for the Jews, they did not, but the combination of malaria, unbearably hot sun, and thirst took its toll on the Jewish ranks. By September, however, General Allenby needed their help. Most of the Jews experienced their first warfare as Allenby's army drove the Turks northward. The push was completely successful. The Turkish lines were smashed. On October 31, 1918, the Ottoman Empire sued for peace.

British military historians have acknowledged the Jewish legion's contribution to Allenby's victory. From their station in Jericho, the Jews joined in the drive in the western sector of the front, which started a few days after Yom Kippur. According to records in the British War Office, the Thirty-eighth, Thirty-ninth, Fortieth, and Forty-first battalions of the Royal Fusiliers—about a thousand men—were part of the forces that moved into Damascus. They are credited with capturing 13,400 prisoners, hundreds of guns, and all types of ammunition.

A total of about five thousand Jews saw active service and provided the nucleus of the postwar defense force in Palestine. In terms of the future homeland, the Jewish legion was a training exercise. When the war ended and the Arabs (ironically, often with British connivance) attempted to drive the Jews out, the well-trained legionnaires joined the Haganah (the Jewish army) and the Palmach (the special strike force) to fight for Jewish survival.

In the vacuum left by the Turkish defeat, the British found themselves playing a powerful role in the Middle East. Not only was Great Britain the pivotal force between Arabs and Jews but also the protector of the Suez lifeline and the first great power caught in the ascendant complications of oil diplomacy. Despite the Balfour Declaration, the overriding interest of His Majesty was to keep the Suez out of hostile control and to seize the opportunity to develop Middle Eastern petroleum reserves. Arabs, not Jews, controlled the oil and surrounded the Suez. Realistically, the Jews no longer seemed important.

Colonel Patterson was one of those who discerned the subtle change in British policy. "To the observant onlooker," he wrote, "it was quite evident that the hostile policy pursued by the administration must inevitably lead to outbreak against the Jews."

The Arabs, too, sensed the change in policy and were emboldened by it. With the Turks gone, Arab nationalism began to flourish. The Arabs now saw the Jews as usurpers of their land, and Colonel Patterson was right in his foreboding. In April 1920, within the ramparts of the holy city of Jerusalem, the British military looked the other way during a three-day series of pogroms. Consistent with this policy, the Balfour Declaration was, by British orders, never published in Palestine. Patterson reported that an unnamed military governor stated that "in case of anti-Jewish riots in his city, he would remove his garrison and take up a position at a window where he could watch—and laugh at—what went on."

In Jaffa, Arab anti-Zionist harangues were bellowed from the steps of the

military governor's office, while British soldiers stood by. Not surprisingly, the Arabs in Jerusalem, during the orgy of rape, murder, and pillage, cried out, "El dowleh ma'ana" ("The government is with us")."

There was a French factor as well. In February 1920, when the Arabs attacked four small, almost unarmed Jewish settlements in upper Galilee, one of their purported aims was to drive the French away from the vicinity of the lands that would someday be Syria and Lebanon. The Jews fled from the village of Hamarah to Metullah and finally to a compound at Tel Hai. There the Arabs demanded to be allowed to enter, assuring the Jews they would not be harmed because the Arabs were seeking only French soldiers. As a goodwill gesture, the Arabs were admitted inside the village. As soon as the gates were opened, however, hundreds of Arabs poured through and greeted the Jews with point-blank fire. Many Jews were felled by bullets before they realized what was happening. One of those shot was the great hero Joseph Trumpeldor. As he lay dying, this soldier of almost legendary stature uttered, in Hebrew, his last words, making light of his own death— "Ain diva" ("It doesn't matter").

In the besieged settlements of Kfar Gileadi and Metullah the villagers believed themselves to be the innocent victims of a fight between the Arabs and the French. With only a skeleton force of former legionnaires to protect them, some felt a strategic retreat was essential. A bitter debate followed between those who saw any retreat as dooming the *yishuv* and those who felt it was better to live to fight another day. The latter group prevailed by a narrow margin in a local referendum. The precious soil of Galilee was abandoned.

The decision proved to be a wise one. The French subdued the Arabs, and by the winter of 1920 the Jews were back on their farms at Kfar Gileadi and Metullah.

Meanwhile, Jabotinsky had organized an ad hoc Jewish self-defense corps that attempted to come to the aid of beleaguered comrades in Jerusalem. The British would not allow his forces to enter the city nor allow the trapped Jews to get out. Many were killed and hundreds were wounded. Their homes were burned and looted.

When the reign of terror was over and the British had restored order, it was not Arab leaders but Jabotinsky and his followers who were arrested and imprisoned. The indictment charged "banditism, instigating the people of the Ottoman Empire [which still nominally existed] to mutual hatred, pillage, rapine, devastation of the country and homicide in divers places."

As Jabotinsky was led off to prison, the Allies confirmed the Balfour Declaration and declared a League of Nations mandate over Palestine.

For the Jews the future was clear. Their survival lay not with the British but with themselves.

4

Fleeing Hitler: The Treacherous Journey

AFTER THE ESTABLISHMENT of the Palestine mandate in 1920, British policy toward the Zionist movement was to fluctuate for eighteen years. For the Jews, however, the peaks of hope seemed with each fluctuation to be lower and the valleys of despair ever deeper. As Arab nationalism became more belligerent, the settlers in the *yishuv* found themselves in increasing danger. No less than four British commissions from 1923 to 1939 attempted—unsuccessfully—to resolve the Palestine question. The Jews' best hope was to expand their economic and political beachhead through immigration. With the rise of Nazi Germany, this hope became doubly urgent; for not only were Jews needed in Palestine, but they needed to escape from Hitler as well. The barbarities of the Nazis in Germany and in Austria after the *Anschluss* had ignited the fires of anti-Semitism throughout Central and Eastern Europe.

Hitler, whose intent to debase the Jews was proclaimed as Nazi policy even before he seized power, was as good as his word. Within weeks of his accession in January 1933, he had removed Jews from the universities, the professions, and public service jobs, and he had even ordered a boycott of Jewish shops. What started as harassment became oppression and, by 1936, continuous violence. Jews were beaten, tortured, and imprisoned. Nazi gangs murdered thousands of them and went unpunished. After the *Anschluss* the Austrians rivaled their conquerors in barbarity. William L. Shirer, an eyewitness in Austria, described what he saw in his great work *The Rise and Fall of the Third Reich*:

> For the first few weeks [after the *Anschluss*] the behavior of the Vienna Nazis was worse than anything I had seen in Germany. There was an orgy of sadism. Day after day large numbers of Jewish men and

61

women could be seen scrubbing Schuschnigg signs off the sidewalk and cleaning the gutters. While they worked on their hands and knees with jeering storm troopers standing over them, crowds gathered to taunt them. Hundreds of Jews, men and women, were picked off the streets and put to work cleaning public latrines and the toilets of the barracks where the S.A. and the S.S. were quartered. Tens of thousands more were jailed. Their worldly possessions were confiscated or stolen. I myself, from our apartment in the Plosslgasse, watched squads of S.S. men carting off silver, tapestries, paintings and other loot from the Rothschild palace next door.

In those weeks one hundred and seventy-six thousand Viennese Jews were desperately seeking to leave the country that many of them had known as home for generations. Exactly thirty-two visas to Palestine were available.

This pitiful statistic was symbolic of the complex moves on the chessboard of history, moves that brought the Jews ever closer to the checkmate of decency. In theory the League of Nations had authorized the British mandate over Palestine in order to lay the groundwork for a Jewish homeland, as assured in the Balfour Declaration. Whatever Great Britain's original intentions, the humanitarian and practical underpinnings of the declaration had vanished, as far as Britain was concerned. The Arabs, with their massive oil reserves and their potential for disruption of the vital Suez area, had, quite simply, become more important than the Jews. That this change in British attitude paralleled the rise of Hitler is one of history's crueler ironies.

Unable to rely on Great Britain for protection, the Jews of Palestine depended increasingly on their highly organized (although officially illegal) defense systems. The Haganah was the most widespread and was officially affiliated with the Jewish Agency, the acknowledged representative of a majority of Palestine Jews. But the more militant settlers, imbued with the spirit of Jabotinsky, called themselves Revisionists and created their own military organization, the *Irgun Zvai Leumi* (National Military Organization).

Both organizations were acutely aware of the perils confronting the Jews of Europe as the Nazi philosophy swept from Germany, through Austria, and into the minds and hearts of latent anti-Semites in Poland, Czechoslovakia, Hungary, and Romania. Often the Jews in Palestine, viewing the situation from afar, were more convinced than the Jews of Central Europe of the dangerous reality. But in both the Holy Land and Europe some foresaw the ultimate truth: that for a Jew to remain in Nazi territories meant death. Haunted by this terrible vision, they worked against overwhelming odds to spirit some four hundred thousand of their people out of Europe through various tortuous escape routes to Palestine.

As war became a probability and as more and more European Jews realized the life-and-death nature of their situation, they found themselves further endangered by a worldwide attitude ranging from apathy to hostility.

Almost every country had an immigration quota, and none of them saw fit to make adjustments to save a doomed people. The appalling irony was the situation in Palestine itself. While the Jews in the new homeland welcomed the refugees from Europe, the immigration quotas for Palestine were not set by the Jews who lived there but by the British Foreign Office. Even before the infamous White Paper of 1939 that virtually choked off immigration, His Majesty's Government had set absurdly low quotas.

Did the world show any compassion for the trapped Jews of Europe? Under an initiative taken by President Franklin D. Roosevelt, representatives of thirty-two nations assembled in the elegant resort of Évian-les-Bains on the French-Swiss border in July 1938. The conclave proved to be a textbook exercise in hypocrisy. The question on the floor was how the nations of the world could save the beleaguered Jews of Europe. Under British pressure, however, the conference would not even permit an appearance by the man who knew most about the urgency of the situation, Dr. Chaim Weizmann, president of both the World Zionist Organization and the Jewish Agency.

Each representative rose to express his country's sorrow over the plight of Europe's Jews and the reasons why his country could not go beyond its fixed quotas. Even Myron Taylor, Roosevelt's representative, hewed to the same line. The conference had received the official blessing of the American Federation of Labor on the condition that the United States not import Jews who would compete for American jobs. Among the participants there were only three exceptions. Holland and Denmark, already glutted with refugees and so close to Germany as to offer little safety, were willing to accept more, as was the tiny Dominican Republic. Then the conference, astoundingly, formalized its resistance in the resolution relieving all participants of the obligation of making any financial contribution toward "involuntary emigration." In short, all refugees would be expected to support themselves. Inasmuch as Germany allowed no Jew to leave with more than 10 reichsmarks—less than $5—self-support was initially impossible. The door to escape had been slammed shut by the very conference that was supposed to open it. The whole shameful affair was discreetly reported on page 13 of the *New York Times*.

Hitler's propaganda minister, Paul Josef Goebbels, was gleeful. To his mind the Évian conference seemed to confirm what he had suspected: the rest of the world found the Jewish presence as odious as did the Nazis.

One Jewish leader, the legendary Ruth Klüger, told the authors in 1977 that the Évian fiasco was the final turning point: "Because it ended in nothing—and I will say this to my dying day—this was the official signal of the civilized world to Hitler to go ahead and kill the Jews. It gave him the freedom to act as he wanted."

Mrs. Klüger and hundreds—perhaps thousands—of Jews and non-Jews were now freed from all illusions. If the Jews were to be rescued, the whole process would have to be accomplished in defiance of every authority, and the only possible haven for large numbers of refugees was Palestine.

Thus, as the rescue effort was set in motion, the barriers to its success were

fourfold: first, world indifference, as evidenced in the Évian conference; second, Nazi cruelty and its echo among the anti-Semites of the neighboring states; third, official barriers in the countries in which, or through which, the rescues were to be accomplished; and, finally, the chilly intransigence of the British government, which systematically blocked the exit routes to Palestine.

The breakdown of relations with Great Britain was especially bitter. Except for one regretted episode in 1936, the Jewish Agency had taken the position that it would sanction no illegal immigration. In the spirit of the Balfour Declaration, Ben-Gurion and Weizmann had pinned their hopes on a liberalizing of immigration policy by the British. But in 1936 the quota, instead of being increased, was cut in half—from sixty thousand a year to thirty thousand. Even then Weizmann and Ben-Gurion did not lose faith. Illegal immigration, they thought, was jeopardizing the safety of the immigrants and further exacerbating relations between the Jews and Great Britain.

By 1938, the Revisionists, who had never felt bound by the Jewish Agency's policies, had already organized clandestine transportation to Palestine. In the wake of the disillusionment that followed the rigid British policy as well as the fiasco at Évian, the more moderate adherents of the Jewish Agency and its military arm, the Haganah, reluctantly decided to organize their own rescue system. Ben-Gurion did not officially support them, but he all but agreed not to interfere, "and when the boat arrives, I shall go down to the shore, take off my shoes, wade into the water and help the boys disembark the newcomers and bring them to shore on my own back. But then I shall go directly to a meeting to have you all disciplined for your utter irresponsibility." The right to immigration, Ben-Gurion said, was not negotiable. Only the methods were in question.

The rescue missions that took place from 1938 through 1941 involved an intelligence system of incredible complexity. Its heroes and heroines and its martyrs, known and unknown, must number in the thousands. This stirring record is marred only by the damaging rivalry between the militant Revisionists (and their military arm, the Irgun) and the larger, more moderate group that owed its loyalty to the Jewish Agency and the army of the Haganah. This is the schism that persists today in the Likud faction of Menachem Begin (once head of the Irgun) and the modern Israeli Labor party.

The authors talked with many veterans of the rescue missions—including Ruth Klüger* of the Haganah faction and William Perl and Mordechai Hacohen of the Revisionists. Each, in a unique way, played a part in delivering—illegally—some of the four hundred thousand Jews who escaped to Palestine from 1938 through 1941.

---

*Mrs. Klüger, who later adopted the Hebrew surname Aliav, died in Tel Aviv on February 22, 1980. For some portions of this chapter dealing with Mrs. Klüger's activities, we are indebted to her book, *The Last Escape*, written in collaboration with Peggy Mann (Pinnacle Books, New York, 1973). We recommend it for a more detailed account of Mrs. Klüger's selfless struggle to free European Jews.

As early as 1937 a Revisionist named Moshe Krivoshein, who had adopted the Hebrew surname Galili, was transporting Jews overland to Greece. There, from the port of Piraeus, the immigrants boarded small boats for the journey to Palestine. The organizers of rescue voyages not only had to raise the money but usually had to risk their personal safety in doing so. Moshe Galili dealt with the underworld—smugglers who, for a price, were willing to smuggle human beings instead of contraband.

Courage and money were the common denominators of every illegal immigration effort for the next decade. The ships available usually charged double or triple the price for legal commerce. The crews exacted wages at about the same scale. Often the crew members were thugs who robbed the desperate passengers of the last pitiful possessions they had been able to bring from their abandoned homes. And the refugees themselves, often with foreknowledge of the ordeal they were to face, endured sealed, stifling railway carriages and jammed, footwide bunks in the holds of ships, without sanitary facilities and with a minimum supply of food and water, which more often than not ran out before the journey was ended.

The tendency of the British, with their Palestine mandate, to reduce the immigration quota just when it needed to be expanded gave a sudden impetus to the illegal immigration movement. By the summer of 1938 Galili had masterminded the clandestine deliverance of nearly a thousand German and Austrian Jews in half a dozen ships to Palestine.

After the *Anschluss* a paradoxical situation briefly existed: the Nazis supported the departure of Jews from Germany and Austria. The chief functionary for facilitating this process was Adolf Eichmann.

There was a method in the Nazi madness. Seizing, robbing, beating Jews, and expropriating their property was a means of financing the German and Austrian economy. By the simple device of this legalized banditry and hoodlumism, millions of dollars of Jewish property were made available to the state. Jewish money and valuables became part of the national treasury. Jewish apartments became available to the pompous functionaries of the Nazi party. Finally, the physical attacks on Jews made them more inclined to realize that their only hope was to get out of Germany or Austria, leaving everything of value for the Nazis to plunder.

William Perl was a successful Viennese lawyer and economist. As a Revisionist, he had a contempt for the patient Anglophilia of the Jewish Agency for Palestine. The Jews needed swifter help than that. He therefore worked with Galili in organizing and financing the escapes to the Holy Land. After the Nazi takeover of Austria, when the situation of the refugees had become acute, Perl found himself working with—of all people—Adolf Eichmann. Their first contact came when Eichmann summoned the acknowledged Jewish leaders to a meeting in which he proceeded to snort and rage that Jews must leave Austria.

This was Eichmann, the failure, the skinny, timorous, cowering youth who could not even complete high school. Thanks to the intervention of a Jewish family friend, Eichmann got a job as a salesman for an oil company. He was not a success at it, and the indignities of his situation were especially

galling to a young man who had boasted that he too came from the Austrian town of Linz, which had produced Hitler. Perhaps it was that tenuous connection that led Eichmann to join the Nazi party in 1932. In three years he was a sergeant in the S.S. and was assigned to seek solutions to the "Jewish Problem." Finally, the young Nazi had found work to his liking. To better acquaint himself with his subject, he studied Hebrew and Yiddish. The party sent him to the Middle East to learn more about Palestine, and while he only got as far as Egypt, he was rewarded for his diligence with a lieutenant's commission. His assignment after the *Anschluss* was to make Vienna *Judenrein*—"free of Jews."

To this end, he summoned Perl before him. Eichmann had expropriated the mansion of the imprisoned Baron Leopold von Rothschild, where the grand salon suited his grandiose purposes as head of the Austrian branch of the Office for Jewish Emigration.

Perl was not happy to have to deal with Eichmann, but he was a realist. The two of them had the same goal—to get the Jews out of the country. This was Perl's paramount concern as he was admitted to Eichmann's office by a jackbooted guard. The slight, erect, and quietly dignified Perl walked toward Eichmann, who was seated behind an ornate table. Eichmann stood up when Perl was about ten feet away. There was neither greeting nor handshake. Instead, Eichmann launched into a tirade about Jews boycotting German goods.

As he spoke, he walked around the table and stood directly in front of his guest. Then he pulled a pistol from his holster and thrust it into Perl's stomach. Perl would tell him who was behind the boycott or Perl would have a "second belly button."

Perl did not know, and Eichmann probably realized this. After a few terrifying seconds the Nazi burst out laughing and thrust the weapon back into its holster.

His visitor did not laugh. He went straight to the point of his visit. "If you want to get the Jews out of Vienna, I am the man who can help you."

Perl's suggestion was that Eichmann and the Gestapo not interfere with the illegal immigration that he, Galili, and the other members of their organization had been directing. The problem, obviously, was not getting out of Austria but facilitating the procurement of documents that would enable the refugees to pass through other countries en route to Palestine. Would Eichmann help?

Eichmann would not. He preferred to make things difficult. "Perhaps it will be possible," he said, "but you will have to make a written request." Perl left in disgust.

Nevertheless, he followed Eichmann's suggestion and filed a written request to the Office of Jewish Emigration. Several weeks passed without a reply. Then, unexpectedly, Perl ran into Eichmann as the latter was inspecting the Jewish community in Vienna. Perl asked if he could have an answer. Eichmann was peremptory. "I am against it."

Perl then went over Eichmann's head and wrote to the central Office for Jewish Emigration, in Berlin. In reply he was given permission to travel to

Berlin to discuss the matter. By the time he left the German capital, Perl had managed to arrange everything, including the right of departing Jews to change the 10 reichsmarks they were allowed to leave with into British pounds—a concession that even he had not expected. There was no change, however, in the stipulation that all wealth except the few pounds was to be expropriated from the emigrants by the German government.

At that time Eichmann was still a relatively minor local functionary whose talents had not yet been tapped by Hitler. When the orders to assist Perl came from Berlin, Eichmann complied. In time, he actually came to depend on Perl; the Nazi became an unholy partner in a desperate enterprise.

Late in 1938 Perl left Vienna for Bucharest. By this time most of the Jewish transports were taking the Danube route in order to transfer to seagoing vessels in Romanian ports. The principal problem was no longer in Vienna but in Romania, where the complications attendant on securing transit visas and exit visas were bottling up the refugees at Black Sea ports. There was the additional danger that the Nazis might at any time turn on Perl and dispatch him to a concentration camp. Such was happening with increasing frequency to many prominent Jews. Romania was then still allied with France and relatively free of Nazi influence.

In February 1939 some kind of a breakdown occurred in the processing of refugees in Vienna. This was apparently caused by a dispute among the transport organizers, as well as between the organizers and Eichmann, as to which Jews were to get the highest priority in the exodus. The logistics problem was immense; there were always more people seeking to escape than the transports could accommodate. When Perl learned of the breakdown, he telephoned Eichmann from Bucharest. What, he wanted to know, was causing the confusion.

"We have a lot of problems," Eichmann replied. "Perl, I would like you to come back to Vienna and straighten things out."

Perl was suspicious. "You don't really think I would come back to Vienna?"

"Look, I will guarantee you free passage. You will be able to leave again."

"No. I am here in a free country, and I have no intention of coming back to Vienna."

Faced with Perl's unexpected intransigence, Eichmann's manner changed completely. He muttered some kind of curse, paused, and his deep-seated animosity was exposed.

"One day, Perl, we will catch you."

And he hung up. He and Perl never spoke again.

Instead, it was the Jews who, one day, caught Eichmann.

Up to this point the Jewish Agency was still officially opposed to the illegal immigration into Palestine that was being actively pursued by the Revisionists. While the Jewish Agency based its position primarily on the political situation, the Revisionists, who tended to be religiously inspired as

well as politically conservative, justified their militant posture on the basis of the Scriptures.

Mordechai Hacohen, a sixteen-year-old leader of the Betar, the Jewish youth organization closely allied with the Revisionists, was an example of a Jew deeply moved by religious convictions. A native of Vienna, he joined Perl in organizing transports. A precocious youth, he was a valuable aide; the Nazis little suspected that someone so young had assumed the responsibilities of an adult.

"Our rationale was not the Balfour Declaration," said Hacohen (now a banker in New York), "but the mandate of the Bible. The Balfour Declaration was just a political document, not based on the Bible, though it recognized the biblical connection of the Jewish people to Israel. We never considered our work illegal because we felt that Palestine was the land of the Jewish people. An American doesn't need a visa to enter America, or an Englishman to get into England. No Jew should be required to get permission from any foreigner to get into his own homeland." This religious zeal permeated the entire rescue operation of the Revisionists.

So, also, did brashness. For example, one of the transports organized by Perl with Hacohen's assistance employed an overcrowded sloop that expected to meet the usual British challenge when it was within the three-mile limit south of the port of Haifa. By prearrangement, the Irgun sabotaged the local electric power plant just as the refugees were being taken into small boats. In the total darkness, the boats were able to slip ashore unseen by the British coast patrol and deliver the refugees into the welcoming arms of the Irgun soldiers.

By the spring of 1939 the onrush of events tended more and more to justify the illegal activities of the Revisionists and to discredit the sincere effort of the Jewish Agency to remain a law-abiding ally of Great Britain. Hacohen cited a gruesomely ironic episode in Vienna. The Nazis, it appeared, supported the Revisionists simply because they were moving the Jews out of Germany and Austria faster than anyone else.

"Many Jews stood in line at the American embassy and the French embassy, trying to get visas. Some of them had to stand all night and all day just to get a number to apply for an application. While they were standing in line, many of them were rounded up by the Nazis and sent off to Dachau. None of those who were waiting for our so-called illegal immigration to Palestine were ever arrested or picked up by the Nazis."

On March 15, 1938, the Germans invaded Czechoslovakia, which had been hopelessly weakened by the ill-fated Munich Pact of the previous September. Several hundred thousand more Jews were now in mortal danger. The trickle of refugees became a flood. The limits on Palestinian immigration imposed by the British had become intolerable, and the tiny quotas doggedly imposed and defended by the "civilized" world were a bitter joke. Hence, illegal immigration into Palestine became literally a matter of life and death for every Jew.

In the years since the Balfour Declaration of 1917, the British had made sincere efforts to establish a *modus vivendi* between Jews and Arabs. In

November 1936 a commission under Lord Peel proposed adjacent Arab and Jewish states. Most Jews reluctantly accepted the Peel proposals; but the Arabs flatly rejected it, and local Arab attacks on Jewish settlements flared up again. The so-called Woodhead Report in November 1938 was a modified version of the Peel proposal, but it reduced the Jewish state to a tiny enclave around Tel Aviv and hence was rejected not only by the Arabs but by the Jews.

Discouraged by these successive rejections, the British government, in a kind of petulant retaliation, responded with its own version of Pax Britannica, the notorious White Paper of May 1939. Because of the imminence of war and the urgent need of Britain to control the Suez and have access to Middle Eastern oil, the document was heavily weighted toward appeasement of the Arabs.

Under the White Paper's terms there was to be no Jewish state—a complete repudiation of the Balfour Declaration—although at some future date there would be a state of Palestine, presumably ruled jointly by Jews and Arabs. The worst part of the White Paper, however, was its restriction of Jewish immigration. A total of seventy-five thousand Jews would be allowed to enter Palestine over the five years from 1939 through 1944. After that there would be no immigration without the consent of the Arabs, which is to say no immigration at all. This meant that the future state in Palestine would be overwhelmingly Arab.

Thus died (or so it seemed at the time) the dream of a Jewish homeland. To relinquish this dream would have been an unbearable concession for most Jews even in the best of times, but in light of the situation in 1939, it was beyond comprehension that the beleaguered victims of Hitler would now be denied their last avenue of escape.

The Jewish Agency and the Haganah at last abandoned their hope of a British immigration policy that would cope with the realities of Nazi persecution. The change did not come about overnight: as early as 1938 one faction saw no future in cooperation with Britain, at least in dealing with the refugee problem. Consequently, preparations for organizing illegal immigration had already been made on a tentative basis.

With the onset of illegal immigration prior to World War II, the legal entry process became known as *aliyah aleph* ("immigration A") and the illegal immigration as *aliyah bet* ("immigration B"). The organization set up by the Haganah to mastermind the illegal process was called Mossad le Aliyah Bet,* or Institute of Illegal Immigration. Its chief in Israel was Shaul Avigur, destined to become a leading, and even legendary, figure in Israeli intelligence.

In Europe the Mossad consisted of exactly ten people, spread over perhaps

---

*Because *mossad* simply means "institute," the word recurs several times in recent history and may cause some confusion. Those who organized the illegal immigration still refer to their organization as the Mossad. In 1951, however, Mossad was also the name given to the Israeli central intelligence organization. Not surprisingly, some of the same people were involved in both.

half a dozen countries—France, Switzerland, Austria, Romania, Bulgaria, and Turkey—although the agents moved from place to place in pursuit of their mission. And lost to history are the names of many non-Jews in Greece, Romania, Bulgaria, Italy, and even in Germany and Austria who risked their lives to help the refugees. Some of them were paid for their services, but to many the money motive was secondary; they were more concerned with helping the victims of Nazi barbarity to escape.

Singling out those Mossad members who contributed the most is an impossible task; it was an era in which bravery seems to have been routine. But certainly among the most colorful were Ehud Avriel, later a distinguished diplomat and cabinet official in the postwar state, and Ruth Klüger, the only woman in the Mossad.

The Mossad was at work by late 1938, preparing to become involved in illegal immigration (at that time the Jewish Agency still opposed it) when Avriel, like Perl several months earlier, was summoned to appear before Adolf Eichmann. Avriel was only twenty-one, the son of a successful merchant. His family was highly intellectual and multilingual and, until the *Anschluss*, had led a comfortable middle-class existence. Although his family was not religious, his parents were fully aware of their Jewish heritage, and in his late teens, Avriel had become a committed Zionist.

Eichmann's behavior, although somewhat different, was just as outrageous as it had been with Perl. By this time the Rothschild Palace had been thoroughly looted by its captors, a dismal sight to Avriel or to any visitor who had known it before its owners were driven out. In his book, *Open the Gates*, Avriel describes his first meeting with the future mass-murderer, now apparently more confident of his power:

> It was a long, still walk until my guard and I reached the large and rather narrow room in which Eichmann waited. He stood at the far end in black boots and uniform, whip in hand, one foot on a chair.
>
> "Closer!" he shouted as I moved toward him. "Closer!" Then, suddenly, like thunder, "Three steps away!" and the whip cut the air with a vicious whistling sound as if to demarcate the line between us. He sat down. I remained standing in front of his desk.
>
> "Progress is too slow," he barked at me. We did not work quickly enough. Why did we get so few people down the Danube and to the Black Sea and through Yugoslavia to the Adriatic and from there to Palestine? And why did we not push more people into England and America? Were we not aware that he had had enough of us? It was time to make the place *Judenrein*—and soon!

Avriel's protest that he and the other members of the Mossad were doing their best was not sufficient for Eichmann. To the latter's complaint that Avriel's organization was taking only the young, the Jew replied that they had to be hardy enough to leap into the water and swim ashore to evade British capture off the shores of Palestine.

"Let the old and sick jump in the water, too," screamed the Nazi. "From now on you will have to take them."

Actually, Eichmann's office did eventually facilitate the acquisition of the vast number of visas and transit visas that were essential to move the refugees down the multinational Danube. Jews were pouring into Vienna now from Poland, where there was a notoriously anti-Semitic government, as well as from Germany and Nazi-controlled Czechoslovakia. The eastern end of Czechoslovakia had become the independent nation of Slovakia, but it was ruled by a puppet government loyal to Hitler.

The Mossad's problems piled up so fast that there was something miraculous in the fact of their being solved for tens of thousands of people, each of whom had to be individually processed through the escape route. There was no secret to the *modus operandi*. It required exhausting work through sleepless nights by a handful of Jews—and an unending quest for money.

"Our work is considered illegal to every government in the world—including our own." That was the warning of Eliahu Golomb, one of the leaders of the Haganah, as he accepted a new recruit into the Mossad. As with other intelligence agents operating with cover stories, arrest meant the end. No other member could expose himself by seeking the release of a luckless captive.

The recruit in this case was hardly typical—a lovely, twenty-five-year-old woman with red hair and an intangible feminine magnetism. Her name was Ruth Klüger. In the space of less than a year she would become a legend—a woman who, with the zeal of a Joan of Arc, would sacrifice every personal need in order to set her people free. She worked herself to the point of broken health, enduring along the way the death of a man she loved in an ill-fated rescue ship, and never yielded to physical weakness or heartbreak.

Mrs. Klüger (she had been briefly married to a well-meaning friend of her family) worked for the Mossad in Romania, having been recruited from Palestine because of her knowledge of languages. She, like William Perl, found Bucharest the ideal headquarters for the Mossad operation because by early 1939 most of the refugee traffic was coming down the Danube for transfer to seagoing vessels in the Black Sea ports.

She arrived in Bucharest only to meet with resentment from other operatives because of her sex and extreme youth. But in a short time, she not only resolved everyone's doubts but became the dominant member of the organization in Romania.

The vagabondage of Ruth Klüger's life, like that of many Jews, had made her a linguist. She was born in Kiev, where she learned Russian and Yiddish. As a small child, she was taken to a town near the Austrian border to live with her grandmother. There she learned German. Later the family moved to Romania, where Ruth acquired the native language. After that, in her university education in Vienna, she mastered French and English. When she emigrated to Palestine in 1936, Hebrew was added to her repertoire.

Ruth's immediate superior in Bucharest was Josef Barpal, known as Kadmon. On one of her first assignments, she had to accompany him on a visit to an incredibly huge—and very rich—Greek shipping magnate known only to the Mossad people as Shamen (Hebrew for "fat"). The meeting was to be conducted in French, which Kadmon did not understand, and so Ruth went

as a translator; she was only to translate and was warned not to get involved in the substance of the discussions.

Shamen told them that he had found a ship that could be used to transport refugees. It was called the *Tiger Hill*. His price was £90 (about $450) per passenger—three times the cost of a legal passage from the Romanian port of Constantsa. The down payment would be £10,000 (about $50,000) with £80,000 (about $400,000) deposit for the rest, £40,000 of which would be returned if the *Tiger Hill* returned safely after its mission.

It was an exorbitant and outrageous price. The Mossad had no hope of raising that much money. Shamen stood firm. Since the issuance of the White Paper, the British had strengthened the patrol off the shores of Palestine. The ship's owner and operator would be taking an immense risk.

Kadmon appealed to Shamen's humanity. Those who were not transported to Palestine would die at the hands of the Nazis. The shipowner's massive bulk rocked with laughter. "This is the twentieth century. We are no longer slaves. You surely can't believe that the German government intends to murder hundreds of thousands of human beings?"

Up to this point, Ruth had obeyed the orders of her superior and merely translated, French to Hebrew. But Shamen's intransigence was more than she could bear. Suddenly, while Kadmon sat back in total astonishment, she poured forth her feelings. She told the Greek of the Évian conference, of how every country found an excuse for not admitting Jews. When Shamen interrupted to question her about quotas, she responded with a bitter story.

The United States, she pointed out, would admit 289 Romanians, Jew or gentile, a year. Consequently, when a desperate Jew went to the United States embassy in Bucharest to apply for a visa, he was given some advice.

"Come back," he was told, "in the year 2003."

"In the morning," said the Jew, "or in the afternoon?"

Shamen laughed and then was embarrassed that he had done so.

The only hope, Ruth exclaimed, was in Palestine. There Jews were welcome. But with perhaps a million seeking entry, the British would admit only five thousand over the subsequent six months.

She showed Shamen a postcard received by the father of a dear friend in Vienna, a young man for whom she had felt a strong affection. The card simply informed the father that his son had died of an unspecified illness in Dachau.

Shamen cut his price to one-third of the original demand. This was at least within reason. Shamen, it turned out, was a decent man.

After that Ruth Klüger was no longer dismissed as a child—or a woman. She had displayed the oratorical persuasiveness and courage that transformed her into a heroine.

The hundreds of vessels that transported the beleaguered refugees to Palestine included well-organized, relatively comfortable passenger ships; converted freighters; yachts; all kinds of sailing vessels; and even a few riverboats, which were not built to endure the choppy seas of the Mediterranean. They were chartered, hired, leased, or purchased—which is to say, acquired

by whatever means was available. The suppliers were rarely motivated by anything other than financial gain. They ranged from shrewd businessmen to the rankest kind of profiteers. Many refugees were put to sea in hulks so decrepit that their owners, after collecting their exorbitant tolls, dispatched their human cargo with the full knowledge that the vessel would probably crumble on the high seas. Hundreds, perhaps thousands, of Jews drowned in the Black Sea and the Mediterranean from no other cause than greed.

Any one of these benighted journeys is a chronicle in itself. But Ruth Klüger's experience with the *Tiger Hill* typifies them. When Shamen agreed to his comparatively merciful price for the chartering of the *Tiger Hill*, the Mossad group in Bucharest had no idea where they would raise the money. Then, should the money be somehow scraped together, there was the problem of secretly converting a freighter into a sort of troop transport, with bunks, however small and uncomfortable; minimal sanitary facilities; medical supplies; and food and water. And even were the ship to convey its cargo successfully to the shores of Palestine, running the British blockade would be the most harrowing part of the journey. The British navy intended to enforce the quotas of the White Paper. Hence, every refugee-laden vessel that arrived had to cope with disembarkation on an ad hoc basis. Some ships were met at night by small boats. The hardiest passengers leaped into the sea and swam to land if the vessel could swing close enough to shore. The ultimate irony was that thousands who endured the sea voyage, usually under appalling conditions of overcrowding, hunger, thirst, and filth, waded ashore onto the Promised Land, only to be arrested and returned by the British military.

All of this was still ahead for the seemingly fortunate passengers of the *Tiger Hill* if the Mossad could raise the money. Their best hope was an extremely wealthy banker named George Mandel. Ruth agreed to approach him, although not with much hope. He refused most appointments, and it was possible that in his role as a member of the power establishment of Romania, he did not want to get involved in helping refugees. But he was a Jew.

Ruth, as a young and lovely woman, was both burdened and blessed by her appearance, although perhaps more of the former. Many of the functionaries whom she met propositioned her. At one point a police detective threatened to turn her over to the authorities on a trumped-up charge if she refused his offer to "take care of her." But her appearance seemed to be in her favor when she wanted to see important people. After all, she melted the heart of Shamen.

At Mandel's office she was the beneficiary of an incredible stroke of luck. While she was waiting to see Mandel's assistant (at this point her prospects of seeing the banker himself were still dim), she noticed a familiar face in the line at one of the teller's windows. It was a man she refers to as Stefan (she has never revealed his real name), on whom she had had a schoolgirl crush some eleven years earlier, when she lived in Romania. He had been handsome then; he was handsomer now in his early middle age. Ruth knew he had married and had several children. He was also an important man in

business circles. In desperation, she walked over and spoke to him. He recognized her immediately, and his recommendation to Mandel's staff was sufficient to gain her an audience with the banker.

But that was not all that happened. Ruth's marriage had all but dissolved in her absence, and Stefan was unhappy in a lifeless union of many years. He and Ruth fell instantly and passionately in love. Yet, for all its intensity, the secret of Ruth's mission and the scarcity of her time were to constantly thwart their passion.

When, thanks to Stefan's intervention, Ruth was shown into Mandel's inner sanctum and told him she had come to discuss the Jews of Europe, Mandel was furious. He was a busy man, and indeed his bearing was that of the imposing, powerful executive—conservative dress, handsome features, gray at the temples.

"Don't throw me out; *hear* me out."

He heard her out. She warned him that war was imminent, that the Jews in Europe would be trapped. For £10,000 (about $50,000) now, he could save fifteen hundred of them. Could he live with himself if he were to look back upon this time and know that when he had a chance to help, he had not?

Mandel was not impressed. His secretary entered; it was time for his next appointment. Mandel asked Ruth to leave. It was time to play her trump card. She handed him a secret telegram sent before the notorious *Kristallnacht* ("Night of the Broken Glass") of November 10, 1938. In supposed reprisal for the killing, by a young Jew, of a secretary of the German embassy in Paris, the Germans had beaten and murdered Jews all over the Reich, smashed windows, and looted and burned Jewish shops, homes, and synagogues.

The telegram was a top-secret message to the Nazi leadership from Reinhard Heydrich, chief of the security service of the S.S. It proved that the *Kristallnacht* was a carefully orchestrated plan, calculated to justify the arrest of thousands of Jews and even the creation of concentration camps.

Mandel was clearly shaken. Very quickly, almost secretly, he asked her to return at six o'clock that evening, when the bank would be closed. He would notify the guard.

She spent the afternoon on a picnic with Stefan. It would be their only leisurely meeting. Then, at six o'clock, she was alone with Mandel. It turned out that at the earlier meeting he had been more stirred by Ruth's words than his cool demeanor had indicated. He questioned her again about the Mossad and then revealed to her the horrors of a pogrom in Poland he had endured in his youth, when his fiancée had been raped and murdered before his eyes. He told Ruth that he was deeply moved by her question about how he would feel if he had allowed Jews to die when he might have saved them. He knew, in fact, even before Ruth arrived for their evening meeting, what he was going to do.

From Shamen, Ruth had gotten a ship. Now, from Mandel, the rich banker, she had gotten the £10,000 that would enable the *Tiger Hill* to embark on its mission.

The sailing date was set for August 1, six weeks away. The logistics prob-

lems were staggering. No one was certain yet how many souls, would be crammed aboard the ship. Some were in Vienna awaiting passage to Constantsa, the Black Sea port from which the *Tiger Hill* would depart. Others were already in Romania. Still others were in a sealed train bound for the Polish-Austrian border. There was the confusion of passports and visas. Some were real, some were false, some authorized passage through real, although unreachable, countries like Panama. It did not make much difference so long as the papers permitted departure from Europe. From then on, the mission was illegal in any case.

The *Tiger Hill* was being refitted in the Romanian port of Braila. The conditions under which the passengers would travel were inhumanly crowded, and yet it was essential to permit as many aboard as possible. The bunks were boards two feet wide and five abreast. In the men's quarters only two feet of space were allowed between each bunk and the one above it. Not enough to raise one's knees and barely enough to raise one's head. The women were given an extra foot of vertical separation.

The departure had to be on time because crewmen had been hired and fuel and supply deliveries were scheduled as of August 1. But to the people of the Mossad, there was more than a practical reason for the early deadline. They were convinced (Ruth especially) that war would come to Europe any day. Once the armies began to move, the doors of escape would slam shut. Every minute counted.

When the refitting was nearing completion, the passenger list had to be scaled down. Shamen had insisted his ship could carry 1,500. Even with the tiny, cramped bunks, however, there was room for a maximum of 760 passengers. This allowed only minimal space even to move between the bunks. A person needing to relieve himself during the night or to vomit from seasickness would, in some cases, have to crawl over four bunks just to reach space to stand up.

Ruth, using the "cover" of a Palestine real estate agent, was able to visit the offices and homes of rich Jews in Romania. With Mandel's initial contribution as an example, she managed to raise huge sums of money. Most of the Romanian Jews were not worried—or pretended not to be worried— about the possibility of the Nazi scourge reaching them. Their contributions were in the nature of noblesse oblige—helping those poor souls unfortunate enough to live in countries under the German heel. Ruth could not even persuade her own brother and sister, still living in Romania, of the impending danger. They resented her for entreating them to leave their comfortable, prosperous homes for the unknown perils of a journey to Palestine. They considered Ruth an alarmist. Even her faithful Stefan was skeptical.

The most agonizing part of the whole escape plan was deciding who, from among a hundred thousand candidates, would be on the coveted passenger list of the refugee ships. There was no agreement even among the handful of Mossad members who gathered in Bucharest to make up a passenger list. The first talk was in terms of nationalities. Shipping Romanian Jews would be most feasible. They would not have to be spirited across national boundaries with false papers overlooked by heavily bribed officials. Money, after

all, was limited. On the other hand, which Jews were in greatest danger? Certainly those in Germany and Austria. Now, however, the mantle of hate had been dropped over Czechoslovakia, too. Eichmann was already there, setting up a new Office of Jewish Emigration. He had stated publicly that seventy thousand Jews must leave Czechoslovakia immediately or face being shipped to Dachau. Czechslovakia's common border with Romania would make the escape possible.

But what about Poland, with 3 million Jews, the greatest concentration in the world? Already threatened by a viciously anti-Semitic government and almost certain to be soon at the mercy of the Nazis, did not the Polish Jews deserve first priority?

The conversation turned again to Romania. If the number of Jews within a country was to be a consideration, Romania had more than any country except Poland—seven hundred and fifty thousand. The Romanian people had a long history of hatred of Jews, sometimes latent, sometimes erupting into brutal pogroms. One of the Mossad members recalled, as a child, coming home from school to find his mother hanging from a tree in the backyard. At first he thought she had invented a new kind of swing or some kind of game. When he came closer, he saw that she was dead.

After hours of argument that went far into the night, the little party reached agreement—at least in principle. They would seek to embark on the *Tiger Hill* those Jews in the greatest immediate danger. This seemed to give priority to Germans and Austrians but did not solve the problem of how to get them to the port of Constantsa, where the ship would be waiting.

Thenceforth it was a matter of contacts from the various operatives. The passenger list was described in agreed-upon codes in each phone call. The passengers were "wedding guests." An agent in Warsaw had five hundred guests ready to go to the wedding, all with the necessary papers. Most of the Mossad group in Romania agreed that the Polish Jews were in imminent peril. They would be Hitler's first target when the war started. Then a few Germans were added, and some Russian Jews stranded in Bulgaria.

Then, just a few days before the scheduled sailing, the whole project collapsed.

Great Britain, alarmed and angry at the number of Jews breaking through the blockade of Palestine, took measures to deal with the government of Romania. If any more refugee ships were permitted to sail from Romania, if any more refugee railway trains were allowed transit through the country, His Majesty's Government would cancel a large promised loan to the government of Premier Armand Calinescu. Economics, as usual, took precedence. The train from Poland would be stopped at the border and the refugees sent back to Warsaw. To die.

The authors have acquired from this period several score of top-secret memoranda to and from various officials of the British Foreign Office. The messages reflect near-panic over the situation; and yet, in the British tradition, they represent a desperate search for a *legal* means of intercepting the transports before their human cargo could be unloaded in Palestine. Follow-

ing is a typical example; it is dated July 6, 1939, and is from A. W. G. Randall of the British Foreign Office to an unnamed functionary in London:

> I would suggest that the Romanian minister, when he next calls on the Secretary of State, should have impressed on him the gravity with which H.M. Government are compelled to regard this question and should be requested to represent this to his government, with an earnest hope that the Romanian Government will fulfill their undertakings to us in this matter.

From another memo of the same time:

> The traffic has been organised to a large extent by the Revisionists, partly for political reasons and partly for the sake of the profits to be made from the heavy fares charged.

Nowhere in the thousands of words is there a hint of any understanding that the illegal immigrants were going to Palestine not to annoy the British but to save their lives.

It would seem that with the avowed British respect for life and freedom, their soldiers and sailors might have looked the other way when the pitiful refugees waded ashore. They did not. Why?

> This traffic is causing the most serious embarrassments to His Majesty's Government and the Palestine Government.

On July 7, 1939, an aide memoire was issued by the Foreign Office:

> In this instance it is particularly difficult to explain why the Romanian Government have failed to carry out their assurances of effective action and His Majesty's Government would accordingly be glad if Monsieur Tilea [the Romanian minister to Britain] would be good enough to bring the above facts to the attention of his Government and express the hope that measures will be taken as a result of which it may be expected that a practice, which is causing grave embarrassment to His Majesty's Government at a time when specially friendly relations exist between the Romanian Government and His Majesty's Government, will cease.

The pressure was applied not only to the Romanians but to the Poles as well. His Majesty's Government asked assurance from Poland that no Palestine-bound refugees would leave Polish ports nor be allowed to cross Poland en route to embarkation in neighboring countries. On July 10 a memo politely but firmly demanding such action was sent by C. J. Norton, the British ambassador in Warsaw, to the Polish Ministry of Foreign Affairs.

The minutes of a British Foreign Office meeting of July 12, written in longhand, contain the following passage, underlined:

This illegal immigration has got to be stopped somehow. And I think we need not be too scrupulous about our treatment of this traffic in human beings.

The problem was apparently that the British had no legal right to intercept the ships before they reached the three-mile limit, and once they had gotten that close, many refugees managed to steal ashore by night. Thousands of them were getting through the blockade. Hence, the Foreign Office explored the legal precedent established when Prohibition was in effect in the United States. At that time the British accepted the right of search and seizure beyond the three-mile limit of the United States coast in return for the right to transmit liquor under seal through American ports. After exploring this as a legal recourse, the British rejected it, primarily because of the mixed registry of the ships. Although the ships may have been owned by Romanians or Greeks, they were often of foreign registry, according to the flag-of-convenience custom. An agreement with Romania, for example, could only apply to ships flying the Romanian flag, few of which did.

Another possibility explored by His Majesty's Government was to bring pressure to bear on British insurance companies that were covering the ships involved in the refugee trade. This proposal, too, was abandoned. Finally, the efforts to establish legal justification went back to the statutes of the slave trade, which stipulated that by reciprocal agreement, slave ships could be intercepted on the high seas under certain conditions. These agreements, alas, had been abrogated in 1919. The Foreign Office reluctantly concluded "that we must uphold the view that action outside territorial waters is impossible without agreement."

If indeed the British could not look the other way because of "embarrassment," why were they embarrassed? A secret telegram, dated July 15, to the British ambassador to Yugoslavia is revealing:

Situation regarding illegal immigrants into Palestine has become extremely serious. Recently nearly 1,800 illegal immigrants were arrested in a few days and nine further ships are believed to be en route for Palestine with five thousand passengers. *Continuance of illegal immigration is having disastrous effect on Arab and Moslem opinion both in Palestine and in Moslem countries.* (Italics added.)

With war seeming almost certain, it is not surprising, and possibly even understandable, that Great Britain, faced with a threat to her own survival, was thinking of the Suez Canal and of Arab oil instead of the plight of the Jews. British motives, however, were of little comfort to the Jews hoping to escape on the *Tiger Hill*.

The stories filtering back from Palestine were increasingly discouraging. True, refugee ships were evading the sea patrols and their passengers were

getting ashore. But the British were now enlarging their beach patrols. The Arabs, taking their cue from the British, were also waiting on shore. A Jew who had endured weeks in the crowded, stinking hold of a rolling ship, might plunge into the waters of the Mediterranean by night, swim or wade ashore, and barely set foot on his Promised Land before being arrested and interned by soldiers of His Majesty or seized and mauled—and usually turned over to the British—by Arab brigands. That was the chance they nevertheless had to take.

The most immediate problem was at the embarkation point, where, at last, Romania was yielding to Great Britain's pressure. The trainload of Jews from Warsaw was to be stopped at the Romanian border. The *Tiger Hill* was to be impounded. By order of Premier Calinescu, it would not sail.

It was George Mandel, the banker and principal financial backer of the project, who told Ruth Klüger of Calinescu's decision. Ruth, her strength sapped by weeks of exhausting work, was near hysteria. She demanded that Mandel use his power to force Calinescu or some influential cabinet officer to rescind the order. Mandel knew better. The situation was the product of top-level diplomacy between mighty nations. The *Tiger Hill* and the hapless Jews who were to be its passengers were only pawns.

But Ruth was sure that to these inconsequential refugees, the impounding of the *Tiger Hill* was the same as a death sentence. She refused to accept it. Armed only with money withdrawn from the Mossad's limited bank account, she made a hasty train and taxi trip to the point on the Polish border where the trainload of Jews was to enter Romania. A massive bribe to the station master of the border town ensured that the train would go through to the port of Constantsa. He would tell the authorities that his telegraph was not working and that he never received the orders to turn the train back.

Meanwhile, in Constantsa, two of Ruth's Mossad comrades, Meir Cotic and Moshe Orekhovsky, were trying to persuade the local port officials not to impound the ship, because the order would soon be rescinded. The officials were skeptical, but the arrival of the train from Poland seemed to indicate that perhaps Cotic and Orekhovsky were right. Obviously the Romanian government would not have allowed the train to continue to dockside if the voyage had been canceled, or so the Mossad pair argued. The officials agreed to withhold the impoundment for three days.

This gave Ruth some precious time. She was able to arrange an appointment with George Tatarescu, the former premier, now downgraded to minister of the interior. It was a risk, because she was fearful that he would regard her as an outlaw and have her arrested. He was gruff and unsympathetic. Leaving his office in a rage over his unconcern with the refugees, Ruth knew she would have to go higher.

Mandel took her to a dinner party where some of the richest and most influential Romanians were fellow guests. Again, the indifference to the plight of the Jews, amid the ostentatious and frivolous display of wealth, embittered and infuriated her. One guest appeared somewhat concerned when she took him aside, but his sympathy proved to be based on the hope of a quid pro quo—his influence in exchange for Ruth's body. She told him

bluntly that she was interested in saving eight hundred human beings. He told her just as bluntly that there was nothing he could do.

Her goal was to reach the powerful and ruthless Calinescu, King Carol's Prime Minister. Her agitation and frustration were more than she could bear. Unwilling to endure the superficial banter of the bejeweled guests, she asked Mandel to take her back to her hotel. He refused, if for no other reason than that he suspected—correctly—that she had been working so hard that she was literally starving. Sit down, he told her, and dine with the guests. Exhausted, she did as he said. It turned out that not only was the dinner delicious, but from the aimless dinner chatter there emerged a thread of hope.

The conversation had drifted to the subject of Father Gala Galaction, the priest who had translated the Bible from Greek and Hebrew to Romanian. It was known as "King Carol's Bible." Cautiously joining in the talk, Ruth learned that Father Galaction was a writer and teacher of Hebrew and a student of Jewish history and that he was known to King Carol II.

Carol, like most European monarchs of the period, wielded his absolute power only by the careful balancing of the political factions in his country. Calinescu was a strong leader, but he still answered to the king. Carol was vulnerable in few areas, but his sexual appetites, in both quantity and variety, were voracious. He had divorced his wife, Princess Helen of Greece, and lived openly with his favorite courtesan, the beautiful, red-haired, green-eyed Magda Lupescu.

The well-publicized passion of Carol and Magda was remarkable in one respect. In a country where anti-Semitism was rampant, breaking occasionally into bloody pogroms (seemingly with Carol's tacit approval), he nonetheless had chosen a woman who was Jewish.

At the mention of Father Galaction, Ruth's hopes soared wildly, beyond the imagination of a less determined person. Through the priest she would gain an audience with King Carol himself. She left the party with a letter of introduction to Father Galaction, supplied by a somewhat bemused hostess.

The next morning she was standing in the presence of the white-bearded, blue-eyed priest, an imposing man with an unmistakable kindness in his expression. He was delighted to practice his Hebrew with Ruth; they were friends almost immediately. As for an audience with the king, however, Father Galaction pleaded that he was powerless. He himself had only met King Carol once, and that was to present the monarch with the Galaction translation of the Bible. He did, however, know Colonel Sidorovici, the king's aide-de-camp. He would do what he could to arrange an appointment with him that afternoon.

Unfortunately another crisis arose. Cotic phoned to say that the officials at Constantsa had changed their minds; they were going to commandeer the ship. Ruth urged Cotic to find Mandel and get some more money. Then she hurried off to her appointment wondering if, despite her efforts, she was seeing Sidorovici too late.

The royal palace was within walking distance of the hotel. Once within its awesome walls, Ruth found herself rehearsing her appeal to the king's aide-de-camp. Surprisingly, when she announced herself in an outer chamber, Sidorovici himself came to greet her. When they were in his private office, he proved to be uncommonly kind and sympathetic. He had a deep respect for the courage of the Zionists. Then came the bombshell: "The King will see you now."

The astonished Ruth for once had achieved far more than she had expected. Why, when others wait months or years to see the king, or never see him at all, was she accorded this breathtaking honor?

Sidorovici was clear on that point: She was a beautiful female. "You may have heard that the king is partial to redheads."

Indeed. Lupescu was a redhead. The king was waiting in his Casa Nuoa, the informal villa he had built behind the splendor of the palace itself. Presumably it was because he found the formality of the palace oppressive. Ruth wondered if perhaps the real reason was that his assignations could here be accomplished more discreetly. And what was in store for her? Sidorovici had given her a quick lesson in curtsying and in addressing the king in the third person: "His Majesty knows" or "if His Majesty would prefer," and don't ask questions of the king.

An officer ushered Ruth and Sidorovici into a small library. "His Majesty will be down in a few minutes."

"How long will I have?"

"Twelve minutes," said Sidorovici.

Ruth was thinking: twelve minutes to save 760 people.

Her thoughts were interrupted by the reality of the king's arrival. Despite her panic, she was impressed.

"He was one of the handsomest men I ever saw," she recalled some four decades later in a conversation with the authors. "He was not in uniform, but in a trim, gray business suit. He was tall, blond, with gray eyes—I can still remember him so well."

He held out his hand. She touched it and curtsied as she had been taught a few minutes earlier.

"Madame Klüger, assayez-vous, s'il vous plait." She obeyed: she and Sidorovici took two chairs facing Carol's library desk. The entire conversation was in French. Carol offered coffee or an aperitif. Ruth declined. She did not want to waste a minute in drinking or in small talk.

He broached the subject first. "I understand you want me to help you with your illegal activities."

Cautiously, she responded. She said His Majesty would have an opportunity to be remembered in history for his compassion. "Your Majesty is known and loved as a man who cares about people."

Her approach did not seem to work. Premier Calinescu, he explained, acted in the best interests of the king's people. In a voice rising in apparent anger, Carol questioned her right to appeal to him.

"I can't be involved in fighting Germans and the British, too," he said.

"How can you come here and ask me to help you rescue Jews. You are not rescuing *my* Jews. The Jews of Romania are safe. Why am I asked to interfere to rescue Polish Jews?"

The time was up.

"I'm sorry, there is nothing I can do. I do not wish to discuss the matter further."

As she had defied Shamen to procure a ship and Mandel to raise money, Ruth kept talking, in defiance of the orders of a king. "Please, Your Majesty. You will not be fighting the Germans; you will be helping them. They want to get rid of their Jews. As for the British, they won't publicly object to saving Polish Jews—they can't afford to publicize such an attitude. They know these people have committed no crime except that they were born Jews. For that and that only, they may die."

Carol seemed to lose interest, but at least he did not have her thrown out. Obviously, though, she was getting nowhere. She took the greatest gamble of her life, a one-in-a-thousand chance that, she felt certain, might result in her being arrested and shot.

Magda Lupescu, after all, was Jewish.

"Your Majesty, what would you say if someone very dear to you would be in the same danger because he or she has been born of the Jewish faith?"

The king was in a rage. She had broached the one subject forbidden in the royal presence. "His eyes could have killed me," Ruth recalled, "and poor Sidorovici was trembling, because I had put him in a terrible spot, but I had no other resort."

King Carol seemed suddenly to gain control of himself. "Sidorovici, see that Mrs. Klüger is given some coffee."

The sudden shift from rage to a mundane request for some coffee puzzled Ruth. While Sidorovici was briefly out of the room Carol began, inexplicably, to chat amiably. Had she lived long in Bucharest? Did she know Romania well? Would she enjoy a vacation at his summer residence?

After all, she was a lovely redhead.

Sidorovici returned, followed by a butler with a cup of coffee. Apparently, for the moment, the time deadline had been suspended.

Carol looked at his aide-de-camp. Ruth was concerned for Sidorovici. Was he now in serious trouble?

"Sidorovici, what do you think of Mrs. Klüger's request?"

His response surprised Ruth. "I think Your Majesty should comply."

"Oh? For what reason?"

The colonel spoke eloquently about the saving of more than seven hundred lives and said that this act would not be a precedent. Romania would not be a haven for Jewish refugees.

"To save even one life, sir, is a privilege not granted to every man."

Ruth now felt she could speak. "Your Majesty, there is a line in the Talmud: 'He that saves a single life, it is as though he has saved the entire world.'"

Carol was more realistic. If the *Tiger Hill* sailed, it would be because the officials had been bribed with *baksheesh*. In short, he was saying it could sail,

but his excuse to the British could be that its departure was without his approval: bribed officials had acted in defiance of his orders.

There was no way of knowing whether Carol had acted out of passion for Ruth or compassion for the refugees, but the fact was that he had agreed. Ruth's desperate gamble had succeeded beyond her most extravagant expectations.

This twenty-five-year-old woman, who looked even younger, went to Constantsa to see the *Tiger Hill* sail into the night. Then, wearied from weeks of little sleep, a relentless physical pace, and inadequate food, she collapsed. For one week she was delirious and confined to her hotel room by a doctor's orders. In moments of consciousness she would phone Orekhovsky for word of the *Tiger Hill*. Toward the middle of August, when Ruth was rapidly recovering, she heard bad news. The British had spotted the ship and were following it.

Days of anxiety were eased only by visits from Ruth's devoted Stefan. Both of them still planned for their elusive hours of love and peace.

On August 16 Ruth and her Mossad comrades went to the World Zionist Congress in Geneva. The keynote address was given by the great Chaim Weizmann, the gentle scientist who was the acknowledged leader of world Zionism. Dr. Weizmann acknowledged the catastrophic nature of the Jewish situation. But so profound was his belief in human decency that he failed to chastise the civilized world for its indifference. Although he finally conceded the necessity for illegal immigration, his apathy infuriated the Mossad group.

The conference enabled the group to get some information about the *Tiger Hill*, but the news was gloomy. The ship had been turned away from Palestine, was short of water, had a lengthy sick list, and now, incredibly, was steaming off course to rescue the passengers of another refugee ship, the *Prosola*, which was sinking.

Where, in God's name, would the benighted vessel find room to take on several hundred more passengers?

Ruth had to wait until early September to receive the final news of the trouble-tossed *Tiger Hill*. A young man from Palestine came to visit her in Bucharest with the dual purpose of enlisting her aid in finding arms for Jews and reporting on the long-silent refugee ship.

The *Tiger Hill*—overburdened with the *Prosola*'s passengers, drained of food and water, manned by a near mutinous crew, rampant with sickness, and mourning two passengers dead of disease—tried to make a landing off Ashdod, on the southern coast of Palestine, where the British patrols were thought to be less vigilant.

The day of the attempted landing was September 1, 1939. Early that morning, Hitler's armies had invaded Poland. The years of tension—when the world asked, "When?"—were over. War was a reality. As the Nazi panzers moved against the hapless Poles like a knife through butter, the *Tiger Hill* was making its secret approach to the shore of the Promised Land. A few passengers were put over the side in a small boat. They were mistaken about the lack of British resistance. Almost immediately a patrol boat that

had been watching noiselessly in the predawn sea caught the refugee boat in its searchlights. There was a burst of fire. Two passengers, a Czech doctor and a young Pole, were killed. Except for the defenders of the Polish front, they were the first casualties of World War II.

Some of the passengers panicked. This was especially true of those rescued from the *Prosola*, who had not been as well conditioned as the *Tiger Hill* refugees to expect a harrowing and dangerous landing even under the best of conditions.

The ship managed to back off from the shore until it was beyond the three-mile limit, where the British patrols could only watch and wait. The question was one of strategy. If they could not disembark at relatively isolated Ashdod, was there any hope at all?

The Mossad representatives, in consultation with some of the leaders among the *Tiger Hill's* original passengers, decided on a bold plan. If they could not sneak in unobserved in an isolated spot, why not attempt just the opposite? They would ram into the shore at Tel Aviv, the most heavily populated and most thoroughly guarded shore in Palestine. Perhaps, because it would be so unexpected, the maneuver would succeed.

It did.

Not only did it succeed from the standpoint of surprising the British, but the presence of so large a ship offshore had aroused the Jews in the Tel Aviv area. When the *Tiger Hill's* nose rammed the beach, thousands of members of the *yishuv* were there as a welcoming party.

The passengers, despite their hunger, sickness, and exhaustion, leaped over the side and out of the cargo doors into the water, swimming and wading toward the sacred soil of Eretz Yisroel. Some screamed with joy as they were greeted by their rescuers on the shore.

The British police and soldiers were soon on the beach among the Jews, but they were overwhelmed by the numbers of the rescuers and—perhaps because they were British—they were unwilling to shoot in cold blood. A few of the passengers were seized and interned but were free within a few weeks. Except for the two that died at sea and the two that were shot in the landing attempt at Ashdod, all the rest, 1,159 refugees from the *Tiger Hill* and the *Prosola*, reached their destination.

We have recounted the story of the *Tiger Hill* not because it is unique but, on the contrary, because it is typical of hundreds of such vessels. And in terms of the total number of refugees that reached Palestine from the Nazi-controlled lands, the passengers from the *Tiger Hill* represent only a few early arrivals. The pathetic shiploads of homeless and destitute Jews were to continue their mournful trek well into the war years. A new illegal wave began again in 1945, this time consisting of the ragged, fear-dazed survivors of the Holocaust. Not until the creation of the State of Israel in May 1948 could a Jew set foot on the new homeland without interference.

For the pathological anti-Semitism of World War II, history tends to point the finger of blame at the Germans and, indeed, the Nazis are deservedly singled out as the most culpable. But as Hitler lighted the first

fire of hatred, millions of Romanians, Hungarians, Czechoslovakians, and other Central and Eastern Europeans were all too willing to fan the flames. The political factions known as the Iron Guard in Romania and the Arrow Cross in Hungary were to be guilty of atrocities that, for sheer barbarity, matched the worst excesses of Nazi Germany.

In the spring of 1940, half a year after the successful Nazi invasion of Poland, the so-called Phony War ended with the German blitzkrieg westward. Denmark, Norway, Holland, Luxembourg, Belgium, and France fell in rapid succession. Great Britain stood alone, seemingly next in the path of the invincible Nazi war machine.

Romania, at first hoping to remain neutral, soon found itself under assault from both parties to the unholy German-Soviet alliance. They had already gobbled up Poland like two wolves going after a carcass. Romania's turn was next. The alliance with Britain at the war's onset became meaningless, since Britain was now the solitary defender of the West. The Soviets announced that they would reclaim Romanian Bessarabia, which had been ceded by Russia in World War I, and also, as a sort of reparation, the northern part of the province of Bukovina, which had never been Russian.

The Jews in these provinces (which included most of the members of Ruth Klüger's family), fearful of the spreading Nazi influence, for the most part either stayed where they were or fled toward the Soviet Union. They hoped that their chances of survival, although dismal in any case, might be better under the Russians. The Romanian troops, fleeing in panic before the powerful Soviet army, noticed that many Jews were not leaving and concluded—or found it convenient to conclude—that the Russian take-over was achieved with Jewish complicity. The Romanian soldiers, in the midst of their flight, vented their fury on the Jews. Hundreds were shot down as traitors to Romania.

Nor was that the end of the dismembering of Romania. As a reward for its loyal support of the Nazis, Hungary was permitted to seize the entire province of Transylvania, over which Romanians and Magyars had squabbled for a thousand years. With the transfer of territory went one hundred and fifty thousand Jews, now under the yoke of Nazi-controlled Hungary. And finally, Bulgaria, Romania's neighbor to the south, demanded, with German backing, southern Dobruja. In a matter of weeks, Romania had lost more than a third of its territory.

King Carol's dependable premier, Calinescu, was assassinated by the Iron Guard. The king, although possessed of some administrative ability and a few decent instincts, could not survive the dismemberment of his country. He was eventually forced to appoint a pro-Nazi premier, Ion Antonescu. The new premier's first act was to oust King Carol, who represented the last fragile thread of legitimacy and political respectability. The emergence of this fascist strongman brought to the surface the latent anti-Semitic hostilities of the citizens, specifically from the anti-Semitic Iron Guard.

Romania immediately embarked on one of the worst campaigns in history against the Jews. Antonescu's decrees immediately deprived Jews of every

civil right, including ownership of property and even employment itself. Overnight they became derelicts.

In October 1940 Antonescu formally allied his country with Germany and Italy. The German army took over Romania's Ploesti oil fields, and a large military "mission" moved into Bucharest. Romania had become a captive nation without a shot being fired.

In the midst of all this turmoil, as if the earth itself could not support the agony on its surface, a devastating earthquake struck Bucharest. Hundreds were killed, and thousands injured. The casualties included many German soldiers staying in earthquake-vulnerable hotels. Ruth, who had rented a room in a small house, was not hurt; surprisingly, every member of the Mossad contingent was unharmed.

The chaos following the quake played into the hands of the swelling Iron Guard and its adherents. Decent Romanians, including almost every civilized leader who spoke out against the atrocities, were murdered. Since many houses were smashed by the temblor, looting was rampant. Jewish houses were the preferred targets.

The depravity reached its nadir with the rounding up of about a hundred Jews who were then tied together and taken to a local slaughterhouse. They were stripped, their heads were chopped off, and their bodies, stamped with the word *kosher*, were hung on meathooks.

One of the victims was Moshe Orekhovsky, Ruth's friend and perhaps the bravest and gentlest of the Mossad contingent. A colleague had been forced to identify him. He found Orekhovsky's head with a dozen others in a basket.

A few days later, warned by a telephone call from George Mandel, Ruth escaped Iron Guard fanatics by jumping from a second-story rear window of her house as the marauding mob was coming in the front door. Met by Mandel's limousine, she was driven across the border into Bulgaria and eventually made her way to Istanbul. There she and her surviving Mossad comrades, as well as the Revisionist group, set up headquarters to continue their rescue work.

There were successes and disasters. Even though Great Britain had her back to the wall (her people were greatly admired by the Mossad contingent), she continued to divert naval forces to harass the rescue ships. In December 1940 the *Struma*, carrying eight hundred passengers bound for Palestine, was bombed and sunk in the Sea of Marmara. Only one person survived, and in the gruesome confusion of war, no one knew whether the ship had been sunk by the Germans or the British.

In that same month, Ruth was awakened in her hotel room by one of her colleagues in the middle of the night. He told her that a small sailing vessel jammed with refugees had sprung a leak and was sinking rapidly just outside the harbor of Istanbul. Ruth joined her comrades in a rush to the water's edge. They plunged into the icy waters of the Bosporus to help drag the struggling passengers ashore. Of the 360 aboard, only 91 were saved. The tragedy mocked the name of the vesssel—the *Saviour*.

On either the *Struma* or the *Saviour*, Ruth learned later, had been her beloved Stefan. He did not survive.

Ruth Klüger's career did not end with the last of the prewar and early wartime rescue ships. For many years thereafter she served in a dual capacity, as a secret agent for the British (as the war progressed it became apparent that for all their failings, the British would prevail over the Germans) and as a fund-raiser for the Jewish Agency. She was eminently successful in both areas. As an agent, she was aided by her seeming youthfulness and her femininity. As a fund-raiser, she effectively utilized the same qualities that had persuaded such skeptics as the shipowner known as Shamen, the complacent banker George Mandel, and Carol, King of Romania.

How important were the illegal rescue missions of the Revisionists and the Mossad le Aliyah Bet? According to Eliahu Dobkin, the immigration expert of the Jewish Agency, the two hundred thousand illegal immigrants changed history. As quoted by Peggy Mann in the introduction to Ruth Klüger's thrilling story, *The Last Escape*, Dobkin stated: "There is no doubt but that it would have been impossible for our nation to come to statehood, and to survive without the illegal immigration."

5

Iraq,1941:Fighting for the British

DAVID RAZIEL, commander in chief of the Irgun, and Yaacov Meridor, leader of the Irgun's Tel Aviv section, were about to risk their lives on behalf of his Britannic Majesty, George VI. In the dark days of 1941, when Hitler was winning on every front, Raziel and Meridor had reluctantly accepted the confluence of British and Jewish interests. No matter that the British had virtually repudiated the Balfour Declaration; when it came to a choice between Hitler or His Majesty being in control of the Middle East, the latter was obviously the lesser evil.

The risk took the form of a projected daredevil mission into Iraq to sabotage the Basra oil fields, which had fallen into the hands of the Germans. For the British it was a bizarre situation. The Royal Air Force (RAF) could easily have bombed the wells and the adjacent refineries. In fact, on May 1, 1941, President Roosevelt had written Prime Minister Winston Churchill of his concern about the Iraqi oil installations, but, said the president, "I assume production there could be practically destroyed by you in the event of necessity."

Roosevelt did not understand the complexity of the situation. The collapse of Western Europe before the Nazi juggernaut in the spring of 1940 had destroyed the faith of most Arabs in an eventual Allied victory. Hitler, joined by his paper partner, Benito Mussolini, had launched a vast pincer movement to drive the British out of the Middle East. One thrust would be from Italian-occupied Libya into Egypt; the other would sweep from the Balkans, through Turkey and Syria, and into Palestine to link up with the German forces in Egypt. Success would ensure Hitler's control of the entire Middle East, including the Suez Canal and the world's largest oil reserves. Beyond any doubt, the British hegemony in the eastern Mediterranean

would have been ended, and the hope of a victory of the Allies would have been dim at best.

Jews in Palestine, such as Raziel and Meridor, knew that despite the betrayal of the Zionist cause by Great Britain, British rule was infinitely preferable to that of the Nazis. A Nazi take-over of the Holy Land would unleash such a slaughter of the Jews that there would not be enough of them left to continue the fight for nationhood. It seemed that the only inhabitants of the Middle East that the British could count on for help were Palestine's four hundred and fifty thousand Jews. When the war started, one hundred and thirty thousand of them had registered for military service and thirty thousand were actually enlisted in His Majesty's forces. The Arabs, in contrast, observing the German successes in the early days of the war and under pressure from pro-German leadership (especially the notorious Haj Amin el-Husseini, Grand Mufti of Jerusalem), began to back away from further commitments to Great Britain.

The Nazis took ample advantage of this Arab opportunism. Iraq became the principal target of German subversion, since it could supply oil for the German war machine as well as function as a staging area for the march into Egypt. With the Nazi successes in Europe, Iraqis, as well as Pan-Arabists, began to feel that Britain's cause was lost and that the future of Arab independence was more secure with the Germans. Rashīd Ali el-Kilani, the Iraqi prime minister, continued to pay lip service to the Anglo-Iraqi alliance until the early spring of 1941. But then, Rashīd Ali was overthrown, presumably because of his unwillingness to break completely with the British. In April he was restored to power, but this time as a committed pro-Nazi. All pro-British elements were ousted from the government and the army. With the proclamation of the end of British "tyranny," the movement grew violent. Hundreds of Jews and Christian Assyrians were slaughtered, and the small British diplomatic mission in Baghdad was surrounded and held hostage in the British embassy.

In response, the British, entering through the Persian Gulf, moved a small force of several companies and armored vehicles, plus a few fighters and bombers, to a base near the Basra oil fields, 280 miles southeast of Baghdad. There was already a large British air and military base at Habbaniya, 60 miles west of the capital. The Nazis, meanwhile, were permitted to move thirty aircraft to a base close to Baghdad and began systematically bombing the British installations.

General Sir Archibald Wavell, the British Middle East commander, was determined to prevent the Basra oil installations from supplying the Nazis, but he, unlike Roosevelt, was only too well aware of the complications. When the pro-Nazi coup took place in Baghdad, the anti-British faction remained adamant in its threat against imprisoned Britons in the embassy. The word was passed: the hostages would be slaughtered if the oil fields were molested. Wavell was seemingly faced with a Hobson's choice. He could keep Iraqi oil out of the hands of the Nazis only at the risk of scores of innocent British lives.

There was, however, one feasible alternative—to destroy the oil installa-

tions not by an overt military attack but by sabotage, which could not so easily be blamed on the British. The task would require agents to steal into the oil region and blow up the facilities. Ideally, Wavell would like to have entrusted the mission to Arabs loyal to Britain, but there were none he could depend on.

There was nowhere else to turn but to the Jews, more specifically to the Irgun, with its coterie of audacious and enterprising Zionists. To have to seek the Irgun's help must have been difficult for Wavell. While he was not openly anti-Semitic, his reputation was that of a man without much fondness for Jews. According to a letter from Churchill to his colonial secretary dated March 4, 1941, Wavell, "like most British officers, was strongly pro-Arab."

There was no official contact between the Irgun and the British anywhere, although they worked together informally in Cairo, especially in matters relating to intelligence. Before the German invasion of Russia in June 1941, the Irgun was principally concerned with Soviet penetration into the Middle East. As the Soviets backed away to meet the greater threat on their home front, the Irgun turned its attention to helping the British identify and expose the considerable number of hired assassins that Hitler was employing in Egypt.

In Palestine there were five top Irgun commanders. The leader of the largest and most important section was Yaacov Meridor, a slight, wiry, fair-skinned agent in his early twenties. Some years later, during the post–World War II struggle for Israeli independence, he was to become a thorn in the British side. While he has written extensively on the period 1945–1948, he has revealed little of his exploits during World War II, when he was in the service of the British. Not until October 1977, in our meeting with him, did he disclose the full details of the events in 1941.

The story he told us began in the summer of 1941 when a Palestinian named Yitzhak Berman was summoned to the offices of the British Middle East high command in Cairo. Berman (currently a lawyer and member of the Knesset, the Israeli parliament) was then the Irgun's unofficial contact with General Wavell. He was given a verbal message to carry to the Irgun headquarters in Palestine. The message, as Meridor remembers it, was as follows: "The British Army in Cairo has arrived at the conclusion that the only reliable group and possible source of armed help to the British forces [in the Middle East] can come from the Jewish population."

In effect, Wavell was appealing to the *yishuv* to lend its full support to the Allied war effort. Obviously, the Jews already knew the peril of the Nazi alternative. But, in return for their support, they wanted a British commitment to a postwar Jewish state. The Jews were sophisticated enough to know that Wavell could not make promises on behalf of the Foreign Office, but Wavell did go as far as he could. The Jews (especially the Irgun, whose help was urgently needed) received unofficial assurances that their service to the Allies would not be overlooked when the Axis was defeated. Wavell, speaking personally, went even further. On behalf of the army, he pledged, "You are going to have your state."

Wavell's assurances were fraught with irony. Even as he spoke, the British mandate authorities in Palestine were hunting down and jailing members of the Irgun, usually for illegal possession of arms. The situation exposed the ambivalence that has characterized the British attitude toward Jews since the beginning of the Zionist movement.

The general message transmitted to Berman for all Palestinian Jews was supplemented with a specific request. Wavell's headquarters needed Irgun agents to destroy the Iraqi refineries. The British officers came right to the point. The refineries and the oil fields could not be allowed to remain in the hands of the Nazis. They were in easy range of the RAF, but such an attack would probably doom the captives in the British embassy, including many women and children. On the other hand, if the Irgun could sabotage the facilities, the British could disclaim responsibility and perhaps English lives would be spared.

This was the message that Berman carried to Tel Aviv for the commander in chief of the Irgun, David Raziel. Raziel had been married only a few days before and was enjoying the closest thing to a honeymoon that an outlaw (in British eyes) could afford by living with his bride under an assumed name in a small Tel Aviv apartment. He never stayed in one place very long because the mandate police were constantly looking for him. If he were caught, the least he could expect would be a long jail sentence.

After listening to Berman's message, Raziel thought about it for a while and then summoned Meridor. The commander of the Tel Aviv section of Irgun met his chief at Raziel's parents' home on the late afternoon of Tuesday, May 14, 1941. After explaining the situation, Raziel said that he thought he should respond to the British, "Yes, we are ready to do what you want. We are ready to help the war effort. But we want a declaration. We want something in writing. We don't want to risk the disclaimer of your verbal promises after the war is over."

Raziel was thinking aloud. On sober second thought, he realized—and Meridor agreed—that it was unrealistic to make such a demand. Wavell could not sign such a statement without the concurrence of London. There was no time even to press the issue. The larger and more immediate issue was to defeat the Nazis. Thousands of Jews had already enlisted in the British army to fight fascism. Meridor reluctantly told Raziel, "I don't think we should wait for any official declaration."

The upshot of this was that Raziel and Meridor decided to take on the dangerous assignment themselves. They did not consult anyone else. Time was short and preparations were complicated.

The preparations included the recruiting of two young eastern Jews, remembered only as Tarsi and Ahroni, who had been carefully trained by the Irgun to pass as Arabs. They spoke the language without an accent; and they were familiar with Arab customs and Moslem rituals.

There was a touch of whimsy in Raziel and Meridor's next step. They needed explosives and timing devices but did not know if the equipment would be available in Iraq. Hence, they stole the material from a British supply depot in Palestine. The obvious question follows: Since they were

working with British military intelligence, why did they not simply requisition what they needed? The reason was twofold: first, they were afraid that bureaucratic delays might hold up their mission, and second, stealing from the British was such a well-established habit that it seemed easier that way. Early in the morning of Sunday, May 17, the four saboteurs were picked up in Tel Aviv by a British intelligence officer in civilian dress. With their explosive and detonating devices in two innocent-looking suitcases, they were driven to the British air base at Telnof, a half hour away. An RAF transport plane was waiting for them.

"We were brought into a plane full of British generals," Meridor recalls. "They were being transferred to the Jordanian front. They all sat together in the forward section, studying their maps, and not one word was exchanged." Meridor speculated that the generals must have assumed that he and his colleagues were on a secret mission and so maintained their silence. The noisy transport lumbered along for two hours and finally landed briefly at an airfield in Jordan. Quickly it was off again to Habbaniya, the main British base in Iraq.

The desperate plight of the British brought on by the Nazi thrust into Iraq was immediately apparent to Raziel and Meridor. The Luftwaffe had been pounding the area every ten or fifteen minutes, and the base was a shambles. Bombing was not the only problem. Some Iraqis who were allied with the Germans had attacked Habbaniya with tanks and one mechanized brigade. The base was surrounded, and artillery fire was coming unpredictably from all directions. The base had been saved from destruction only by bursting dams and diverting water from the nearby Euphrates River, creating a moat around the slightly higher area of the base. For the moment, at least, there was no danger of the facilities being completely overrun.

The situation was so crucial as to endanger the plans to sabotage the refineries. When Raziel and Meridor explained their mission to the British commander, a young, sandy-haired colonel, he responded with a burst of sardonic laughter.

"Look," he said, "right now my problem is not the oil fields. I have worries more urgent than that. I don't even know what's happening one mile from here." He explained that he had been dependent on paid Arab informers. When the tide of battle turned in the Germans' favor, the informers vanished. British intelligence had been blinded.

"My first priority," said the commander, is to know where the enemy is and what is happening between here and Cairo. Right now I know nothing." His face reddened. "Do you understand? *Nothing.*"

A day or so earlier a small British force had attempted to capture Feluja, a fairly large Iraqi village across the Euphrates. It was in the hands of Iraqi forces loyal to the Germans and supported in their defense by German aircraft. Under threat of counterattack, the British had started to retreat back to Habbaniya. Most of them made it back across a nearby bridge, but the Germans bombed the escape route in time to trap a ten-man platoon near Feluja. No one knew if they had survived or not.

Raziel volunteered to take his three comrades across the river in an

attempt to make contact with the trapped soldiers. The commander gratefully accepted the offer and supplied one of his officers to vouch for the identity of the Jews.

On Tuesday morning the party of five set forth in two canoes paddled by Iraqis. Raziel and Tarsi were in the first; Meridor, Ahroni, and the British officer were in the second. The morning was bright and clear. The canoes had barely pushed off when a flight of Luftwaffe planes bore down on the settlements on each side of the river, bombing and strafing. The men in the canoes thought that they would be mowed down at any moment by the relentless German fire. But the canoes were apparently too small to be noticed, for they crossed the river without mishap.

The experience was enough of a scare, however, to persuade Meridor that they should not tempt Providence. The German planes had disappeared only momentarily. Meridor convinced Raziel that he and Ahroni could complete the mission. Raziel, Tarsi, and the British officer could return to the base while everything was still quiet. The Irgun chief agreed. With Tarsi and his Iraqi crew, Raziel pushed off and headed back across the river, leaving Meridor and Ahroni in hostile territory.

From that moment, nothing went according to plan.

Leaving their own canoe and its paddlers at the water's edge, the two men began to walk along the shore. The villages had been abandoned as a result of the German bombing. Meridor was sickened by what he saw—the huts shattered by bombing and pockmarked from machine-gun fire. And everywhere were rotting bodies, the dead deserted as the living fled inland and away from the settlements that had been targeted by their proximity to the river.

In a few minutes he found the trapped soldiers unhurt. They had taken refuge from the bombing in a large abandoned house. They could offer no information as to the whereabouts of the Iraqis who were fighting on the side of the Nazis. The two Jews scouted the surrounding area briefly, but other than learning something of the surrounding terrain, they gathered little useful information. Meridor decided to return to the canoes for the dash back across the Euphrates.

When they reached the river bank, paddlers and canoes had disappeared. They had either been frightened by the possibility of more German strafing or simply deserted.

"It was a very unpleasant situation," Meridor said, some thirty-six years later, understating a grizzly experience.

The British platoon elected to stay and await a better opportunity to get back to Habbaniya, but Meridor and Ahroni, defying the odds, decided to wade and, if necessary, swim back. It was an agonizing experience. For several hundred feet they struggled through waist-deep water, pushing aside bloated bodies of both human beings and animals. When the water grew too deep for wading, they made further progress by clambering over half-submerged tanks and military vehicles. When that was impossible, they clung to the floating bodies as if they were life rafts, the dead ensuring the survival of the living.

As they completed their gruesome crossing and crawled onto dry land, they were spotted by another flight of planes. They dove into the muck of the river's edge until the planes had passed.

The worst was yet to come.

When Meridor and Ahroni arrived, sick with exhaustion, back at Habbaniya, they were greeted by a pale and weeping Tarsi, who clenched his fists and cried out, "The commander is dead."

Spotting Raziel's canoe returning, the base commander had sent a car to pick up the little group at the water's edge. On the way back a German plane spotted them and strafed the vehicle. The British officer was killed instantly. A second later a piece of shrapnel came through the roof and struck Raziel full in the face, just below the left eye, and he died in a few seconds. The sergeant driver was struck in both legs (they were later amputated). Only Tarsi survived, miraculously unharmed.

Meridor felt the sudden, oppressive weight of anger, fear, and responsibility. He was now head of the entire Irgun. The awful irony of the situation overwhelmed him. He had suggested Raziel return to Habbaniya mainly as a safety precaution. Now he was alive and Raziel was dead.

From the relative security of 1977, he still recalled that day with visible pain. When he returned to the base, he was exhausted and tried to sleep. "At first, I couldn't sleep. Then, when I did sleep, I felt as if someone was strangling me. I didn't think about the Irgun. I thought about my friend, David Raziel. I thought about his life, his bride, his family, and his parents. How could I go back to face them?"

He would doze off and then awaken to the nightmare of reality, his body bathed in sweat. "I felt that all of a sudden I knew the burden was on me. There are the biblical stories of Moses receiving a message from God. This happened to me, but not in the form of God. It was very strange, but the voice or vision said, 'You are the man and you are going to lead the Irgun. From now on it is your responsibility.' Once again I felt as if I were choking. I wanted to escape, but I couldn't."

When he arose next morning, Meridor's sleep seemed not to have rested him but exhausted him, as if instead of sleeping he had been running all night. He had an immediate and intensely personal problem to resolve. He knew that Raziel was a devout Jew, that his parents were orthodox, and that his uncle, Rabbi Rosenson, was widely respected in Palestine. Orthodox law requires that burial take place no later than sundown of the day after death. Hence, Meridor felt it essential that Raziel's body be returned to Eretz Yisroel immediately for burial.

The British authorities explained that they could not grant the request unless there were an order from London—which was not likely. Reluctantly Meridor allowed his fallen chief to be buried in a metal casket in the military cemetery at Habbaniya. He was identified with his cover name, Captain Ben-Moshe. The understanding was that at the first opportunity his remains would be transferred to Palestine.

The graveside services in the alien land were, for lack of any other clergy, presided over by an Anglican chaplain, with Meridor and his young com-

rades, Tarsi and Ahroni, echoing in Hebrew and then reciting the Kaddish. As it turned out, ten years were to pass before the remains of David Raziel were exhumed and returned to Israel, the state he did not live to know, where he was reburied with full military honors.

The day after the services at Habbaniya, the British commander suggested that under the tragic circumstances, Meridor and his group would probably like to return to Palestine. Meridor refused. He had cast his lot with the British and was determined to stay and do what he could. He told the colonel he felt sure that he could provide information on the location of enemy forces, especially between Habbaniya and Baghdad. All that he needed to accomplish the intelligence mission were sufficient food, plenty of Iraqi currency, and Arab disguises for Tarsi and Ahroni.

Meridor had decided that the best means of getting the information he and the British needed was to send his young colleagues to Baghdad. So, about a week after the ill-fated venture across the Euphrates, Tarsi and Ahroni, in Arab dress, began the fifty-mile trek to Baghdad—on foot. Meridor accompanied them on the first few miles of their journey and, as they walked, repeated their instructions. They were to pose as Palestinian refugees from Jerusalem. They were to claim to be friends of Haj Amin el-Husseini, the pro-Nazi Grand Mufti of Jerusalem. They were carrying a message from the Mufti to his allies in Baghdad.

When the two young Jews fully comprehended all their instructions, Meridor wished them Godspeed and sent them off into the hazards of a hostile country. Within a few miles Tarsi and Ahroni were stopped at an Iraqi military checkpoint. The Iraqis seemed suspicious, but the Grand Mufti, a favorite of Hitler, was held in awe throughout the Middle East. To offend friends of the great Haj Amin el-Husseini would have been a blunder.

Nevertheless, the Jews were not allowed to pass without certain routine checks. They were asked to drop their trousers to determine whether they were circumcized. Since both Moslems and Jews practice circumcision, this test proved only that they were probably not Christians.

The next test was more of a challenge. If they were indeed Moslems, what did they know of their faith? The Iraqis wanted to hear the prayer chanted at a wedding. The well-trained Jews complied flawlessly. And the prayer at the death of a parent? Again Tarsi and Ahroni were equal to the challenge. There were more questions on the Koran. These were no problem. They were freed and sent forth on the road to Baghdad.

For the rest of the journey the disguised travelers saw increasing indications that the "triumph" of the Nazis was a mirage. Iraqi soldiers had deserted the army in droves, trading their uniforms for civilian clothes. They had blended into the civilian population. They had no faith that the German supremacy would last and were terrified of a military showdown with Great Britain. Tarsi and Ahroni concluded that an offensive move against Baghdad would meet with little resistance.

During the absence of the two spies, British forces at Habbaniya were reinforced by two companies of Indian Gurkhas, a considerable morale-builder for the soldiers who had been facing an uneasy situation. Meridor,

however, was little comforted. Still in a state of shock over Raziel's death, he was now worried about the long absence of Tarsi and Ahroni. He was sure they were dead.

But they returned jubilant after a little more than a week. A proud and emotional Meridor brought them before the British commander. They had penetrated all the way to the outskirts of Baghdad and had seen absolutely no signs of any organized military opposition.

Partly on the basis of this information, the British, just three days later, launched an offensive from Habbaniya toward Baghdad. It was an effortless campaign. The Iraqis had no stomach to fight the British and scattered before their oncoming forces. Rashīd Ali el-Kilani, who had embraced the Nazi cause as a safe political move, was forced to flee. He and the Grand Mufti, who was temporarily in Baghdad, boarded a German plane that took them directly to Berlin. All German forces left the country, and the leading members of the anti-British Iraqi faction were interned for the duration of the war. Four of them were tried in British military courts and hanged.

There was considerable irony in the outcome, insofar as the Jews were concerned. Raziel, Meridor, and their two young comrades had gone to Iraq to sabotage the Basra oil installations, a mission that proved to be unnecessary with the collapse of the anti-British opposition. And yet the British success stemmed in no small part from the intelligence gathered by the Irgunists, who had diverted their efforts from oil-field sabotage to a probing of the defenses of Baghdad. Then, the ultimate twist of fate—the death of David Raziel, the powerful leader of the Irgun in a minor incident of no tactical consequence.

Even after the success of his mission and the routing of the Nazis, Meridor could not turn his thoughts from Raziel.

"We went back to Palestine, three unknown soldiers bereft of our commander in chief. These were the most difficult days of my life because David Raziel was not only a man, a leader, he was *the* commander in chief of the Irgun. Like Begin later, he was the kind of man who expressed the hope of a generation. He inspired men and women to believe in the concept of a national homeland and thus to be prepared to fight and, if necessary, to die for Eretz Yisroel."

Meridor's major problem as the man thrust into leadership was to hold the Irgun together while expanding its activities. But first of all he fulfilled a promise to write a short account of the Iraqi mission to be deposited in the Jabotinsky Museum in Tel Aviv. With this obligation to history completed, Meridor, who had never regarded himself as more than an interim commander, began the search for a permanent leader of the Irgun.

The political structure of the future Israeli state was foreshadowed by the paramilitary factions that emerged during World War II. In the full spectrum of the Zionists fighting for a Jewish state, the Irgun represented a faction leaning to the political Right. During the war the Irgunists gave reluctant support to the British as long as the Nazis remained an immediate threat. On the far right was an offshoot of the Irgun, the militant Lohame Herat Yisroel (Fighters for the Freedom of Israel), founded by Abraham

Stern and generally—and invidiously—known as the Stern Gang. Stern himself was killed by the British in 1942, but his organization continued to live by terror and assassination through 1948, always intractably anti-British. The Stern Gang's excesses contributed to the growth of anti-Jewish sentiment in Britain both during and after the war.

While the survivors of the Stern Gang were never an important factor in Israeli politics, the heirs of the Irgun represent, to this day, the right wing of the Knesset, and the descendants of the Haganah, the largest pre-1948 Jewish paramilitary organization, tend to align themselves with the political Left, although there are, of course, some notable deviations.

The Haganah was the military arm of the Jewish Agency, the embryo of the future government of Israel. No Jewish militants were completely trusted or accepted by the British, but the Haganah, with its more moderate posture and its willingness to cooperate throughout the war, acquired a semilegal status. This was never true of the Irgun, despite occasional cooperation, exemplified by Meridor's exploits in Iraq. And there was prolonged, bitter rivalry between the militant Irgunists and the larger and more widely accepted Haganah, a rivalry that eventually came close to igniting a fratricidal war.

Just as the threatened German take-over in the Middle East had brought the Irgunists Meridor and Raziel temporarily into the British fold, so it was to do to the brave, but troublesome, members of the Haganah. On February 1, 1941, the British released from the jail in Acre some Irgunists and several members of the Haganah, including a charismatic Zionist named Moshe Dayan, all of whom had been imprisoned for various offenses against the mandate authority. The most common offense was illegal possession of arms.

The former Haganah prisoners became part of a countrywide unofficial collection of daredevils. They assumed the dual function of protecting Jewish settlements from Arab attacks and participating with the British in selective commando operations. The commander was Yitzhak Sadeh, one of the most colorful of Haganah's senior officers. Two company commanders were to become political and military leaders in the years to come—Dayan and Yigal Allon. Their assignemtns in 1941 included work with intelligence patrols along the Syrian border where the Vichy French, puppets of the Nazis, were massing. Several of them, including Dayan, became involved in border skirmishes. It was then that Dayan lost the sight of his left eye. His other wounds were serious but not critical.

This was in the same period that had seen Iraq fall briefly to the Nazis. The threat of a German invasion of Palestine was still taken seriously. Nazi subversion was making inroads into the Middle East and Field Marshal Erwin Rommel was advancing in North Africa.

The political department of the Jewish Agency operated its own intelligence-gathering section, known as Special Services, under Reuven Shiloach, a cool, tough, and methodical soldier-leader. The British, whatever their reservations about cooperating with the Jewish Agency, had to be realistic; the possibility of total Nazi occupation of Palestine could not be discounted.

Consequently British Middle East intelligence approached Shiloach with a proposal. In anticipation of a German take-over, Shiloach was asked if the Jewish Special Services could set up an underground network that would become operative should that gloomy event ever occur. The network would gather military information on the enemy and transmit it to British intelligence. In exchange for these services, the British agreed to finance training and equipment.

Shiloach agreed and even knew whom he wanted to direct the operation. It was Moshe Dayan, recuperating uncomfortably in a Tel Aviv hospital from the loss of his eye. Dayan, despondent, unemployed, and in physical misery, accepted Shiloach's proposition immediately. Later he wrote: "That was one problem solved—how to support my family. It also gave me a psychological lift. I had a job, a salary . . . my spirits soared and my body began to gradually accustom itself to its new state."

Dayan, not long out of a British jail, was now on His Majesty's payroll—a monthly salary of £20, plus £5 (about $25) for the rent of a small combined office and apartment in Jerusalem. From this base Dayan set to work establishing branches at Tel Aviv, Haifa, Hadera, and Kibbutz Maoz Chaim in the Bet She'an Valley, near the Jordan River, south of Galilee. Each "cell" included a commander, an intelligence team, and a radio operator equipped with a small transmitter. The training of the radio operators was especially thorough, including the techniques of receiving and transmitting, the use of codes, and applied theory so that they could maintain the equipment.

By the fall of 1941 the intelligence network was taking shape. Dayan was kept busy going from station to station, briefing the squad commanders on the intelligence needs of their patrons, the British, who were paying the bills, and suggesting areas of future investigation. Contingency plans were drawn up, and "safe houses" were established.

The system was under the nominal control of Great Britain; the officer in charge was Colonel Reid from the British Middle East Intelligence Command, assisted by a civilian deputy named Hopper, who served as liaison with Dayan. The British soon referred to the system as Dayan's network.

With the Nazi threat receding in the Middle East, it was inevitable that by late 1941 the network would be put to alternative uses. From the standpoint of the Jews, the network's value increased as it provided more intelligence to the Jewish Agency as well as to the British. The British enjoyed the expertise of Dayan. They accepted his suggestion that Arab-speaking Middle Eastern Jews be trained to assume the identity of their Arab cousins. In the same manner, Jews from Germany were recruited for missions in Nazi-occupied Europe, while Polish Jews were trained for duty in Poland. For example, the network supplied four radio operators of various nationalities to be parachuted behind German lines in Europe and Africa. Others were sent to points along the different escape routes out of Europe, to assist Jews fleeing from the Nazi persecution. Some of them were to enter legend as martyrs.

One of those most entitled by character and motive for recognition as a

martyr was the Italian-Jewish nobleman Enzo Sereni, who had left Rome in the late 1920s to live in Palestine. He was a founding member of the Kibbutz Givat Brenner, south of Tel Aviv. Sereni was socialist by inclination, bitterly opposed to Mussolini's Fascisti, and a deeply religious Jew. He believed his socialist ideals complemented his Judaic beliefs and consequently found in Israel's labor movement a reflection of his concept of the ideal society.

During the sporadic Arab rioting of 1936–1939, Sereni, essentially a man of peace, believed that he could change things by persuasion. Repeatedly he entered Arab villages unarmed, to plead the cause of peace between Arabs and Jews.

In 1941 during the brief Nazi take-over in Iraq, Sereni helped to establish an underground escape route for Jews who were faced with slaughter in Baghdad. He and a small group of comrades risked their lives in a daring mission across Syria and into Iraq.

Sereni also made his services available to the British as a broadcaster of war news to the people of his native Italy. He regularly spoke to the Italians, informing them of Allied successes and urging them to remain courageous. He supplemented these broadcasts by editing an Italian-language antifascist newspaper that was distributed to Italian prisoners of war.

Sereni offered his services to Eliahu Golomb, the effective head of the Haganah from 1931 until his death in 1945, to assist in the training of Jews to parachute behind enemy lines in Europe. The training program was carried out effectively, but Sereni was increasingly distressed by a sense of guilt. He felt that if he could send young people off on such dangerous missions, he should be willing to do the same, even though he was forty years old. Sereni decided to discuss his feelings with Golda Meir, who was then a member of the Histadrut (the Jewish Labor Council) and a friend and co-worker of both Golomb and Sereni.

"Don't go," Golda pleaded. "First of all, you are too old and much too valuable here. Please, be reasonable for everyone's sake, and stay."

Sereni could not be dissuaded. As he left, he took Mrs. Meir's hand, looked into her eyes, and said, "You must understand. I cannot possibly stay behind when it is I who send so many others. Just don't worry. I give you my word of honor we will meet again."

Only in the next world, perhaps. A few days later Sereni parachuted into Italy and was speedily captured. He died in Dachau at the hands of the Nazis.

Such were some of the exploits of the Haganah, the relatively moderate faction of the Zionists. At this period the Irgun was seeking a leader to replace David Raziel. Meridor's search first of all took him backward in time.

In 1939 he had visited Poland on behalf of the Irgun, using an assumed name and forged documents. His purpose had been to negotiate with the Polish government, first, to get its support for the establishment of a Jewish state and, second, to obtain armaments for two military divisions. Warsaw

agreed to both requests, with one condition. The Irgun must agree to evacuate 1 million Polish Jews to Palestine. In effect, the Poles were saying, "We'll help you if you'll help us get rid of a million Jews."

There was a barrier to the plan beyond the control of the Irgun or the Poles. The plan had to be approved by Britain. In the face of Arab objections, Whitehall took a dim view of a million new Palestinians. The plan was vetoed.

Although Meridor had failed in his grand design, his visit, quite by accident, included another incident that was to have a far-reaching effect on the history of the Jewish state. Meridor's father lived in Warsaw; the son, of course, paid his father a visit. In the course of their conversation, the elder Meridor told his son of a member of the Irgun who was "a fantastic speaker . . . a very young man. I was very much impressed with him."

The father could not remember the young orator's name but could describe him. He was a slight, bespectacled man, a disciple of another great orator, Zeev Jabotinsky. Meridor's interest was stirred, and he soon found out the name of the man who had so captivated his father. An active Zionist since his early youth, the man had several times visited Palestine. In 1941 he was imprisoned briefly in Soviet Lithuania for Zionist activities. That same year, when Raziel died, Meridor knew he wanted this young Pole to take command of the Irgun. His name was Menachem Begin.

In 1941 Begin was not in Palestine but in a Siberian prison. With his candidate for leadership not available, Meridor's interim command was to last two and a half years. His organization and the Haganah were busy working toward their common goal, the creation of a Jewish state. Unfortunately their methods remained so unalike that the original schism between them proceeded to widen. The Haganah represented the spirit of Ben-Gurion, essentially socialistic and communal in its philosophy. The Irgun was fiercely individualistic, politically conservative, and more belligerent. The two groups would, in time, be shooting at each other.

The militancy of the Irgun had an ironic twist. As dedicated as were its members to the Zionist state and as violently as they opposed the emerging anti-Zionism of the British, the Irgun did not seem dedicated enough to the wild-eyed, anglophobic adherents of the Stern Gang. Consequently, Meridor's trusted chief of intelligence, Israel Prizker, was gunned down by the Stern Gang because apparently he did not seem to hate the British enough. The Sternists believed that Prizker was cooperating with British intelligence and thus threatened the Stern Gang.

The intelligence network of the Irgun was divided into three sections: Arab, British, and Jewish. Arab informers, who easily blended into the landscape, supplied intelligence not only about their brethren but in many cases about the British mandatory police. The police themselves were sometimes cooperative. A few of the police were Jewish auxiliaries who provided information to both the Haganah and the Irgun.

The most valuable intelligence, surprisingly, came from policemen in good standing. They happened to be of Irish or, less often, Welsh origin, and

they identified the Jewish struggle for independence with their own nationalistic uprisings back in the British Isles. On several documented occasions, the Irgun received warnings from British policemen of plans to raid its illegal arms caches and was able to hide the contraband before the police arrived.

On occasion the common goal of the Haganah and the Irgun brought them together in spite of their animosities, especially in the early days of the war. "There was always a link," Meridor told us. "When we felt the Haganah could be harmed by the British, we notified them, and they would extend to us the same courtesy. But generally I would say the relationship was a strained one. Mutual suspicion prevailed. But the farther the Iraqis went into the war and the more we learned of the extermination of the Jews in Europe, the more we decided that the fight for unlimited legal immigration could not be postponed until after the war. The Haganah was willing to wait. We were not."

In 1943 the Soviet Union let Begin go to Palestine and join a Polish unit that was stationed in the Holy Land under Soviet command. Soon after he arrived, Begin deserted the unit and took over the Irgun command that had been tendered him. Meridor had no qualms about yielding his powerful position to a man he considered more capable. "Yaacov kept the flame alive," Begin wrote. "His position was difficult, sometimes intolerable. . . . When the time came, he did not hesitate, great and modest man that he is, to hand over his command to one who had placed himself under his orders."

Neither Meridor's heroic exploits in Iraq on behalf of Great Britain nor his dedication to the concept of a Zionist state produced any gratitude from the British or the rival Zionists of the Haganah. On February 13, 1945, he was arrested.

The arrest was not entirely unexpected. The leaders of the Irgun knew they were regarded as enemies by the British. Meridor had even taken some precautions to forestall the possibility. He lived in a small house in an orange grove near the village of Raanana and carried a passport identifying him as Meyer Silverman.

From time to time representatives of the Haganah had pressed him, for his own safety, to abandon the Irgun and the stigma of its militant opposition to British rule. He was actually urged to seek refuge in a kibbutz, disown the Irgun, and switch his loyalty to the Haganah.

On that February evening there was a knock at the door of his house. Meridor's wife went to answer it. A voice speaking Hebrew with an English accent demanded to be let in. Meridor was not inclined to resist. He suspected correctly that his house was surrounded. He went to the door himself and opened it.

"Is your name Yaacov Meridor?" The speaker was a tall man in plain clothes, backed up by six uniformed British policemen. They were composed and formal.

Meridor saw no point in lying. He conceded he was the man they sought, fully aware that an armed Irgun officer could be hung.

"Then sign here," said the spokesman. Meridor complied, putting his signature on an arrest document. A second paper describing his rank in the Irgun and his role, as well as his alias, was produced.

"Is this information correct?" Again, Meridor knew that denials were useless. He signed it. Immediately, he was handcuffed and led away. He would not see his wife or children again for three years.

The British took him to Cairo for days of interrogation by intelligence officers. They wanted to know the names and whereabouts of his Irgun comrades. Even under threat of death, Meridor told them nothing.

He was sent to a prison camp in the Sudan for several weeks and then to a more primitive stockade in Kenya. He made three attempts to escape. The third one, in March 1948, was successful. He went via the Belgian Congo to Europe. When he arrived in Israel in May, he was a free man because Israel was a free country.

But being back home with his family did not erase all the bitterness. To this day, Meridor believes the Haganah was responsible for his capture. "I was handed over by the Haganah personally to the British. Only they knew where I was hiding. Without the help of the Haganah it couldn't have happened."

6

The American Underground: Helping the New State of Israel

In May 1945 World War II ended with some 6 million Jews dead and more than a hundred thousand emaciated survivors in displaced-persons (DPs) camps in that portion of Germany occupied by the Allies. For the most part, the DPs comprised the fortunate few who had survived the death camps in Poland and Czechoslovakia. Only after Germany surrendered did the full truth of the Holocaust gradually emerge. As a result, Zionism acquired new support from Jews who had previously based their survival hopes on assimilation. In particular, American Jews embraced Zionism with far more determination than before the war.

David Ben-Gurion, as head of the Jewish Agency, was convinced that a reservoir of financial, technical, and political support was available in the United States. The war in Europe had been over for less than a month when Ben-Gurion came to the New World to meet with Zionist groups, warning them that the establishment of the new state of Israel could not take place without arms, money, and skills from America. The most significant meeting was held on a sweltering Sunday, July 1, 1945, in an apartment on West Fifty-seventh Street in New York City.

The host was Rudolf G. Sonneborn, a wealthy business executive and son of a prominent Jewish family in Baltimore. At the request of Ben-Gurion, Sonneborn had hastily called together Jewish leaders from all over the United States. Nineteen of them responded and were on hand at midday to hear what Zionism's most powerful spokesman had to say.

The short, rugged Ben-Gurion, standing without jacket or tie in the midst of the successful, well-dressed assemblage, presented his case with a combination of emotion, assurance, and a stark recognition of the facts. His message was simple: The refugees in Europe had no place to go but Palestine; no

other country was prepared to admit them. Further, they were needed in the future homeland to build the population sufficiently to achieve a viable state. Jews could expect no help from Great Britain toward the goal of statehood and very little help from the United States. With the expected termination of the British mandate within a few years, the Arabs could be expected to take over all of Palestine. The Jews would have to fight.

No specific course of action was decided upon at the meeting. Instead, each of those on hand pledged their willingness to help when called upon. Thenceforth, the group was known as the Sonneborn Institute. In time, each member was called on to contribute money and work. The institute was the nucleus of an effort that fanned out over America. Operating largely in secret and sometimes illegally, the institute became involved in intrigue at every level—from the halls of the United Nations to the grass roots of America.

The Sonneborn Institute was, to be sure, not the only organization laboring for the dream of a new state, but it was the most pervasive. Hence, it was the institute that in the early summer of 1947 called on one of the shrewdest undercover operatives of this formative era. His name was Nachum Bernstein, by profession a lawyer, by experience a superb secret agent. And, strangely enough, Bernstein had acquired his detective-story skills as an accidental by-product of his law practice.

Bernstein, a native New Yorker, had been raised in a family with strong Zionist inclinations. At the age of twelve, he was president of the Young Judea Club in his neighborhood. His choice of a profession, however, was prosaic. He became a lawyer and by the late 1930s was known as one of New York's brightest legal minds. From this conventional path he inadvertently veered off into a specialty that would mark him as a unique contributor to the founding of Israel.

In the early 1940s the major life-insurance companies in the United States were smarting under what seemed to be an epidemic of fraud arising from false heart disease claims. The client would claim a chronic heart condition, present medical testimony to uphold his claim, and thereby benefit from a system under which insurance companies waived future premiums for such cases. The companies estimated the cost to them at billions of dollars.

Bernstein's firm was hired to investigate the perpetrators of the frauds. The evidence gathered over four years included information obtained through bugging, wiretapping, and surveillance. More than a hundred doctors and lawyers were convicted. The defendants, however, appealed, and the case went all the way up to the Supreme Court, which overturned the convictions on the constitutional basis that wiretapping without a court order was an invasion of privacy. The entire case was then retried without the wiretapping evidence. The defendants were again convicted, and most of them were sentenced to jail.

As a result of his experience in the insurance cases, Bernstein had become an expert on bugging, wiretapping, and surveillance techniques. When he faced induction into the army or navy in World War II, he offered his services to the Office of Special Services (OSS). He was quickly accepted and

assigned to the OSS Department of Police Methods—surveillance, wiretapping, bugging, microfilm work, breaking and entering, safe-cracking, and a variety of other techniques. Eventually he was promoted to head of the department. He ended his OSS career as a teacher of these techniques at a training base near Ellicott City, Maryland.

From such experience were the skills of Nachum Bernstein fashioned. In 1947, now out of the OSS and working again as a lawyer in New York, he was approached by Sonneborn, who wanted Bernstein to teach intelligence-gathering to a group of young recruits bound for service with the Haganah. Bernstein was willing and tried to enlist the help of some of his former OSS colleagues. Oddly, a former Jewish associate turned him down, but an Anglo-Saxon graduate of Yale with the impressive name of Geoffrey Mott-Smith joined up willingly. Mott-Smith had a brilliant mind, utilized in the OSS for cryptography. On his return to civilian life he became a grand master at chess, teaching and organizing chess tournaments all over the world. He also had the unusual accomplishment of proficiency in Hebrew.

Bernstein had another special skill that he offered to the Jews in Palestine. Toward the end of World War II the United States developed what is known as the one-time pad cipher system. It was perfected too late to be of much use in the war, but Bernstein had become familiar with it. Until this development, most ciphers revealed the frequency with which each letter appeared in a message and hence were eventually breakable. The one-time pad system had the double advantage of not reflecting letter frequencies and of being very easy to teach. The agent transmitting the cipher did not have to understand it—he just had to follow directions. Bernstein persuaded Mott-Smith to translate the one-time pad into Hebrew. Thenceforth, tough young Haganah recruits learned cryptography from a Yale gentile in a synagogue on West Sixteenth Street in Manhattan. Down the hall Bernstein was teaching bugging, wiretapping, and surveillance. Both men wore yarmulkes in the classroom.

In the winter of 1948 Bernstein flew to Palestine to help organize a more sophisticated intelligence system in the Haganah. But he made the most spectacular use of his talents in New York in late November 1947 as the United Nations neared the historic moment of its vote on the proposed partition of Palestine.

The partition plan was the product of the United Nations Special Committee on Palestine (UNSCOP). Following in the wakes of the Balfour Declaration, the British mandate, and the various schemes of the 1930s and formulated in the face of bitter British opposition, it was remarkable that UNSCOP at last offered a package that could be brought to a vote. Even the eleven members of UNSCOP were divided. Canada, Czechoslovakia, Guatemala, the Netherlands, Peru, Sweden, and Uruguay supported the partition plan, while India, Iran, and Yugoslavia opposed it, in favor of an Arab-Jewish federation. Australia abstained.

The portioning out of Palestine in the UNSCOP plan was a geopolitical jumble. The Jews were awarded a thin coastal strip from Acre southward to

Ashdod. Below that the coastline was to be Arab territory—a kind of extended version of today's Gaza strip. The entire center of Palestine west of the Jordan River was awarded to the Arabs with the exception of the Jerusalem-Bethlehem area, which was to be internationalized. The Jewish coastal strip was to be contiguous with the huge triangle of the Negev, south of the city of Beersheba. In the north, the land immediately adjacent to the Sea of Galilee was assigned to the Jewish state; it was connected to the coastal area by a corridor only two miles wide. The northwestern section of Palestine was to be Arab territory but not connected to the central Arab portion. On a map, the territories appeared to have been laid out by a drunken cartographer.

Because they believed that for the present this arrangement was the best they could get and because the plan provided for a relatively large flow of immigration, the leaders of the Jewish Agency decided, with some reluctance, to support it.

Not so the Arabs. Howard Sachar, in *A History of Israel*, notes with some sympathy the plight of the Arab leadership. When David Horowitz and Abba Eban of the Jewish Agency met with Azzam Pasha of the Arab League on October 14, 1947, Azzam noted sadly that any Arab leader returning to Cairo or Damascus after having made a deal with the Zionists would be dead within hours. Hence, any attempts by Zionist leaders to provide guarantees against any attempted expansion of Jewish territories were met with sullen rejection.

From the onset of the postwar Palestine problem, President Harry Truman had seemed to be moved by a sincere and intense concern for the victims of the Holocaust. He tended to favor partition and the creation of a Jewish state out of a sense of humanity. At the same time, he was too much of a politician not to be aware of the importance of the Jewish vote in the United States. However, occasionally he felt particularly abused by too much pressure from American Jews, and the times when his support for them wavered was, ironically, when the Zionist lobby overplayed its hand. But the real opposition to partition resided in the State Department. Secretary of State George C. Marshall, although more flexible than his staff, was more concerned than the president about alienating the Arabs and jeopardizing American access to half of the world's oil.

This was not the only problem foreseen by the State Department. There was a genuine fear that partition would only loose the fury of all the surrounding Arab nations on the relatively tiny Jewish enclave and wipe it out. Neither Marshall nor British Foreign Secretary Ernest Bevin believed the Jews could defend themselves. To the Jews, however, this was no issue. They had complete faith in their ability to defend their part of Palestine, despite the doubts of most of the rest of the world.

The vote in the United Nations was thus seen as the pivotal decision, perhaps the most important political act in the history of Judaism. With international sanction for a Jewish state, Palestine's Jews could build an economy, shelter immigrants, and, if necessary, fight for existence.

On October 9, Truman made up his mind to support partition. This policy

was officially announced before the General Assembly on October 11 by Herschel V. Johnson, the United States member of the UNSCOP. The Jews, of course, were overjoyed, and the Arabs furious. The Jews were also realistic. While the United States was certainly influential, the votes for partition were not certain. (A two-thirds vote was required to approve the UNSCOP plan and the accompanying political and military conditions.) Truman stood by his convictions despite Arab threats to cut off oil supplies to the United States and to destroy the new state the day it was created. The Soviet Union opted for partition only because at that time the Russian leaders considered British hegemony in the Middle East a greater threat to Soviet influence than the independent Jewish state that could replace British power.

Thirty-one votes were needed to launch a state that would provide Jews with a homeland after two thousand years of exile. Nachum Bernstein knew the count would be close and that both the Arabs and the British would use every kind of pressure, threat, and ruse available to swing the decision against partition. As the time for decision approached, a preliminary count indicated that three more votes were needed for a Jewish victory, and at least five countries were still uncommitted. Obviously, both sides would take extraordinary measures to capture those votes.

Bernstein, the master secret agent, swung into action. He needed to learn at first hand what the British were thinking.

Every day His Majesty's representatives were conveyed in a hired limousine between their Manhattan apartment headquarters and the temporary General Assembly hall at Lake Success, Long Island. This long journey seemed, to Bernstein, to provide an unusual opportunity. First, he found out the name of the firm that leased the limousine. From the state of New York he requested the firm's corporate records (always available for public inspection). Some of the owners, he noted, were Jewish.

Bernstein tracked down one of the Jewish owners and telephoned for a meeting. The man was agreeable but obviously puzzled. Bernstein went to his office and got right to the point.

"How would you like to be instrumental in the creation of a Jewish state, in saving the Jewish people."

His overwhelmed host was a slight man with squinting eyes, a sharp nose, and a pencil-thin mustache. He did not look like the Messiah and obviously did not feel like one.

"Me? I don't know what you're talking about. I'm nobody."

"But you own a limousine business, don't you?"

"I own the controlling interest, yes."

"And you lease a limousine to the British UN delegation?"

"That's right, but I don't know what you're getting at."

"Who pays the driver, the British or you?"

Bernstein carefully explained how the efforts of the British to block partition could only be thwarted if the Jewish Agency could find out where the British were applying pressure and whose votes they were trying to win. To know this required listening to their private conversations. And since the entire delegation was together on the trips between Manhattan and Lake

Success, what they talked about en route could obviously give a clue to their plans.

The limousine magnate was still unconvinced. "I can't help—I have no money."

"I don't want your money," Bernstein responded. "I want to talk to the limousine driver and have access to the car at night."

"I don't understand."

"I intend to install a tape recorder in the car, and teach your chauffeur how to turn it on and off."

At last the little man understood. "And you'll be able to know what the British are saying."

"Now you've got the idea."

"That would be risky—but for this cause I'd be willing to take the chance."

The tape recorder was to be hidden in the trunk, directly behind the back seat. The driver could control it, and Bernstein was sure the British would never detect it.

The chauffeur was given $100 to assure his cooperation, the tape recorder was installed as planned, and the whole system worked without a hitch. Every evening, when the limousine returned to the garage, the tape reel was removed and transcribed. By seven o'clock each morning, the transcriptions were in the hands of the Jewish representatives at the United Nations.

Essentially what the tapes revealed was the point of focus of the British pressure for antipartition votes. The countries they hoped to swing included Greece, China, Haiti, the Philippines, and Liberia, all of which were at that time fence-straddling.

"They were always talking about who they'd tried to meet that day, and where they were succeeding and where they were having trouble," Bernstein recalled. "We had a lot of good contacts and we were able to apply counterpressure to swing the votes back again—in favor of partition."

Bugging the British, however, was not the only undercover operation. Bernstein and his associates managed to get their microphone right into the headquarters of the Arab delegation in the McAlpin Hotel. This was the suite of Faris el-Khoury, senior delegate of the Arab League.

Once again, Bernstein appealed to the loyalty of a Jew who was in a position to help. In this case it was a house detective who happened to be passionately concerned with the outcome of the vote.

The eavesdropping operation was made possible by the existence of a steel column with an open-work filigreed capital in an archway between two rooms of the suite. When the Arabs were away from the suite, the detective, with Bernstein's help, cut away a small portion of the ornate design, slipped a microphone behind it, and then welded the filigree back in place. The wires were run behind the column and through the ceiling to the room above.

"The Arabs were always testing for microphones," Bernstein recalls, "but in this case the microphone was inside a steel column, which prevented their equipment from detecting it."

As with the British, the Arab conversations consisted mainly of discussions of whose arm could be twisted.

The overheard conversations were not without their humorous touches. Today Abba Eban, the former foreign minister of Israel, is known worldwide for his mellifluous voice, for speeches delivered with such a refined Oxonian lilt as to rival the vocal qualities of the most established English aristocrat. In 1947 the young Abba Eban, who had indeed been a don at Oxford University, used the given name Aubrey and was relatively unknown. When he made a major speech before the United Nations General Assembly, the British delegation seemed more distressed by his English than by his message. "Who was that bloke who spoke today?" one of the delegation asked. "I don't know," another replied, "but it seems he was a don at Oxford or Cambridge." Another delegate commented, "Well, I'd like to know how he learned to speak the King's English better than anyone in our own delegation."

The partition vote took place on November 29, 1947. Thanks primarily to Truman, the United States was committed, as were the Soviets for their own reasons. Most of the doubtful nations, notably France, supported the partition plan. Of the Western nations, only Greece was opposed, apparently because of large colonies of Greeks in North African countries. The vote was thirty-three to thirteen, safely above the needed two-thirds majority.

After two thousand years, the Jewish state was a geographical fact, although given an illogical and seemingly indefensible shape. With virtually every Arab state ready to spring at its throat, the great question was whether it could become a viable political entity.

The worldwide rallying of Jews to defend their new homeland is one of the epic stories of history. On the great stage of world politics it involved the decisions of statesmen and generals. But from the lives of ordinary people came some fascinating anecdotes.

At the corner of Hanover and Lombard streets, in the midst of Baltimore's lavish downtown renewal area, stands the new, massive, but architecturally dreary, Federal Court House. This structure and others in the vicinity have replaced the shabby warehouses and loft buildings that once dominated this area close to the bustling waterfront. There is a certain whimsy in the replacement of a warehouse by a federal hall of justice, for it is probable that some thirty years ago a federal crime was committed on this very spot.

Surviving physical surroundings are often the anchors of memory. If the bulldozers had not razed the old building, if the corner looked today as it did then, perhaps more Americans would remember what happened there. In the light of current perspectives, the nature of the crime—if indeed it was a crime—transcends the federal statutes, and the criminals are now properly revered as brave and dedicated men and women. Many of them survive. One of them, Mose Speert, remembers it as if it were yesterday. After all, he owned the warehouse.

Speert was one of the handful of Jewish leaders who had attended that historic meeting in the New York apartment of Rudolf Sonneborn in July

1945. Within two years of that modest beginning, a vast network of enterprises had sprung up in anticipation of the birth of Israel. Ships had been bought and refitted to rescue the refugees in the DP camps. Provisions, from nails to airplanes, had been gathered to send to Palestine.

When the United Nations voted to partition the Holy Land into Jewish and Arab enclaves, Britain was expected to surrender its mandate of three decades and to leave the Jews to fend for themselves. Once hailed, because of the Balfour Declaration, as the prospective midwife of the new Jewish state, Great Britain, now thinking more of oil and Suez, was arming the Arabs, who vowed that the new State would be stillborn.

The Jews of the *yishuv*, as Ben-Gurion had told the Sonneborn group, needed more Jews to fight and work, and they needed tools, fuel, and guns. In the stockpiles of the world there was a surfeit of guns from the overflowing armories of the recent great war. The major suppliers, however, as well as the willing Jewish purchasers, had to deal with embargoes, restrictions, profiteers, and sabotage.

One day Mose Speert had an idea. His warehouse had been used mainly for the storage of liquor, but he had just retired from the wholesale liquor business. He still used the building, however, for another of his business ventures, a small furniture and appliance store in downtown Baltimore.

Why not, he thought, send out a confidential, word-of-mouth plea for privately owned guns? He reasoned that millions of former soldiers and sailors had brought a variety of firearms home with them. By now, he imagined, multitudes of wives and mothers were pleading with husbands and sons to get the guns (not to mention the hand grenades, ammunition, and knives) out of the house.

Mose Speert decided to discuss his arms-collecting idea with David Hacohen, one of the most respected leaders with the Sonneborn group. (Hacohen later served as Israeli ambassador to Burma and then deputy mayor of Haifa.) Hacohen had all the zeal of the other members of the Sonneborn group, as well as an exceptionally level head. Speert persuaded him to come to Baltimore, for ideas such as his could not be discussed on the telephone or through the mails.

The two men closeted themselves in Speert's office at the warehouse.

"What do you think of this?" said Speert. "We desperately need guns—and there are millions of guns available—now."

Hacohen seemed unreceptive.

"Yes? Just where?"

"Thousands of our young men have come home from the war, and they've all brought souvenirs with them—you know, all kinds of guns and weapons. I think we can send out the word and acquire a lot of them."

Now Speert's guest was almost hostile. "I'm afraid that's ridiculous. You couldn't get enough to make it worthwhile."

Speert responded rhetorically. "You really think so?"

Hacohen's objections were becoming firmer. "Furthermore, it would be risky. It would be a violation of the law, and I wouldn't want to antagonize

the United States, which, so far, is friendly to our efforts. I don't want to get involved in something illegal."

Speert laughed inwardly. He knew that all of the Sonneborn group, Hacohen included, were involved in illegal activities.

Hacohen continued. "And even if you tried to do it, you couldn't get enough guns to justify the risk."

Now it was time for Speert's surprise.

"Well, before you came down, I thought I would experiment with this idea. So I passed the word around quietly to a few friends. I said we needed guns and anyone who wanted to donate them should bring them to my warehouse, but they should be sure all the weapons are kept hidden. "Now, let me show you the results."

With that he led Hacohen to a small room behind his office and snapped on a light. "There you are."

There were hundreds of pistols, rifles, hand grenades, and knives of every description.

Hacohen was clearly impressed. "How long did this take you?"

"Exactly three days."

"I have to admit I am amazed."

"And just think, David. If I can gather up this many weapons by simply passing the word quietly to a few friends, think of what we could do with a secret appeal all over the country?"

Hacohen still had to be cautious. "We're getting into something here with a lot of dangerous ramifications."

"I realize that."

"Well, I'll tell you what we'll do. Don't make any effort to collect any more guns now. I'll go back to New York and discuss it with our people there. As soon as possible, I'll call you."

Speert did not have to wait long. Four days later, he answered the phone to an unfamiliar voice, a man who was speaking for Hacohen.

"We'll be needing the hardware supplies that you mentioned. Please continue to provide as many as you can."

"I understand," said Speert, quietly jubilant.

Now he could expand the appeal. The word was passed through his circle of friends in the Baltimore area to anyone who was considered to be a friend of Zionism. Jewish war veterans were prime targets, and they responded enthusiastically.

A cascade of arms, conventional and exotic, began to pour into the warehouse, carried in boxes, under blankets, in suitcases. The small room behind Speert's office could not hold the arsenal. And yet it was out of the question to store the weapons in plain sight.

Speert therefore conceived a novel means of hiding them. Several dozen cases of kitchen cabinets destined for his furniture store were stored in one end of the warehouse. Speert built a high partition, enclosing an area about twenty by thirty feet, in one corner of the cavernous room. The kitchen cabinets were placed against the partition so that the entire area appeared to

be solid with cabinets. By sliding one or two of the packing cases aside, he could reach the door into the partitioned area.

The contraband included not only guns but even cases of ammunition. Speert acquired a convoluted respect for the initiative of the American GIs and sailors. How, he wondered, did they manage to convey such massive quantities of armaments from the camps and bases they left on being discharged from the service?

"We even acquired an antiaircraft gun," Speert recalls. "How the hell they ever stole that I'll never know. It took three people to carry it, even after it was dismantled—a monster, eleven or twelve feet long."

Not all the contraband was worth collecting. There were hundreds of Japanese pistols and rifles that were of different caliber from standard American and European weapons and hence were useless.

The weapons continued to arrive for several months. Not all of the donors were Jewish. A substantial number of non-Jews were anxious to contribute to the Zionist cause and perhaps others were glad to dispose of weapons that had become burdensome to have in the house.

The arms collection took a frightening turn one day when an agent of the Federal Bureau of Investigation (FBI) called upon Speert. He asked a few perfunctory questions about what was in the warehouse but left without so much as a warning, let alone any accusations. The visit alarmed Speert, however. Apparently there was at least an inkling in the FBI that something mysterious was happening in the warehouse. Speert believes that from that time on, his office and home telephones were tapped.

Zionist groups in New York, most of them under the guidance of the Sonneborn Institute, had purchased trucks that came to Baltimore from time to time to haul the arms to New York. This was perhaps the riskiest part of the operation. The drivers did not always know what they were carrying, and if they had been intercepted by the police, both the truck and its cargo would have been confiscated and the drivers arrested.

During a visit to New York, Speert was sitting with a friend when an idea occurred to him. The Zionist-owned trucks were too risky. The solution would be to rent the trucks. The owner would not be responsible for the activities of the persons renting the truck, and so the truck would not be confiscated even if the cargo was seized. Furthermore, the rented trucks, usually bearing the name of the owner, would attract less suspicion.

That was the procedure followed thereafter. Speert was at one point carried away by his zeal and decided he was not doing enough for the cause. He feared for the safety of the young men making the trips between New York and Baltimore; like a good general, he decided he ought to share the risk with the troops. So one day he loaded the trunk of his own car with weapons and took the cache to New York. "It was only because I couldn't ask others to do it if I hadn't done it at least once myself."

While Speert reached the secret warehouse in New York safely, Sonneborn did not appreciate this act of "heroism." He was furious at Speert for running the risk of exposing himself, and hence the whole operation, to the police. Properly chastised, Speert did not try it again.

On a visit to New York sometime in the spring of 1948, Speert received a phone call from one of his employees. The Baltimore police, armed with a warrant, had searched the warehouse. The system of blocking off the space in which the arms were deposited with the wall of kitchen cabinets worked perfectly. The policemen had made a cursory search and left none the wiser.

Speert, however, decided that the police search was the last straw. The arms-running was getting too risky. He had no desire to go to jail or, more important, to have the operation uncovered. If the arsenal in Baltimore were exposed, it might open leads for the police and the FBI that could jeopardize all the activities of the Sonneborn Institute throughout the United States. The only safe course was to get all of the weapons out of the warehouse and terminate the project. By now the consequences of stopping were no longer significant, since deliveries of weapons had tapered off. Apparently the available supplies of guns had been exhausted.

One final, frightening experience was still ahead for Speert and his gun-runners. When he informed the New York contingent that the police seemed to be on his trail and that he wanted all of the guns out of the warehouse, he was promised a truck large enough to clean out the supply completely. The truck, a small moving van, arrived two days later. By this time Speert was getting decidedly edgy. He imagined that he was being followed and the warehouse was being watched, and possibly, this was not just his imagination.

When the truck, manned by three ebullient Palestinian Jews, pulled up to the front of the warehouse, Speert quickly directed it around to an alley in the rear, where the loading could take place in relative secrecy. Speert was aware that a solitary man in his shirtsleeves had been standing across the street for several hours and had seen the truck arrive. Was he a detective or an FBI agent? If he was just loitering, why did he stand on one corner for so long?

Speert had to gamble on the man's being harmless. In any case, the stranger could not observe what was happening in the alley on the other side of the building.

The truck was almost as wide as the alley. The driver pulled it carefully between the two buildings and stopped it with its rear end opposite the big warehouse door. The loading took almost two hours—from about noon until 2 P.M. More than eight hundred items—including rifles, revolvers, automatic pistols, knives, bayonets, and a few machine guns, plus boxes of ammunition—were piled into the truck. There were no hand grenades. The shippers had decided they were too dangerous, and all such donations had been politely refused.

The heavy work, straining the muscles of even this young and determined crew, was just about completed when the men froze in their tracks. From the end of the alley, heading toward the front end of the truck, came one of Baltimore's downtown mounted policemen.

To make matters worse, it was no ordinary policeman, but Officer William McKeldin, whose brother, Theodore Roosevelt McKeldin, was then

mayor of Baltimore and was about to become a two-term governor of Maryland. Officer McKeldin was known for his impeccable honesty as well as a gentle affability. In other words, he could not be bought.

The only necessity in Speert's mind was to make sure McKeldin did not get any closer to the truck. If he became suspicious, all was lost. Speert had only one card to play. He knew McKeldin personally (as did almost everyone in downtown Baltimore) and decided to take the initiative.

"I was so scared I wasn't sure I could even talk," Speert recalls. He had visions of one policeman making a discovery that could lead to exposing the whole nationwide underground operation, so vital to the survival of the Jews in Palestine.

Straining to appear relaxed and friendly, Speert sauntered up to the approaching policeman.

"Good afternoon, Officer McKeldin."

"How are you, Mr. Speert?"

"Just fine." Was his anxiety showing? Speert wondered. "Say, I wonder if I can ask you a favor."

"Why, sure."

"We're about to pull this truck out of here, and as you can see, there's just about room for it to clear the buildings. Could you move your horse out of the alley?"

"Of course," replied McKeldin, a perfect gentleman. He turned the horse around and rode smartly back to the main street.

"Thanks very much, officer."

"Don't mention it. Have a good day." The policeman disappeared around the corner.

Speert still shudders when he recalls the incident. "We all died a thousand deaths," he told us, "but within a few more minutes the truck was loaded and off to New York."

There is a minor historical twist to the incident. Officer McKeldin was unwittingly contributing to a favorite cause of his renowned brother. Theodore Roosevelt McKeldin was the only Republican ever elected to two consecutive terms as governor of Maryland and, as a liberal Republican, became one of the most popular politicians of this century in his home state. He was not only a champion of racial justice but also a champion of Israel. A spellbinding, if somewhat affected orator, he supported the Zionists with unflagging zeal, making speeches for Israel bonds and for the cause of the new state. Today he is honored in Israel by the Theodore R. McKeldin National Forest and the McKeldin Wing of the Hadassah Hospital in Jerusalem. (Of course, politically it did not do McKeldin any harm that Baltimore has one of the highest proportions of Jews of any large American city.)

Speert never again used his warehouse to store arms, but his idea of a direct, although clandestine, appeal to the public was tried all over the country. This appeal was not entirely based on what had happened in Baltimore. It was more of a spontaneous movement. Fund-raisers representing the Sonneborn Institute found that offers of guns often paralleled offers of money. The Baltimore experience was matched by other secret arms depots in

almost every major city. Since it was illegal to ship firearms through the mail, donors far from New York often shipped them in innocent-looking trunks or footlockers by Railway Express. Others were dispatched as caskets, and a group in Denver even shipped arms in oil drums, topping them off with a layer of plaster of paris and an inch or so of heavy oil.

The vast surpluses of World War II provided the Zionists with some exceptional bargains. The United States, switching from guns to butter, had millions of dollars worth of precision machinery for making guns and ammunition. Sold under the supervision of the War Assets Administration (WAA), the special agency set up to dispose of the seemingly useless glut of war matériel, the machinery was marketed as scrap, priced at as little as a hundredth of its original value. The WAA little realized that the matériel purchased by Zionist groups would be shipped to Palestine to create a badly needed indigenous armaments-manufacturing capacity.

STRUCTURE OF ISRAELI INTELLIGENCE SERVICES-1948

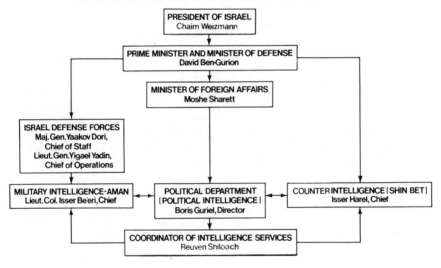

7

Safecracking in Haifa,1948

THE STATE OF ISRAEL was proclaimed by Ben-Gurion on May 14, 1948. Immediately four Arab armies invaded it. On June 11 the United Nations voted an arms embargo applying to all belligerents. By July, Israeli Foreign Minister Moshe Sharett was positive the British were secretly supplying huge quantities of arms to the Arabs in violation of the embargo. Israel's desperate quest for arms was destined to be a labor of Sisyphus if the British offset every Israeli gain with more guns for the Arab states. While Israel could do little physically to stem the flow of arms to the Arabs, proof of Britain's transgression could expose it to worldwide contempt before the forum of the United Nations and perhaps force a change in its policy. What Sharett needed was documentary evidence.

One of the difficulties was in drawing the line between legal and illegal arms transactions. The government of Prime Minister Clement Attlee admitted making some shipments. He justified these, however, as fulfilling commitments that antedated the embargo. Other countries, of course, were violating the embargo to the benefit of the Jews, notably Czechoslovakia. But the newborn state of Israel could at least claim the moral justification of the right to survive. As the war began, the Israeli defense consisted mainly of rifles and an air force of Piper Cubs. Against the established military machines of the Arab states, the future of Israel looked bleak indeed if its own buildup were exceeded by British contributions to Israel's enemies.

Sharett was unable to convince the American State Department of the British embargo violation. Secretary of State Marshall either did not believe Britain was guilty or, for diplomatic reasons, did not want to be in the position of making such an accusation. Marshall was also embroiled in a schism within his government that would not be fully revealed until the release of

116

secret 1948 documents in 1976. United States foreign relations were being conducted by two rival camps. On one side were President Truman; his counsel, Clark Clifford; most of the United States delegation to the United Nations; and Truman's handpicked representative (later ambassador) to Israel, James G. McDonald. On the other side were Marshall (although he apparently made some efforts to reconcile the two camps), Undersecretary Robert Lovett, and most of the department policy-makers. Truman was intensely committed to the survival of the new state of Israel. Although he was accused of simply courting the American Jewish vote (obviously, the president was not unaware of this political reality), Clifford insisted that Truman's concern was a humane one.

"From the outset," Clifford said in 1976, "the [State] Department Office of Near Eastern and African Affairs made it its business to block Harry Truman from implementing a policy that was animated by his deepest human instincts." Recently declassified documents tend to confirm Clifford's view. Even prior to the partition in November 1947, Loy Henderson, head of the Office of Near Eastern and African Affairs, wrote to Marshall that the participation and the setting up of a Jewish state was opposed by "practically every member of the Foreign Service and of the Department who has been engaged with the Near and Middle East." Clearly, Sharett was trying to deal with a divided administration.

Ernest Bevin, the union boss who had been transformed into foreign secretary, had completed Britain's 180-degree turn from the 1917 Balfour Declaration. Noah Lucas writes that at the time of the partition agreement, "the British role became one of trying to influence the outcome of the expected war in favor of the Arabs." There were signs of developing panic in Bevin's behavior as he came to realize that Britain had bet on the wrong horse. McDonald found Bevin "an unbelievable liar." McDonald recalled the foreign minister's reaction to Truman's announcement of his *de jure* recognition of Israel (sixteen minutes after the creation of the state on May 14): "His bitterness against Mr. Truman was almost pathological. It found its match only in his blazing hatred of the Jews, the Israelis, the Israel government." Predictably Britain did not recognize the new state.

The partition of Palestine was accepted by Israel despite its bizarre dimensions. The whole enclave resembled a letter *G* that encircled the Arab portion. Jerusalem was designated an international zone in the center of the Arab land. The Arab attack that followed the Jews' declaration of their portion as the new state of Israel proved to be a strategic error, for Israel quickly expanded its enclave.

The Israelis were furious when Sweden's Count Folke Bernadotte, acting as a mediator for the United Nations, proposed an armistice that would have awarded Israel eastern Galilee, which Israel had quickly captured, but deprived it of the Negev. In short, Bernadotte proposed to take away from Israel what it already possessed, part of which it had gained through bloody sacrifice.

Bevin immediately embraced the Bernadotte plan. The State Department did likewise (although the Truman faction did not), leading many Ameri-

cans and Israelis to believe that both the department and Bernadotte were in the pocket of Ernest Bevin. There were two reasons for backing the Bernadotte plan, according to its adherents. One reason, still prevailing thirty years later, was the fear of alienating the Arabs and thus disrupting Middle-Eastern oil supplies. This danger was in the forefront of British thinking and of almost equal concern to many American policy-makers. The other reason, in retrospect almost laughable, was the fear in the State Department that immigrants to Israel would include a coterie of Russian-trained agents who would establish a beachhead for Communism in the Middle East. In time, of course, Israel proceeded to become a bulwark of Western democracy instead.

In the late summer of 1948, as the Arab armies suffered disastrous defeats in their attempts to overrun Israel, Bevin, perhaps in blind sincerity, told Marshall that Arab losses were caused in part by the United Kingdom's strict adherence to the embargo, in contrast to the embargo's lax enforcement in other countries.

To the Israeli government and to Sharett as its foreign-policy spokesman, the British posture was an outrage. By September 1948 Sharett had acquired intelligence reports indicating that His Majesty's Government had authorized arms shipments not justified by existing treaty obligations and had stated as much in secret documents. The problem was where, in the whole world, such a document could be found and how it could be acquired or, more bluntly, stolen. It was a needle-in-a-haystack possibility. The search was rendered more difficult by the near-total evacuation of Palestine by British forces at the conclusion of the mandate on May 14, 1948. Most of the military posts and police stations had been handed over to the Arabs. This, in itself, was another reason for Israeli bitterness.

There was one conspicuous exception. In Haifa the Attlee government maintained a small consulate. In the absence of British recognition of the state, the consulate was bound by protocol to admit only that it was a "liaison office to Jewish authorities." The consul himself was an amiable old-line career diplomat, Cyril H. A. Marriott. Tall, fair-haired, and blue-eyed, in his early fifties, he was once described as the stereotype of the British colonial administrator. The Israelis who knew Marriott liked him and felt a little sorry for him in his essentially untenable position. Ambassador McDonald recalls that in a conversation with Joseph Linton, an Israeli representative in London, Linton "spoke with amused resignation of the British consul in Haifa, Cyril Marriott, who, whenever he had occasion to communicate with the Provisional Government of Israel, addressed his letters to the 'Jewish Authorities, Tel Aviv,' and as regularly had them returned, unopened." McDonald's choice of an adjective to describe Marriott was "hapless."

During the difficult days of the summer and fall of 1948, the virtual war between Israel and Great Britain forced Marriott into the life of a recluse. He ventured out into Haifa only to visit the headquarters of the Bernadotte peace mission in the Haifa Zion Hotel. Visitors to the consulate were few. The Karamon family, prominent Arabs in Haifa, were personal friends.

Other occasional visitors were Haifa Mayor Levy and Police Chief Norman Stavi.

Almost as a matter of routine, the Political Department of the Israeli Foreign Office, which is to say Sharett's intelligence agents, kept close tabs on Marriott. The department was headed by Boris Guriel, an agent cast in the mold of so many leaders of the time. A native of Latvia, Guriel was a battle-seasoned veteran of years in the Haganah. He was highly educated and multilingual. Guriel knew that Marriott's isolation was broken about every two weeks when he disappeared for a day or two. Usually he flew to Cairo via Cyprus.

If Marriott's burden was relieved by breaks in his routine, his eight British guards enjoyed no such interludes. They lived in the gloomy basement of the three-story consulate, whereas Marriott's office was on the first floor and his living quarters were on the second. While there was, in spite of the war, some night life in Haifa, Marriott, because of the tensions, had ordered his staff not to fraternize with any of the citizens of Haifa, Arab or Jewish. They did not obey the order. All of the guards were former members of the mandatory police, and many of the Jews in Haifa had been their comrades. When Marriott was away, the guards usually strayed away from their consulate-prison to eat and drink with their old friends—and to complain of their homesickness, the monotony of their jobs, and their resentment of Marriott's antifraternizing decree.

The situation was made-to-order for a daring intelligence move on the part of the Israelis. The General Assembly was scheduled to meet in the Palais de Chaillot in Paris on September 20, 1948, to consider Count Bernadotte's peace proposal. Sharett and Abba Eban were to attend as observers (Israel was not yet a member of the United Nations), and Sharett desperately wanted an incriminating piece of paper to discredit Ernest Bevin. Resentment of the British and of Bernadotte was rampant in Israel. This bitterness found an outlet finally in Bernadotte's senseless murder. On September 17, Stern Gang extremists ambushed and assassinated the well-meaning Swede in Jerusalem. Earlier that same day Bernadotte had forwarded his plan to Paris in anticipation of the General Assembly session.

A day or so before Count Bernadotte's assassination, Sharett had met with his intelligence staff to discuss the possibility of acquiring classified British documents. According to Boris Guriel's recollection, Sharett did not order him to procure the needed evidence, he merely indicated how helpful it would be if the foreign minister possessed it.

This exchange of views reveals some fundamental precepts of intelligence-gathering in most countries. Sharett did not order his operatives to find the elusive evidence. To have done so would have been to condone their obtaining it by covert, violent, or other unlawful means. He simply let them know that he needed it. The inference that extraordinary measures would be employed if necessary was drawn by his intelligence agents. It is probable that Sharett expected such an inference.

With the United Nations session only a few days off, Guriel knew he had

to act quickly. His assumption was that if the British had circulated a top-secret memo relating to arms shipments, the only likely place to find it in Israel would be in Marriott's consulate. What had to be done was obvious enough; doing it presented a formidable challenge. Despite the presence of eight guards, the consulate had to be entered, the safe opened, the papers examined, and any telltale documents seized and presented to Sharett.

Fortunately Nachum Bernstein, the former OSS spy who had bugged the British limousine in New York, happened to be in Tel Aviv. Guriel called in his agents for a quick course in breaking and entering from Bernstein, who was very much the right man at the right time.

Obviously the breaking and entering had to be accomplished during one of Marriott's trips to Cairo. The timing would be critical. Marriott was sometimes absent for as little as thirty-six hours, often departing one evening and returning the morning of the second day. As soon as the Israelis observed Marriott leaving Haifa, they passed the word to the guards that a party would be held in the back room of a nearby bar and restaurant. The guards were urged to bring their own female company but were informed, as an additional lure, that there would be other women and plenty of food and drink. Not surprisingly, the guards accepted the invitation to the last man. The party was to be a convivial affair, not a brawl that might draw attention to the guards' desertion of their posts.

An unexpected turn of good fortune was the presence in a Haifa jail of an internationally famous safecracker. A Jewish immigrant from Poland, he had served time in Polish prisons for pursuing his vocation. When he arrived in Israel, he was apparently unable to alter his life-style and once again was incarcerated for safecracking. This time he was recruited into the service of his new country.

One of the noteworthy things about planning for the exploit was that a great number of people had to be let in on the secret. For example, the local Haifa police had to acquiesce in the temporary release of the safecracker. Keys had to be acquired for the consulate doors. Detailed drawings of the interior of the consulate were prepared.

Some twenty-four hours after Marriott's departure, at about nine o'clock in the evening, the guards started turning out for the party. Within an hour the consulate was totally unguarded. The employees of Haifa's electric system were cooperating, too. Power to the consulate was cut off, eliminating the danger of someone unexpectedly or unintentionally turning on a light.

The invasion force consisted of Guriel, three agents (two of whom happened to be twin brothers), and the safecracker. All of them carried flashlights; the safecracker was equipped with an elaborate set of lock-picking tools.

Silently and carefully one of the operatives slipped a key into the basement door of the consulate. They all felt a sense of relief as it opened easily. Following their prearranged route, they crept along to the stairway that went up to Marriott's office. Again, a key in a lock and another door opened. Probing about with their flashlights, they found the office in the kind of

disarray that an occupant might indulge himself in if he expects to be the next person in the room. There were papers strewn on the desk, and a raincoat thrown over the back of a large chair. And in the corner of the room, behind the desk, one of the flashlight beams revealed a small, squat safe.

The safecracker was ordered to his task. While two of the agents turned their lights on the safe, he brought forth his elaborate set of tools. For a man who had not been told why he was doing this, nor even who his employer was, he showed a patient pleasure in his craft. At first he seemed so self-assured that it seemed as if he would make short work of his task. Unfortunately, his sense of assurance did not last long. He tried a dozen ways to solve the combination with no success. While the agents became increasingly uneasy, the safecracker grew angry and frustrated. Nothing seemed to work. For more than two hours he struggled. By 1 A.M., time was closing in. No one could predict when the first of the guards would come back or even when Marriott might return from Cairo.

There was just a chance, Guriel thought, that the vital document might be somewhere else in the house. Leaving the safe expert sweating and muttering, he began probing through Marriott's papers, drawers, cupboards, and bookcases. Predictably, the search was fruitless. By two o'clock their situation was becoming desperate.

Two contingency plans had been drawn up in case of such a failure, both of them inherently hazardous. One was to bring a mobile crane from a Haifa shipyard (the crane operators had also been brought in on the secret operation), attach its cables through a window to the safe, and haul it away without attempting to open it inside the consulate. The crane was not expected to attract attention because it was frequently trundled through the streets of Haifa on a variety of public-works projects. The whole operation, however, would require time, and it was already late to be starting. The second plan was to bring in a rather unwieldy portable electric generator that powered an electric cutting torch. In this case the danger would come from the noise of the generator and the smoke and smell created by the cutting operation.

Guriel decided to put both plans into effect, one as a backup to the other. The crane was summoned, and it began its slow trek to the consulate. The generator was wheeled into the building, and the safecracker, no stranger to this tool, immediately set to work. He cut through the heavy metal quickly. Within a few minutes he had sliced a hole six inches in diameter into the strong box. The crane, no longer needed, was ordered back to the shipyard.

In high excitement, Guriel reached inside and clutched a handful of papers. He had grabbed every loose paper in the safe, including some money, about 500 Egyptian pounds. Guriel quickly vetoed a suggestion from his accomplices that the foursome share the loot; money was not to be touched. What was most important was to peruse the papers to see if any of them pertained to the arms embargo.

With one of the agents holding a flashlight, Guriel started rifling through the documents. He had barely started when a sound down the street froze them with fear. The guards, drunk and singing, were returning to the con-

sulate. Leaving tools, equipment, and everything but the papers behind, they fled. Guriel noticed, however, that the safecracker, even in his haste, took time to rub each doorknob with his handkerchief to obliterate any fingerprints. He was no amateur.

By prearrangement an accomplice was waiting to drive Guriel to his Tel Aviv apartment, some forty miles away. En route Guriel tried again to look through the papers, only to be thwarted this time by a strange and sickening smell arising from them. Apparently the metal-cutting process, with its intense heat, had generated fumes that had impregnated the paper. Perhaps excitement and exhaustion also contributed, but the smell made Guriel ill. Once again he had to put them aside without knowing if his mission had been successful.

It was six o'clock in the morning by the time he reached his apartment. In utter exhaustion he fell into his bed and into a nightmarish sleep, the papers still clutched in his hand. He had been sleeping only for a few minutes, or so it seemed, when he became aware that the telephone was ringing. In a daze, he picked it up.

"This is the foreign minister. Have you been to Haifa?"

A mumbled affirmative.

"Come to my apartment immediately."

Boris Guriel was in the presence of Moshe Sharett. The foreign minister was skimming over the papers one by one. He seemed unimpressed. Guriel was uneasy. He and Sharett were not the best of friends, and both of them seemed to resent their interdependence.

Sharett, reaching the bottom of the pile, glowered angrily.

"No use, no use. You have wasted your time."

Then Sharett was suddenly silent. Guriel noticed his eyes widen. "My God."

The foreign minister read aloud: "This consignment should be seen as in excess of our regular supplies made within our agreement, which has expired."

He was scanning a top-secret document issued by the British Foreign Office on August 24, 1948, and addressed to the British envoy in Baghdad. It was also addressed to all British Middle East missions, including Marriott, care of the British embassy in Cairo.

The final paper proved to be equally sensational. Also addressed to the envoy in Baghdad, it advised him of a shipload of military supplies en route to the Hashimite Kingdom of Jordan, a nation "endangered by Jewish aggression."

Sharett told Guriel that he was leaving that day for the General Assembly session in Paris. Guriel suggested that he first have copies made of the two secret papers. Sharett replied that they were so important and so confidential that he did not want to risk making copies. He would take the papers with him and prove to the world that the British had betrayed the United Nations.

Then the foreign minister pressed a firm warning on his intelligence chief. "Keep this Haifa adventure to yourself. Don't tell anybody what you found." Sharett paused. "Not even Ben-Gurion."

Sharett retreated into the bathroom to get ready for his journey. He shouted his final orders through the closed door.

"Don't forget the warning I gave you when you indicated you might embark on this Haifa search. It is your responsibility and yours alone. I never heard of it, and I know nothing about what happened in Haifa last night. Go home and get some sleep. Shalom."

Guriel was bound by Sharett's orders not to reveal the particulars of the plan. But he did take the liberty of having the event inscribed by name, at least, in the official history of the Jewish National Fund. He called it "Operation Nachum" in honor of the master spy Nachum Bernstein, who had taught Guriel so much about the art of intelligence.

Marriott's discovery that his office had been pillaged understandably enraged him. He called Police Chief Stavi to file a complaint and to berate the chief for the ineffectiveness of his police force.

Although he and Marriott had always been mutually cordial, Stavi's reply was formal and to the point: "Our police have been given a list of foreign missions to keep under surveillance, and we accept our responsibility for their security insofar as this is possible. Your mission, however, is not on the list. You do not recognize the Provisional Government of Israel but claim to be in liaison only with 'Jewish authorities.' We don't know who these 'Jewish authorities' are. I'm sorry."

Marriott was to be transferred within a month or so to Switzerland, where he served as consul general. When, in early 1949, Israel sent a consul general to Switzerland, he found Marriott still bitter, although most of his rancor was directed at his own guards. He could not understand how these eight men—his own countrymen—could have left the consulate unguarded. Guriel has no recollection of the manner in which the guards were punished by their own government, but when the consulate was closed, they were all sent back to England. A year or so later, one of them, perhaps as a reward for his timely absence during the break-in, was hired by the Israeli legation in London. Such are the wages of nonfeasance.

Sharett, accompanied by Abba Eban, carried his evidence to the United Nations sessions in Paris on September 20. The Israelis' goal was to persuade Secretary of State Marshall not to support the Bernadotte plan. The American delegation had been in utter confusion. On September 21 Marshall, addressing the assembly, called Bernadotte's handiwork "a generally fair basis for settlement of the Palestine question." He had, however, neglected to clear the speech with President Truman. The president, away from Washington on his reelection campaign, received the news when he was, of all places, in New York City, where there were a million Jewish votes. He was enraged. He could not, however, discredit his own secretary of state. Truman therefore called the Bernadotte plan "a sound basis for the adjustment of differences."

The debate over the plan continued throughout October and into early November and was complicated by the apparent ambiguity in the United States position. Britain tried to force through a resolution that would apply sanctions to Israel if it did not withdraw from territory (principally in the

Negev) conquered since the Bernadotte borders had been proposed. The United States managed to have the resolution watered down to require withdrawal to temporary boundaries based on negotiations with Bernadotte's successor, acting mediator Ralph Bunche.

Bunche was willing to face reality. By this time his military advisers had convinced him that Israel was strong enough to take over all of Palestine, sanctions or not. He accepted a token withdrawal from the Negev. The British were furious, but their diplomatic endeavors were not as effective as the reality of Israel's power.

Meanwhile, Sharett and Eban had protested to various United Nations delegations about the British violation of the arms embargo. Apparently they did not have a formal meeting with Marshall until November 13. At that meeting, according to Marshall's memo, Sharett assured him that Israel had received no men or arms from the Soviet Union, but he freely admitted that men had come from all over the world to assist Israel and that munitions had been purchased and received from Czechoslovakia, France, and Switzerland.

Then Marshall wrote: "Mr. Shertok* added that Israel had definite evidence that the British were not supplying the Arabs with men and arms. I told him I had heard reports to this effect, had investigated them and was convinced that the British were not supplying the Arabs with men and arms."

It is difficult to determine why Marshall, even after Sharett's assurance that he had "definite evidence" (undoubtedly the documents Guriel had stolen in Haifa), was not "convinced."

On November 3, Harry S Truman had won a dramatic, upset election victory over Thomas E. Dewey. Despite their reservations about the State Department's vacillation, most Israelis were delighted over the reelection of a president who had so swiftly granted them recognition as a nation. Not the least of these well-wishers was President Chaim Weizmann. He expressed his warm congratulations to Truman, his hopes for the building of Israel as a haven for persecuted Jews, and his "deep pain" at the behavior of the British in supporting the Arab states, "who were sent against us by the British almost like a pack of hired assassins . . . even as I write we are receiving constant reports of Great Britain rearming the Arabs to enable them to restart hostilities against us."

In further debates there was little mention of the arms embargo. Sharett's documents had neutralized it, and both sides were acquiring arms with impunity. As for the Bernadotte plan, the Israelis were spared having to fight against it when the Arabs, too, rejected it. This was a blunder on their part, because the Israel that finally emerged included western Galilee, the Negev down to the port of Elath, and western Jerusalem. In January of 1949 even Great Britain abandoned its irrational struggle and officially recognized the State of Israel.

---

*Like many Israelis, at the insistence of Ben-Gurion, Shertok was soon to abandon his European name in favor of a Hebraic name, Sharett.

8

Escape from Iraq,1947-1950

ON A MOONLESS NIGHT early in 1947, a battered old Boeing C-46, a World War II relic, taxied out to the end of an unlit runway of Baghdad's airport. The craft spun around to its starting position and paused briefly to test its engines in the usual manner of propeller planes before takeoff. To the Iraqis at the guarded airport this was a routine operation.

During that brief pause, however, the plane was accomplishing its real and desperate mission. While the engines roared, the doors were thrown open and from the brush on each side of the runway some fifty Iraqi Jews scrambled toward the plane and were quickly hauled aboard. They were fleeing a land where Jews had lived continuously for twenty-five hundred years—the oldest diaspora in the Middle East. Their ancestors had been driven out of Jerusalem by the Babylonians about 586 B.C.

For much of this epoch Jews had lived peacefully in Baghdad. With their customary communal coherence and zeal for education, they prospered in an alien land. From time to time there were uprisings against them and sporadic persecutions, but the Jews persevered and survived. The most serious threat to their existence came in the twentieth century when, in 1919, Britain assumed a mandate over Iraq. The British control coincided with the wave of rabid nationalism that swept over the Middle East with the disintegration of the Ottoman Empire. When the mandate ended in 1932, nationalistic fervor took the form of violent oppression and persecution of those who were not Iraqi Arabs. The small Assyrian community was set upon, and hundreds of people were slaughtered. The Assyrians were Christians, which set them apart religiously as well as ethnically. The one hundred fifty thousand Iraqi Jews knew they were in peril and, indeed, subject to wanton attacks on their communities; many of them died, but somehow most of them

125

managed to survive until the pro-Nazi coup in 1941. In the forty-eight hours after the take-over, Arab mobs swept through the Jewish communities, especially the large one in Baghdad, killing Jews on sight, raping the women, and setting fire to houses. All the synagogues were demolished.

To some extent, the Jews had, characteristically, anticipated the danger, and the Jewish Agency, operating from Palestine, had established a covert cell in Iraq. When the pogrom took place, plans were already under way to arrange for the migration of the Jews to Palestine. There, at least in the *yishuv*, the new immigrants would be welcome. This was the first priority of the Haganah.

The Jewish Agency's second objective was to organize some kind of self-defense system for the endangered Iraqi Jews. Self-defense was hardly possible when the attacks came from the Iraqi police or the army, but spontaneous attacks from unorganized mobs could be effectively repulsed. A certain number of rifles were spirited into the various communities, and with these, as well as with knives or clubs, the marauders could be kept at bay.

The third responsibility of the Haganah was to establish an intelligence apparatus in Iraq. The Jewish Agency needed to know as much as possible about the military, political, and economic developments in the country. When the pro-Nazi government took power, the message to Tel Aviv was clear: the only safe course for Jews was to get out of Iraq.

During the war years, however, the safe course was rarely available. The Jews enjoyed a modest respite from imminent danger when the Nazi-controlled government was overthrown in the restoration of British military superiority. While the hatred of the Jews was not extinguished, it had to hold itself in check, in the face of military realities. The Haganah's intelligence operatives were constantly observing the national mood, trying to outguess the Iraqis so that any action directed at Jews could be forestalled.

The Haganah's intelligence mission was unusually dangerous, and many agents were uncovered and captured, usually to face jail, torture, or death. Stories of torture are numerous, and while some may be apocryphal, their persistence indicates a measure of truth. One widely related story involved a unique torture devised by the Iraqis. A captured agent, reluctant to answer questions, was put into a hole in the ground slightly larger than his body, with only his head above ground level. The hole was filled with water up to his neck, and he was then ordered to reveal his activities and his accomplices. When he refused to answer, blood-sucking leeches were thrown into the water. Shortly they were attacking the bare skin of the prisoner, sucking away his lifeblood. In agony, with his strength ebbing, he was asked the questions again. The leeches had broken his resistance; the Iraqis gained the information.

One agent who was never caught was an Iraqi Jew named Shlomo Hillel, who later rose to a high position in the Israeli government. In 1976, when we interviewed him, he was minister of police. He told us the story (never before published in English) of how a handful of brave people saved the lives of thousands of Iraqi Jews.

Hillel, who was born in Baghdad, was still in his early youth when the mandate ended and the Iraqi hostility toward the Jews, despite their two and a half millennia of residence, rose to the boiling point. Among the edicts directed against Jewish citizens was prohibition of the teaching of Hebrew. Hillel's father decided to emigrate to Palestine.

"We were one of the lucky families," Hillel told us. "We had some capital, and at that time Jews were permitted to take their liquid assets with them when they left the country. The greater difficulty was in entering Palestine." Nevertheless, the Hillel family managed to travel overland and, despite the British restrictions against immigration, to sneak across the border into the Promised Land.

As a native Iraqi, Hillel never forsook his friends back in the land of his birth. During the war, passage from Iraq to Palestine was relatively easy because Palestinian soldiers in the British army conducted an effective "underground railroad." Since there was constant British military traffic between the two countries, refugees were smuggled out regularly in army trucks. The Jewish Agency also played a part in assisting the Iraqi Jews, employing Arab smugglers for this traffic in human cargo.

With the war's end, the Iraqis recovered control of their own borders and emigration became much more difficult. Hillel, deeply concerned, offered his services to the Jewish Agency. He wanted to go to Iraq to facilitate the emigration of those who sought to leave before another onslaught of Iraqi persecution could occur. He was assigned to the agency's political department, which was essentially an intelligence unit.

The means Hillel used to return to Iraq was left to his own inventiveness. "Since I was an Iraqi by birth," he told us, "I decided to return to my own country to claim my citizenship. Therefore, I simply walked over to the Iraqi consulate in Jerusalem and told them I was brought to Palestine as a child and that I wanted to return home." Hillel did not tell the consular officials that he was a Jew. They either did not realize it or, because he paid them enough *baksheesh*, chose not to ask.

"I took the plane from Lydda Airport and was in Baghdad within a few hours. But the moment I passed through immigration, I got rid of my passport so that they would not discover that I was a Jew who had come from Palestine illegally."

Thenceforth, Hillel had to carry out his task as an underground agent. He was taken in and kept hidden by a Jewish family that was willing to risk harboring him. "They wanted to be active in our movement," Hillel said, "and this meant secretly teaching Hebrew to restore the Jewish roots of the children and to make plans to get them out of the country. We had to start from nothing—the British were gone, their trucks were no longer available—to find new ways and means to bring our people out of Iraq and then into Palestine."

The thousand miles between Baghdad and the border of Palestine was largely a wasteland, a rocky, barren plateau. Most of the route is across the vast Syrian Desert, which actually covers the western part of Iraq, the

northern tip of Jordan, and most of southern Syria. Only on its fringes do nomadic tribesmen manage to eke out a fragile subsistence, mainly as goat farmers.

These extremely poor desert people were easy prey to offers of money for almost any reason. When they were approached by representatives of the Haganah about smuggling Jews into Palestine, they were only too glad to take on the job. They were not, however, without guile. They asked a high price—£100—for the safe passage of every individual, and they got it. The Jewish Agency, which furnished the money, had little choice. The charge, equal to about $400, was not fixed. "Sometimes we had to pay double that amount and other times a little less," Hillel recalls.

The Arab smugglers were not always able to keep all of their loot. They had to give suspicious officers at military checkpoints along the route a certain amount of money for looking the other way.

The means of disguising the Jewish refugees varied. The most effective cover-up was literally that; the Jews would lie on the bed of a truck and would be covered over with bales of hay or straw. Another technique was to supply Arab garb to the Jews and pass them off as members of Arab families. Most Iraqi Jews were fluent in Arabic; they were, after all, lifelong residents of an Arab country and were indistinguishable from their Arab escorts.

Generally, the smugglers were dependable, since one safe delivery meant more offers and more money. There were occasional betrayals: some Jews were left in the desert to die, and others were turned over to the police, probably by Arabs who feared the consequences of being caught smuggling. But the records indicate that more than five thousand Jews did arrive in Palestine. The number who died en route is not known.

Some time in 1947 Hillel, who had slipped back into Palestine, was approached by two American soldiers of fortune—or rather, airmen of fortune—who had acquired a surplus C-46 cargo plane. Hearing that planes were needed by the Jewish Agency (although they were not certain for what purpose) and anxious to make a few dollars, they offered their services to the Haganah.

Haganah officials approached Hillel with an idea. They suggested the plane could be hired to make clandestine landings in some level area of the desert outside of Baghdad, pick up refugees, and fly them to Palestine. Hillel approved of the plan in principle, but he was fearful of the danger if the plane tried to land on some untested desert flatland. He had a better idea that did not involve any landings in uncharted territory.

The pilots were asked if they would be willing to take the risk of smuggling Jews out of Iraq. They were quite willing—for a price. The price, however, was reasonable compared to the cost and danger involved in the overland exodus: £5,000 in gold for each planeload of fifty passengers.

Hillel rode along with the two Americans (who were not Jews) as a representative of the Haganah and as a guide. The plane took off from Lydda Airport, bound for Baghdad. En route Hillel told the pilots that the original plan—to land first at Baghdad and then in the desert—was too risky. He

suggested an alternative scheme: simply land at Baghdad, take on some meaningless cargo, and, under cover of darkness, taxi to the end of the runway and, in the pause to warm up the engines, take on fifty Jews alerted to stand by.

The ruse worked perfectly, not once but perhaps half-a-dozen times. For many of the Jews on the flights, the journey took on a spiritual significance. They believed it was the fulfillment of the biblical prophecy that they would be taken to the Promised Land on the wings of a bird.

All of the danger was not in the departure. The British were just as vigilant in blocking immigration by land and by air as they were the shiploads of Jews off the Mediterranean coast. Hence, landing in Palestine had to be accomplished far from British military installations. The site selected was close to the village of Yavniel, a few miles southwest of the Sea of Galilee. A field was cleared of boulders, holes, and hillocks to provide a relatively smooth surface for the cargo plane to land. The departure from Baghdad was always at about 2 A.M. so that the landing at Yavniel could take place at dawn. There was never a mishap, proving, as Hillel claimed, that a C-46 could take off or land almost anywhere.

The airlift was remarkably successful. In combination with the trek across the desert, Hillel and his colleagues masterminded the escape of eight thousand to ten thousand Jews. Then, suddenly, on May 15, 1948, the Iraqi rescue operation came to an abrupt halt.

On that historic morning in May, Israel declared itself an independent state. Immediately, the five surrounding Arab nations—Egypt, Jordan, Syria, Iraq, and Lebanon—launched their attack. Egyptian planes bombed Tel Aviv, and King Farouk's Egyptian armies marched northward toward what they fully expected would be their own version of the Final Solution.

The Jews still in Iraq—some one hundred twenty thousand—were in immediate danger. No longer simply non-Arab Iraqis, they had been transformed overnight into nationals of an enemy state.

The intelligence reports from Baghdad were alarming. Hillel remembers them: "We received messages that the persecutions of the Jews in Iraq was becoming intolerable. They were sent to prison by the scores for no reason whatsoever, just for the fact that they were Jews. They were beaten, some of them to death, in prisons. It was really a horrible situation, and I have to say that at that time the memory of what had happened to the Jews in Europe during the Second World War was very fresh in our minds. We knew we had to do something to support the Jewish community there during this trouble and once again to do our utmost in order to open new roads for their deliverance." Israeli intelligence had three agents in Baghdad. Hillel decided it was essential that he somehow join them there. Since he could not travel directly to Baghdad, he conceived a scheme to reach his destination via a complicated, roundabout route.

One of the common skills of almost every intelligence agency in the world seems to be the ability to produce false documents. Hillel was shortly in possession of a forged North African passport and documents identifying him as the representative of a company doing business in the Middle East.

With these in hand, he went to Paris to talk to an acquaintance, a selfless Catholic clergyman, the Abbé Glaceberge, who had helped to rescue Jews during World War II. Glaceberge's antecedents were at least partly Jewish. The two men, pooling their experiences for a common goal, came up with a desperate plan.

Hillel proposed to get the Jews out of Iraq by taking them eastward, instead of westward, into the relatively friendly confines of Iran. The problem was how to get them across the guarded border. Here Glaceberge's knowledge meshed with Hillel's plan. In the early 1930s, when the Iraqis had attacked their Assyrian community, most of those who escaped had fled across the border into Iran. The Assyrians were Christians who had subsequently formed new communities and monasteries in Iran close to the Iraqi border. Glaceberge was personally acquainted with many of the Assyrian leaders. If Hillel could get the Jews to the border, the Assyrians could probably escort them safely into Iran.

So intense was the abbé's concern about the Jews that he volunteered to join Hillel in Iran to help carry out the mission. Hillel flew immediately to Tehran; Glaceberge joined him there a week later. Together they went to the Iraqi frontier to visit the Assyrian monasteries.

Their first contact with the Assyrians was disheartening: the communities were besieged from two directions. Although the Iraqis were their deadliest enemies, occasionally the Assyrians suffered raids from the Iranians in their new country. This sometimes necessitated their escaping back into Iraq for temporary sanctuary. This perilous existence, however, had made the Assyrians experts at crossing the border undetected, and they were happy to share this knowledge with Hillel and Glaceberge. In the last analysis, the Assyrians proved to be helpful allies who contributed a great deal to the success of Hillel's mission.

Through intelligence connections in Baghdad, the Iraqi Jews were informed that if they chose to attempt to escape, they would be met at the Iranian border. The distance to the border was relatively short—about eighty miles—and the way was nothing like the tortuous westward escape route. From the time the first group of Jews was spirited into Iran, Hillel decided the best hope for Iranian acceptance was for the refugees to deal honestly with the police. A group of them went immediately to the nearest Iranian police station and identified themselves as refugees from Iraqi persecution. "We do not want to be a burden on your country. All we want is permission to leave Iran, so we are requesting a *laissez-passe* [transit visa]."

The historic hostility between the Iranians and the Iraqis worked to the refugees' advantage. The Iranian authorities were kind and helpful, as if ascribing to the old adage "The enemy of my enemy is a friend."

With the State of Israel a reality and the British mandate ended, the problem was no longer that of breaking through a British blockade but finding temporary lodging for the thousands of Jews who crossed the border, providing them transport to Israel, and finding the money to pay for it all. At first the "visitors" to Iran were lodged in available inns and hotels, but this space was soon exhausted. The problem was solved by utilizing one large

space that was already the property of the refugees—the Jewish cemetery near Tehran. On this hallowed ground, primitive structures were constructed to serve as embarkation quarters for the Jews arriving from Iraq and bound for Israel. One of Hillel's associates was deeply moved by "the sight of youngsters playing in the snow among ancient Jewish tombstones." To him this was a symbol of Jewish continuity. From mid-1948 to the end of 1949, thousands of refugees were processed through this unique staging area between an ancient diaspora and the Promised Land.

The route was at first by plane or ship to Europe and thence to Israel. This was a long, expensive journey that strained the available resources of the Jewish Agency and the State of Israel.

Eventually it became essential to find a more feasible route, even if a small risk was involved. Hillel was asked to explore the possibilities. His response was to purchase some small Iranian planes to serve as transports. The aircraft were limited in capacity and range but, under the circumstances, were the best alternative to the roundabout journey via Europe.

The risk was in the decision to overfly the Arab countries between Iran and Israel. Potentially, that was extremely dangerous. If Arab intelligence learned that Iranian planes loaded with Jews were violating their airspace, the aircraft would be blasted from the skies.

To divert Arab suspicion and present a seemingly routine appearance to the operation, the Iranian-registered plane would file a flight plan indicating it was traveling without cargo to Beirut or Cairo. While cooperating, Iranian authorities pretended not to notice, and twenty to twenty-five Jews would board the plane. It would then take off on its "authorized" flight toward either Cairo or Beirut, which necessitated flying over Iraq, Jordan, and sometimes Syria. Toward the end of the route, the plane would veer off to a small airport in Haifa, where the refugees were joyfully disembarked. The "empty" plane then continued on to Cairo or Beirut, in accordance with its flight plan.

The unique evacuation system worked well for several months, until all the Jews in the graveyard refugee camp had been transported to Israel. But for all the thousands that had escaped Iraq, there were still more than one hundred twenty thousand facing an uncertain future in the growing hostility of their Arab environment.

Hillel had begun to grow wary of the air-evacuation system. There was evidence that the authorities in Cairo and Beirut were becoming suspicious. The flight controllers began to ask embarrassing questions of the pilots. Given the departure time from Tehran and the arrival time at the announced destination, plus the speed of the plane, there was a time gap. How could the pilot explain it? Constant excuses such as headwinds or detours to avoid bad weather began to sound less credible. Rather than have the whole scheme exposed, Hillel elected to put an end to the flights, which had continued into 1950.

Back in Baghdad, the man chiefly responsible for organizing the movement of the Jews to the Iranian border was Mordechai Ben-Porat. He was an example of the extent to which Jews were indigenous to the various ancient

diasporas. He traced his ancestry back twenty-five hundred years in the same Baghdad community. In 1945, anticipating the battle for the new Jewish state, he had left Baghdad on foot and walked a thousand miles, through Iraq, Syria, and Lebanon, to Palestine.

After serving in the Israeli army, Ben-Porat in 1950 returned to his former homeland as an undercover agent to help Jews who wanted to leave the country. He had the assistance of some twenty to twenty-five Israeli agents. They were hardly an elite corps; most of them were inexperienced. Their network security was lax and their organization was loose. Yet they had a camaraderie and accepted such discipline as was imposed by Ben-Porat, the man in charge. In cooperation with Hillel in Iran and an American industrialist, most of the Jews remaining in Iraq were conveyed to Israel.

The industrialist was James Wooton, head of the American Near East Company, whose motivation seemed to be both idealistic and financial. Wooton owned a four-engine Skymaster transport with a one-hundred passenger capacity, far larger than the small Iranian planes that had been employed by Hillel. The great advantage of the Skymaster was its range: it could fly from Iran to Israel without violating the airspace of the Arab countries in between. Wooton had his plane fly northwestward to Turkey and thence in a counterclockwise half-circle over the Mediterranean and into Lod Airport near Tel Aviv.

With the pace of the evacuation moving at full speed, the Iraqis became as irrational about their Jews as some of the Nazi-controlled countries in World War II. While holding Jews to be undesirable citizens, they nonetheless punished those attempting to leave the country and sought to track down the agents who were masterminding the escape into Iran. Hillel believes that hundreds of Jews were sent to prison and scores beaten to death in an effort to thwart the exodus. These assaults, so reminiscent of the persecution of the Jews by the Nazis, were widely reported by Western correspondents, and the result was a worldwide outcry against the Iraqi cruelties.

In April 1950, perhaps reacting to the criticism from abroad, the Iraqi parliament reversed its policy toward the would-be emigrants. It decreed that provided a Jew would surrender his Iraqi citizenship and forfeit all of his possessions to the state, he would be granted an exit visa. Even this relatively good news was hedged with one restriction. The exit visas provided for emigration to Iran, not for passage to Israel. The Israeli government was determined to change this. They wanted the departing Jews to be flown directly to Israel.

Hillel once again took on a dangerous mission. With Wooton's help, he acquired a British passport identifying him as Richard Armstrong, the name of an associate of Wooton. Hillel's English is not perfect, but he was proficient enough so that the Iraqis did not immediately recognize him as an Iraqi in disguise. He was accompanied by one of Wooton's aides, Ronnie Barnet.

They represented themselves as officials of a British transport company willing to assist the Iraqi government in evacuating its Jewish population.

By this time the leaders in Baghdad had convinced themselves that they were better off without this unpopular minority. A homogeneous population produces fewer chronic dissidents; the expulsion of the Jews would contribute to Islamic religious purity. An even more persuasive reason for ridding Iraq of Jews was strictly material: the wealth and property of the Jews was loot for the government, available as favors for the faithful followers of the leadership.

The negotiations between "Armstrong" and Barnet, on one side, and Prime Minister Tawfig Lel Swedi and Jewish leader Yehiskel Shentob, on the other, were fraught with ironies. Shentob, who participated only because he knew the expulsion of his people was inevitable, had been a classmate of the prime minister. A network of schools in the Middle East, the Alliance Israelite Universelle, had been established in the 1880s by Maurice de Hirsch, a French-Jewish philanthropist. Intended primarily for Jewish students, the school's academic excellence attracted the children of wealthy Arabs as well. Swedi and Shentob had attended the school in Baghdad. Now they were adversaries negotiating a new exodus.

Nor was that the only coincidence. Shentob was Hillel's cousin, a fact that Hillel realized, but that Shentob, apparently, did not. For official purposes, Shentob was talking with "Armstrong." The discussions were in French.

The arrangements were complicated, as Hillel later recalled. "In one and a half years we had to evacuate over one hundred thousand people from their homes. They had to be prepared to leave with only their clothes on their backs and one suitcase. And our comrades in Israel had to be organized to receive this influx."

To add to the difficulties, arrangements had to be conducted in the strictest secrecy. The decision to allow the Jews to leave was made at the highest level of the Iraqi government, without the general agreement of the Iraqi people. If the policy were to become public knowledge and a wave of resentment were to arise among the general populace, the government could have been forced to back down.

A formal contract with the Iraqi government was signed by "Armstrong." The charge for each departing Jew was £14, paid to the Iraqi treasury.

With the flights now legal and a hundred thousand potential passengers, the number of planes was increased. At first the Iraqis refused to allow direct flights to Israel. The planes had to make a useless trip to Cyprus first and then back to Lod Airport. Finally, after a great deal of persuasion, the planes were allowed to fly directly to Israel. This reduced the turn-around time, and the pace of the evacuation was increased.

By the end of 1951—about a year and a half after the legal flights began—all but five thousand Jews had been spirited away from their once-hospitable community in Iraq. Those who remained were mainly elderly people who could not leave their ancient homeland or anti-Zionists who opposed the exodus on principle.

Yahuda Tagger did not, like Lazarus, rise from the dead, but he probably feels at times as if he had lived twice. Who else walking the good earth

today once stood poised on the gallows, the noose around his neck, the trap ready to be sprung? The moment of imminent death followed a long night during which a rabbi had comforted Tagger with the Psalms of David, the prayers of hope. The condemned man had painfully and laboriously written a petition to the International Red Cross asking that his body be returned to his family in Israel. Then, at dawn, he had been led out to the gallows.

Yet it is this same Yahuda Tagger who today tells the story in careful detail. He recalls it without obvious signs of suffering from the effects of this ultimate human experience. He remembers the walk to the gallows, shuffling because of the short chain that linked one ankle to the other. A stocky, powerful man, he was determined not to betray any signs of fear. In his manacled hand he carried the heavy iron ball, whose chain joined the one linking his ankles. He was grateful for the weight. Gravity and the God of Israel had joined forces, he felt, and his neck would snap that much more quickly.

The road to the gallows had been a long one. Tagger was a sabra, a native-born Israeli. He traces his ancestry in Jerusalem back to the early sixteenth century, when the armies of the Ottoman Empire first occupied Palestine.

In 1941, in the midst of World War II, Tagger graduated from secondary school in Palestine and immediately joined the elite fighting force of the Haganah, known as the Palmach. At that time Jews and Englishmen were cooperating, ostensibly in the spirit of the Balfour Declaration but actually by necessity, against the common Nazi enemy.

When the war ended, Tagger enrolled in Hebrew University, where he specialized in history and economics. Again, his studies were interrupted, this time by the 1948 War for Independence. He served on the Jerusalem front during the desperate days when the ancient city was cut off from the rest of the country.

As much as the emerging state needed good soldiers to defend its soil, especially besieged Jerusalem, the leadership was thinking ahead to the need for trained diplomats. The Foreign Office decided to offer a two-year course in Paris and to tap its best-educated soldiers for the training. Tagger, with his good academic record, was an ideal candidate.

He was ordered to report to Tel Aviv, where he joined more than a thousand others for the diplomatic training. All but three hundred were weeded out through preliminary screening of various sorts. The remaining ones took a hundred-question true-or-false test on matters of general information.

Tagger was not only the best but his ninety-nine correct answers overwhelmed everyone else. The next highest score was seventy-five. Through this test the three hundred were cut to a mere fifty. After a final interview, twenty-five, including Tagger, were selected.

But there were those who recognized that school would probably be a waste of time for someone who seemed to grasp subjects as easily as Tagger. His talents were obvious to Asher Ben-Nathan, acting director of the Political Department of the Israeli Foreign Office. Ben-Nathan was midway in a distinguished career that would culminate eventually in his service as ambassador to France.

One day Ben-Nathan approached Tagger and, with a half-smile, asked, "What would your reaction be if I asked you to become a diplomat without even attending classes?"

"So much the better," Tagger replied with no hesitation.

"All right. We are going to appoint you to be an Israeli consul in a certain country. Agreed?"

"Agreed."

"Fine. Now move down to the third room, and they will tell you what your assignment is."

Tagger, amazed at his seemingly good fortune, followed instructions and walked down the corridor to the third room. Inside were two men sitting behind a bare wooden table.

"Mr. Tagger?" one of them asked, offering his hand.

"Yes, sir."

"You are hereby appointed to be Israeli 'consul' in Baghdad."

Consul? But Iraq and Israel were at war.

In fact, he was being asked to take on a dangerous spy mission, Tagger told us, nearly thirty years later in his office in Tel Aviv. "And so I went to Baghdad."

He was to join a small group of Israeli agents who were rescuing Jews and transporting them to Israel. But his main responsibility was the gathering of all types of information.

As with every spy, the cover story was paramount, and six months were devoted to fabricating it.

Tagger looked Semitic enough to pass for an Arab, but unfortunately his knowledge of the Arabic language was only sketchy. This meant he could not pose as a former Iraqi returning to his native land after a sojourn in some other Arab country. There were, however, many persons of Arabic origin who had lived most of their lives in Western countries and thus spoke less than perfect Arabic. Some returned to their native countries for sentimental reasons. This guise was the most plausible for Tagger, or so it seemed at the time.

Tagger was to pose as a former Iraqi who was now an Iranian citizen. The fact that he did not speak the Persian language nor even its Parsi dialect had to be overlooked.

As a cover story, it was a bad choice. If Tagger or his superiors had any doubts, they submerged them because his presence in Baghdad was a necessity.

With the usual forged passport, Tagger flew first to Cyprus, thence to Tehran. There he was met by an Israeli intelligence agent who provided him with Iranian identification papers (also forged, of course).

Tagger acquired a car and drove across the border to Iraq and on to the capital city of Baghdad and took up his duties as chief of Israeli intelligence in Iraq. He directed a network of some twenty-five to thirty agents gathering information, mainly military intelligence.

Information was transmitted to Israel with a secret radio or, in other cases, by letter to one of the several mail-drop addresses in Europe. The

Israeli intelligence also managed to recruit some crew members from commercial airlines as couriers to convey oral or written messages to Israeli intelligence in Tel Aviv.

After two months, Tagger was summoned back to Tel Aviv for consultations and briefing. An incident during the journey itself nearly exposed him, even though the circumstances were, on their face, somewhat amusing. Tagger described it to us: "At the same time we landed at the Rome airport, so did an El Al [Israeli] plane. The two groups of disembarking passengers were walking in parallel paths toward the air terminal. My girlfriend at the time was a hostess with El Al, and she happened to have been on that plane. Suddenly she saw me walking across the apron and, without thinking, rushed over to me, embraced me and kissed me. I had no choice but to brusquely push her aside and proclaim that I did not know who she was and that she had obviously mistaken me for someone else. This brief encounter, however, was witnessed by the Iraqi passengers. Still, I don't believe that this display of rejected affection led to my eventual arrest. That is another story."

Tagger flew from Rome to Lod Airport and immediately reported to his superiors in Tel Aviv. His return coincided with the end of large-scale hostilities between Israel and its would-be conquerors. The War for Independence was over. On January 13, 1949, six days after the Israelis had routed the Egyptians in the last major battle of the war, negotiations began. Late in February the acting United Nations mediator, Dr. Ralph Bunche, presided over the signing of an Egyptian-Israeli armistice agreement. Similar negotiations were conducted with King Abdullah of Jordan and the governments of Lebanon and Syria. By July all of the armistice agreements had been signed, and the Jewish state at last knew peace, however temporary.

With the cessation of hostilities, the Israeli Foreign Office saw new opportunities for stepping up the rate of Jewish emigration from Iraq. But Baghdad was not a signator to any of the armistice agreements, which created a somewhat complicated situation.

When Tagger reported back to Baghdad with new instructions from Tel Aviv, he began to assist Mordechai Ben-Porat with a new immigration program. The activity was hazardous, the perils unpredictable. Privately the Iraqi government was agreeable to letting the Jews leave. Its public posture, however, was that the emigration was illegal and reprehensible. But inasmuch as Iraqi citizens could not help but notice that the exodus was taking place, Iraqi newspapers conceded it by publishing announcements such as "Yesterday four planes left with Jews for an unknown destination."

This hypocrisy did not deter the Iraqis from dealing harshly with the Israeli agents who were abetting the departure of the Jews. From time to time, Jewish agents were arrested and jailed and sometimes hanged. During one of these periodic crackdowns, Tagger and Ben-Porat were arrested.

Tagger, who had gone to extreme efforts to keep himself under cover, does not know how he was discovered, but he suspects he was betrayed by an Israeli Arab: "During the period when I was military commander of Acre in western Galilee, a young Arab waiter served us coffee in our office. Later we

learned that he had moved to Iraq to work with the police as an informer, keeping tabs on the activities of the Palestinian refugees. One day we came face to face in Baghdad. His face was familiar, but I could not remember where I had seen him. On the other hand, he remembered me and later claimed that he had pointed me out to the police as an Israeli officer."

Tagger and Ben-Porat were seized in the former's apartment. Tagger was immediately placed in solitary confinement. He remembers: "In the evening I was taken to a cell adjacent to the torture chamber, where I stayed until dawn. Through the walls I could hear the anguished cries and moans of the prisoners. I was told that the people being tortured were friends and that I faced the same fate unless I cooperated with the police and confessed to my involvement with the Zionist conspiracy. After a while I started to believe that the victims were actually Communists or ordinary criminals, but it made no difference because the cries of pain, whether you are a Communist, a Zionist, or a simple murderer are the same. I do not know how I would have behaved if I were in the other room, and at times I sincerely wished I were. Anything would have been better than to have to listen to the cries of others. It was a form of unbearable torture."

For more than fifty nights Tagger was subjected to the vicarious suffering from the neighboring torture chamber. Each morning he was asked the same question: "Are you ready to talk?" His response was always defiant: "No!"

He shared his solitude with a radio and local newspapers. His captors allowed him this access to the outside world by design. They wanted him to know that a pogrom atmosphere was building up in Iraq. The newspapers and radio reported that five Israeli spies had been caught, that these criminals had been endangering the peace and were guilty of sabotage. Every Friday afternoon one of the Islamic mullahs would end his radio service with the holy exhortation: ". . . and we must hang this Israeli spy." Tagger realized to his acute discomfort that the mullah was referring to him. (Years later Tagger met and talked with this same mullah in prison and conceded, "He was really a gentle person.")

Immediately after the two Israeli agents had been arrested, emigration was suspended for a few days and then was allowed to resume, a moral ambiguity of sorts. Tagger was in prison for abetting the emigration, yet it was allowed to continue day after day, as Tagger well knew from the daily announcements in the newspapers.

"And then for several days," Tagger recalled, "the standard announcement did not appear. Shortly afterward I was taken before the investigating magistrate. I was shown a letter signed by the king's uncle, Prince Abdul Illah. Since the king was not of age, the prince was the regent."

The letter stated: "According to your request, I do hereby command that the transfer of Jews should cease until further notice." The judge explained to Tagger that he had requested the letter from the regent. The reason, as he explained, was that he was certain that some of the other agents sought by the Iraqis were escaping with the emigrants. "My job, my duty, as the investigating judge, is to block this channel of escape and, therefore, I asked for

and received this letter. This order will stay in effect as long as you refuse to cooperate with me in the investigation."

Tagger was faced with a terrible choice. He did not want the escape route to Israel shut off; it was the only hope for thousands of Jews. But his immediate concern was for a young Iraqi Jew already being held in prison and accused of being a foreign agent. The authorities wanted to know if he were a native Iraqi (which he was) because that would mark him as a traitor to his country and almost certainly result in his being hanged.

Assuming the judge's threat was real—and there was no reason to believe it was not—did Tagger have the right to deny freedom to thousands of Jews in exchange for the life of one? There was the real possibility that rising resentment against the Jews would result in a repetition of the 1941 pogroms, and this time the ancient Jewish community might be entirely wiped out.

Despite the danger implicit in his silence, Tagger's first strategy was to take a chance and stall. His decision to hold off was based on one reasonable assumption. Since the Iraqi government was making a lot of money out of the Jewish exodus (from the confiscation of the refugees' property), Tagger believed it would be allowed to resume. He guessed right. After seven days the emigration was permitted again. Tagger had successfully called the judge's bluff.

His silence, however, seemed to assure his martyrdom. The judge was not bluffing insofar as Tagger personally was concerned. Urged once again to talk or die, Tagger chose the latter, and he was sentenced to hang. His own moral decision was that he had no right to save his own life at the expense of a fellow human being—in this case the suspected young Iraqi Jew.

Tagger was transferred to the death cell of the Baghdad prison from which, through a narrow window, he could see the gallows in the adjacent courtyard. On the afternoon of his transfer he was told that he would die early the next morning. Tagger protested: "What do you mean? In this country do you condemn people to death without a trial?"

The officer with whom Tagger was arguing received the prisoner's comments with a mixture of amusement and contempt. "If you are that insistent on formal proceedings, we will hold a military trial tonight, and tomorrow we will hang you."

As Tagger looked out the window, he watched a chilling preview of his own fate. The hangman was busy.

Hope seemed lost. At dusk a Baghdad rabbi entered the jail, stood in the corridor facing Tagger, and began to chant the Psalms of David—the prayers of hope. All night long the rabbi's chanting continued; faithfully he comforted Tagger during his last hours.

At dawn a guard entered the cell to ask if Tagger had a last request.

"Please see that my body is returned to my family."

He was told that the procedure was complicated but that if he would write a petition to the International Red Cross, that organization would try to comply. Tagger was given a sheet of paper and a pen. With a trembling hand he scratched out the petition and handed it to the jailor. A few minutes later

a second guard entered, and the condemned man was led out into the court-yard.

The morning was bright and clear and seemed especially beautiful to Tagger. Struggling with his ball and chain, he staggered up the wooden steps, slippery with the yard mud from the shoes of those who had died before him.

The manacles were removed from his hands, but only so that they could be strapped to his body to keep them from flying outward. He was directed to stand on the trap door, and a bag of heavy sand was attached to his legs.

The executioner offered the condemned man a black hood to cover his head so that his eyes could be shielded from the awful reality. Tagger refused the offer. He had read somewhere that a hero goes to his death with his eyes open.

The noose was slipped around his neck and tightened slightly. Tagger began to recite, almost by instinct, the age-old prayer.

"Hear, O Israel, the Lord thy God, the Lord is One."

He had accepted death.

In this semitrance of expectancy Tagger slowly became aware that he had stood on the trap door for a long time. Minutes passed. Except for an imperceptible mumbling some distance away, all was silence. Five minutes. Ten minutes. Twenty minutes.

One of the attending Iraqi officers approached him and, as if partaking in a miracle, removed the noose from Tagger's neck. Then his voice seemed to boom into the prisoner's ears.

"Our king is very generous. He still gives you the opportunity to stand trial."

The chief of Israeli intelligence in Baghdad was not dead. It took him a few minutes to realize it. The bag of sand was removed, his hands were freed from his sides, and he was gently escorted back down the steps, almost as if a film were being played backward. He was treated with extreme kindness, as if even the hardened Iraqi jailors were aware of his mental suffering at the jaws of death. He was even given a meal better than he had enjoyed for weeks.

This compassion, however, lasted only hours. By evening he was being ruthlessly interrogated again. When he repeatedly answered, "I don't know," he was beaten. Tagger was alive, but otherwise his captors' tactics had not changed.

The change, such as it was, seemed to come from world opinion. The Israeli government had protested through every available channel the ruthlessness of the treatment of the innocent Jews of Iraq. The repercussions of the protest, which had been well publicized throughout the world, may have affected official Iraq policy.

After several days Tagger found himself before the same judge—the one who had condemned him to death, knowing, in all probability, that the sentence and the near execution had been an extreme tactic to force the truth out of Tagger. This time the judge spoke with the voice of forced reasonableness.

"Look here. By now we are all good friends. I will not deceive you. You can be tried for three possible offenses that carry three different punishments. You can be sentenced to death, you can be sentenced to life imprisonment at hard labor, or a third option that will imprison you for only five years. Cooperate with me and I will see that you get the five-year sentence. But the next hanging will, I assure you, not be staged. If you refuse to cooperate you will be executed this time."

Tagger responded that his position had not changed. He would not reveal the identity of any comrades. Once again he was put on trial for his life, this time, however, in a full-dress proceeding to which selected representatives of the press were invited.

It was the outcome of the trial that was the most surprising, especially to the defendant.

"I was represented by Iraqi counsel, and the trial was well covered by the local press. The charges specified that I was an admitted Israeli and that there had been several incidents of sabotage in Baghdad. The prosecution, however, could not prove that I had any responsibility for these and could not even offer evidence that the Israelis were involved. The prosecution asked for a death sentence, and the court usually complied with such a demand, but in this rare instance the prosecution was disappointed. I was given life in prison. It may be that since I had once been spared from the gallows, it would have been tempting the wrath of Allah to condemn me again to this fate."

The government, while tacitly accepting the court's verdict, was not beyond imposing its own revenge. Tagger was kept in the death cell for eighteen months. This kind of incarceration is an eerie mixture of blessings and hardships to the prisoner. He was given plenty to eat.

"The philosophy behind this," Tagger explained, "is that the chap in the death cell is lucky to eat today because tomorrow may be too late." Tagger had so much food that he used the surplus to bribe the guards and arrange to have some of it distributed to other inmates who were hungrier than he. This generosity added to his popularity, already enhanced by the mystique attached to a man who had stood upon the gallows, yet was still alive.

The prison director used a cell next to Tagger's for punishing inmates, and again, Tagger had to listen to the beatings day after day. This was Tagger's greatest hardship. To some extent he turned this hardship into a source of personal satisfaction and a comfort to the prisoners.

The unfortunates being beaten were, for the most part, Arabs. The procedure involved a clash of wills between the prison director and his prisoners. The director, or whoever was administering the beatings, would challenge his victim: "Moan, or even sigh once, and I will stop beating you." This was an indication that both parties regarded an admission of suffering as a victory for the prison authority. Aware of this, the prisoner would answer, "You will not succeed in getting a sound out of me. Seven times you will turn in your grave, and I will not know it." The prisoner would usually be right, because he would lose consciousness without uttering a sound. Tagger believes this explains a great deal about the mentality of the Arab prisoners.

Whatever their mentality, they emerged from the beatings with horribly bruised and swollen feet, because the punishment was usually administered in the form of blows on the soles of feet. In an Arab society, Tagger explained, only women or homosexuals were expected to wash men's feet. Tagger was neither, but he had, to use his own words, "a good Jewish heart" and wanted to help the unfortunate prisoners.

Immediately after the beatings he would warm some water on a small stove, add some salt and soda, and apply the soothing treatment to the battered feet with a cloth compress. He thus gave a measure of relief to the victims, who were surprised and grateful. Many of them were important Arab political figures, members of the nobility who moved in and out of prison in accordance with the shifting sands of Iraqi political opinion. During his eighteen months in the death cell, Tagger's kindness became legendary among both the wealthy, well-educated political prisoners and the common criminals who were his prison mates.

Tagger witnessed many executions and learned of a gruesome form of bribe solicited by the hangman. Each time he sprang the trap, he received a fee of two Iraqi dinars. He was required to share half of this with the director of the prison. (A dinar was then the approximate equivalent of $1.)

In order to increase his income, the hangman offered each doomed prisoner a proposition, in which Tagger was an unwilling but powerless accomplice. The hangman would ask: "So you want a comfortable hanging? Give our friend here five dinars, and if the execution is quick and comfortable, he will give the money." The victims had to bribe the hangman to assure their painless demise.

Tagger took part in the scheme only because he agreed that a quick death was preferable to an agonizing one. The money for the hangman's bonus was raised from all of the prisoners.

The executioner was not totally without scruples. On one occasion in the fall of 1951 the money was offered to him the night before he was scheduled to dispatch two young Iraqi Jews. Surprisingly, he refused the bribe. "Your friends," he explained, "will not be executed in the prison yard. I have been instructed to hang them in the public square as an example to other traitors. Unfortunately I have been specifically instructed to use the harsh method, therefore, in good conscience, I cannot accept your money."

That evening Tagger and his friends spent the long hours before the execution singing Jewish patriotic songs. The next morning they learned that the two young victims' last cry was "Long live the State of Israel."

After eighteen months in the death cell, Tagger was transferred to the Nugart Salman Prison, near the Saudi Arabian border. It was a peculiar sort of institution, run almost entirely by its inmates in a sort of commune. Immediately after his arrival Tagger was given a cup of tea and asked to sign a political protest petition. The Communist prisoners were condemning the involvement of the United States and Iraq in the Korean War. The document accused the United States of waging bacteriological warfare.

Tagger surprised his fellow prisoners by refusing to sign. "Look here," he said, "I do not know if your charges against the Americans are true, and I will not sign a document that may be false." Then, getting down to the

precariousness of his own situation, he added, "Second, there are people in the Iraqi government who still would like to put a noose around my neck, and I am reluctant to give them any excuse."

As a result of his refusal to sign, Tagger was labeled "an agent of international imperialism."

"Life in the prison became very unpleasant," he recalls. A majority of the prisoners, however, were not Communists, and Tagger became their leader.

There was sporadic fighting between the Marxists and the uncommitted. Tagger, as the anti-Marxist leader, took a lot of the physical brunt of the confrontations. He did his best to persuade the factions that the battles were fruitless and that all the prisoners should focus their attention on getting along with the authorities.

As the years passed and Tagger endured the wasting away of the prime of his life, he never seemed to lose his spirit. The authorities developed a respect for him. At first this was demonstrated by inviting him to join with the guards and officers in poker and badminton. Later they began to seek his advice in police and military matters.

On July 14, 1958, when Tagger had been in prison for nine years, the regime of King Faisal was overthrown in a coup led by General Abdul Karim Kassen. The king and Crown Prince Abdul Illah were murdered, and General Kassen proclaimed a republic. The new government officially announced a policy of nonalignment with East or West and formally withdrew from the Baghdad Pact.

It was a mark of the new leader's inexperience that one of the men whose advice was sought was none other than that illustrious prisoner, Tagger. A series of unofficial seminars was organized within the prison walls. Army officers, in ranks ranging from major to brigadier, visited Tagger in groups of two to thirty. Even for Tagger, these were relatively pleasant affairs. His students usually arrived with food and drink.

The revolutionary regime had at least a touch of enlightenment. The officers involved represented all shades of political opinion, and so, there was a fair degree of free speech.

The symposia were incongruous affairs. The "teacher" presided over his "students" encumbered with a ball and chain. But Tagger welcomed the opportunity not only to teach some politics but to cast Zionism in as bright a light as possible.

These weekly dialogues continued for almost a year. The leader and his neophyte statesmen discussed Arab-Israeli relations at length, as well as their own idealistic desire to build a better society for Iraq. It was an educational process for both Tagger and the Iraqis.

One of the regular participants was General Abdul Karim Gadda, the commander of the Third Division, the unit that had stormed the palace and made possible the successful revolution. Gadda was a close friend of President Kassen. The president, in his effort to create a mood of general amnesty, was releasing one by one the leaders of the Communist party who had been imprisoned under the Faisal regime.

Since Tagger had been accused of being a Communist at one point, he felt that as one so accused he had a right to freedom along with the Communists. He approached General Gadda on this basis. It was an interesting gambit. The Iraqis knew full well their prisoner was not a Communist.

Tagger asked Gadda to appeal to Kassen for his release. Gadda asked the prisoner to prepare a request in writing. "I promise you it will reach Kassen's hands. Our president is a good man." As it turned out, there was some goodness in Kassen.

In his plea, Tagger quoted from one of the new president's speeches. Kassen had said, "If we are fighting a war, we are fighting it against our foe's army and not against individuals." Tagger asked, "Is the fact that you are leaving me in prison for ten years a part of your war against Israel or against me as an individual?" Within a few days Tagger received a message informing him that he would have an audience with the president.

The prisoner and the president met in the latter's makeshift headquarters. Still in his prison garb and chains, Tagger stood before Kassen, who was surrounded with medal-bedecked officers. For more than an hour they spoke in generalities. Then the president brought up the issue almost unexpectedly in the midst of the conversation.

"Suppose we were to release you and war broke out between Israel and the Arabs. Would you fight us?"

Tagger knew this was a kind of challenge. He tried to be as honest as possible. "As God is my witness, if I get out of here, I will do my best to bring peace between our people."

Kassen seemed to be playing a kind of game. He turned to his officers. "In case of war would you fight for your country?"

Their answer was predictable—a resounding affirmative. The president then turned to Tagger, who was equally positive: "I would also fight for my country."

Kassen was not annoyed, in fact he smiled in appreciation of the prisoner's lack of duplicity.

"That is a very good answer. You will be released."

After ten years, the Israeli spy returned to his native land.

9

Getting the Intelligence Acts Together:1949-1952

THE EXPLOITS of Israeli intelligence have tended to overshadow the details of its formal structure. This is not surprising, for although an intelligence agency, like an army, must have a hierarchy, it is the dedication of the agents in the field that is the stuff of legends. This is especially true in the case of Israel because the two-thousand-year hope, the century-long preparation, and the final battles for the creation of a Jewish state have created a collective sense of mission unmatched by any people in modern times.

There is, nevertheless, a formal structure. It was established in June 1949, one month after the birth of Israel, and except for a partial reorganization in 1951, the structure has remained essentially the same. The very nature of intelligence, however, ensures periodic stresses and occasional scandals. At its best intelligence activity calls for courage and brilliance; at its worst, it can be a dirty business in which the agents in the field must often perform duties so unsavory that their own governments, while privately condoning or even ordering ugly operations, must publicly disown them. Hence, the lowest-level operative may have to take the blame for misdeeds that were perpetrated as a result of orders from higher up. The ultimate responsibility is often hidden forever in the smoke of burned documents.

The essence of political or military intelligence is intelligence in the broad sense—that is, intellect. This implies, among other things, the ability constantly to outthink, outguess, and outmaneuver one's enemies. Jews, living in the midst of hostile societies for most of their existence, have often developed this skill to a high degree simply as a means of survival.

Simcha Dinitz, the Israeli ambassador to the United States from 1973 to 1979, told us a joke that, while essentially Jewish, carries the weight of a universal parable. Paraphrasing (and slightly embroidering) the ambassa-

dor's version, this is the story: A Jew in czarist Russia was fleeing from the police, who had sanctioned a pogrom in his native village. He boarded a train to Minsk to find refuge with relatives there. Unfortunately the czar's police boarded the train at the next stop and went from coach to coach asking each traveler his destination. Two of the smartly uniformed officers cornered the ragged little fugitive. "Where are you going?" The Jew's immediate impulse was to throw them off the trail by telling a lie. He would tell them he was going to Pinsk so that they would look uselessly for him in that city. But his mind raced beyond this first impulse. He thought to himself, "But they will expect me to lie, so if I say I am going to Pinsk, they won't believe me and will look for me in Minsk. Therefore, I will tell the truth—that I am going to Minsk, in which case they will look for me in Pinsk and I'll be safely in Minsk."

In Israel's brief history, its intelligence agencies have been particularly successful at outthinking the enemy. In telling his story, Dinitz had a particular situation in mind. Before the Six-Day War of June 1967, President Gamal Abdel Nasser of Egypt was moving vast numbers of troops and heavy military equipment toward the Sinai desert. The first assumption of the Israelis was that since all this activity was taking place in broad daylight, Nasser obviously must be only conducting maneuvers and would not be so foolish as to move troops into battle position while Israel could clearly see what was happening.

But Israeli military intelligence did not take the first assumption for granted. To conclude that Egypt was only conducting maneuvers might be precisely what Nasser expected of the Israelis. More careful analysis of the movements of troops and weapons led to second thoughts, that this was a preparation for war. And that, indeed, was the case. By outthinking Nasser, Israel was moved to launch a successful preemptive strike.

When the modern state of Israel was founded on that strangely shaped portion of Palestine in 1948, the means to survive had been instilled through decades of struggle in the garrisons of local communities. The formal intelligence organizations created in June 1948 were the natural outgrowths of the secret Haganah army, the undercover Palmach strike force and the preindependence intelligence service known as Shai. Added to this was the formal experience gained by the thousands of Jews who served in the British army in World War II, hundreds of them in British intelligence, then considered the best such service in the world. While many Jews had been bitterly anti-British because of that country's restrictive Palestine immigration policy, they swallowed the bitterness long enough to join in the fight against Hitler's Germany.

In the three decades that followed Israeli independence, there were to be successes and failures in the intelligence services, as well as both dedicated and unscrupulous leaders. But the path toward the creation of a sophisticated service was relatively unbroken.

The largest service is the Bureau of Military Intelligence of the Israel Defense Forces, often known by its Hebrew acronym, AMAN, but also fre-

quently called the Modi'in, which simply means "information." AMAN has the usual assignment of military intelligence—to determine the enemy's capabilities and its dynamics. This branch of intelligence has some remarkable successes to its credit, as well as two spectacular failures, which are described in later chapters.

The second major branch of intelligence is the Department of Internal Security, or in Hebrew, Sherut Bitahon Klali, which literally means "General Security Service"; it is usually known as Shin Bet, for the first letters of the first two words of its Hebrew name. The Shin Bet is the equivalent of the FBI in the United States, but Israel's chronic insecurity imposes an immense responsibility on the agency. Internal security involves, among other things, keeping tabs on three hundred thousand Arabs who live permanently within Israel's borders. Most of them are loyal, but the harmless Arabs must be differentiated from the small but dangerous minority who are dedicated spies and saboteurs. In addition, Shin Bet must cope with the continuous infiltration of hostile Arabs from bordering or nearby states.

The greatest measure of romance and excitement is attached to the Political Department of the Foreign Ministry and, after 1951, its successsor, the Central Institute for Intelligence and Special Missions. In function, the Political Department and its successor agency were essentially the same, the equivalent of America's Central Intelligence Agency. The post-1951 name, Mossad, simply means "institute," in Hebrew, for the first word in the official title. The term is confusing because Mossad was also the name applied to the organization that sponsored and organized the illegal immigration to Palestine immediately before and during World War II.

Like the military and political leaders in the years of the fledgling state, the chiefs of the intelligence branches tended to be men of heroic proportions. Yet, in the shakedown era of intelligence, when its proper powers and functions in a democracy had not yet been clearly defined, each was eventually to face defeat. The first chief of military intelligence was Isser Be'eri, known as Big Isser because he towered a foot over the bulldog chief of Shin Bet, Isser Harel, or Little Isser, who was only four feet, ten inches tall. The third member of the triumvirate was Boris Guriel, chief of the Political Department (later Mossad).

In theory, all staff members of the intelligence agencies, and especially their chiefs, remain anonymous even after they have been detached or retired. In fact, with the passage of time, many have broken their silence. Harel, a man of commanding physical presence despite his diminutive stature, has become an international celebrity. His book, *The House on Garibaldi Street*, the story of the Eichmann capture, was a best seller and an American television drama. Harel was eventually to move sideways from Shin Bet to become head of the Mossad and finally to control all branches of intelligence as chief of Israeli secret services.

All three members of the triumvirate were ambitious, and there was considerable rivalry and infighting among them. Be'eri was the first to fall—in his case to disgrace, in what was to be known as the Toubianski affair.

Guriel went down to defeat in 1951, fired in a conflict over the relative power of his agency, the Political Department, vis-à-vis the military intelligence agency, AMAN. Harel held on to his power until 1962.

In many ways, Guriel is the most fascinating of these early intelligence chiefs. Like so many Israeli military leaders, he is a person of remarkable intellectual breadth. Born in Russia in 1912, he went to Germany in 1930 to study political science at the Hamburg Institute. There he became active in the organizations of Zionist students called the Kartelyiddische Verbindung, known simply as the KV. After he had received his graduate degree, he was persuaded by his colleagues to emigrate to Palestine and join the secret army of the Haganah. Because of some small experience he had had in the Latvian army before his departure for Germany, the Haganah pressed him into service as a small-arms instructor. Within a few years he was a section commander (the equivalent of a first sergeant). His section was one of the units charged with defending the Jewish sector of Jerusalem in the skirmishes with the Arabs prior to the outbreak of World War II.

A sense of the necessity of military and political intelligence was acquired by fighters such as Guriel and Harel in the daily struggle for survival. Guriel was greatly influenced by the eccentric but gifted British officer, Major Orde Wingate. Motivated by a belief in the biblical gift of the Holy Land to Abraham, Wingate organized the Jews to go on the offensive against the Arabs whose raids harassed them on almost a daily basis.

In 1939 Guriel joined the Palestine Brigade of the British army. He was captured by the Germans in 1942 and languished in a prison camp in Germany for three years. He was released, a wan, half-starved soldier, in May of 1945 and returned immediately to Palestine. The Haganah not only remembered him but knew of his excellent record as a soldier for the British. He was immediately pressed into service as an officer of Shai, the preindependence intelligence agency. By 1948 Isser Harel had become the chief of Shai and Guriel was one of his area commanders.

In June 1948 Ben-Gurion, after consultation with his military commanders and his cabinet, formally established the three branches of intelligence. This was the full chain of command: Dr. Chaim Weizmann, the world-famous chemist and lifelong Zionist leader, was president of Israel. David Ben-Gurion (who was often at odds with Weizmann) was prime minister and minister of defense; through the latter portfolio he exerted control over the Israel Defense Forces, headed by Major General Yaakov Dori, who was the immediate superior of Lieutenant General Yigael Yadin (later to be celebrated as an archaeologist as well as a political leader). Directly under Yadin was Isser Be'eri, director of military intelligence (AMAN). Also, through the defense ministry, Ben-Gurion exerted direct supervision over Shin Bet, the internal-security agency, headed by Harel. The minister of foreign affairs under Ben-Gurion was Moshe Sharett, who, through his Middle East office, controlled the Political Department (that is, political intelligence), headed by Guriel.

As a kind of coordinator of all secret services, but with limited power, was

Reuven Shiloach, a native of Jerusalem and a tough veteran soldier-diplomat. His main task was to ensure an interchange of information between the agencies.

The checks and balances that limit the abuse of power by intelligence agencies in a constitutional democracy were supposedly functioning in Israel, but within two months they were severely tested in the Toubianski case.

This affair has usually been presented as a triumph of law over the abuse of military power, but even today its facts are clouded in uncertainty. That uncertainty involves one of the perennial problems of intelligence: From how high did the order for which Isser Be'eri took the blame come? Even his fellow leaders in the intelligence triumvirate, Harel and Guriel, disagree. To Harel, Be'eri was "a dangerous megalomaniac." To Guriel, he was "responsible and judicious." But perhaps most significantly, to Ben-Gurion he was "a rascal without a shred of conscience."

Be'eri's ordeal began in June 1948 when the Jews lost control of eastern Jerusalem to the Jordanian army but were desperately holding on to the western part of the city. When a United Nations cease-fire began on June 11, Jerusalem had already been cut off from communication with Tel Aviv and the coast. The cease-fire, supposedly to last for four weeks while the United Nations sought an armistice, was observed by neither the Jews nor the Arabs.

The Arabs seemed to have an amazing foreknowledge of the most vulnerable spots on which to concentrate their fire, and the Jews were enduring losses that threatened to become disastrous. For example, a small-arms plant consisting mainly of valuable machine tools was in operation close to the field of battle. It was hit repeatedly. The Jews secretly moved the plant to a new and—they thought—completely secret location. It came under Arab bombardment almost immediately.

The Jews concluded this was not luck; there had to be a spy in the Jewish ranks. Israeli commanders reported this to Ben-Gurion, who summoned Be'eri and gave him an ultimatum: find the traitor. Failure to do so would mean Be'eri would lose his command.

Boris Guriel had been in Jerusalem from late April until June working with the preindependence Haganah intelligence. In June, after the formal creation of the state, he returned to his Tel Aviv home and was appointed chief of political intelligence.

One night he awoke, aware that someone had turned on his light. A worried Isser Be'eri, who had a key to Guriel's apartment, was standing beside the bed. He was in a near panic about the apparent traitor in Jerusalem who was advising the Arabs about the location of major Israeli military installations. He told Guriel about Ben-Gurion's mandate to find the culprit.

The spy, whoever he was, was able to capitalize on a unique situation. The British still owned and operated the Jerusalem Electric Company. The power station was in the Arab-controlled Old City. The company was supposedly neutral, supplying electricity to Jews and Arabs alike. But the amount of power was limited. The power was fed to Jewish and Arab sectors according

to each side's requested priorities. It was a delicate situation; the company knew on which lines to feed the power, but presumably they did not know for precisely what purpose.

The international Red Cross arranged with British and Arab authorities to allow a Jewish officer to cross into the Arab sector to furnish the electric company with a priority list. The officer chosen was Major Meir Toubianski, an engineer who had served in the British army in Palestine during World War II and who was personally acquainted with the engineers in the power station. Toubianski was an admitted anglophile who retained many wartime friendships. He was said to have even adopted British habits and mannerisms.

David Shaltiel, commander of the Jerusalem forces, provided Toubianski with a list of the facilities that required electric power, including hospitals, several bakeries, the Jewish Agency headquarters, and certain military installations. Toubianski in turn supplied the power company with the geographical sectors (not specific installations) to be served. Almost as soon as Toubianski had turned over the information, the Arabs' guns zeroed in on every one of them.

The crisis came when the Arabs bombarded the secretly relocated small-arms plant. The Israelis did not believe the Arabs had any means of learning where the arms machinery had been moved except through a spy. Benyamin Gibli, chief of military intelligence for the Jerusalem area, suspected that Toubianski might be the traitor. At Gibli's direction, two of his officers went to Tel Aviv, where they informed Be'eri of Gibli's suspicions. Be'eri, already under intense pressure from Ben-Gurion, decided to act.

There are marked differences of opinion between various sources about the handling of the Toubianski case from that point on. Guriel believes Be'eri acted under direct orders from Ben-Gurion. Most other sources believe Be'eri's procedures were the desperate actions of an arrogant and ambitious man who was willing to go beyond the law to keep his job.

In late June, Toubianski, on leave from his duties, was seized at his brother's house in Tel Aviv, formally arrested, and taken to the remote village of Beth Jiz, near Jerusalem. Also arrested were three British supervisors at the electric plant, who were turned over to civil authorities of the new state.

Toubianski was tried on June 30 by a kangaroo military court composed of three men, with only Be'eri as prosecutor and witness. (According to Guriel, the court martial was composed of Gibli, Avraham Kidron, and David Karon, all officers under Be'eri's command.) In less than two hours Toubianski was convicted of being a spy and was immediately shot by a firing squad.

The three supervisors at the power company, however, were accorded the full protection of the Israeli system of justice. They were allowed defense counsel and the right to cross-examine their accusers. Ultimately the charges against one were dropped for lack of evidence; those against the second were dismissed. The third was tried, convicted, and sentenced to seven years in prison. Even this sentence, however, was suspended by the Supreme Court of Israel when the defendant's lawyer appealed his case.

This double standard of justice shocked many Israelis, most of all Lena

Toubianski, the embittered wife of the dead officer. She had been given no information about her husband; he had simply vanished. She learned of his death twenty-two days later when she read about it in a newspaper. In desperation she wrote to Ben-Gurion. Part of the letter, quoted by Michael Bar-Zohar in *Spies in the Promised Land*, reads as follows:

> Why did those Englishmen accused of spying get the right to a trial according to due process of law whereby they were allowed counsel, whereas the most basic rights were denied my husband, who was a loyal, ranking officer in the Haganah? If Toubianski ever had a trial, where did it take place, and when? What law justified the verdict? Why was the condemned man given no opportunity to say farewell to his wife and his young son before he was executed? Even the vilest criminal has that privilege.

Mrs. Toubianski hired a lawyer, who assembled enough evidence to persuade Ben-Gurion to conduct a thorough examination of the evidence used against Toubianski and the court-martial proceedings. The lawyer argued that even under wartime conditions, Be'eri's actions were in violation of military law. But more important, he seemed to raise a serious doubt in the prime minister's mind as to the guilt of Toubianski. Ben-Gurion proceeded to conduct his own investigation. In December 1948 he concluded that Toubianski was innocent. The body was exhumed from its lonely grave in Beth Jiz and reburied with full military honors, including a posthumous restoration of his rank of captain. Lena Toubianski and her son were awarded damages, and she was given a lifetime pension.

On January 14, 1949, Be'eri, disgraced by the Toubianski revelations, resigned as chief of military intelligence. Five days later he was arrested and charged with murder. His trial began October 16 and continued until November 23, when he was found guilty.

Once again, the recurring problem of reconciling the procedures of intelligence agencies and the standards of constitutional jurisprudence confused the issue. If intelligence is occasionally a dirty business, the line between what is acceptable activity and what is beyond the pale of elementary decency—as well as legal decency—is almost impossible to draw.

Be'eri, after the court had established his guilt, was given only a symbolic jail sentence of one day and even that was commuted by President Chaim Weizmann, presumably in recognition of Big Isser's long devotion to the Zionist cause. This, however, did not remove the stain of dishonor from Be'eri's reputation. He lived for ten more years, a broken and bitter man. He believed to the end that Toubianski was guilty as charged.

Most histories of this era close the book on the Toubianski case with Be'eri's conviction, which, they presume, represents the victory of the rule of law over the abuse of military power. But was there more to it than that? Does the Toubianski case represent the supremacy of civil power, or does it prove the impossibility of conducting intelligence under any legal or moral strictures?

Was Be'eri silent upon his conviction because he had no reasonable defense or because, true to the code of intelligence, he refused to indict those above him? Was the mere slap on the wrist given Be'eri a tribute to his patriotism, or was it a deal to buy his silence? The masters of the Israeli government and of its intelligence services were great men, but they also had great ambitions and great egos. There was, beyond any question, a clash of ambitions between Isser Be'eri, Isser Harel, Boris Guriel, Reuven Shiloach, Benyamin Gibli, and even Ben-Gurion himself.

The authors persuaded Boris Guriel to unburden himself on the facts of the Toubianski case insofar as he knew them. His story, which follows, casts a whole new light on the machinations of intelligence services:

On the eve of the Be'eri court proceedings' termination, in fact a few days prior to the judgment pronouncement, I received a document which contained startling news concerning the Toubianski case. The document was a transcript of a letter dictated by Mr. John Balfour of the British embassy in Tel Aviv to his superiors at the Foreign Office in London.

John Balfour's assignment to the British mission in Tel Aviv was portentous in the years of the postmandatory period. . . . We carefully observed Balfour's sporadic trips to Amman and Cyprus, where the task force of the British mandatory administration had been concentrated after the British evacuation from Palestine. We knew that Balfour was in contact with Sir Alec Kirkbride in Amman and with the commander of the Arab Legion, General Sir John Glubb. We couldn't overlook Balfour's involvement with the British-instituted Arab League in the Middle East.

Balfour's letter to his London superiors, which fell into our hands at the time of Isser Be'eri's trial, focused our attention on an aspect of the Toubianski case which was beyond Be'eri's role. . . . At the outset of the letter he spoke of Be'eri's trial and of Toubianski's friendly relations with the British officers in the Jerusalem Electric Company at the time of the Jerusalem siege in 1948. His reference to Toubianski was in the tone that his service to the British was well known. He wrote to the effect that Toubianski was instrumental in hindering Jewish control in Jerusalem.

I read and reread Balfour's document. It was in the late afternoon when I phoned Foreign Minister Moshe Sharett's office to present him with the document. But Sharett had left for Jerusalem, so I went to the director-general of the ministry, Walter Eytan. He read Balfour's document and asked me what I was going to do with it. I replied that I intended to submit it to Yaacov Solomon, Be'eri's attorney. Eytan added, "Go."

I rushed to Solomon's office, where I found Be'eri. Solomon was due any minute, so in the meanwhile I spoke to Be'eri, but I did not mention Balfour's letter.

When Solomon came in, I handed him the document, warning him

that he should take precaution in using it, keeping in mind that I was a government official on special duty and was bound to keep documents in tight secrecy. Solomon replied that if I would leave the document with him, he would return it the same evening. In a few hours, he said, he would phone me and I could get the letter back.

I waited in vain that night for Solomon's call.

The next morning, as soon as I arrived at my office, I got a call from Sharett. He wanted to see me at once. When I reached Sharett's study, Eytan was with him. The foreign minister turned to me and asked, "Why did you give that document to Solomon yesterday?" Eytan broke in, "I sent Boris to Solomon."

"We'd better go see the prime minister," said Sharett.

On the way to Ben-Gurion's office, Sharett was excited, trying to encourage me to stand up to Ben-Gurion. I realized that the matter involved his own power struggle with Ben-Gurion.

Ben-Gurion seemed to be in a taciturn mood when we came in. Sharett told him about the document and said I had turned it over to Solomon because Solomon had stood by me when we were together in the Haganah intelligence service.

Ben-Gurion turned sharply to me. "Why did you give out a classified paper? Your task was to collect information, but you are forbidden to divulge any piece of gathered knowledge to any unauthorized person. Why did you violate a primary rule?"

I responded, "When the paper came to my knowledge, I had the feeling that I was in the position of the German officer who knew the truth during the Dreyfus affair. By keeping silent he actually became an accomplice in the crime committed."

Ben-Gurion looked at me grimly, then exclaimed, "I know who Toubianski was, but why did Isser murder him? Do you think he was entitled to do so?"

There was a long silence; then Ben-Gurion dismissed Sharett and me. I was worried, but Sharett was strangely jubilant, hinting that Ben-Gurion had committed a faux pas in his dealing with the Toubianski affair. What struck me as peculiar was that on the way back Sharett did not comment on the substance of the document. For that matter, neither had Ben-Gurion—he had not indicated whether he had any feelings about the implications, the veracity, or the consequences of the document.

A few days later the verdict was reached, and the sentence was imposed in the Be'eri case. It was a surprise, but those who were aware of the Balfour letter realized that Solomon had made use of it. Be'eri, however, refused to testify about the case.

My belief is that the mildness of the sentence—and even that was suspended by the president—was as a result of the presentation of the Balfour document by Solomon to the court. The court may have been swayed by the probability of Ben-Gurion's involvement. The exoner-

ation was granted even before any judicial authority gave its consent to it.

The pro forma sentence—which in fact was an acquittal—accentuated the question of whether Be'eri acted out of his own convictions or whether he did what he did by orders of a higher authority which he would not compromise, because of a sense of loyalty and because he was guided by the state's higher interests.

In 1964, six years after Be'eri's death, Ben-Gurion, responding to a Haifa businessman who complained that in 1948 Be'eri had falsely accused him of corrupt practices, wrote that Be'eri was a "swindler" and a "scoundrel."

The prime minister's character assassination—omitting any facts —triggered a bitter reaction from Beryl Repetor, an old-timer with the Labor party who had maintained a friendship with Ben-Gurion after the prime minister's retirement in 1963. In 1975 Repetor published his memoirs. He vigorously defended Be'eri and contradicted Ben-Gurion's view. "It was a strange thing," Repetor wrote, "that Isser Be'eri, a strong man, reasonable and judicious, who had worked with Ben-Gurion and had been one of his admirers, was, of all men, accused by Ben-Gurion of acting out of expediency in a security matter. I personally, having known Isser well, cannot imagine that in the matter of a death sentence he did what he did solely on his own judgment.

"When Ben-Gurion's letter was published, I just couldn't keep quiet. I went to him and related a conversation I had had with Isser a few months prior to his death.

"Isser refused to talk about it. He said everything in connection with the subject he would take to his grave. Perhaps someday a historian who would examine documents might throw some light, then perhaps it will reveal that he was victimized.

"Ben-Gurion insisted we change the subject."

About that time rumor spread that documentary evidence—an order to Be'eri from Ben-Gurion—existed, but it was never found, despite the efforts of Be'eri's brother and son.

Several American publishing houses had approached Be'eri seeking to publish his memoirs. He flatly refused.

The case remains a mystery. The crux in this case and in the infamous Lavon affair that was to follow is reduced to the ominous question, Who gave the order to try Toubianski?

That is the end of Guriel's version of the Toubianski case. It differs markedly from the version heretofore accepted in most Israeli chronicles. The authors are not in a position to pass judgment on either version. What is more important, however, is the way that the Toubianski case and the disgrace of Isser Be'eri reveal the intrinsic complexity of intelligence operations. The orders to carry out intelligence missions involve enforced secrecy.

Seldom does an operative know from how far up the hierarchy an order originated, nor is he supposed to know. Hence, intelligence often escapes becoming history for lack of any recorded information. Only on rare occasions does a government reveal the details of an intelligence operation.

The tripartite organization of Israeli intelligence set up in 1948—AMAN, Shin Bet, and Guriel's Political Department—was to be shaken up in 1951, and this time it was Guriel's turn to see his career abruptly ended.

The most detailed account of this shake-up is described in *Spies in the Promised Land*, Michael Bar-Zohar's biography of Isser Harel. Guriel would not discuss this part of his career with the authors, and therefore, Bar-Zohar's account, which tends to be pro-Harel and pro-Ben-Gurion, may be incomplete.

Along with Guriel, the key figures in 1948 were Be'eri, who was to resign in January 1949, and Harel. Be'eri was succeeded by Vivian Herzog, who had been Be'eri's deputy and was another veteran of British intelligence. In 1950 Herzog was succeeded by Benyamin Gibli.

Herzog's principal contribution during his brief tenure was to establish a coordinating agency over all three intelligence functions. The coordinating body was a commission, headed by Reuven Shiloach.

By 1951 Guriel had accomplished what he believed he was supposed to do: he had built up a substantial worldwide intelligence and espionage system. He had agents throughout the Middle East, Western Europe, and the United States. Some of his Middle Eastern agents were competing with the military intelligence operatives of AMAN. It was this rivalry with AMAN that was to contribute to Guriel's downfall.

Guriel believed passionately in political intelligence. Whereas the roles of military-intelligence and political-intelligence services overlap frequently, they are essentially seeking different kinds of information. Military intelligence seeks to know the *capability* of the armed forces of an enemy or potential enemy—the strength of its army and navy, the location of its bases, the technology of its weapons. Political intelligence is concerned less with capability and more with *intent*; this requires knowledge of the subject country's politics, its power structure, the policies of its leaders, its national psyche. "We had to know which way the wind was blowing," Guriel told Bar-Zohar.

To carry out such an assignment, Guriel's men had to blend into the power society of each country. They had to be at the parties, in the offices, at the restaurants where the power elite mingled. This often required high living—or rather the appearance of high living. Guriel's rivals in the other intelligence services thought his agents were having too much fun in Paris and Geneva—or so it appeared.

Shiloach, as coordinator of the secret services, carried the complaints about the Political Department to Moshe Sharett, the foreign minister, who had never been much of an admirer of Guriel. Sharett called in Shiloach and Guriel to thrash out the situation. Guriel strongly defended his quest of political intelligence and the methods his agency used. Sharett, who felt there was a critical need for more emphasis on military intelligence, was not

convinced. He empowered Shiloach to come up with a solution. Shiloach decided to dissolve Guriel's Political Department.

Guriel protested directly to Ben-Gurion, who gave him a sympathetic ear and then proceeded to enrage Guriel and his agents when he threw his weight behind Shiloach's decision. The prime minister then met with Commander in Chief Yigael Yadin, Sharett, Shiloach, and Walter Eytan, director of the Foreign Ministry. The Political Department was reduced to a minor agency to study political problems but deprived of its worldwide intelligence network.

In its place was created the organization that has given the most romantic luster to Israeli intelligence—the Mossad. Shiloach was selected to be its chief. Its official existence began in October 1951.

The upheaval caused a brief, but potentially serious, rebellion within the disbanded Political Department. Guriel and his agents felt they had been betrayed in a power struggle. Guriel resigned, as did most of his operatives. Shiloach warned them that if they did not return to duty, they would be permanently banned from employment in any branch of the government. But the real concern was the collection of secret information in the hands of Guriel's men. In time, most of them capitulated, either joining Mossad or signing a pledge not to reveal the secrets they had gathered as foreign agents. In later years, Guriel was openly contrite about his brief defiance of authority.

The assignment of Shiloach to a position of power in the secret services was irritating to the ambitious Isser Harel. Circumstances played into Harel's hands. Shiloach, despite years as a fighter and an intelligence leader in the Haganah, proved to be a poor administrator as he tried to build a new Mossad from the ruins of Guriel's Political Department. According to Bar-Zohar, even Shiloach's own deputy turned against him, but mainly Shiloach felt the pressure from Harel, who told him bluntly that he was incapable.

Ben-Gurion apparently was concerned about Shiloach's performance. In September 1952, less than a year after he had engineered the creation of the Mossad, Shiloach resigned. He was succeeded by Isser Harel, who moved over from his post as chief of the Shin Bet. In addition, he took over Shiloach's coordination of all the secret services. For the next decade, Harel was to be the most powerful man in the intelligence agencies and, in fact, because he had Ben-Gurion's ear, one of the most powerful men in Israel. But the establishment of a permanent organizational structure did little to eliminate the competition between agencies.

10

The Spies Who Went Too Far: The Lavon Affair

ON THE AFTERNOON of July 23, 1954, Philip Nathanson, a clean-cut nineteen-year-old, was standing in line to buy a ticket to the movie at the Rio Theatre in Alexandria, Egypt. Except for his stylish slacks and blazer, he was not markedly different from the other patrons.

Suddenly, Nathanson cried out in agony, dropped to the sidewalk, and was engulfed in smoke. His clothes seemed to have caught fire. Bystanders tried to tear the flaming clothes off him. Hassan el-Mandadi, a police captain, came to the rescue. With a policeman's efficiency he was able to remove Nathanson's jacket and beat out the smoldering clothes under it. Nathanson was seriously, although not critically, burned.

From this small incident the greatest fiasco in the history of Israeli intelligence came to light. Whereas the operations that preceded it and those that were to follow were typically characterized by initiative, brilliance, and, most important, success, this one was a unique failure. Its details kept unraveling for seven years, bringing to light arrogance, ignorance, and betrayal. Ultimately, when the whole truth was finally exposed, its sordidness reached the cabinet of the great Ben-Gurion, forcing the father of Israeli independence to resign as prime minister. To this day all the facts are still not known, and they probably never will be. The whole, long imbroglio is known as the Lavon affair.

Philip Nathanson was a Jewish spy and saboteur in Egypt. He was acting on dubious and misguided orders from military intelligence. That afternoon he had intended to set fire to the Rio Theatre with an incendiary device in an eyeglass case in his trouser pocket. The eyeglass case contained a small quantity of potassium chlorate plus, in a rubber condom, a few drops of sulfuric acid. When the acid ate through the rubber, the mixture caused a

brief but intense fire—enough to start a blaze in a movie theater. Somehow in Nathanson's case the device, which had worked well on earlier occasions, ignited too soon.

Moshe Sharett found it was not easy to be the prime minister who succeeded the legendary Ben-Gurion. So absolute was the emotional hold of the old warrior on the people of Israel that even when he took a "leave of absence" in the fall of 1953, his successor soon realized that the real power still rested with the temporarily retired Ben-Gurion at his Negev retreat in the village of Sde Boker. Sharett's task was all the more difficult because everyone knew that he was not Ben-Gurion's first choice as successor. Ben-Gurion had preferred the more solid, if less intellectual, Levi Eshkol. Eshkol, however, did not want the job, and it went right to Sharett almost by default. The irony in the succession was that Sharett had fought at the side of Ben-Gurion for decades and confessed to near worship of the Israeli hero. But the old man, for his part, had reservations, not about Sharett's intellectual capacity, but about his inner drive.

One of Sharett's legacies from Ben-Gurion was his defense minister, the arrogant, ambitious, and brilliant Pinhas Lavon. Ben-Gurion had held the defense minister's portfolio as well as the prime minister's, and Lavon had been his assistant. Strong, hard-driving men had always appealed to Ben-Gurion. While it is doubtful that he liked the cynical and officious Lavon, certainly he respected him. This loyalty to Lavon was one day to nearly destroy Ben-Gurion.

But in 1954 Lavon was the retiring prime minister's choice for the defense post, and Sharett reluctantly acceded to his predecessor's wishes. Within weeks he had reason to regret it. Lavon approved a retaliatory raid on an Arab village in Jordan from which, it was suspected, attacks were being launched into Israel. The retaliation was unnecessarily ruthless. As many as eighty villagers were killed, including many women and children. When it was disclosed, the revolting incident shocked the world. Sharett, who publicly had to defend the raid, had not been consulted. Ben-Gurion had been, however, and had approved of the action, although its excesses may have privately shocked him. The action did not shock Lavon, who publicly joked about it.

In the midst of this, Sharett had to deal with a boiling international crisis that posed a direct threat to Israel's security. On July 22, 1952, a group of young Egyptian officers had staged a coup that overthrew Farouk, their overweight and degenerate monarch. Among the grievances that the officers held against Farouk was Egypt's miserable performance against Israel in the 1948 war. Power appeared to have been wrested by General Mohammed Naguib, an intelligent liberal, and there was hope, especially in the United States, that his rule would create a pro-Western regime.

Actually, Naguib was a figurehead; real power was in the hands of the fiery young Colonel Gamal Abdel Nasser. Nasser, a Pan-Arabist, sought a united front against Israel. He was not, however, a satisfactory leader to the religious zealots of the Muslim Brotherhood who tried twice to assassinate

him. In April 1954 Nasser was elected prime minister and took de facto power from Naguib, who was eventually ousted on the trumped-up charge that he was cooperating with the Muslim Brotherhood.

Despite the bitterness between Israel and Great Britain that still existed over British support of the Arabs in 1948, the British military contingent guarding the Suez Canal was regarded by Israel as a buffer protecting the Israelis against another assault from Egypt. Early in 1954 Nasser began overtures to the British about a withdrawal of troops from the canal zone.

This possibility of leaving Suez in Nasser's hands caused deep concern in Sharett's cabinet, but it was the convoluted brain of Pinhas Lavon that seemed to demand a wholly irrational solution. Although there is little direct evidence of what went through Lavon's mind, he apparently, without consulting Sharett, decided that extreme measures were necessary to dissuade the British from leaving Egypt.

His plan—if indeed it was his plan—involved sabotage against British and American facilities in Egypt on the assumption that this would be blamed on either Egyptian anti-British extremists or the Muslim Brotherhood. The British, by the reasoning attributed to Lavon, would then have second thoughts about their impending negotiated departure in the face of Egyptian instability. A radicalized Egypt would force Britain to change its mind in order to keep the Suez Canal open.

The so-called Lavon plan would be carried out by Israeli spies trained and ready in Egypt under the direction of AMAN, the Israeli military intelligence organization. AMAN was not part of Mossad, the central intelligence organization, and the AMAN agents presumably were enjoined from sabotage except in wartime.

Mordechai Makleff, army chief of staff in early 1954, considered Lavon "a dangerous man." A hint of Lavon's thinking process was revealed when Makleff confided to Ben-Gurion that Lavon had suggested that sabotage in Jordan might help stir up trouble between the Jordanians and Americans. On the basis of such information, Ben-Gurion began to have doubts about his support of Lavon, but through the summer of 1954 he made no effort to force the defense minister out.

The spy cells in Alexandria and Cairo were first organized by an AMAN agent named Avraham Dar. Because Dar originally came from England and affected an upper-class deportment, he was able to operate under a false British passport bearing the name John Darling. His cover was that of a British businessman. Under that cover he organized spy cells composed of young Jewish Egyptians; they were then equipped with transmitters and code books. For the most part, the spy cells were on standby.

Early in 1954 Dar was replaced by a man who was to become one of the most mysterious, controversial, and villified figures in the annals of Israeli intelligence. He was Austrian-born Avraham Seidenwerg, who had emigrated to Palestine in flight from the Nazis in April 1939. Eventually he chose a Hebrew name, Avri El-Ad. To this day, no one knows whether El-Ad is a cruelly misunderstood hero who took the punishment for Lavon's blunder or one of Israel's archtraitors. The second judgment currently

prevails, and El-Ad now lives in the United States, a refugee from his own country.

El-Ad's record as a fighter for Israeli independence is impressive. He joined the Haganah soon after his arrival in Palestine. In World War II he was selected for the Palmach, the elite commando force of the Haganah. In 1943, when the Jewish stake in defeating the Nazis was paramount, he joined the British army, where his service record was beyond reproach. At the end of World War II he was honorably discharged from the British army and rejoined the Haganah. When the 1948 war broke out, he was assigned as an intelligence officer of the Palmach Sixth Battalion. After the Jewish victory and the creation of the State of Israel, he served in various military posts, eventually becoming an instructor of infantry, with the rank of major.

Then, suddenly, a seemingly minor offense turned El-Ad's life around. He was charged with theft of military property, a refrigerator that El-Ad claims was abandoned by the Arabs. He was court-martialed and discharged from the army. His reserve rank was reduced from major to private.

To this day, El-Ad believes he was framed by a jealous senior officer, that the so-called theft was an innocent mistake that supplied the senior officer with an excuse for getting rid of El-Ad. In contrast, Isser Harel, chief of the Mossad at that time, told the authors that El-Ad "was a very questionable character, an unreliable man . . . to a certain degree I think he was a liar."

Since AMAN operated in partial independence from the Mossad, Harel was unaware that shortly after El-Ad's discharge, he was hired by military intelligence to take over Dar's role in Egypt. The chief of AMAN was Colonel Benyamin Gibli. El-Ad had been sought out and hired by Gibli's second in command, Lieutenant Colonel Mordechai Ben-Zur, known usually by the nickname Motke. The hiring had been done with the knowledge of Avraham Dar.

Why did military intelligence seek out a court-martialed officer? In retrospect, Isser Harel had developed his own theory, as he told the authors in an interview in 1977: "I think they hired him because they believed he would be willing to do something risky to rehabilitate himself. But they didn't know that with a man of this kind, with a weak character, that a critical moment would not bring out the best in him. They should never have given him the chance."

Harel pointed out that in late 1952, when El-Ad was offered the intelligence mission, he was completely down on his luck. He had not been able to find a steady job, and he and his wife had been divorced (although, oddly enough, they had continued to live together and later remarried). By his own admission, a job in military intelligence offered the solution to all of his problems—joblessness, military disgrace, and a broken marriage.

From this nadir, El-Ad began to rise. He loved the AMAN training in espionage and sabotage, completing in four months training that normally requires at least double that time. Colonel Gibli and Ben-Zur were pleased with the man they had hired. He seemed to have a passion for excitement

and an enjoyment of danger. As he explained to his superiors, he had learned to live with danger, first as an Austrian Jew under Hitler and then as a Palestinian Jew surrounded by Arabs. He described himself as a "soldier by instinct."

In January 1954 an unusually handsome young man named Paul Frank arrived in Cairo and presented himself as a German manufacturer's representative. At that time Nasser was anxious to do business with technologically sophisticated German manufacturers. Paul Frank was very welcome. Blond and blue-eyed, he was the quintessential German in looks, manners, and mannerisms. He had traveled on the same ship as the German ambassador to Egypt and become acquainted with the diplomat's associates and eventually with the ambassador himself. This connection gave Frank an entrée into the Egyptian ruling class. Within a few weeks he was making business deals.

Paul Frank was only one of a veritable army of German technicians and businessmen who had been encouraged to come to Egypt by President Nasser. Many of them were former Nazis, now out of favor in their homeland but equipped with skills valuable to the underdeveloped Egyptian economy. In addition to the attraction of his other accomplishments, Frank was able to ingratiate himself with powerful Egyptians because of his seemingly spontaneous and profound anti-Jewish attitude. Paul Frank was, of course, Avri El-Ad.

El-Ad had been dispatched to Germany in the spring of 1953. With the identity papers of a real Paul Frank, who was half Jewish and then living in Israel, El-Ad was able to acquire not only a German passport but a birth certificate. He got the passport from the consulate in Zurich by convincing the German consul's first secretary (whom El-Ad suspected was a former Nazi) that he had been a member of the Hitler S.S. who had parachuted into Palestine during World War II. In the small town of Willmars, near Frankfurt, he was able to get a copy of the real Paul Frank's birth certificate, which fortunately said nothing of his mother's Jewish ancestry.

El-Ad's own account of his months in Germany expresses his bitter hatred of the Germans, especially former Nazis. The reader of his book, *Decline of Honor,* will be thoroughly convinced at this point of his absolute loyalty to Israel. Furthermore he was—if his own account is to be believed— unusually imaginative and resourceful in establishing his cover and making the connections that would enable him to function as a businessman in Egypt. He agreed to represent a German industrial firm seeking to sell military equipment to the Egyptians.

His superiors in AMAN, however, were not entirely satisfied with El-Ad's performance. He appeared to them to be operating too independently and without sufficient communication with his headquarters in Tel Aviv.

To some extent, El-Ad was at this point the victim of interservice rivalry in Israel. AMAN, as the chief military intelligence agency, was not under the direct command of the Mossad, the central intelligence organization. Isser Harel, as chief of the Mossad, resented the independence of Gibli's

AMAN. The Mossad was a geographically more widespread organization, so that agents abroad who belonged to AMAN were often forced to make use of Mossad office and communications facilities. This gave Harel some knowledge of what was going on in AMAN. He desperately wanted—for sound reasons—to bring all intelligence under a central control, which is to say, under Harel. He did not like or trust the judgment of Colonel Gibli. In the end, Harel, his ego and his thirst for power aside, was to prove that his doubts were soundly based, and the entire intelligence establishment was to be unified under Harel's command.

In Egypt, El-Ad's success seemed boundless. His chance meeting with the ambassador and his quick acceptance as a friend of Egypt were such that Frank "couldn't believe his luck." He was a capable manufacturer's representative, and his personal friendships reached to the very top of the power structure, even including the future prime minister, Zakariah Mohieddin, and, most remarkably, Colonel Osman Nuri, the chief of Egyptian military intelligence. In retrospect, Israeli intelligence officials in both AMAN and the Mossad were to wonder if the latter friendship was perhaps too sincere.

By the spring of 1954 the Israeli government was desperately fearful of the consequences of the British withdrawal of its military garrisons from Egypt. In May, El-Ad was summoned to Paris for a secret meeting with Ben-Zur, the deputy military intelligence chief who had originally hired him. At this meeting Ben-Zur apparently relayed the orders for the sabotage that was to create such an Israeli domestic disaster.

One of the first principles of intelligence is that an operative does not ask who originated his orders; he obeys his immediate superior. But El-Ad, by his own account, tried to find out. He asked Ben-Zur if it were Chief of Staff Moshe Dayan and was told (or so he reports) that it was "higher." El-Ad guessed it was Lavon, only to be told that it was someone even higher than that. Both men discounted Prime Minister Moshe Sharett as the perpetrator, perhaps aware of the contempt Lavon had for Sharett. Although Ben-Gurion was in temporary retirement, Israelis took it for granted that even without a formal role he functioned as highest authority. El-Ad's impression was that the order for the sabotage came from Ben-Gurion.

All of the evidence, circumstantial and direct, indicates that El-Ad was wrong and that Lavon was the original perpetrator of the sabotage plan, with Colonel Gibli, his intelligence chief, a willing follower. The defense minister had a record of thinking in terms of violence. The ruthless retaliatory raid on the Arab village in early 1954 betrayed that tendency. And, as has been noted, it is a matter of record that he advocated in Jordan the same kind of sabotage he later unleashed in Egypt.

Lavon was apparently convinced that fires and bombings in Egypt would create sufficient chaos to force the British to reconsider removal of their Egyptian forces. His plans called for the sabotage not only in British and American installations—embassies, consulates, libraries—but in public gathering places such as railroad stations and movie theaters. Michael Bar-Zohar, in his biography of Ben-Gurion, calls the plan "astonishingly

naive and dangerous." To Isser Harel, any such scheme was not only dangerous but illegal under Israeli law. Military intelligence operations were not supposed to be involved in sabotage in foreign countries except in an active state of war. El-Ad and his men, as far as Harel was concerned, were only on standby in Egypt.

Nevertheless, El-Ad left Paris with his orders from Ben-Zur, and he intended to carry them out. But to what purpose? Was he truly acting on behalf of Israel, which is to say, Defense Minister Lavon? Or had El-Ad, who seemed to be perpetually short of money, been tempted by his Egyptian friends to become a counterspy, willing to betray Israel? Was his friendship with Nuri, the Egyptian intelligence chief, the skillful achievement of a masterful and loyal Israeli spy or an equally skillful betrayal of Israel by an unprincipled man who would do anything for an adequate payoff?

According to El-Ad's own record, his orders from Ben-Zur did not stop at sabotage. He and his small Egyptian intelligence cell were to be prepared also to carry out assassinations of Egyptian leaders from Nasser on down.

Here is how he describes his mission in *Decline of Honor,* which is largely a defense against the accusation that he was disloyal to Israel:

> Whatever the ramifications of my country's scheme, my task was clear: Take command of the Alexandria cell and render it operational for immediate sabotage action. (The Cairo cell would be activated later.) And at all times I must be prepared to deliver death—on order. My objectives were to spread sedition and unrest—and poison the political atmosphere against Egypt in the international arena. Sabotaging Anglo-American establishments would disrupt America's courtship of Nasser by making it appear as if Egypt's populace was actively subverting his promises. These violent acts would throw Egypt backward into internecine warfare; force Nasser to crack down on the extremists opposing his rule; and give England's Parliament cause to retract her intent to abandon the Suez Canal to a man unable to control his countrymen. Keeping the British 80,000-man garrison along the canal would give Israel more time, more protection from any impulsive Egyptian move.

El-Ad also expresses a distaste for the possibility of having to carry out assassinations: "We haven't come very far if we, as the chosen people, had to resort to assassinations. To do this was to align ourselves with the Arab mentality." He concedes, however, that he was a "made-to-order killer." He worried prophetically about the "puniness" of the network he commanded because "in intelligence operations dishonor lies not in the commission of the act so much as in its discovery."

In Alexandria, El-Ad lined up his Israeli-trained agents. They were all young—in their late teens or early twenties. One of them, Victor Levy, was in charge of the projected Alexandria sabotage. His accomplices were the luckless Philip Nathanson and, tentatively, Reuben Dassa and Shmuel

Azar, the latter pair being uncertain at first of their willingness to participate. Sought, but not recruited, was young Eli Cohen, who was later to become the greatest spy in Israel's history.

El-Ad came up with one excellent idea (at least, he claims credit for it). The signal from Israel as to when the actual sabotage should take place would not come by coded wireless message to the limited commercial receivers they had set up in an Alexandria apartment. It would come instead through a sequence of words included in a humdrum program on cooking from the powerful radio station, the Voice of Israel.

On the morning of July 2, 1954, Levy and Nathanson dropped thin envelopes of explosives through the mail chute of Alexandria's general post office. A fire was started, at least one postal clerk was injured, and the post office was closed for several days. The actual damage is unknown because the news of it was censored by Egyptian authorities. The date of the sabotage is important because in the recriminations that were to follow, how or by whom the order was issued was never certain.

This was not true in the next case. On July 9 the Voice of Israel's broadcast advised a listener to "add English cake or some cake of that sort" to her coffee party. El-Ad had no doubt of the hidden message: Commence sabotage against British or American institutions or installations.

In Cairo the projected operation involved other agents. These included Dr. Moshe Marzouk, a practicing physician who, according to El-Ad, had wanted to be head of the Egyptian venture in place of El-Ad. As a courier, the spy ring had recruited Victorine Ninio, an exceptionally lovely young woman.

On July 14, El-Ad dispatched the now-willing Azar and Dassa to the United States Information Agency library in Alexandria and Nathanson and Levy to the one in Cairo, which was adjacent to the United States embassy. In each case the agents planted their crude incendiary devices behind books. In each case the damage was not serious, but the shock to Egyptian, British, and American public opinion was considerable.

Acquiring the chemicals and explosives was a continuing problem. Azar helped to solve the problem by stealing a bottle of sulfuric acid from the technical school where he was a teacher. El-Ad (if we are to believe his own account) was more daring. He managed a dangerous nighttime break into an Egyptian explosive bunker from which he was able to steal a hand grenade and a brick of TNT.

In the midst of all the preparations, El-Ad was still pursuing his successful career as a German manufacturer's agent. He was mingling daily with top-bracket Egyptian society and the oversized German business and technical establishment. His friendship with Colonel Nuri progressed to the point where Nuri actually offered the fake Paul Frank an intelligence assignment. What has never been known is whether El-Ad accepted the offer.

The final strike was to involve five targets on July 23 and one on July 24. The time was considered ideal. On these dates the Egyptian people would be celebrating the anniversary of the monarchy's overthrow. Theaters and public places would be overflowing with people in a holiday mood.

On July 23, Dassa and Azar were to start fires in the Rivoli and Radio movie theaters in Cairo, while in Alexandria, Nathanson and Levy were to plant similar incendiary devices in the railway station and in the Metro and Rio theaters. On July 24, El-Ad reserved for himself the prime atrocity. With the hand grenade and the TNT brick, he had fashioned a particularly gruesome device. He bound them together, with a string attached to the pin of the grenade. His plan was to drop this into a mailbox in the crowded central square of Alexandria, with the string hanging out of the letter slot. Obviously some curious passerby would eventually pull the string, setting off a massive explosion that would turn the mailbox into a thousand shards of metal. "The makeshift grenade would fell or maim scores of people," El-Ad writes in his book with what seems to be genuine pride.

The Cairo mission went flawlessly. A fire of some dimension was started in the Rio Theatre, while the device in the Rivoli caused mostly smoke. Both theaters were emptied, but there was no panic.

In Alexandria, Nathanson and Levy planted one of their incendiary devices in a suitcase in the railway station. Here, too, damage was minimal but enough to bring out the fire brigades. The two theaters were next on the schedule.

On the morning of July 24 El-Ad drove to Alexandria to plant his diabolical bomb and to check out the success of the railway and theater sabotage. He drove past the Metro Theatre, curious about the damage. This was to have been the second of the two targets. El-Ad was surprised to find no fire damage—in fact, no sign that anything had happened. Somewhat worried, he headed for Nathanson's apartment, where the transmitters, receivers, and other secret equipment were hidden. On the street, he passed Azar, who had just arrived from Cairo.

Azar gave his chief the news that would lead to six years of disruption in Israel: "Nathanson has been arrested."

The incendiary eyeglass case that had ignited too soon had upended the entire sabotage plot. Within a few hours the police had tracked down Levy, who was also arrested.

In Nathanson's apartment the Egyptian police found photographic equipment and a tiny transmitter fitted into a hollowed-out book. Levy was grilled and possibly tortured until he confessed to his complicity in the operation. Within less than twenty-four hours, Dr. Marzouk, Azar, Dassa, Victorine Ninio, and Eli Cohen were arrested, although Cohen had not been involved at all. Also taken into custody was an Israeli spy named Max Bennett, who was on an entirely separate mission.

The most mysterious and incomprehensible aspect of the whole roundup was that Avri El-Ad (still Paul Frank, a German, to the Egyptians) was not arrested nor even questioned. He took his time making plans to leave. He sold his car and did not actually depart for Germany until two weeks after the Nathanson incident had triggered the collapse of the mission. This seeming immunity of the principal agent of the whole fiasco confounded El-Ad's Israeli superiors and led eventually to the suspicion that he had actually betrayed Israel by becoming an Egyptian double agent.

NACHUM BERNSTEIN—"Teacher of spies," he masterminded the bugging of the British U.N. delegation limousine and the Arab U.N. headquarters in New York in 1947.

PINCHAS LAVON—The headstrong defense minister, whose decision to sabotage American and British installations in Egypt (while blaming the Egyptians so as to discourage a British pull-out from Egypt) caused a scandal that eventually forced Ben-Gurion to resign as prime minister.

YAACOV MERIDOR—He conducted a daring mission into Iraq for the British in 1941. He later was Menachem Begin's predecessor as chief of the militant Irgun Zvai Leumi (National Military Organization).

SHLOMO HILLEL—By land and air he directed the rescue of as many as 100,000 Jews from Iraq, from 1947 through 1951.

ISSER HAREL—Only four feet ten inches tall, he nonetheless became the most powerful figure in the history of Israeli intelligence, heading first the Shin Bet (counter intelligence) from 1948 to 1952, after which he became chief of the Mossad (central intelligence) and eventually, while remaining in his Mossad post, serving as coordinator of all intelligence services.

MAJOR GENERAL ABRAHAM "BREN" ADAN—One of Israel's most celebrated tank commanders, he, armed with exceptionally accurate intelligence and using skillful tactics, defeated Egyptian tank units that outnumbered his tanks by as much as three to one.

YEHUDA TAGGER (in 1948)—As chief of Israeli intelligence in Baghdad during the War for Independence he, too, helped Jews escape from Iraq, but was caught, arrested and given a reprieve as he stood on the gallows waiting to be hung.

ADMIRAL SHLOMO ERELL—As commandant of Israeli naval forces in the 1960s, he was instrumental in the development of the superb and unique missile boats that are the backbone of the Israeli navy.

ADMIRAL MORDECHAI LIMON (WITH DAVID BEN-GURION)—A former Israeli naval chief, he was in charge of European arms procurement in Paris when the missile boats escaped from Cherbourg. The French, convinced Limon masterminded the escape, ordered him out of France.

ADOLPH "AL" SCHWIMMER— He was an American pilot who found and purchased the surplus planes for Israel's nascent air force, then was the driving force behind the establishment of a sophisticated aircraft industry in Israel.

A MISSILE BOAT OF THE SAAR IV CLASS—This is an advanced version of the boats developed and built in France from 1965 to 1968, the last five of which were spirited out of Cherbourg harbor by Israeli crews after the French government had attempted to impound them.

ISRAEL'S KFIR FIGHTER—Developed by Israel Aircraft Industries, it is considered the equal of any fighter aircraft in the world.

When news of the arrests reached Israel, Prime Minister Sharett was justifiably enraged. Since he had known nothing about the sabotage operation, he believed he was speaking the truth when he called it a plot to discredit and "harass the Jews in Egypt." Isser Harel was enraged, too, but in his case his anger was on learning the truth—that at least some of the arrested Jews were indeed involved in an irresponsible sabotage scheme. It was Harel who had to tell Sharett that his indignation was misplaced. The experience was humiliating to Sharett: an operation of sweeping, worldwide significance had been carried out without the knowledge of the head of the Israeli government.

Ben-Gurion himself did not learn the truth until several weeks after the arrest of Nathanson. His faith in Lavon, whom Ben-Gurion had handpicked for the Sharett cabinet, was shattered. In his journal he wrote that Lavon was guilty of "criminal irresponsibility." He confided to a friend that Lavon had vastly exceeded his authority.

When the extent of the disaster was realized, its perpetrators began running for cover. Gibli and Lavon each accused the other of lying. Gibli insisted Lavon had given the order for the operation on July 16, while the defense minister claimed he had not even discussed it until July 31, which was not only after the final sabotage attempts, but after the Egyptian agents had been arrested. The evidence indicates that both were liars, that Lavon's order was probably given July 23. This, however, explains very little, since El-Ad had initiated the first sabotage on July 2, presumably on the basis of instructions from Ben-Zur, Gibli's deputy, back on May 26. Ben-Zur was obviously acting on orders from Gibli, and the latter must have assumed he was carrying out Lavon's wishes. One unusual aspect of the whole affair was that the military chief of staff, General Moshe Dayan, was visiting in the United States through most of this period. He apparently was unaware of Lavon's plans.

Lavon purported to show his interest in a full and fair inquiry by asking Sharett to appoint an independent commission to conduct a secret investigation of the whole matter. Sharett accepted the suggestion, appointing two distinguished public servants whose honesty and impartiality were presumably beyond questioning. They were Supreme Court Justice Yitzhak Olshan and former Chief of Staff Ya'akov Dori.

One of the key witnesses summoned before the so-called Olshan-Dori Commission was, not surprisingly, Avri El-Ad. At this point occurred one of the most reprehensible episodes of the entire sordid affair. Gibli and Ben-Zur, faced with Lavon's conflicting version of the sabotage, wrote to El-Ad. They ordered him to commit perjury, by stating that he was not involved in the post-office and library assaults on July 2 and 14. He was also to alter his diaries and reports accordingly, a sort of historical cover-up. When El-Ad arrived in Israel, he was met by Gibli's staff and was further briefed on the details of the proposed perjured testimony.

Gibli went one step farther to protect himself. He had apparently written to Dayan in the United States, advising the chief of staff of the Egyptian operation. In keeping with intelligence custom, Dayan read the letter and

destroyed it. Gibli then had the original carbon copy destroyed and falsified a carbon copy that added a phrase stating that the raids were on the orders of Lavon. Consequently, when the commission started taking testimony in December, Lavon, who had placed great hope in its investigation, found the deck stacked against him. Faced with public disgrace, he threatened suicide, in effect an attempt to turn a secret inquiry into a public scandal. The Labor party leadership and the cabinet retreated from any accusations.

Unfortunately, the Olshan-Dori Commission, puzzled by conflicting testimony, was unable to reach any absolute conclusion. Essentially what it said was that it believed Gibli did not cause the action in Egypt to take place without an order, yet it could not prove that Lavon had given such an order.

The inconclusive verdict infuriated Lavon, who had hoped for vindication. His rage was such that he threatened to make a public demand for an inquiry by the Knesset, thereby once again posing the possibility that this closely guarded secret would be made known to the world. This amounted to a kind of blackmail by Lavon, and for a long time, it worked. The party leadership decided to turn to the man who, for this group, represented the ultimate authority—David Ben-Gurion. He was not equivocal; despite his past support of Lavon, the old man now said flatly that Lavon must be ousted. Some news of the meeting leaked to Lavon. Surprisingly, he offered his resignation. But there was a catch—to wit, the same blackmail. On resigning he would carry his case to the Knesset. Once again Sharett and the party leadership were entrapped by the wily Lavon.

Now the defense minister sought to destroy those whom he believed had betrayed him, Gibli and Shimon Peres, the young director-general of the Defense Ministry. This time, at last, Sharett called Lavon's bluff. On February 17 the defense minister put his tail between his legs and resigned. He was replaced by that most powerful man, Ben-Gurion, back into action once more, although nominally only as defense minister.

The agony of the secret machinations within the government was exacerbated by what had happened in Egypt. Nathanson, Levy, Azar, Victorine Ninio, Dr. Marzouk, Dassa, and two Jews not connected with El-Ad's caper, Max Bennett and one known only as Carmona, were all languishing in jail. Ninio tried to commit suicide by jumping from the window of an interrogation room. She suffered only a broken leg. Carmona hanged himself in his cell; Bennett killed himself by puncturing his veins with a rusty nail. The trial of the rest was internationally publicized. It coincided almost precisely with the secret Olshan-Dori investigation in Israel. On January 28 the world heard the verdict of the military tribunal. Dr. Marzouk and Azar were sentenced to death. Nathanson and Levi received life sentences, and Dassa and Ninio fifteen years.

The death sentences brought pleas for clemency from all over the world, including from Pope Pius XII and Edgar Faure, foreign minister of France. The Egyptians, however, were not inclined to be merciful in the light of such a flagrantly destructive mission. Dr. Marzouk and Azar were hanged at dawn on January 31.

The lid clamped on the story in Israel was blown off by the confessions and the evidence in the Egyptian trial. The scandal was to run its course for nearly six more years before all the revelations of deception were to pull down an Israeli government. And only slowly did the Israeli authorities uncover the paradoxical role of Avri El-Ad. He was to emerge as either a ruthless traitor to Israel or a scapegoat for high-level blunders.

If there was one Israeli who was furious and resentful over the Egyptian fiasco, it was Isser Harel, chief of Mossad and generally conceded to possess the most skillful intelligence mind in the new state. Harel had always been proud that despite the necessity for covert, dangerous, and even distasteful activities in connection with foreign and political intelligence, he had managed to respect the limits of intelligence in a lawful state. The mind of a Lavon, a Gibli, an El-Ad was beyond his tolerance.

In 1977, more than twenty years later, he was still angry over the excesses of the agents in Egypt and their masterminds in Israel. "They didn't have any right to give any order to do something active there at the time," he told us. "They had no right to take their authorization from anyone but the prime minister, and head of military intelligence had no right to act without coordinating with me. I had an active organization myself, and all of them could have been endangered."

Harel did not question the right of military intelligence to recruit and train agents for work as spies and saboteurs, but the sticking point as far as he was concerned was that they could not be activated except in time of war.

Despite Harel's low opinion of El-Ad, the more important issue was where the ultimate responsibility lay for the reckless orders given to the Egyptian cell—"and that was with military intelligence." It was even more incomprehensible to Harel that military intelligence—which is to say AMAN, under Benyamin Gibli—had allowed El-Ad to go to Germany and disappear there, apparently living under his German cover name of Paul Frank. Why was no one trying to track down El-Ad and find out what went wrong?

"I wanted him back," Harel told us. "I didn't suspect him of being a traitor at that time, but I considered him a security risk because as head of a sabotage group whose name was known, he could be a very simple target for assassination or be kidnapped by the Egyptians or arrested by the Germans. I wanted him returned, but for some reason military intelligence didn't want to take him back."

When El-Ad had been living in Germany for three years as Paul Frank, still ostensibly an Israeli agent, an unusual coincidence not only revealed his whereabouts but cast a deeper suspicion on his activities. In 1957, Mossad agents contacted a German whom they believed could be trusted to carry out some espionage assignments in Egypt. The man was unwilling to take on the mission, but he suggested someone else whom he believed to be equally capable. This man, the German said, was especially qualified because he had made close friends of the Egyptian intelligence staff in Bonn and so would not be suspected. The man in question, known to the Germans as Paul Frank, was none other than Avri El-Ad. His Israeli superiors were shocked to learn

that in Germany he had become close friends with Admiral Suleiman, the Egyptian military attaché in Bonn, and he had remained in touch with Colonel Osman Nuri, the chief of Egyptian military intelligence.

Why was a man sentenced to death in absentia by an Egyptian military court now hobnobbing with the very people who had prosecuted him? Did the Egyptians still not know that Avri El-Ad and Paul Frank were the same?

For Isser Harel, the news raised the specter of a gross betrayal. Perhaps the fire that was prematurely ignited in Philip Nathanson's eyeglass case, accidentally exposing the whole Egyptian sabotage ring, was not the actual cause of the fiasco. Perhaps El-Ad had engineered the case for failure. Perhaps El-Ad was a double agent, in the pay of the Egyptians while seeming to work for Israel. This would explain the swift arrest of everyone involved except El-Ad and the totally unexplainable manner in which El-Ad had calmly taken two weeks to leave Egypt.

"We began to suspect," said Harel, "that it wasn't because Nathanson had been caught red-handed. That was just an excuse by the Egyptians to round up the group."

At the time that El-Ad was discovered in Europe, Harel's fear that he was a double agent could not be confirmed. Many years later, when some of the prisoners in Egypt had served their terms and returned to Israel, they reported their belief that someone in the group had betrayed them although they were not certain that it was El-Ad. Meanwhile, the enigmatic saboteur continued to conduct his export-import business in Germany, still in the pay of AMAN and still presumably awaiting further assignment. To his business associates he was Paul Frank, an opportunistic German willing to do business with both Israel and Egypt. Twice he returned to Israel for briefing. AMAN had become a vastly different organization. Gibli and Ben-Zur had been fired. The new director of military intelligence was Jossi Harel. He was no relation to Isser Harel, although, coincidentally, he was very much under Isser's influence as the latter strained to extend his control over all branches of intelligence.

By this time both Harels must have harbored serious doubts about El-Ad's stability, if not his loyalty. They knew he had had several meetings with Osman Nuri in Germany. According to El-Ad's book, he met with Nuri because the Egyptian intelligence chief offered him a job as an Egyptian agent. El-Ad claimed he had entertained the offer because it presented a unique opportunity to become a double agent for Israel. Isser Harel, however, had his doubts. He suspected that El-Ad had seriously weighed working for Egypt because he was offered a great deal of money.

It is essential to understand the dual identity of El-Ad in 1955 and 1956 in order to fathom the feasibility of his actions. He was, in Germany, still Paul Frank, a highly successful businessman involved in the sale of various manufactured goods to Egypt and Israel. In actuality he was Avri El-Ad, the man who had led the abortive sabotage caper in Egypt, for which his comrades had either died or been imprisoned. El-Ad, as a name, not as the man known to the Egyptians, had been sentenced to death in absentia, after his seemingly too-casual departure from Egypt.

Which man—Avri El-Ad or Paul Frank—did Osman Nuri think he was dealing with? That depends on whether El-Ad is viewed as a traitor (as Isser Harel eventually saw him and still considers him today) or as a successful intelligence agent who maintained his cover so skillfully that even Osman Nuri never knew that Avri El-Ad and Paul Frank were the same.

El-Ad's contention is that Nuri offered him a job as an Egyptian intelligence agent because he believed only that Paul Frank, a German businessman with a history of interest in Egypt, could serve Egypt well as an international agent. The belief of the Mossad was to the contrary: that Nuri knew that Paul Frank was El-Ad and that he had betrayed Israel by becoming an Egyptian double agent, and therefore quite reasonably assumed that El-Ad was willing to continue to serve Egypt.

The Israeli authorities allowed El-Ad to stay on in Europe until 1957 for a variety of reasons, including the long terminal illness of his father in Vienna. During his brief return visits to Israel, El-Ad made an effort to regain the army rank he had lost in 1951 after the stolen-refrigerator incident. The restoration was eventually granted, but possibly only as a means of keeping El-Ad unaware that he was the subject of a continuing investigation and that the evidence of his complicity with the Egyptians was closing in on him. Israeli intelligence authorities, including Isser Harel, decided that they would have to bring him back to Israel permanently for fear that he would sense their suspicions and attempt to flee to Egypt.

In November 1957, Avri El-Ad voluntarily returned to Israel, the pain of his father's death presumably having stunned him into a determination to tell the "truth," insofar as he knew it had not been told before the Olshan-Dori Commission three years earlier—the truth about the perjury he had committed at the orders of his superiors, Ben-Zur and Gibli. His resolve may have been a counterattack to the charges building against him, although his ostensible goal was to clear Lavon from the scandal created by the false testimony engineered by Gibli and Ben-Zur.

There was thus a two-tiered issue. One was the question of whether Lavon had been responsible for the Egyptian fiasco. The other, the higher one, was whether, regardless of who was responsible, military intelligence had exceeded its authority and thereby endangered the state. Isser Harel was concerned with both issues, but primarily the second one; he was determined to bring about creation of a central authority to coordinate foreign, military, and domestic intelligence operations. Needless to say, Harel intended to be that central authority.

What El-Ad did not understand was that in his anxiety to clear himself by exposing Gibli and Ben-Zur, he was walking into a trap laid by Isser Harel. When Jossi Harel wired him to meet him in a Tel Aviv café on December 15, El-Ad assumed it was something routine. Actually, Jossi, no longer chief of AMAN, was acting on orders. He picked up El-Ad in front of the café and took him to a military security post. It was the end of the road for El-Ad. He would not be free again for twelve years.

Almost immediately he found himself subject to a fierce interrogation by Zvi Aharoni of Shin Bet. Aharoni called him a traitor, an indication that

El-Ad was already suspected of high crimes. After a long grilling El-Ad insisted on a lie-detector test. The AMAN authorities complied and were surprised. To every question relating to his loyalty to the State of Israel, El-Ad answered that he was indeed completely loyal, and the polygraph seemed to confirm that he was telling the truth.

Meanwhile, El-Ad persuaded his captors to allow him to return to his flat to pick up some personal possessions. Surprisingly, they agreed. In the brief moments that he was alone in his flat, El-Ad managed to gather up a number of documents, including the 1954 letter from Gibli ordering him to name a false date for Lavon's alleged order to carry out the Egyptian sabotage. He put the letter and other papers into a suitcase, quickly handed them to a neighbor, with careful instructions that an old El-Ad friend, Peter Landesman, should be summoned to take the suitcase to Landesman's home. He also asked the neighbor to summon Gibli on the safe assumption that Gibli would be loyal to his former agent.

On his return to AMAN headquarters, El-Ad, now being treated like a common criminal, was transferred to a small Shin Bet jail. He was ordered to summon his wife home from Austria, but in the phone conversation he conveyed the good wishes of a family that did not exist—whose name was in fact that of a prison where El-Ad's father had been imprisoned by the Nazis. His wife understood. She did not come home.

El-Ad's imprisonment and interrogation continued for a month. To questions asked about the Egyptian sabotage, the suspect legitimately refused to answer; he had been sworn to secrecy in the Olshan-Dori investigation. But he was not so bound by inquiries about what happened after that, such as the unexplained contacts with Osman Nuri in Germany. The effort to coerce him into confessing his complicity with the Egyptians became unbearable to El-Ad. He threatened suicide, and his captors took the threat seriously, but only temporarily. A few days later the psychological pressure was augmented by handcuffs and a transfer to the Ramla Prison. Clearly, the Shin Bet thought it was closing in on a traitor. A bill of complaint was drawn up, giving the government the basis on which to seek a court order to confine and interrogate El-Ad further. The formal charge was that he had contacted Egyptian agents with the intent of harming the State of Israel. The judge urged the defendant to seek the advice of a lawyer.

As the weeks passed in the miserable conditions of Ramla Prison, where El-Ad was in something close to solitary confinement, he kept hoping that Gibli and Ben-Zur would come to his rescue. He made an effort to contact them through his brother-in-law, Svi Swet, and his sister, Ruth. She warned El-Ad that his confinement was the result of the obsessive hatred of Isser Harel, the Mossad chief who was still outraged at the audacity and the stupidity of the Egyptian operation.

Then, one day, Swet told El-Ad that he was free to tell the truth—presumably meaning the real story of how Gibli, Ben-Zur, and El-Ad had conspired to place the blame for the sabotage fiasco on Foreign Minister Lavon. El-Ad assumed that Swet had seen Gibli, who was no longer going to challenge the right of the prisoner to defend himself. On this assumption,

El-Ad finally told the story of the falsified diary that had made it appear that Lavon had given the sabotage order before he actually did.

The Shin Bet inquisitor, now Chayim Victor Cohen, was impressed enough to ask El-Ad to repeat the story before a formal military inquiry board. At last, El-Ad rejoiced, his innocence would be proved by the comparison of the real and the fake letters, and his long ordeal would be over. When the board was empaneled, El-Ad was distressed to see that the stenographer was none other than Isser Harel's secretary. The Mossad boss, he concluded, was still out to get him.

Ben-Zur, the suspect told the board, had the real letter, which would prove that the deception had originated with Ben-Zur and Gibli and that El-Ad had been forced to participate.

A few days later, when it was Ben-Zur's turn to testify, he flatly denied there were two letters. El-Ad was flabbergasted. Even worse, the Shin Bet then produced the fake letter that El-Ad had put in his suitcase to deliver to his friend Landesman. Obviously, the Shin Bet had observed his last-ditch effort to dispose of his papers. Nevertheless, El-Ad told the whole story of how he had been ordered to commit perjury at the Olshan-Dori inquiry.

Ben-Zur returned to the stand to state that El-Ad was a liar, that his story of the framing of Lavon was totally false. Without the letters to compare, El-Ad was trapped. He was sent back to Ramla Prison.

The case against him became more serious than ever and for a damning reason. When the Shin Bet agents recovered his suitcase, they found in it photographs of a supersecret "violet file" of AMAN. Thereupon, formal charges were filed against El-Ad. They included unlawful contact with Egyptian agents, unlawful photographing of the violet file, and unlawful possession of the violet file photographs. El-Ad was in no position to deny the contact with Nuri. The question was why he had contacted him. As for the photos, El-Ad claimed they were planted among his belongings in order to trap him. His trial opened before a three-judge tribunal.

Almost immediately, Avri El-Ad's former friend, Motke Ben-Zur, was exposed as a liar. He denied conspiring with El-Ad to falsify the diary so as to place blame on Lavon, and he denied warning El-Ad not to come home to "make a clean breast of the whole affair." The warning, it is true, was cryptic, hidden in a seemingly meaningless anecdote about the head of the Spanish Olympic team deciding not to go to Russia when the Russians offered him only a one-way ticket. Its meaning did not escape El-Ad at the time and, despite Ben-Zur's protests, was perfectly clear to the judges. Testimony by other officers further confirmed the conspiracy. But proving that a dishonorable clique of intelligence officers had conspired to save their own skins was not, in the long run, much help to the defendant. The tribunal still had to hear from Isser Harel, the most powerful, effective, and respected intelligence leader in Israel's history. Since the founding of the state, he had been successively head of the Shin Bet (internal security), chief of the Mossad (central intelligence), and, finally, chief of the secret services, which gave him centralized control over Shin Bet, Mossad, and AMAN, the last being the service that was, in effect, on trial.

The antagonism between El-Ad and Harel was intense. To the powerful security chief, El-Ad was "a liar" and "a questionable character in every aspect." In contrast, El-Ad saw Harel as a power-mad Napoleon, a man of "molelike ugliness" who "was permitted to exaggerate so obviously and lie so freely that I became concerned about the court's impartiality."

In cross-examination Harel fumed at the implication that secret AMAN documents found in El-Ad's possession might have been planted to frame him. He pointed out that every defendant brought to trial by Mossad had been convicted with legal evidence, and the mere suggestion that his organization would frame anyone was "infamy."

The final arguments of the defense lawyer presented the defendant as a man who had repeatedly risked his life for his country and was now being unfairly tried to protect those above him. In contrast, the prosecution pictured him as a traitor without conscience who sold out his country to the Egyptians.

El-Ad was found guilty in August 1960 and later sentenced to twelve years in prison, including the nearly three years he had spent incarcerated between his arrest and his trial. The punishment was far more severe than the gloomiest prediction of his counsel. To the bitter defendant, the trial was a proof of Israel's corruption. He saw it as a conspiracy between one of the judges and Isser Harel, a face-saving attempt by the state.

For El-Ad, the story was ending, but for the government of Israel, for Pinhas Lavon and Ben-Gurion, it was only beginning. While presumably clearing up the issue of whether Israel's Egyptian agents had been betrayed, it opened for those within the government (but not to the public, since the trial had been conducted in secret) the question of whether Lavon had ordered the ill-fated Egyptian sabotage and whether military intelligence officers at the highest level had conspired to place the full blame upon him.

More than six years had passed between the July 1954 sabotage and El-Ad's sentencing in November 1960. In the interim, Israel, along with England and France, had fought the aborted Sinai campaign against Egypt. Although it had been militarily successful in terms of the performance of Israel's armed forces, it was stalemated when the United States condemned the action of the three nations. The campaign ended with Nasser still in power and the Suez Canal in his hands.

Lavon, although he had been forced out of the defense ministry in 1955, remained, through his incredible energy and resourcefulness, a powerful force in Israel. The sop for his expulsion from the cabinet was the job of chief of the Histadrut, the politically powerful labor-union federation. When El-Ad's trial revealed the probable perjury on the part of Ben-Zur and the falsifying of documents by Gibli so as to blame Lavon, the former defense minister demanded that he be summarily and publicly "cleared" of blame. This Ben-Gurion refused to do: "I am neither judge nor investigator."

Once again Lavon tried the tactic he had threatened twice in 1955—to take the issue before a committee of the Knesset and hence before the public. This time Ben-Gurion did not try to stop him. The old man's passivity in the

face of such a state-shaking scandal is attributed by Bar-Zohar to his "advancing age and weariness."

Lavon was as good as his word, and at last, in June 1963 the six-year-old Lavon affair exploded before the public. Ben-Gurion's silence meant that the public heard more of Lavon's side of the story. Emblazoned in the newspapers, the scandal was a profound shock to a nation that had justifiably regarded its intelligence services as the finest in the world.

Everything seemed to go against Ben-Gurion. His closest aides, Shimon Peres and Moshe Dayan, were both out of the country. Meanwhile, Lavon, in testimony before the Knesset Foreign Affairs and Defense Committee, attacked Dayan and Peres, implying they would not defend him as they should because of political considerations.

The public's reaction was especially emotional because the entire matter had been successfully kept secret for so long. No one had known the real reason why Lavon had resigned back in 1955; now the truth was coming out. The highest officers of military intelligence were implicated in forgery and perjury.

Ben-Gurion, attempting to stay above the battle, was finally enraged when Lavon apparently released to the press a secret correspondence between them in 1955. He now became Lavon's enemy. He wanted a judicial inquiry into the affair, but his cabinet forced a ministerial investigation on him. Ben-Gurion, behaving like a beaten man, did not oppose the investigation by his own cabinet. In effect, he settled for a political solution instead of a judicial one.

The investigation proved to be haphazard, and astoundingly, Lavon was completely cleared. The cabinet approved the findings despite Ben-Gurion's furious objections over the lack of judicial proceedings. Even his loyal associates in the cabinet did not vote against it; they merely abstained.

Ben-Gurion would have no part of this, and on June 16 he promptly resigned. The Lavon affair had overthrown the most revered leader in the long history of Zionism and the founding of the State of Israel. He would return a few months later for his last brief tenure as prime minister, but his effectiveness as an active leader had been destroyed. Only as a retired elder statesman would he gradually regain the reverence of the people that now marks him as the George Washington of Israel.

In his fall from grace, Ben-Gurion was able to pull Lavon down with him. He hinted that Lavon should be ousted as secretary-general of the Histadrut. Ben-Gurion's Mapai party (the largest in the Labor coalition), in an effort to appease the angry old man, forced Lavon out of his job and into permanent political eclipse. Lavon, too, had been destroyed by the affair that bears his name.

The Lavon affair is a textbook study in the abuse of the power of intelligence in government. In many general ways, although the particulars are vastly different, it resembles the American abuse of intelligence in the restoration of the shah of Iran to his throne in 1953, an error for which Americans paid dearly twenty-six years later.

The problem with an assessment of the Lavon affair is that even today all the facts are not known. There was not really one issue, but two. First there was the question of whether Lavon, either by direct order or by implication, set the Egyptian sabotage plan in motion. It has never been established whether he did indeed mastermind the attacks on British and American facilities and other public targets or whether this was a high-handed abuse of power by the chiefs of Israeli military intelligence, who may or may not have believed they were acting in accordance with the wishes of their minister of defense. Whatever the origin of the orders, there is no doubt but that Gibli, the military intelligence chief, and Ben-Zur, his deputy, behaved in a deceitful and cowardly fashion after the mission proved a disaster.

Beyond this administrative issue is the question of the character of Avri El-Ad. It must be remembered that El-Ad was not convicted of being a double agent. His conviction was based on his having in his possession films of documents of a supersecret military intelligence file. The perjury he committed in the 1955 Olshan-Dori inquiry was reprehensible, but it was based on orders from his superiors. In *Decline of Honor,* El-Ad devotes 354 pages to a far from successful attempt to prove he was a scapegoat. The book is marred by great loopholes in his defense and by extruded reasoning to fit such defense as he does present.

To Isser Harel, symbol of the greatest achievements of the Israeli secret services, El-Ad is both specifically and generally an example of what can go wrong in intelligence. In an interview of many hours with the authors, Harel repeatedly returned to what he considered a fatal error: the hiring of El-Ad in the first place. To put a man with a questionable background in a sensitive intelligence post was, to Harel, indicative of incredibly poor judgment on the part of the military security chiefs. Likewise, the unleashing of El-Ad and his Egyptian secret agents on a sabotage mission was not only foolhardy but illegal under the laws of the state.

In sum, there was, first, a mission that was, in itself, reckless, irresponsible, and illegal in its abuse of power. Second, the man hired to carry out the mission was at best ill-suited for it and at worst an immoral opportunist who betrayed his country. In the history of Israeli intelligence there have been errors in judgment and serious miscalculations. But the Lavon affair was unique in its total wrongness; it is no wonder that when it was finally exposed to the public, the innocent and the guilty were both destroyed.

11

Confusion in the Sinai, 1956

IF ISRAEL'S INTELLIGENCE had correctly assessed American intentions, Israel would never have gone to war against Egypt in the Sinai campaign of 1956. The war was launched under the assumption that the United States would not intervene, thus allowing Israel to achieve two important goals: first, the breaking of the Egyptian blockade of Israeli shipping through the Strait of Tiran at the entrance to the Gulf of Aqaba and, second, the crushing of Egyptian fedayeen (guerrilla) bases in the Gaza Strip, from which frequent and bloody raids against Israeli villages were launched.

As it turned out, Israel was able to achieve both of these objectives before, in a posture of high moral authority, President Dwight Eisenhower and his secretary of state, John Foster Dulles, were able to persuade the United Nations to force an Israeli withdrawal. Eisenhower backed up his position with a threat to impose a variety of military and economic sanctions—in short, an end to the vital interdependence that the United States and Israel had shared since 1948.

It is no wonder that Israeli intelligence was confused, for the Eisenhower administration itself was split into two camps: the practical military men, who saw in Israel's attack a chance to rid the world of Egypt's Nasser, and the statesmen, who considered a moral position before the world of greater long-term importance.

Nasser, who had seized power in Egypt in 1952, embodied one face of Egypt's historic split personality. On the one hand, Egypt is the most populous nation and the natural leader of the Arab world, its prophets destined to lead the Pan-Arab revival. On the other hand, it is the heir of the cradle of civilization, the keeper of a flame that outdazzles mere Arabism, a heritage

175

that transcends the temporal yearnings of the vast and disorganized Arab nations.

David Ben-Gurion had long feared most of all the ascendancy of an Egyptian-led Pan-Arabism. He dreaded the day when a leader would arise who would put Arab primacy ahead of Egyptian cultural pride. Nasser was such a man, described by Michael Bar-Zohar as "the great leader who would unite the Arabs and launch them into a holy war against Israel."

In pursuit of this goal, Nasser triggered two wars during the years he was in power—the Sinai campaign of 1956 and the Six-Day War of 1967—and lost both of them. The Sinai campaign was unique in that it brought together, in the face of Egyptian aggression, three nations that had little in common except their fear of Nasser—Israel, Great Britain, and France. The self-proclaimed president of Egypt had managed to offend all three: Egyptian raids had harassed Israeli villages; in 1953 Nasser had closed the Strait of Tiran to all Israeli flagships; and in 1955 he closed this vital waterway to all ships bound for the Israeli port of Elath, regardless of nationality. France was being challenged by Nasser's support of anti-French revolutionaries in Algeria. Great Britain was the most affronted of all: in June 1956 Nasser seized and nationalized the Suez Canal, through which passed one-quarter of all British imports.

France recognized Israel as a friend before Great Britain, under Anthony Eden, would concede any commonality of interest with an upstart nation whose very existence had exposed the creeping impotence of Britain in the Middle East. Despite the Balfour Declaration, Israel ultimately had had to achieve independence with opposition, not help, from Great Britain.

Confronted with the fact of Nasser's ambition, the three nations were drawn into an unwilling and tenuous alliance. By late 1955 Ben-Gurion had all but made up his mind that war was inevitable. By the summer of 1956 France and Great Britain were forced to conclude that their security required the overthrow of Nasser. The strategy was the only issue.

The war plan they agreed upon was disingenuous at best. Israel would march into the Sinai, toward the Suez Canal and also toward Sharm al-Sheikh, where Egyptian garrisons controlled the Strait of Tiran. French and British forces would land at Port Said, ostensibly as "neutral" protectors of Suez from both Egypt and Israel. The final outcome, the three nations hoped, would be the defeat of the Egyptians and the overthrow of the troublesome Nasser.

What they did not assess correctly was the reaction of the United States or, for that matter, of the Soviet Union. This intelligence failure was disastrous for Britain and France; only Israel was to emerge from the conflict with positive gains.

A step backward into history is necessary to understand the historical currents that Nasser represented. Israeli intelligence had been measuring him since 1948, five years before he and his young officers overthrew the corrupt and increasingly ineffectual regime of King Farouk. From 1951 onward, Isser Harel had maintained a special-services unit in Egypt, sepa-

rate from the military intelligence cadre that was responsible for the Lavon fiasco.

But what is probably most remarkable about Israel's accumulated knowledge of Egypt is that much of it was culled from a scholarly analysis of open Egyptian sources. Every Arabic newspaper, periodical, and radio broadcast was analyzed by Jewish intelligence specialists, who prepared daily summaries for the prime minister's office. Over and over again the information carried the same message: Nasser was a man to fear. And yet there were strange ironies in his rise to power.

Here was a man from the Egyptian middle class (the son of a post-office clerk) who, by force of his own ability, ambition, and charm, had become the leader of 22 million Egyptians. On the road to power he first championed the cause of Egyptian independence and, when that was assured, embraced the concept of a great Arab nation.

Nasser was one of the rare members of his economic class to be admitted to the Egyptian army's Officers' Training College. After he received his commission, he organized a clandestine army group known as the Free Officers. Composed mainly of officers of junior rank, the group had a dual objective. The first was to remove the obese King Farouk from his throne; the second was to drive the last vestiges of British colonial rule from the land of the Nile.

Perhaps because Nasser saw Great Britain as the immediate adversary, his sympathy was with the Nazis in World War II. And as strange as this might seem in retrospect, an even stauncher ally of the Nazis was Nasser's faithful follower and alter ego, Anwar el-Sadat. With funds channeled through the Grand Mufti of Jerusalem (an avowed ally of Hitler), Sadat hired assassins to liquidate British officers. Sadat reemphasized his pro-Nazi sentiments and his zealous anti-Jewish, anti-Zionist convictions on numerous occasions until as late as 1972.

Although Nasser and Sadat were the real leaders in the Free Officers coup in 1952 (Farouk was ousted without a shot), the man they thrust forward as the titular leader was General Mohammed Naguib. He was an officer with a sincere desire to introduce democracy to Egypt, an intelligent moderate who presented an excellent face to the Western powers. It is probable, however, that Nasser never intended Naguib to play more than a transitional role. In 1954 Naguib was ousted, and Nasser, at thirty-six, became the new president of Egypt.

What kind of man was now dominating the Arab world? In an earlier assessment, the CIA described him as a man of "vanity, obstinacy, suspicion, avidity for power. His strengths are complete self-confidence, great resilience, courage and nervous control, willingness to take great risks, great tactical skill and stubborn attachment to initial aims . . . he gets a boyish pleasure out of conspiratorial doings. He has a real streak of self-pity. While a patient, subtle organizer, he can lose his head."

At that time David Ben-Gurion was not privy to the CIA's appraisal, but the information flowing through Israeli intelligence was just as alarming. For the ultimate reason to fear Nasser, however, Ben-Gurion had only to

turn to the Egyptian's published writing. In his *Philosophy of the Revolution*, Nasser had outlined his grand design. He promised and predicted an Arab dominion from the Atlantic coast of Africa to the frontier of India. Egypt's Ministry of Information was even more candid. The ministry produced a map showing Spain, half of Africa, and—of course—Israel as part of the future Arab domain. Once again the question of Israel was her survival. For England and France it was control of the Mideast, including the oil supplies and the vital Suez Canal. From the standpoint of the United States there was the possibility of dangerous conflict with the Soviet Union, the long-range big power rivalry over strategic interests—especially oil—in the Middle East.

In February 1955 the United States sponsored (although it did not participate in) the Baghdad Pact, which provided for mutual-defense agreements between Iran, Pakistan, Iraq, and Great Britain.

The Soviet reaction to such an encirclement was to reach out to Egypt. On September 27, 1955, Nasser announced that a commercial agreement had been signed with the Soviet satellite Czechoslovakia, to exchange Egyptian cotton and rice for Czech arms.

The Soviet alliance encouraged Nasser to be bolder, especially in standing up to Israel. Since 1953 no one had challenged his blockade of ships flying the Israeli flag from passage through the Strait of Tiran, the entrance to the Gulf of Aqaba, at the head of which lies the Israeli port of Elath. Now he went further, blocking the strait to all shipping bound for Elath. This was not only a clear violation of international law regarding freedom of the seas; it was, to Israel, an act of war.

Although Ben-Gurion hoped to find a political solution, he was forced to explore the means of reopening the Strait of Tiran, by force, if necessary.

The blockade had been made possible by gun emplacements at Sharm al-Sheikh, the town on the southernmost tip of the Sinai. Sharm al-Sheikh was a long way—nearly 140 miles—from the nearest part of Israel. Hence, any military action by Israel would involve a large force and a long journey.

Nevertheless, the possibility had to be considered and, therefore, a military-intelligence expedition was mounted to explore the long overland route down the Sinai to Sharm al-Sheikh. The group selected for the treacherous journey was made up entirely of volunteers and included engineers and surveyors. Traveling mainly by night, the little band was in constant danger of being discovered by Bedouins, whose nomadic habits made it impossible to predict where they would appear. The Israelis carefully bypassed the little village of Taba in the Sinai, only a few miles southwest of Elath. The one thing they were certain of was that if even a wandering Bedouin had spotted them, the Egyptian army would have soon been on the scene.

Beyond Taba, there was no settlement for seventy miles. The coastal town of Dahab, two-thirds of the way down the gulf, was the most dangerous point on the journey and the detachment swung wide around it to avoid being seen. Forty miles farther on, they sighted the village of Ras Nasrani, on the outskirts of Sharm al-Sheikh. The expedition had now completed half of its mission. There was only the return journey. The survey of the terrain

was later to be of crucial importance. In his autobiography, Dayan wrote that "the results of the survey would make possible the extraordinary trek of one of our brigades in the Sinai Campaign a year and a half later."

As Israeli preparations for war continued, John Foster Dulles did not seem to comprehend that Nasser was rapidly proceeding toward an alliance with the Soviet Union. When, in August 1955, the CIA tried to persuade him that Egypt and the Soviet Union were negotiating an arms deal that would change the military balance in the Middle East, he refused to believe it. Only when the existence of the arms became public information did Dulles acknowledge the truth and set about trying to change Nasser's mind. To this end, he dispatched his top Middle East CIA agent, Kermit (Kim) Roosevelt, who had supported Nasser when the latter outsted his puppet Naguib. But Nasser was not sentimental about such friendships, and Roosevelt's mission was a failure. What Dulles did not understand was that the Soviets, unlike the United States, were willing to aid and abet Nasser in his grandiose plans to create a great Arab nation.

To Israel, the Pan-Arab movement and the Czech arms deal were nothing less than the most serious threats to its existence in its brief life. There was no doubt in the minds of Ben-Gurion and Dayan that the Czech arms were for use against Israel. It is a reasonable assumption that Israel's leadership debated the advisability of allowing the Egyptian buildup to continue.

The only way to properly assess the situation was to set the Israeli intelligence organizations to obtaining the facts. Agents fanned out over eastern and southern Europe, along the transportation routes of which arms might be moving toward Egypt. Surreptitiously they observed the loading of military cargo aboard freight cars and ships. A remarkable inventory of the number and types of arms was compiled. By the time the last tank had been unloaded in Alexandria and the last plane had landed in Egypt, the Israelis had an accurate assessment of their enemy's military potential.

In his autobiography, Dayan revealed the thoroughness of Israeli intelligence. The government knew from tanks, to guns, to jets, to naval vessels, and even to spare parts, just how much Soviet-bloc equipment had been delivered. The quantity was alarming: there had been a quantum jump in the armaments Egypt could array against Israel.

The causes of the strained relationships between the big powers and the Middle Eastern countries were complex, as they remain to this day. The American-controlled Arabian-American Oil Company (Aramco) was feeding the coffers of King Saud of Saudi Arabia. He, in turn, was pouring money into the Arab states of Lebanon, Syria, and Iraq and encouraging them to oppose the Baghdad Pact. Thus, American money was being used to undercut an American-sponsored alliance. No wonder Anthony Eden was confused. He wrote that "America's, that is Aramco's, money was being spent on a lavish scale to abet communism in the Middle East."

For America, and especially for Secretary of State John Foster Dulles, the situation was confusing at best. One of the historic oversimplifications subsequently heard is that if only the United States had agreed to help Egypt build the Aswan High Dam on the Nile, Nasser would have clutched Amer-

ica to his bosom and the lasting friendship would have changed history in the Middle East. In fact, Nasser asked for American help on the dam only after he was deeply involved in arms trade with the Soviet bloc. Hence, his "invitation" must be seen as a form of blackmail. Nevertheless, Dulles decided that the wisest choice would be to provide aid for the dam. On December 16, 1955, he announced that the United States, with some help from Great Britain, would allocate the bulk of the financial support and technical assistance necessary for the project.

But this announcement settled nothing, since there was strong opposition in Congress to the Aswan financing. In addition, Nasser unilaterally made several changes in the agreement, demanding financial aid considerably beyond the original American proposal. Then, on May 16, Nasser established diplomatic relations with Communist China at a time in history when any contact with a presumably hostile power was unthinkable to Americans. A few days later he concluded a second major arms deal with the Soviet Union. Rumors spread in Washington that the Soviets had told the Egyptians that they would be willing to finance the dam.

Many Americans felt that Nasser had been deceitful. They were outraged that after the United States had made a promise in good faith to help build the Aswan Dam, Nasser was using the promise to coax a better deal from the Soviet Union.

Consequently, when the National Security Council convened in late May, its members, especially George M. Humphrey, Eisenhower's powerful secretary of the treasury, breathed a sigh of relief on hearing Dulles recommend that the Aswan Dam offer be withdrawn. Eisenhower, mindful also of the mood of Congress in an election year, went along with the recommendation. On July 19, 1956, Dulles informed Egyptian Ambassador Ahmed Hussein that the United States was withdrawing its support of the dam project. Nasser's response was swift. Only seven days later, on July 26, before a cheering crowd of tens of thousands in Cairo's Independence Square, Nasser announced that he had nationalized the Suez Canal.

This act of defiance caught the Western world totally by surprise. Nikita Khrushchev, then first secretary of the Communist party, was delighted and quickly proclaimed Nasser a "Hero of the Soviet Union" and a "revolutionary democrat."

Israel was not surprised; it had been desperately seeking to purchase more arms in anticipation of some move by Nasser. At this point, in the late spring and summer of 1956, America's hypocrisy was showing. While Britain and France had agreed to sell Israel a modest amount of arms, the United States had refused to do so despite evidence of the cascade of military equipment pouring into Egypt from the Communist bloc. In his autobiography, Abba Eban referred to the American stance as "the paradox of Dulles' position." The secretary of state seemed to have no objection to other countries supplying Israel—"actually he would rather have liked this to happen." But the United States would not do so itself.

The basic reason behind this refusal was that omnipresent constant in the recent history of American diplomacy in the Middle East: reluctance to

offend the Arab world. Eban, at this time ambassador to both the United States and the United Nations, was concerned that "America's official rhetoric was giving currency to the idea that Israel was not the victim of Arab hostility" and that Washington felt the Jewish state was "endowed with spoils, some of which it could part with without any loss of vital interests." In effect, Washington seemed to be suggesting that for the sake of "peace," Israel should have been willing to make some territorial concessions.

With the aid of American and Israeli intelligence, Eban was able to convince Dulles that Soviet MIG-15s were being delivered to Egypt. It seemed as if the United States was about to reconsider its position when there occurred a clash between Israel and Syria over the use of Lake Tiberias (Sea of Galilee). Although the lake was entirely within Israeli territory and was an essential resource for drinking water, irrigation, and fish, Syrians were shelling boats on it.

The Israelis responded with a raid across the Syrian border that left seventy-three Syrians and six Israelis dead. The United States, distressed by the ferocity of this response, backed away from any commitment to Israel.

In February 1956 Eban appeared on the CBS television program *Face the Nation* and openly discussed his alarm about the flow of arms from the United States, the Soviet Union, and Great Britain to the Arab states. Said Eban, angrily, "Bombers to Egypt to terrorize our cities? Yes. Fighters to help Israel ward off those perils? No."

When the war was still a year and half away, Israeli intelligence detected signs of planning for guerrilla warfare to be launched by Arabs in the Gaza Strip. And, in fact, in April 1955 the Egyptian General Staff made a decision to embark on a campaign of terrorism and harassment against the Jewish state. It originated a special unit under the intelligence branch of the Egyptian army, based in the Gaza Strip and soon to be known throughout the world as the fedayeen, meaning in Arabic "those who sacrifice themselves." The name truly reflects the dedication and fearlessness of many of those who joined the fedayeen. Israeli intelligence agents soon determined that three camps were set up west of the city of Gaza, close to the Mediterranean shore. There were seven hundred men in the first contingent. They were paid nine Egyptian pounds per month, with cash bonuses for every border crossing into Israel. There were additional bonuses for every successfully completed act of sabotage or murder.

The targets were primarily civilian settlements and installations—farms, pipelines, roads. Scores of Israeli civilians were killed. Throughout 1955 and early 1956 the attacks increased in ferocity. In one six-day period in April 1956, twenty-six raids took place within five days. The Israelis responded by striking back at the fedayeen camps, but with limited success.

Ben-Gurion appealed to General E. M. Burns, the Canadian chief of staff of the United Nations Truce Supervision Organization. There had been, in theory, an armistice between Israel and Egypt since 1948. General Burns was charged with enforcing the armistice terms, but it was unrealistic to

believe he could be entirely successful. Ben-Gurion also made a plea to Dag Hammarskjöld, secretary-general of the United Nations.

Later, in his book *Between Arab and Israeli*, General Burns spoke of the peace-keeping problems. "It was never possible," he said, "to prove that the orders for the Fedayeen or any other marauders to enter Israel and commit terrorist acts came from Cairo. When challenged on this point by me or the secretary-general, the most that would be admitted was that the raiding could be stopped by the authorities, not that it had initiated them."

Burns may have lacked hard proof of Egyptian responsibility for the raids. Ben-Gurion, however, had documentary proof. Israeli intelligence had intercepted and sent on to Jerusalem a letter from Mustapha Hafez, chief of Egyptian intelligence in the Gaza Strip, to the governor of the Strip. The letter was written on behalf of Yunes Mabrak, who was being charged with murder in the local Gaza court. Part of the letter reads as follows:

> The above mentioned [Yunes Mabrak] is a representative of our office and one of the most faithful; he is a man who can be trusted with important and dangerous missions. He was an example of heroism and supreme courage in his dedication and readiness for self-sacrifice on behalf of Egypt and the Egyptian armed forces.
>
> The above mentioned volunteered for the Palestinian fedayeen forces and, infiltrating into Israel, carried out with his comrades acts of sabotage, dynamiting, and killing. The following are some of his actions which are worthy of praise:
>
> A. On August 29, 1955, he carried out the following deeds:
> 1. Killed three workers in an orange grove at Bet Hanun.
> 2. Murdered a mechanic in the electric power station at Bet Hanun.
> 3. Blew up the main pylon of the Voice of Israel Overseas radio station. (Map reference 12721448).
> 4. Attacked the farm settlement of Juala (M.R. 12781438) near Zarnoga in the vicinity of Al-Kabeiba, in which one man was killed, four were wounded, one building was destroyed, and damage inflicted on the village cooperative store.
> 5. Ambushed a convoy of vehicles at M.R. 12951486.
>
> B. On August 30, 1955, he carried out the following deeds:
> 1. Ambushed a vehicle near the village of Ajur and killed three people. The vehicle was destroyed.
> 2. Attacked the village of Tzumeil (M.R. 13001190) and blew up one of the buildings.
> 3. Ambushed a vehicle on the Plugot–Ben Govrin road.
> 4. At the same site, he ambushed three army vehicles.
>
> C. Since the above-mentioned is one of the accused in the murder trial No. 26/55, and taking into account his wonderful

deeds, we request that merciful consideration and appreciation be given to his past record of sacrificial actions so that a way may be found to help him as far as possible. It will also be possible to use him in the future if he sees that the authorities appreciate the results of his courageous deeds.

We therefore request that you deal compassionately with our representative and that you close the file against him.

Mustapha Hafez
Commander, Palestine Intelligence

Such harassment of Israel, plus Nasser's brash decision to nationalize the Suez Canal, was sufficient to unite Britain, France, and Israel in their unlikely common cause. The objective of the two Western powers was to force Nasser to back off and restore the canal to British control or, should he fail to do that, to produce an upheaval in Egypt that would result in Nasser's overthrow.

France had an additional reason for trying to force Nasser out. The civil war in Algeria was draining France's resources. The anxious men in the Elysée Palace knew that the Algerian rebels were getting weapons and money from Nasser as North African agents of his Pan-Arab design. The French also, as Shimon Peres suggested to the authors, conceded more dependence on Israel than did Britain, because of Israel's potential capacity to challenge Nasser and divert the aid he was sending to the Algerian rebels. "There were even some French officials concerned about Israel and her security," Peres told us. At that time, Dayan was army chief of staff. Peres was director-general of the Defense Ministry.

Even before the fateful day in June 1956 when Nasser seized the canal, Dayan and Peres had completed an arms deal with France. The canal seizure, however, brought the issue to a head. There were urgent consultations between the French and the British. The French defense minister turned to Israel for help in what it did best—providing intelligence information.

Dayan wrote that "what the French wanted from us was up-to-the-minute information on the strength and locations of the Egyptian formations (land, sea, and air)." Israel was able to oblige in great detail. For the time being, the two Western allies did not ask for Israel's participation in the military planning.

Aware that something was in the wind, John Foster Dulles flew to London and met with British Prime Minister Anthony Eden on August 2. Presumably, the CIA station chief had alerted Washington of some impending military action. Eden told Dulles that "the only language Nasser understood was force," according to Leonard Mosley, author of *Dulles*, who interviewed Eden in 1976. Surprisingly, when Eden told the American secretary of state that "the situation would come to a head sometime in October," Dulles interrupted, insisting he "did not want to know anything about the Anglo-French plans. It was better that way." Perhaps the secretary of state could deflect Arab anger if he could claim ignorance of Eden's plans.

The means by which Israel became involved in the Sinai campaign is

almost bizarre. According to Shimon Peres, he was in Paris in August working out the secret arms transaction with the French military. Without warning, "the French defense minister, Maurice Bourges-Maunoury, casually asked me if Israel was interested in an Anglo-French military operation against Egypt."

Peres's first impulse was to say yes, but of course he had to consult Ben-Gurion in Jerusalem. Bourges-Maunoury, meanwhile, pressed more questions: "How long do you think it would take the Israeli army to cross the Sinai and reach the canal? Our staff reckons about six weeks." Peres differed: "I think we could overrun Sinai and reach the canal in *one* week." That confident response ended the conversation. No commitments were asked, and none given.

Ben-Gurion, apprised of the French query, was interested, but he did not trust the British. There were abundant historical reasons not to, and then too, there was Britain's loyalty to Jordan. But on balance, there were practical reasons for believing Great Britain would cooperate with Israel.

Washington's reaction was another worry for the Israeli prime minister. While he felt certain that Britain and France would not move without the approval of the White House, his intelligence sources were not able to offer him any assurance of this.

A key figure in any Israeli decision was the ubiquitous Isser Harel. In 1956 he was head of the Mossad and coordinator of all intelligence services. Two decades later, the authors discussed the events of 1956 with him.

Harel was still convinced that the United States had no advance intelligence of Israel's involvement in the Sinai campaign. But if the United States did know, Harel told us, he had assurances from Ben-Gurion that there would be no interference. Ben-Gurion's belief in noninterference by the United States was, in turn, apparently based on similar assurances from Bourges-Maunoury to Shimon Peres.

The fact that the Americans did intervene is explained by Harel in this way: "If they had known in advance of the operation, they would have acted in a different way. Eisenhower had the political power to stop the campaign before it started. The president did not act, only because he was not aware of our plans. Yes, we fooled your president, and he was furious."

But on the evidence available to the authors, it seems clear that Eisenhower did know about the campaign in advance. The president's fury might very well have been staged to protect America's image in the Arab world.

Prior to the war, Dulles had tried to persuade Eden to forgo the military option. The secretary of state, despite his misgivings about Nasser, did not believe force was the the solution. And he had an alternate proposal—the "Suez Canal Users' Club." This would be an international body formed to manage, maintain, and operate the canal. Dulles did not envision using force to keep the canal open; consequently, when Nasser heard about the plan, he laughed it off.

By the end of August 1956, it was apparent to the world's major intelligence services that France and Britain were preparing for war. Reserves were called up in England, and the British navy sent reinforcements to

Malta. French paratroop units were placed on alert, and a naval strike force was being assembled at Toulon. French citizens in Egypt were being alerted to leave the country.

In spite of these virtually open military preparations, an examination of CIA files (obtained under the Freedom of Information Act) does not reveal any official concern, at least until September 5, 1956. (This does not necessarily mean that the CIA had no information as to war preparations; the available files simply do not mention the preparations.)

Early in September, France's Bourges-Maunoury again pressed Shimon Peres for a decision as to whether Israel would join France and Britain in attacking Egypt. He emphasized that an affirmative response would mean that the three states would have to engage immediately in detailed military coordination.

Peres was anxious to join France, and so was Dayan, but the decision was Ben-Gurion's. Peres sent an urgent coded message to Jerusalem and then waited impatiently for an answer. Meanwhile, Britain suggested a delay in the projected military action. But the French did not believe any delay was advisable. Bourges-Maunoury then sent a handwritten letter to Ben-Gurion urging that their two countries cooperate in the venture.

Ben-Gurion's response, in a personal letter, was a somewhat oblique commitment. Israel would be interested in a joint policy with France in the Middle East even without Britain, but details would have to be worked out. But the Israeli prime minister had finally given tentative approval to the Sinai campaign. On September 24, 1956, Peres left France to return to Israel for consultation.

In the late summer, President Eisenhower and the National Security Council gave increasing attention to the thickening clouds in the Middle East. Recently declassified top-secret minutes of the National Security Council meeting of Thursday, September 6, 1956, recorded with the president and secretary of state present, under the title "Significant World Developments Affecting U.S. Security," read in part: "Noted and discussed an oral briefing by the acting director of Central Intelligence [General C. P. Cabell] on the subject, with specific reference to the probable repercussions of British-French military action in the Suez crisis." Under the same heading on September 20, the council was briefed "on the situation with specific reference to the Arab-Israeli situation."

On September 19, 1956, CIA director Allen Dulles, brother of John Foster Dulles, submitted and circulated a top-secret document under the heading "Special National Intelligence Estimate No. 30-5-56." The paper was titled "The Likelihood of a British-French Resort to Military Action Against Egypt in the Suez Crisis." All the service intelligence organizations had participated in the preparation of the document, and it was concurred in by the Intelligence Advisory Committee.

The report was inconclusive about the probable British and French course of action in the Middle East. The CIA felt that "at least for the immediate future the United Kingdom and France will almost certainly seek to keep

the way open to the use of force." The temptation "to resort to military action against Egypt will probably be great over the next few weeks." On the other hand, the report continued, "at this stage of the crisis, we believe that the UK-French resort to military action is likely only in the event of some new and valid provocation, such as major violence to British and French nationals and property in Egypt."

The report's prediction was that as long as the United States continued to oppose the use of force, the British and French would not resort to it. If the United States were to change its mind and sanction the use of force, "Eden would move" against Egypt. Mosley, in his Dulles biography, reports that "Eden insisted that John Foster Dulles had appeared to give his agreement, if not his approval, to the Suez operation."

The weakness of the intelligence report was that it did not reveal—and perhaps did not have sufficient knowledge of—Israel's involvement with France. By this time, alert intelligence agents should certainly have been able to ferret out France's shipment of planes to Israel and ask—why?

Is it possible that the CIA fell victim to the weakness of many such agencies—that is, making the facts they gather conform to preconceived notions? An example of such thinking is illustrated in a CIA memo, originally classified top secret and dated September 27, 1956:

> The present tension has also spawned a mass of rumors and press reports.
>
> A. These claim there is a joint Israeli-UK-French military plan for Israeli partition of Jordan and occupation of the Gaza Strip, preliminary to Franco-British military intervention in the Suez Canal Zone.
>
> B. This flood of reports, in our view, actually reflects present extreme Arab nervousness and suspicion, rather than genuine information confirming the existence of such a plan.

To be sure, there were no plans for Israel to partition Jordan and occupy the Gaza, but there was an ongoing dialogue between France and Israel, as well as conversations between France and Britain, that would eventually lead to the United Kingdom's joining in the effort to denationalize the canal.

On the evening of September 28, an Israeli delegation slipped out of Lod Airport for a secret visit to Paris. Led by Foreign Minister Golda Meir, it included Shimon Peres, Transport Minister Moshe Carmel, and Army Chief of Staff Moshe Dayan. The next morning, a Sunday, in the Montparnasse home of Louis Mangin, an aide to the French defense minister, the Israelis were received by Bourges-Maunoury, Foreign Minister Christian Pineau, and members of the Ministry of Defense.

Pineau told the Israelis that the Russians were extending their influence in Egypt and that Soviet naval officers were even acting as pilots to help the Egyptians operate the Suez Canal successfully. The French were therefore ready to use force rather than allow the Soviet Union to usurp control of the

canal. Accordingly, said Pineau, the French planned an invasion in the middle of October, before the onset of the winter weather and while the Mediterranean was still calm enough for an amphibious assault.

The Israelis wanted to know if the French had assessed the possible American and Soviet responses. Pineau said hard intelligence information was lacking, but John Foster Dulles had been advised of the possibility of the assault, including the probable Israeli involvement. According to Pineau, Dulles responded that it was all right "but not before the end of the year." In effect, as the French foreign minister saw it, Dulles was saying he was not in favor of the invasion, but if it was delayed until after the elections in the United States, his country would not interfere.

If this account is true, John Foster Dulles was withholding from his brother, Allen, chief of the CIA, vital intelligence information. The CIA memo of September 27 does not reveal that the agency had any knowledge of the French-Israeli joint military planning at that time.

For their own political reasons, the French wanted the attack to take place before the American presidential elections. Pineau reasoned that Eisenhower would be reluctant to take any action against America's allies just before his reelection bid, since such opposition would make it appear that Eisenhower was siding with the Soviets.

By late September, Britain, under Anthony Eden, still had not come to a decision about its participation; the delay complicated the French plans. To destroy the Egyptian air force and to bomb airfields, runways, and installations required more bombers than the French had. They needed British help. As the Israelis and the French continued their military negotiations, the United Kingdom finally promised a decision by the middle of October.

Meanwhile, Dayan, through Israeli intelligence, was able to provide the French with accurate figures on the strength of the Egyptian air force—150 MIG fighters and 40 Illyushin bombers. Their tentative plan called for Israeli armor to operate east of the Suez Canal, with its air force providing cover. The French were expected to operate in the canal zone and to neutralize the Egyptian airfields west of the canal. In addition, the French would have the responsibility for engaging and destroying Nasser's navy, while the Israeli navy would defend its country's coast. It was agreed that Paris would dispatch a group of military experts to Jerusalem to determine if French aircraft could operate from Israel's airfields. The French would also anticipate Israel's further military requirements with the expectation that France would furnish additional military hardware.

Good intelligence agencies spy on their friends as well as their enemies, and the Mossad was no exception. In 1956 Israel had an informant in the American embassy in Paris. That is why Israel knew within twenty-four hours after it happened that a prominent French political figure opposed to the impending Sinai assault had visited the American embassy. He told the American who listened that the Sinai war was imminent and that he hoped to stop it because he believed it would be a disaster.

Obviously, Ben-Gurion or his intelligence chief, Isser Harel, knew of this

embassy visit, but for unfathomable reasons, they apparently did not believe it. Both, as was previously shown, were convinced they were deceiving the Americans.

An even stronger case can be made that the Egyptians, too, were blind in the face of the evidence. The Egyptian embassy also had a visitor. The event was later reported by Mohammed Hassanein Heikal, former editor of the influential Cairo newspaper *Al-Ahram*. The visitor was a Frenchman who was offering information—for money. He told his bewildered hosts that the French and Israelis were planning a military strike against Egypt. Although they were skeptical, the Egyptians paid him. A few days later the visitor returned, this time with detailed military information, but demanding more money. The Egyptians threw him out.

On his return to Israel late in the evening of October 1, 1956, Dayan reported to Ben-Gurion on the progress of the talks in Paris. The prime minister agreed that military preparations and consultations with the French should continue, but the final decision regarding Israel's participation was still pending. The target date for the invasion was October 20. In spite of the uncertainties, the General Staff was given an early warning by the prime minister. Preparations were made for calling up reserves, but actual mobilization was deferred. When a French military delegation came to Jerusalem on October 4 to meet with Ben-Gurion and his staff, Shimon Peres made a suggestion that was tentatively accepted—that French planes and military hardware be delivered to Israel on a loan basis. If the campaign did not take place, Israel would either return the equipment or pay for it.

The tentative battle plan required some careful intelligence from the Israeli army. Nasser's army was known to be encamped near the border of southern Israel in the Sinai. Dayan proposed to drop parachute troops behind the Egyptian lines and then follow up with armored units that would bypass the main Egyptian army and cut off its supplies. This meant that Israeli tanks would have to avoid existing roads and travel over uncharted sand dunes, a potential hazard to heavy vehicles that could get bogged down and be sitting ducks for the enemy. Such a course of action would be impossible without a careful study of the terrain. In his autobiography Dayan wrote:

A request came in from the southern command for authorization to carry out patrols in the Rafah region to test sand dunes for tank movements. Fearing this might draw unnecessary attention, I authorized only one patrol, and that only after being assured that it would make its way along the pebbled bed of the wadi. Not more than two men would actually walk on the sand, and they would be fitted with Bedouin sandals made in Hebron so that their footprints would not stand out against those of habitual Arab smugglers.

This bit of tactical intelligence paid off, since during the invasion no Israeli tanks were to be trapped in salt marshes.

As the battle preparations progressed, a mutual warmth and trust developed between the French and the Israelis. Not so in the case of the British and the government of their former mandate. Eden's government, almost as if embarrassed by the enforced cooperation, preferred to deal at arms' length with the Jews, using the French as intermediaries whenever possible.

To Whitehall's dismay, Ben-Gurion proved to be a masterful negotiator, with both patience and force. When the British put forth an unacceptable proposal, he would frequently launch into a political and philosophical analysis of the future of the Mideast. On other occasions, Ben-Gurion's temper would flare up and he would doggedly maintain his position.

The plan had advanced to the point where the negotiations seemed to take on a momentum of their own. On the morning of October 22 a plane taxied up to the terminal at Villacoublay airfield, and from it stepped Ben-Gurion, Dayan, and Peres. At 4 P.M., they were closeted in a villa near Sèvres, on the outskirts of Paris with Prime Minister Guy Mollet, Foreign Minister Pineau, and Defense Minister Bourges-Maunoury. At 7 P.M., British Foreign Minister Selwyn Lloyd and a senior aide arrived.

The Englishman seemed unable to find any common ground with Ben-Gurion, almost as if it were embarrassing for a representative of Her Majesty to have to negotiate with the leader of the Jewish state. The debate between Briton and Jew became acrimonious.

Nevertheless, two days later an agreement for the three-nation Sinai campaign was hammered out. The plan of October 24 provided that "on the evening of October 29, 1956, Israeli forces would launch a large-scale attack on the Egyptian forces with the aim of reaching the canal zone the following day." The British and French would issue an ultimatum to both the Israelis and the Egyptians demanding a cease-fire and a withdrawal of their respective forces to a position ten miles on each side of the canal. The Egyptian government would be required, in order to guarantee freedom of transit through the canal by ships of all nations, to agree to a temporary occupation by Anglo-French forces of a buffer zone along the canal separating the belligerents.

Of course, it was anticipated, the Egyptians would reject the ultimatum, giving Britain and France a pretext to bomb Egyptian airfields and use other military action to enforce Nasser's compliance to the edict.

The agreement was certainly a neat package, but could it be delivered? From the military standpoint, Israeli commanders were confident of success. Ben-Gurion was a little less confident. He worried about Egyptian bombers raining destruction on Israel's cities. Most of all, however, he worried about the reaction in the United States. Would Israel's probable gains in what Ben-Gurion regarded as a war of self-defense be reversed by opposition from Eisenhower and Dulles? Clearly, Ben-Gurion and the Israelis, as well as Britain and France, underestimated Eisenhower's hostility toward the whole Sinai plan.

There is overwhelming evidence that the preparations for the Sinai action could harldy have escaped the attention of American intelligence. There was a massing of British troops at Cyprus and Malta. There was naval activity

in the French ports of Marseilles and Toulon. And, as noted earlier, Anthony Eden, on August 2, told John Foster Dulles of the Anglo-French plans and predicted that "the situation would come to a head sometime in October." Hence, any claim by the secretary of state that he or President Eisenhower had not been forewarned by August 2 is simply not true. Dulles did not even have to rely on 10 Downing Street for information. He had reports from the CIA, headed by his brother, and abundant military intelligence. The pictures taken by U-2 planes over the Anglo-French staging areas gave substance to Eden's admission that he was preparing for war.

At the same time, the U-2—that famous spy plane that was eventually to get Eisenhower in trouble with Khrushchev when the Soviets shot one down—was contributing to Mideast intelligence. Richard M. Bissell, a tall, scholarly economist who had been assistant director of the CIA and organizer and director, with Tracy Barnes, of a successful revolution in Guatemala, was in charge of the U-2 project. He stated in a letter to the authors that "I was authorized by the DCI [Director of Central Intelligence] to arrange for U-2 surveillance over Egypt, Israel and other mainland areas in the Middle East. At least one or two missions overflew Cyprus and Malta, but the main focus was on the mainland."

Overflight of Communist territory had to be approved in advance by the president. But Bissell told us that "there was no such requirement with respect to the Middle East, though I believe [the president] was made aware that such surveillance was carried out periodically."

With all this, Eisenhower made an announcement that, in hindsight, at least, seems almost mysterious in its import. On October 12, with preparations for war gathering momentum in France and England, the president seemed to see just the opposite. He said he had "good news from Suez." He then went on to report that "it looks like there is a very great crisis that is behind us. I don't mean to say that we are completely out of the woods; but I talked to the secretary of state just before I came over here tonight, and I will tell you that in his heart, and mine at least, there is a great prayer of thanksgiving."

There seems to be no evidence of anything that could explain Eisenhower's optimism, unless Dulles had reported that the invasion would probably not take place until after the election. That would be "good news from Suez."

Perhaps the official optimism could be traceable to C. Douglas Dillon, the American ambassador to France. He was told by a member of the French government that an attempt to topple Nasser would be launched right after the American election. In fact, Eisenhower's aides actually prepared a statement for release after the election calling on both sides to cease their military preparations and allow the diplomatic process to continue.

During the same period, Israeli military intelligence reported that Iraqi forces probably had entered Jordan. Israel had already warned Jordan that if this happened, the Jewish state would consider moving against Amman.

Eisenhower's confusion seemed to be confirmed when later, in his book

Waging Peace, he wrote: "The Israelis, for some reason we could not fathom, were mobilizing. High-flying reconnaissance planes revealed that the Israelis had sixty Mystere planes, not twelve as the French had reported to us."

It is difficult to accept at face value the first part of the president's statement. Egypt was clearly an immediate threat to Israel's security, since Nasser had blockaded the Israeli port of Elath and was massing troops in the Sinai. One cannot believe that the president of the United States could not "fathom" Israel's reasons for responding.

On Friday, October 26, the CIA noted the unusually heavy traffic in coded messages between Paris and Tel Aviv. The mobilization of Israeli forces was now proceeding rapidly. Alarmed, Allen Dulles called for reports from his CIA station chiefs in London, Paris, Tel Aviv, and Cairo. American intelligence was abundantly staffed in these cities; the London chief alone had four hundred agents under his command. What Allen Dulles found disquieting was the absence of communication from British and French intelligence. Normally, there was a high degree of cooperation among the traditional allies.

Meanwhile, Nasser was getting nervous at the possibility of more foes than he had anticipated. He transmitted his alarm to the Soviet Union, which was then preoccupied with crushing the Hungarian uprising of 1956. If the three nations attacked Egypt, he was told, the Soviets would hold well-publicized military maneuvers, but that would be all. The Hungarian situation left the Soviets with neither the ability nor the inclination to help Nasser.

Eventually, Allen Dulles was forced to conclude that a British-French-Israeli assault on Egypt was imminent, based mainly on his own sources of intelligence in the French cabinet, from which he had learned that such an assault agreement had been reached by the three powers. Even with this evidence, however, Allen Dulles was loath to believe that the British would be so willing to jeopardize their relations with the Arab states.

The U-2 evidence was nonetheless pretty convincing. In Leonard Mosley's biography of the Dulles family, he writes: "Richard Bissell produced U-2 pictures of British convoys assembling in Malta and Cyprus and French ships taking on supplies in Marseilles and Toulon, and dryly remarked that they were hardly there for a regatta." When the authors pressed Bissell to verify this report, his response was: "I do not happen to remember the incident related by Mosley in which I was alleged to have displayed photographs of British and French shipments. If it occurred, the president would almost certainly have been informed of the evidence. I do remember at least one U-2 mission that went over Marseilles and Toulon, so the Mosley account could be accurate."

Were the British, French, and Israelis aware of the U-2 overflights? There are reports that the British filed a formal objection to the passes over Cyprus. Bissell did not recall any such protest. "If, in fact, such objections were transmitted, I am sure the president would have been informed of them." As to the issue of British and French objection to the U-2 flights, "I will point

out that the main reason it was felt that overflights in this area could be conducted freely was the belief, which we believe was borne out, that only Israel among the Middle Eastern countries had the capability to detect U-2 overflights. I seem to remember that the Israelis did detect them more than once but chose not to voice any official objection."

On Thursday evening, October 29, President Eisenhower received intelligence reports that the Israeli army was mobilizing. After conferring with John Foster Dulles, Eisenhower sent a cable to Ben-Gurion that he was "disturbed by reports of heavy mobilization on your side" and urged "that there be no forceable initiative on the part of your country which would endanger the peace."

But there was, not surprisingly, a great deal of hypocrisy in the whole situation, as is so often the case in international dealings. For the fact is that by this time the Joint Chiefs of Staff were fully aware of the intentions of the prospective belligerents. According to the chief of naval operations, Admiral Arleigh Burke, the Pentagon wished them success. Dr. Ray S. Cline, whose resemblance to Santa Claus belies his long CIA association (he was deputy director from 1962 to 1966), told us that "in general we knew what was going on, but preferred not to officially know. We hoped that they [the British, French, and Israelis] would get the campaign over before we, for political reasons, would be forced to react."

But even better evidence of the confusion of purposes is available. While Eisenhower was fussing and fuming with Ben-Gurion, the United States organized a Florida-to-France airlift of extra fuel tanks to increase the range of the French Sabre jets.

At the same time, at the port of Haifa, camouflaged French ships unloaded two hundred heavy-duty trucks. These were to be used to supplement Israeli civilian transport that had already been mobilized. Nearly every bus, nearly every private car, and delivery trucks of all descriptions were requisitioned by the Israeli army. A mostly civilian army would go into battle with, appropriately, mostly civilian transport; there was no alternative.

The Sinai war began Monday, October 29. At five o'clock in the morning a car from the American embassy stopped at the Alzaroff Street gate of the Ministry of Defense in Tel Aviv. The American consul was carrying a thick sealed envelope containing another message from President Eisenhower to Prime Minister Ben-Gurion.

The president felt "obliged to emphasize the dangers arising from the present situation, and request most earnestly that your government do nothing that might threaten peace." Shortly before noon Jacob Herzog, head of the American section at the Foreign Ministry, had completed the draft of a reply, which he delivered to Ben-Gurion.

The responsibility for the tensions, the message to Eisenhower said, lay in Nasser's expansionist policy in the Near East; the organizing of terrorist raids into Israel; the closing of the Suez Canal and the Gulf of Aqaba to Israeli shipping; and "the creation of a united command by Egypt, Syria and Jordan" dedicated to the destruction of the State of Israel.

It was at this point, upon the outbreak of the Sinai campaign, that the behavior of the Eisenhower administration becomes, in retrospect, confusing, contradictory, and mendacious. Despite months of intelligence reports and communications between the United States and the principals, on the evening of October 29, Eisenhower appeared before the American people on television to report that "the United States was not consulted in any way about any phases of these actions. Nor were we informed in advance." The president was reporting on a dual crisis: the Hungarian uprising had just been crushed by Soviet tanks, and now the Sinai was aflame.

A few days later, Secretary of State John Foster Dulles, with his usual air of moral rectitude, added, "We had no information of any kind. . . . The British and French participation also came as a complete surprise to us."

Allowing for the exigencies of diplomacy, security, and politics, which may at times necessitate deceit, the fact is that the president of the United States and his secretary of state were unabashedly lying. The uncovered records of intelligence—Israeli and American—leave no room for any other verdict.

This verdict is underscored by the fact that if anyone in the world other than the combatants was in a position to know what was about to happen, it was Allen Dulles, John Foster's brother and director of the CIA. Years later, in an interview with Andrew Tully, author of *CIA: The Inside Story,* the CIA chief attempted, not very successfully, to set the record straight.

"My brother said the State Department was taken by surprise," he told Tully. "That was only technically correct. What he meant was that the British, French, and Israeli governments had not informed our ambassadors. But we had the Suez operation perfectly taped. We reported there would be no attack by Israel on Jordan, but that there would be a three-nation attack on Suez. And on the day before the invasion the CIA reported it was imminent."

No evidence better confirms the confusion in Washington than the remarks of Major General George Keegan, who is now retired but was, when we interviewed him, the chief of intelligence for the United States Air Force. General Keegan's knowledge of what actually happened is based partly on his familiarity with intelligence evaluation, but on at least one climactic occasion, he was there to observe and listen:

> About seven weeks before the 1956 war, there were a number of attaché reports from France, from Egypt, from Israel. These clearly warned the president of the United States that the Israelis, the French, and the English were planning an attack against Egypt. There were more than a dozen of those reports over a seven-week period. As time went on, the content and the nature of those reports grew more explicit—such information as the specific departure of certain French fighter-bomber wings, their destinations, and the dates when they were ready to move into attack positions. The president was the recipient of this information, as were the intelligence organizations of the country.

I was aware, because of the position that I had at that time in the mid-1950s, that Mr. Eisenhower asked the Joint Chiefs of Staff and the CIA for several appraisals of that information and asked for Joint Chiefs of Staff recommendations on the preferred course of action to be taken by the United States. I am aware that in response to those actions, Mr. Eisenhower communicated on several occasions by telegraph and by personal telephone call with Mr. Eden. First of all, he inquired whether the British were planning an unusual initiative in the Middle East, then later giving Mr. Eden veiled warnings that he should be very, very careful.

And on the event of the attack itself, there were telephone calls from Mr. Eisenhower, of which I have personal knowledge, in which he attempted in the most forceful way to persuade Mr. Eden to be very cautious and, in effect—as I understand the thrust of these conversations—to dissuade Mr. Eden from attacking Egypt.

To my knowledge there were three separate Joint Chiefs of Staff evaluations of the developing situation, and in each of these, the Joint Chiefs of Staff studied the intelligence and came up with some firm recommendations for the National Security Council.

I don't recall the specific details of those recommendations. What I recall generally is that the Joint Chiefs of Staff on at least two occasions unanimously recommended to the NSC that if such an attack were mounted by England, Israel, and France, it would be in the best security interests of the United States to let that attack take place without any interference from the United States because of the absolute, paramount importance of seeing Nasser eliminated from the leadership of Egypt.

It was the general judgment, held widely throughout the government, that Nasser was a dictator, that he was an ideologue, that he was a revolutionary, that his principal interest was in leading the Arabs through another cycle of so-called holy wars, that at the same time he was promoting radicalism and promoting revolution abroad, and that he was exporting revolution throughout Africa and throughout the Arab peninsula.

He was generally considered to be a danger to the United States' interests in the Mediterranean. So for a variety of similar reasons the joint chiefs—on at least two occasions, to my knowledge—recommended that if such action takes place, it would be in the best interests of the United States not to intercede. This means a policy of "do nothing" so that the British, the Israelis, and the French might succeed, thereby helping to bring a more enlightened regime into Egypt; to provide the kind of leadership that might have helped to promote stability in the Middle East.

General Keegan was here articulating that split that separated the Joint Chiefs of Staff, with their realistic military view of the danger from Nasser, from the moralistic view of John Foster Dulles and the State Depart-

ment, a view that apparently held sway with President Eisenhower. In other words, whatever the threat posed by Nasser, Eisenhower and Dulles did not want to take a pragmatic position that was, in effect, "prowar." To Israel, it was more a matter of survival, in which morality played a small part. To a lesser extent, Great Britain and France saw it the same way.

The human intensity of the clash of views within the Eisenhower administration was recalled in the most dramatic terms by General Keegan, who was an eyewitness:

There was a National Security Council meeting on the eve of the attack. I recall that meeting very clearly—it occurred one or two days before the attack. The president was present at the meeting. The Joint Chiefs presented their position which was, I think, about as I described it.

In the midst of the meeting I recall that John Foster Dulles entered the White House from the north entrance. He came into the room. He was not wearing a hat; he looked quite disheveled. He was very excited and he was carrying a sheaf of papers in his hand. He walked into the room and said to the president, "I have to see you immediately."

The president got up from his chair. He walked not completely outside the room, but he walked toward the door. I recall Mr. Dulles saying, "We cannot let this thing happen. It is imperative that we let the British know we will not support such an aggression."

As I recall—I'm sure imperfectly after all these years—the thrust of Mr. Dulles's remarks were that the United States could never be a party to, or even be accused of, having sanctioned an unjustified and unprovoked aggression by one group of powers against another, particularly in the Middle East, where from Morocco to Casablanca to Cairo the United States had for more than a hundred years been looked upon as the last sanctuary of freedom in the world and therefore the defender of liberty in all of its constitutional and other forms.

Mr. Dulles—by this time nearly shouting—said the moral implications of the United States taking a position that would not be in the moral tradition of the United States would be something we could never live down.

Mr. Eisenhower returned to the table, and I presume from what then transpired that the president agreed with Mr. Dulles. Then, when the attack came, the United States very quickly introduced a resolution in the United Nations condemning the aggression. I later heard it said, from members of the Joint Chiefs who were in attendance at that meeting, that the indecision on Mr. Eden's part, once the attack had been joined, was in large measure induced by the pressure that the United States had brought upon him and was now bringing upon him in the United Nations to cease and desist.

On November 5, 1956, twelve hours after the last shot of the Sinai cam-

paign had been fired, the Soviet Union joined in the chorus for an immediate withdrawal. Soviet Premier Nikolai Bulganin sent sharp and threatening notes to Britain, France, and Israel, demanding their withdrawal from Egyptian territory. In his autobiography, Moshe Dayan asked, "Who knows whether this Sinai campaign would have been launched if the Russian messages had been sent to Britain, France and Israel before the 29th of October?"

The same, of course, could be said about the interference of the United States. If Israel acted from ignorance, however, it was no less fortunate. Despite American intervention, the blockade of the Strait of Tiran was broken, and the raids from Gaza came to an end.

Perhaps that is why, at the height of the attack, Ben-Gurion spent some time wondering if his worst fears of American intervention would be realized. Then, concluding there was nothing more he could do about it, he took a nap.

12

The Superspies: Wolfgang Lotz and Elie Cohen

WOLFGANG LOTZ* might have been admired by Adolf Hitler as the ideal Nordic type. Blue-eyed, fair-skinned, muscular, he had just enough red in his blond hair to suggest a man of power and vitality. In his manner there was a hint of arrogance; it was not difficult to imagine that he could have been an officer in the notorious Nazi S.S.

In contrast, Kamal Amin Taabes had the swarthy skin of a man whose ancestors had toiled under the hot sun of the eastern Mediterranean. With his sharp features, his curly, close-cropped hair, and his carefully trimmed moustache, he was exceedingly handsome and conventionally Arabic, although the dark eyes, to those who knew Taabes, suggested both a gentleness and an inner strength. Superficially, however, he resembled many of the Muslim soldier-politicians of the Middle East.

Both Lotz and Taabes were Israeli Jews. Both were daring and incredibly effective spies. Taken together, they are a perfect example of how the ethnic variety of the Israeli people has enhanced the state's ability to find the right spy for the right role.

Taabes's real name was Elie Cohen. A martyr for Israel, Cohen probably made the greatest single contribution of any agent in the annals of Israeli intelligence. Lotz, who, by a mere stroke of fortune, is still alive, now uses

---

*Some material in this chapter, notably reported conversations, comes from three outstanding books: *The Champagne Spy*, Lotz's own account of his espionage in Egypt, and two accounts of Elie Cohen's experiences, *Our Man in Damascus*, by Eli Ben-Hanan, and *The Spy from Israel*, by Ben Dan.

the Hebrew name of Ze'ev Gur-Arie.* His story is equally remarkable.

Both men were intensely dedicated to the survival of Israel, blessed with the ability to function under constant tension and—most important of all—gifted with exceptional intelligence. Both made their contributions to the Israeli government during the period 1960–1965. Their principal legacy was the Israeli success in the Six-Day War of June 1967.

Wolfgang Lotz had two special attributes. One served him well as a spy; the other literally saved his life when he was arrested in Egypt. First, he was the son of a German gentile theater director and a German Jewish actress. Of this legacy, Lotz said, "I inherited a certain degree of acting ability from them both—a vital asset to my profession in Egypt. I developed a sort of bombastic charm, was an excellent raconteur and a good mimic. I played the part of a wealthy, charming, and generous man with good connections and a ready sense of humor."

The other attribute was almost unique for a Jew. Lotz was not circumcised. There was no particular reason for this except that his father was not a Jew and his mother was not religious. While Christian men may or may not be circumcised, for Jews circumcision shortly after birth is a religious ritual based on God's covenant with Abraham in Genesis, Chapter 17. Lotz was ten years old in 1931 when his parents were divorced. In 1933, after Hitler seized power in Germany, his mother fled with her son to Palestine. It was a harsh and difficult change from the glamorous life of Berlin, especially for a young woman with no strong ties to her Jewish heritage and not even a faint knowledge of Hebrew.

Young Wolfgang fared better than his mother. He found the new land an exciting challenge. At twelve he went to agricultural school, where he became fascinated with the training of horses. At sixteen, when Arab assaults on the Jewish settlements were growing bolder, he joined the Haganah. Recognizing the skill of Lotz as a horseman, the Haganah chieftains assigned him the task of escorting on horseback the buses that traversed hostile territory on journeys to and from the agricultural station at Ben Sherman.

At the outbreak of World War II, Lotz, now a linguist who had mastered Hebrew, Arabic, and English to supplement his native German, had the temperament of a restless warrior scholar. He brashly falsified his age to join the British army, which at the time was the lesser of many evils for a dedicated Zionist. He was assigned to the North African front, an accidental circumstance that, along with his horsemanship, was to pave the way for his future adventures.

After the war, when the State of Israel was struggling to be born, Lotz spent three years in a dull administrative job for the Haifa Oil Refineries. When the State of Israel finally came into being and was immediately

*In 1946 Lotz had married Rivka Gur. When Rivka's brother, Arie, was killed in 1948 in the War for Independence, the Gur family, Lotz included, adopted the surname Gur-Arie as a tribute to him. Even when Lotz's marriage was dissolved, somewhat bitterly, in 1968, Lotz continued to be known in Jewish circles as Ze'ev Gur-Arie.

attacked by its Arab neighbors, he joined the Israeli army, was given a lieutenant's commission, and put in command of a company composed mainly of new immigrants. His unit endured months of harrowing, bloody conflict. By the time the Arab armies had finally been defeated, Lotz had made his decision to remain a soldier.

Wolfgang stayed in the army through the period of the Sinai campaign in 1956. He had risen to the rank of major and commanded an infantry brigade that captured the town of Rafah in the Negev. Sometime after the conclusion of the Sinai war, the inner councils of Israeli intelligence decided to develop Lotz as an espionage agent. He was approached and asked to take on a dangerous assignment.

"Looking back now," Lotz wrote in his autobiography, "I realize that my choice as a potential spy was in fact no accident and showed the Israeli secret service at its shrewdest. Although I was only half Jewish, I was nationalistic and was used to serving my country. Because of my German background I could easily be passed off as a German. I was blond, stocky, and thoroughly Teutonic in gesture, manner, and looks. I was a hard drinker and the very epitome of an ex-German officer. These qualities, combined with my inherited acting ability, made me a predictable enough choice. I would take orders, I was unlikely to be easily scared, and I would certainly not indulge in any dangerous introspection on my forthcoming predicament."

Where Lotz's talents were needed was in Egypt. Although this ancient nation was thoroughly under the control of the revolutionary Nasser government, it was still glutted with wretched and apathetic peasants and ruled by a central clique that thrived on privilege, intrigue, and corruption. The old traditions of the degenerate Farouk were not so easily discarded. It was fertile ground for a spy who could pose as a rich and influential former Nazi.

The United States was inclined to look upon Nasser as an enlightened despot who could bring stability to the troubled crossroads of the world. Israel, in contrast, saw him as a leader more and more fascinated with the concept of Pan-Arabism, as anti-Jewish and a decided threat to Israel. He brought numerous Germans, many of whom had been Nazis, into Egypt as technical and economic experts. Inevitably pressure began to build up against Egypt's one hundred thousand Jews. The pattern of Nasser's actions against Egyptian Jews resembled the Nazi pressures in the 1930s—removal of civil rights, confiscation of property, capricious criminal charges, and eventually expulsion or imprisonment. The Sinai campaign had capped the fate of some of the oldest Jewish settlements in the world. The Jews were all but forced to leave Egypt, and most of them went to Israel.

In February 1958 Nasser fashioned a tenuous (and, as it turned out, fruitless) union between Egypt and Syria. These two powerful border enemies of Israel assumed a stance of increasing militancy. Another war seemed inevitable, and the survival of Israel rested on its ability to probe the capability and intentions of the so-called United Arab Republic.

Lotz, imbued with a temperament that seemed to crave excitement, proved

to be an ideal trainee for the treacherous world of a foreign agent. More than that, his history was such that he almost seemed destined for his assignment. When he had served with the British army in North Africa, he had taken part in the interrogation of prisoners from Rommel's Afrika Korps and so had acquired a unique familiarity with the smallest details of life as an officer with Rommel, as well as considerable knowledge of Egypt. This happenstance perfected Lotz's cover story, which ran as follows: He had been a German officer from the Afrika Corps. The postwar situation for ex-Nazis was such that he emigrated from his native Berlin to Australia, where he was an owner and breeder of horses. Finally, believing the situation in Germany to be less hostile, he returned to his homeland.

From this point on Lotz merged his cover story with his actual experience. Now thoroughly trained as an Israeli agent, he returned to Germany a loyal German, weary of his exile in Australia, who longed to reestablish himself in the land of his birth. In other words, insofar as his German connections went, he was able to tell the truth. This led to a unique situation: Lotz was a spy, a secret agent of a foreign power, who used his own name and genuine identification papers.

For a whole year Lotz stayed in Germany, playing the part of a former Wehrmacht officer, living first in Berlin and then in Munich, devoting most of his time to his interest in horses but also mentally cataloging the information for his cover story in Egypt. He had also learned in great detail the arcane complications of the Egyptian security system, in which there was so much suspicion and intrigue that agents watched other agents and espionage was backed by counterespionage and counter-counterespionage. All in all, Lotz learned the Egyptian security establishment was active, ruthless—and incompetent. Egypt was a land where "everybody is watching everybody else."

In late December 1960 Lotz arrived in Cairo to find that his briefing was so thorough that "a picture had suddenly sprung to life." He wrote, "As I walked the streets I could immediately detect the 'public eye,' the cornerstone of the GIA [Egyptian General Intelligence Agency]: the Egyptian people. They sat on every corner, outside every door, outside every shop—idly watching. Their communal retina was something that was intrinsically part of the Cairo streets, the hubbub of the coffee houses, the chatter of the stories, the hustling on the pavements. It was as if the whole city was a slumberous, watchful animal."

Lotz penetrated the ruling circle of Egypt with ridiculous ease. With the assistance of his hotel manager, he was conveyed like an honored visitor to the most exclusive riding academy in Egypt, the Cavalry Club in Gezirah. He had barely begun to inspect the horses when he was approached by the honorary president of the club who was none other than the Egyptian general of police, Youssef Ali Ghorab. Lotz, with his thorough knowledge of horses and horsemanship, quickly won the man's respect. By evening Lotz was the center of attention at a cocktail party given by Madame Wigdane el-Barbary, one of the most astute hostesses in Egypt.

Ghorab, for all his pompous mannerisms, proved to be a steadfast friend,

to the point where Lotz became fond of him and worried about the ultimate fate of a man so thoroughly bedazzled by a foreign visitor. Ghorab opened doors for Lotz to important contacts and helped his German friend bypass miles of Egyptian red tape. Lotz played his part by lavishing expensive gifts on Ghorab and his family—an accepted way of acquiring and keeping friends in Egypt.

For six months Lotz allowed himself to be absorbed into the social whirl of upper-class Cairo, abetted by the totally unsuspicious General Ghorab. Riding was the principal form of recreation among the most privileged Egyptians. Consequently, Lotz welcomed Ghorab's suggestion that he buy some horses and stable them at the Cavalry Club. This was a sort of final arrival into the echelons of high society.

Now it was time to get to work. In preparation for the active part of his mission, Lotz returned to Europe, where a rendezvous had been prearranged with his Israeli superior (who has never been identified). His wife, Rivka, was privy to this arrangement, and she and her son moved to Paris in order to meet with Wolfgang periodically. He made several trips back to Paris (via Germany to protect his cover), but according to Rivka, they did not discuss his mission. She knew enough, however, to be aware of the mental strain imposed on him. "Scared? Of course he was scared," she told the authors. "Who wouldn't be?"*

In preparation for his return to Egypt, Lotz was given detailed operational instructions, a lot of money (to maintain the extravagant life-style that was so important to his cover), a tiny radio transmitter concealed in the heel of a riding boot, and a code book cleverly concealing its true information within a tome on the breeding of horses.

His duties were made clear: "I was now ready to begin work in earnest— my immediate objectives being to locate Egyptian fortifications, to assess the military buildup, and to fully investigate the impending arrival of the German and Austrian aircraft and rocket constructors."

Lotz was on the train from Paris when he ran into what he describes as "a cliché-ridden, fictional situation." No spy story is complete without the introduction of a beautiful and mysterious woman. There she was in his railroad compartment, tall, blond, blue-eyed, "with the kind of curvaceous figure I always had a weakness for." In a short time they were engaged in conversation. She was a German girl who had been an assistant hotel manager in Los Angeles and was now back in her native country to visit her parents.

They fell in love almost immediately, and Lotz proceeded to break all the rules. Within three weeks he was—as reported in his own memoirs—married to her and had revealed his occupation and his mission. Among the

---

*In regard to Lotz's domestic life there are substantial differences between his own account and that of Rivka, his Israeli wife. According to Lotz he was divorced before he went to Egypt, while Rivka states they were divorced in 1968. Inasmuch as the facts are not germane to this story, the authors did not press for a clarification of an intensely private matter.

fellowship of secret agents, a woman is regarded as a natural enemy. Even with the best of intentions, they are alleged to have, by chance remarks, sent many a spy to the gallows. It may have been rationalizing, but Lotz convinced himself (and eventually his superiors) that Waltraud (for that was her name) as a devoted wife would enable him to live a more conventional life in Cairo, attracting far less suspicion than if he were a forty-year-old bachelor. Furthermore, Waltraud, to her new husband's delighted surprise, was enchanted with the prospect of assisting him in a dangerous mission. As a member of a family that had escaped from East Germany, she asked only one thing—assurance that he was not working for a Communist country. He told her he was working for Israel. They drank a champagne toast to Israel.

A few days later, having left Waltraud in Munich temporarily, Lotz arrived in the harbor of Alexandria expecting to face the dreary routine of Egyptian entry procedures. He need not have feared, for once again his devoted comrade, General Ghorab, was on the spot to welcome him. The official barriers were thrust aside.

"Rusty, my friend, my dear friend, welcome home to Egypt."

Lotz could not have fashioned a more accommodating arrival. He was now "Rusty," and Egypt was "home." He replied graciously, "He who has once drunk from the water of the Nile shall always return."

The general arranged to have Lotz's Volkswagen removed from the ship and transported to Cairo. The visitor could accept nothing less than a ride in Ghorab's car.

"What's new?" Ghorab asked. Lotz told him that he had married and that his wife would arrive in a few weeks. Ghorab was delighted. Then he told Lotz of something immediate—a welcoming party that night in Heliopolis. Knowing that such affairs usually last out the night, Lotz joked, "It will be a wild night."

"Why worry? You can sleep it off tomorrow."

There was just one inconvenience: at 6 A.M. Lotz was to make his first transmission to Israel, even though it was to be a simple "Arrived safely." He managed it on time.

Waltraud arrived three weeks later at a hotel room turned into a forest of flowers; the largest bouquet, of course, was from General Ghorab. Others came from the German expatriots whom Lotz had met during his half-year in Egypt. Waltraud worried that Egyptian officialdom might become suspicious of her husband's lack of visible income. He reassured her: they could check on the earnings of the Germans who were actually working in Egypt, but they had no way of checking on the wealth of a man who, obviously, was independently well-off. They expected him to spend money—"There is nothing Egyptians love more than ostentation."

He explained how he coaxed information from them: "My system is to get several of them together at a party, give them a damn good meal and plenty of whiskey—which most of them love but can't afford to buy—and then they soon start talking among themselves about matters concerning their military duties. You'd be surprised what one can get out of such casual conversations."

There were other assets in Lotz's methods: "The drink makes them careless. It's all so damned simple. Another thing is they don't realize that I speak Arabic. They think I know only a few simple phrases, and they feel quite free to talk in front of me on subjects that they would not mention before others. But sometimes when I get one of them alone, he will also speak to me about secret or confidential matters. That's because they like to show off. Most of them have a terrible inferiority complex, and all the time they have to prove to themselves and to others how big and important they are and how much they know. They all think I was an officer in Rommel's Afrika Korps and so love to discuss military subjects with me. The fact that I am on intimate terms with a few bigshots around here places me automatically above suspicion in security matters. Some of them even seek my professional advice."

Waltraud was perceptive. "You really do enjoy this, don't you?"

Undoubtedly, she was right. Lotz's incredible success as a spy rested on his ability to rise above the fear and tension, to eschew conventional morality, to make friends of people he disliked, and to use people he really liked.

When it was all over, Lotz summed up his approach to the job: "After all, it was war, and war is not a game."

Waltraud moved easily into the social whirl. At the Lotzes' first party the guests included Madame el-Barbary, known as Danny, a free spirit long since estranged from her wealthy husband; Franz Kiesow, a German economist, and Nadia, his Egyptian wife; General Ghorab, of course, and two other generals of special interest to Lotz—Abdel Salaam, who had given the all-night party for Lotz on his return from Germany and was in charge of all troop and munitions movements, and, amazingly, Fouad Osman, chief of security for rocket bases and military factories.

As their level of alcohol intake increased, the guests began to abandon the small talk and dwell upon their troubles. Lotz zeroed in on Abdel Salaam, who was known as Abdo. "What have you been doing with yourself lately, Abdo?"

On cue, Abdo poured out critical information to an Israeli spy. He was busy transferring an armored brigade from Cairo to the Suez. He complained about incompetent staff officers.

Lotz baited him. "Well, let me know when you're starting the war, Abdo, and I'll stock up with whiskey."

The general told his friend the war would have to wait. There was "enough war matériel to conquer the whole Middle East," but the army was in a scandalous state. There was an abundance of Russian planes and armor, but the leaders were "like a bunch of children with a new football. Even the best football is no good if the team doesn't know how to play." Morale was low, training was bad, "and our whole concept of battle tactics is antiquated." And so went Abdo's litany. It could scarcely have been more pessimistic.

When will there be war, Lotz wanted to know.

Not soon. "But it will come, that's certain. It will come as surely as I'm half drunk now and have to go home."

Back in his hotel room, Lotz compiled what he had learned for a 6 A.M. transmission. He decided to go to the Suez for a closer look. When Waltraud asked to come along, he decided it would be a good idea. With fishing tackle and bathing suits they would be just two more tourists.

First, however, there was the matter of Waltraud's riding lessons. She was a good pupil, and the Cavalry Club was the center of the social activity of almost everyone in the circle of friends Lotz had acquired. Typically, Lotz had proceeded to turn even this affiliation into a positive asset. But there was yet another dividend.

The track where his trainer, Maurice, exercised his horses was at Heliopolis, adjacent to the largest base for armored units in Egypt. In the center of the oval track was a fifteen-foot tower for the owners to watch their horses work out. The base was so close to the track that Lotz needed only to pretend he was watching the horses when, actually, he was taking note of the movements of armored units in and out.

If they were leaving, Lotz could make a reasonable guess as to their destination just by observing the road they were taking. Sometimes he would confirm his guess by following for a while in his car.

It seemed as if similar opportunities just tumbled into Lotz's lap. One of his acquaintances was Colonel Omar el-Hadary, commander of the cavalry unit at the huge Abassia military garrison. Lotz had expressed interest in buying some more horses but was holding off for lack of a place to stable them. Colonel el-Hadary was equal to solving the problem. Stable them at Abassia, he suggested, and he would provide passes for both Lotz and his wife.

Only once did Lotz fear—briefly, as it turned out—that they had uncovered him. He was at a party given by a senile former Nazi, Johann von Leers, who had been given sanctuary in Egypt. Also present was the mass-murderer Dr. Haus Eisele, a physician who had conducted "scientific" experiments on human guinea pigs in the concentration camps. In Egypt he was serving as physician for the Germans working in the aircraft plants on behalf of Nasser.

In private conversation, von Leers wanted to know if Lotz had met Eisele in Germany. When his guest reminded von Leers that he had served in the Afrika Korps, von Leers's reply froze Lotz's blood: "I quite appreciate your telling this story to everybody. . . . It would be extremely stupid to tell them the truth. Might be dangerous, too."

Lotz protested. He was telling the truth.

Von Leers smirked at him. "Come now, Lotz. You are clever. But you don't have to play this game with me."

Again Lotz, now desperately trying to cover his fright, insisted he was hiding nothing.

"All right," said von Leers, "if you don't want to put your cards on the table you don't have to, my dear Obersturmbannführer. I shall certainly not be the one to give you away."

Lotz was totally confused but immensely relieved. Von Leers actually believed he had known Lotz in Germany and that he had been a lieutenant

colonel in the S.S. ("I remember you very distinctly looking very smart in the black uniform of an Obersturmbannführer.") Lotz's denials were fruitless. Von Leers could not be shaken in his belief that Lotz was a top Nazi in hiding. But he was sympathetic. "Don't deny it, my dear boy. I am happy you are one of us, and I will keep your secret. None but a chosen few shall know about it, I promise you."

Lotz finally concluded that von Leers's mistake would be helpful. First, he felt confident that von Leers, despite his pledge of secrecy, would repeat it. Lotz would continue to deny it every time it turned up, but the Germans and the Egyptians, too, would believe it, and Lotz's prestige would expand.

It turned out exactly as Lotz had thought; only the young German professionals who were not Nazi sympathizers grew slightly cool toward him. In time he abetted the story by leaving false documents confirming von Leers's contention where Egyptian intelligence would come across them. So he was accepted as a former Storm Trooper who, for reasons of his own, falsified his background. It was much better than being suspected of being an Israeli. For example, one could go fishing in the Bitter Lakes, a highly sensitive area, unmolested.

After two years in Egypt, Wolfgang and Waltraud had leased a farm ten miles from Cairo in the Nile Delta, conveniently near an Egyptian experimental rocket base. Every shot was a roar that Lotz could not miss. More important, however, were the spacious villa that they had rented near Giza and the parties for which they became famous. Egyptian officialdom and the German technicians constantly talked shop about their progress with military hardware. When Lotz pretended to show little interest, they seemed all the more determined that he should listen to their tales of successes and failures. Israeli intelligence was fed a continuous stream of vital information. When the small transmitter in Lotz's boot heel began to falter, he was provided with a much larger one, this time concealed in a bathroom scale. The transmissions were made from the master bedroom, the only room where Lotz could conceal himself without arousing suspicion on the part of the servants.

In the spring of 1964 Wolfgang and Waltraud had to return to Europe for a briefing in Paris. Their excuse was an invitation from an Italian millionaire to whom they had sold two horses, and their exit was conveniently handled by General Ghorab. From Rome they moved along to Paris and a series of secret meetings. There Lotz was asked about a dummy military airport near the Cairo-Alexandria desert road. Lotz assured Israeli intelligence that despite the unlikely display of so many planes the airport was not a dummy.

On his return to Egypt, Lotz received an urgent Israeli request to determine whether a rocket base near Shaloufa was a dummy or the real thing. The only solution was for Wolfgang and Waltraud to take another one of their "fishing" excursions to the Bitter Lakes. By a process of elimination, they had concluded that the base must be located within a certain area.

The Lotzes set off on their jaunt looking for all the world like typical

tourists. When they reached the road leading from the shoddy town of Suez to Ismailia, Waltraud took over the wheel so that Wolfgang could scan the desert landscape. Eventually they came to a side road guarded by a soldier at a sentry box. As they continued past, the soldier seemed to pay no attention.

Then Lotz decided to embark on the most daring escapade of his career, one that mingled brashness and luck—typical, in short, of most of his adventures. The plan was to turn around and fake an engine breakdown close to the sentry. But when they returned, the sentry's holster was hanging on a nail and the sentry was yards away, squatting on the sand, relieving himself.

At Lotz's order, Waltraud, instead of stopping, swung into the side road and gunned the engine. The sentry, pulling up his pants, shouted at them, but they roared on. They passed a jeep load of soldiers going the opposite direction. The soldiers, once they reached the sentry, realized what had happened, and the jeep swung around in hot pursuit. Lotz made another quick decision.

"Get us stuck. Quick—off the road."

"Hold on to something," said Waltraud. "Here she goes."

They were stuck.

The soldiers piled out of the jeep, machine guns at the ready. Lotz pretended to be berating his wife for stupid driving. In Arabic a soldier asked what they were doing there. The couple indicated they did not understand Arabic. Lotz replied in English. There was no successful communication, but Lotz, demanding help, refused to move.

The sergeant ordered his driver to the base headquarters to report the incident to the duty officer. He and the other soldiers remained to keep Wolfgang and Waltraud under guard. Waltraud, with her flair for excitement, was amused. Lotz took a more serious view of their plight. It was possible that they would have to exploit their connections to extricate themselves, which might leave a residue of suspicion.

The jeep returned within a few minutes, bearing a captain with a revolver on his hip. He spoke English. "Good morning. What is this all about?"

Lotz assumed the role of an outraged tourist. He demanded help in digging the car out of the sand. The captain was not concerned about the car. He wanted to know how they got into the base. Lotz continued to feign indignation.

"What do you mean, how did we get in? In our car, obviously. We came from Cairo. As to what we are doing here—if it's any of your business—we are on the way to the Bitter Lakes for a swim. Is that a crime? Do you know that these soldiers threatened to shoot us? When I get back to Cairo, I shall complain about this at police headquarters, where I have many influential friends."

The captain did not show any sympathy. He told them they were not on the road to the Bitter Lakes and demanded their passports. The car was searched, with special note taken of the camera and the roadmap. Lotz maintained his pose.

"If this is the way you treat well-paying tourists in your country, not many will come here, I assure you."

The captain decided to escort Lotz and his wife to the base headquarters, to confer with the colonel in charge. This entailed driving past the rows of rocket launchers, thus confirming for Lotz everything he had wanted to know.

Seated outside the colonel's office, guarded by a sergeant-major, Wolfgang and Waltraud waited while the captain went in to confer with his commandant. Too late, the captain was made aware of the blunder he had made by escorting two questionable people past all the secret installations. They could hear the colonel exploding: "You idiot! Are you out of your mind! Next thing you will be inviting them to an inspection of the installations."

Lotz knew they were still in danger. Ushered before the colonel, they were alarmed by his intransigence. He told them, "You may be spies or saboteurs for all I know."

The spy was reluctantly forced to go to the limit of his important connections to disentangle himself. The commandant was not impressed with Ghorab's name. Lotz tried General Fouad Osman. A call to Osman's office was futile. He was out. Lotz suggested Colonel Mohsen Sabri, an officer in state security. Although the commandant was suspicious, he put in a call. In a few minutes, Colonel Sabri, after talking to the commandant and to Lotz, straightened the matter out. Regular army officers were always in awe of security people. The commandant was almost contrite. He apologized. Lotz graciously forgave him and commended his men's vigilance. Then came a call from General Osman, who had come back and learned of Lotz's plight. He talked briefly to the commandant and then to Lotz. There were jokes and much laughter. "So you're spying on our missile bases!" Osman concluded the conversation by inviting Lotz to a stag party. "It will be most interesting."

At lunch the chastened commandant called Lotz "Colonel." Lotz assured him he had only been a captain in the German army.

"I will not pry into your affairs. Yours is a secret to be proud of. The S.S. they say, was the crème de la crème of the German Reich." As Lotz expected, von Leers's "secret" was getting around.

Then the "colonel's" eyes lit up.

"We, too, will have a great Arab Reich some day," said the commandant. "Installations like our missile base here will help to destroy Israel soon. Now you understand why we guard it so carefully. The Israelis have an excellent intelligence service. They must not learn anything about this until we strike the final blow."

"Now," said the commandant, "let me show you around."

On February 22, 1965, Lotz had been in Egypt for more than four years. The great disillusionment of the country at that time lay in the failure of German technicians to produce the armaments that Nasser expected. The Egyptians blamed the Germans; the Germans protested about the incompetent Egyptian bureaucracy. Friction between the Germans and their hosts

increased. Once, at a party given by Lotz, a group of the Germans came near to a brawl with some of the Egyptians. According to Rivka Gur, as the Nasser regime was courted by Soviet Russia, all Germans in Egypt were investigated.

On that February day Lotz had been to a party given by his old friend General Ghorab. When he arrived at his villa at Giza, he noticed four cars parked in front of his house. As Wolfgang and Waltraud emerged from their car, the occupants of the other cars piled out. Before he could protest, Lotz heard his wife scream and then was stunned by a blow on the head. The Egyptians had found him out.

The opposition of Jordan and Lebanon to the State of Israel has been sporadic and indecisive; the implacable enemies on Israel's borders have been Egypt and Syria—at least prior to President Anwar el-Sadat's "peace offensive" in 1977. What Lotz did to uncover vital security information in Egypt, Elie Cohen did in even more spectacular fashion in Syria. The two spies were at work at almost the same time, but in personality and *modus operandi* they were completely different. Where Lotz was an effusive extrovert, Cohen was a quiet, scholarly, almost gentle zealot. He shared with Lotz an intense desire to contribute to the survival of Israel.

Cohen was born and grew up in Egypt, the oldest son of a Jewish family of Syrian origin. From his earliest school days Elie was an exceptional scholar. He had a quiet wit but was occasionally almost a recluse. He studied Judaic law and customs and was also a gifted linguist. At an early age he had mastered Hebrew, Arabic, and French. He possessed an unusually retentive mind; often, as a game, he would study an object for a few minutes and then cover it and attempt to draw it from memory. His friends and teachers described him in various ways: he was "strange"; "brilliant"; even, to one teacher, "a genius." His only hobby was photography, an interest that was to serve him well later.

Late in his schooling Cohen began to lean toward mathematics and physics and hoped for a career as an electrical engineer. To this end, he passed the entrance examinations and was enrolled in Farouk I University in Alexandria. As he grew older, he became increasingly aware of the struggle for a Jewish homeland. In 1944, when two young Palestinian extremists murdered Lord Moyne in Cairo in an effort to call attention to British restrictions on immigration into Palestine, Cohen conceded his admiration for them and their fortitude in refusing to name their accomplices even as they went to the gallows.

From this period onward, Cohen worked ceaselessly for the Zionist cause to the extent that Egyptian authorities forced him to leave Farouk University. Cohen then earned his living as an accountant while leading a second, secret life. He was one of a group of Jews working through a fake travel agency to provide European jaunts for Egyptian Jews—jaunts that eventually brought them illegally into Palestine. The outbreak of the 1948 war frightened a large proportion of its Jews into leaving Egypt, one way or

another. All of Elie's family escaped, although he chose to stay and remained in Egypt for another six years.

In 1953 Cohen became peripherally involved in the ill-advised and ill-fated bombings that led to the Lavon affair. Fearing Nasser's growing power and a British withdrawal from Suez, young Jewish zealots, Cohen among them, decided to bomb British and American facilities. Their assumption was that if the bombings were made to seem as if the Egyptians had carried them out, Britain and America would be awakened to the danger posed by Nasser.

This plot turned into a fiasco, and the perpetrators were caught. Cohen himself was questioned and freed after the Egyptians were unable to prove his direct involvement.

The 1956 Suez campaign, pitting Israel, Britain, and France against Egypt, made life intolerable for the Jews remaining in Egypt, and Elie had to escape. Early in 1957 he joined his family in Israel. His reunion was not entirely happy. The years of separation and Elie's involvement in radical underground activities in Alexandria had created a barrier that was never completely surmounted. He again studied languages, adding Spanish, German, Greek, and Italian to his repertoire. He read constantly on electronics. Eventually he found a job as a translator for the Ministry of Defense, but ironically, his exceptional talent in languages could not mask his weakness in Hebrew. He knew the classic language but had not mastered its colloquialisms. He was discharged and moved into a more mundane task as an accountant for the Histadrut, the central Israeli trade-union organization. In August 1959 he married a lovely refugee from Iraq named Nadia. On the surface, his life seemed complete.

What Cohen did not realize was that while he was working for the Ministry of Defense, a double process of desire and recognition was taking place. He had been translating Arabic newspaper dispatches into Hebrew, and even though he was inadequate to the task, he became imbued with the idea that he could learn more about the Arab countries if he were there, ferreting out information. The Israeli secret services, however, have a general rule that they do not accept volunteers—another way of reasoning that a desire to serve in such a capacity does not necessarily qualify an applicant. In fact, such fervor to take on the work of a secret agent may indicate that the applicant's emotions will cloud the rationality that is essential to such a task. Cohen was acquainted with a captain of military intelligence who rebuffed his efforts to be considered. What Cohen did not know was that simultaneously he was being closely observed as a possible intelligence agent for the Mossad, the branch that directed foreign operations.

It was after he had left the ministry and had taken on the humdrum accountant's job for the Histadrut that he was approached. One evening, early in 1960, a man named Zalman, whom he had known only as a fellow translator, came to his home and, after making his apologies to Nadia, asked Elie to go for a walk. As soon as they were on the street, Zalman asked Elie if he would join the intelligence service, probably for assignment in Europe or

an Arab country. Elie responded enthusiastically, with the reservation that he would prefer an Arab country to Europe.

A few days later he was introduced to a man known only as Yitzhak in a shabby third-floor Tel Aviv apartment. Yitzhak warned him, as Zalman had done, that the assignment would mean leaving his wife (who was expecting a baby) for a long time and that he could tell no one, not even his wife, the nature of his mission. (Ben Dan, in his book on Elie Cohen, speculates that in reality no secret agent could be expected to keep all his secrets from his wife, but the warning was offered as a matter of policy.)

After intensive questioning, Yitzhak was satisfied that Cohen had no illusions about any glamour in the job. It was dangerous, grueling, and tedious work. The pay was modest and the rewards were never public. He liked Cohen's attitude, and Cohen, for his part, was elated about his new work. He had to begin by telling a lie to Nadia—that he was going to work for a commercial firm that would be assigning him to other countries from time to time. Perhaps she sensed what was happening, but she asked no difficult questions. The most difficult problem for Elie was explaining a trivial change. He had to grow a moustache, a symbol of virility to Arabs, but the joking explanation to his wife was that he had decided to sport the moustache until she produced a son. Their first and second children were girls, which fact allowed Elie to maintain this ruse.

The new Mossad agent's target was Syria. At that time the Syrian Golan Heights, a series of steep slopes rising over the fertile tableland of Galilee, were studded with Syrian military emplacements from which rifles and mortars rained their fire on Israeli farmers in the kibbutzim below. The situation was untenable for Israel. war with Syria seemed a probability, and inside military intelligence was desperately needed. Short of war, the least that was needed was detailed information on the Golan emplacements.

Those who are unfamiliar with the techniques of foreign intelligence might be surprised to learn that two years of intensive preparation preceded Cohen's active intelligence work. Approximately one year was spent in training within Israel, and another year abroad perfecting the elaborate cover story that would give Cohen credibility among the Syrians.

Early in 1960 Cohen was formally accepted as a Mossad agent in training. He was told by his mentor, Yitzhak, that he was free to change his mind and drop out at any time prior to the beginning of his actual assignment. Likewise, the Mossad could decide that he did not measure up. His training was meticulously thorough, and both physically and mentally rigorous. At the start he had to learn to walk the streets of a city (in this case, friendly Tel Aviv) while being shadowed, to be aware that he was being followed, to recognize his pursuers while not letting on to them that they had been spotted, and to elude them.

The next important phase of his training was a "sample" assignment in Jerusalem. He was given a false French passport and ordered to learn, through his false identity, as much as he could about the State of Israel. Cohen passed this test with flying colors. He made friends easily, even endearing himself to a wealthy couple by helping them with their disabled

car by the roadside. They invited him to a party where the guests were influential Israelis. As a French tourist, he was off to a good start.

But the worst was ahead of him. He returned to his hotel room to be greeted by a phone call from a furious Yitzhak, who wanted to know why he had been away so long. It seemed that a car was already waiting outside the hotel to take him to an airfield for a return trip to Tel Aviv. Cohen protested that he was exhausted and needed sleep, but Yitzhak was coldly unsympathetic. "There's no time to lose." He provided Elie with a description of the waiting driver and that was all. As Elie again pleaded for some time to sleep, Yitzhak hung up.

Cohen was taken not to Tel Aviv, but to Haifa; the pilot said those were his orders. In Haifa the trainee was met by two mysterious men who refused to answer any questions. The confused Cohen was asked if he would like a smoke. He accepted it gladly, took a few puffs, and passed out.

He awoke with a bright light shining in his face; he seemed to be in some kind of a prison. He was conscious of feeling sick and desperately thirsty. There was a pitcher of cool water on the floor nearby. Cohen reached for it, only to have a man emerge from behind the light and kick it away. He was told he was a prisoner of counterintelligence and they wanted to know what he was doing in Jerusalem on a false passport. When he refused to answer questions under the glare of the light, he was ordered to stand and strip and was thrust into a tub of frigid water. He still would not talk. When he thought he was about to pass out from the cold, they removed him, massaged him somewhat, and threw him into something just as bad—a sort of dungeon that reeked of excrement. The interrogators demanded to know his real identity, convinced, they said, that his passport was fake (which, of course, it was). The ordeal continued for twenty hours until a needle thrust into his arm induced a welcome sleep.

This time, when he awoke, he was back in his hotel room in Jerusalem. Yitzhak never conceded that the ordeal was a test, insisting that Elie had been picked up by another branch of the secret services that did not know that he was on a tryout exercise for Mossad. When he returned to Tel Aviv, however, he was commended. Then he went home for a happy ten days. In his absence Nadia had given birth to that first child, who was named Sophie for Nadia's mother.

In September 1960, Elie's testing was over. Everything henceforth was in preparation for a specific mission. Cohen was to go to Syria, but the perfecting of his mission was to require fifteen more months of exhaustive groundwork.

The new spy took on his mission after a year of tense border clashes between Israel and Syria. Early in 1960 Syria had stepped up her harassment of the Galilee, striking particularly at a kibbutz called Tel Katzir at the foot of the Golan Heights. The bombardments had killed numerous Israeli farmers and destroyed many of their homes. In desperation, Israel sent an expedition up into the Heights. It successfully wiped out several of the most threatening Syrian emplacements. But the long-term picture was gloomy. The Soviet Union was supplying the United Arab Republic (the

name for the brief and unsuccessful union of Egypt and Syria) with massive quantities of arms, especially tanks. Syria was now Israel's most dangerous enemy, and better military intelligence was vital if Israel was to survive the expected Syrian onslaught.

Cohen's new name was Kamal Amin Taabes. The preparation that he was required to make and the odyssey that preceded his actual intelligence work were incredibly meticulous—far more detailed than the preparations of Wolfgang Lotz. His false background was this: He was the son of a Syrian who had moved to Lebanon. Kamal Amin Taabes was born in Beirut but went as a small child with his family to Alexandria. His father had never renounced his Syrian citizenship and had always urged Kamal to return there. But Kamal first went to Argentina, where he joined a brother in the textile business in Buenos Aires. The textile business failed, but Taabes developed a highly successful export-import firm in Argentina. After that he achieved his lifelong dream of moving to his father's country, Syria.

All this was imagination, but it was carefully crafted to fit in with Elie Cohen's background and knowledge. His father, of course, had come from Syria, and Cohen had lived in Alexandria. But he had to fill in the gaps in a process that would begin with a real trip to Argentina. To start with, he had to become a Muslim—or as knowledgeable in the faith as a real Muslim. He was sent first to the town of Nazareth, one of the most heavily Arab communities in Israel. There, under a short-term false name, he pretended to be an Arab student from Jerusalem seeking instruction in his religion. Under the direction of an unsuspecting sheikh, he became a better-informed Muslim than most of the Prophet's real disciples.

He had to learn to speak Arabic in the Syrian dialect, a process abetted by hours of listening to Damascus radio. Because he would first have to live in Argentina, he had to perfect his Spanish. And he spent exhaustive hours learning to install, operate, and repair the sophisticated miniature transmitting and receiving equipment he would be using in Syria. He studied Syrian politics through books and current newspapers. And he watched hours of films on Syria—documentaries, newsreels, and anything else on film that would familiarize him with his adopted country.

Eventually the process was so effective that Elie Cohen actually began to think of himself as Kamal Amin Taabes. Even his wife noticed the change. She also suspected that he was involved in a spy mission, but she did not ask any questions.

Argentina was the ideal country for Cohen to begin his existence as Kamal Amin Taabes. A polyglot nation, its national groups were clannish, often making no effort to break their old traditions and merge with the new country. A half-million Arabs lived in Buenos Aires alone. Because of Argentina's liberal immigration policy, it was easy to enter the country and disappear. However, this also made the country a tangled web of intrigue. The Arab countries, especially, maintained extensive espionage and counterespionage operations there.

In early February 1962, Cohen left Israel from Lydda Airport, after telling Nadia he was going off on a business trip. His first stop was Zurich,

where he met with Israel Salinger, chief of Mossad in Europe. In Switzerland, Elie Cohen made the final transition from his real identity to that of Kamal Amin Taabes. He turned all of his clothes over to Salinger and disposed of anything else that might betray his Israeli origins. Salinger provided him with a Swiss bank account, a commonplace with Argentine businessmen. Lastly he was given a perfectly forged passport in his new name and a box number in Zurich through which he could write to Nadia. The long training and preparations were over, and the spy was now at work.

A lone, slightly apprehensive Middle Easterner strolled along the festive Avenida Nuevo de Julio, the showplace street built by the ousted dictator Juan Peron. He had been ordered to meet an agent at a certain café at 11 A.M. The meeting, with "Abraham" (who identified Taabes from a photograph) was brief but substantive. He was told to take lessons to improve his Spanish. Taabes's cover job was as head of a shipping firm. He was told where his office was and what his phone number would be. Abraham would provide him immediately with business cards and letterheads. Finally, he was given the names and addresses of prominent Arabs who could often be found at the Islam Club of Buenos Aires or at restaurants that catered to Middle Easterners.

Within a matter of days Taabes had fallen into the routine. He was frequenting the Islam Club and, on his second day there, fell into conversation with Abdullah Latif Alheshan, editor of *The Arab World*, the leading Arabic weekly in Buenos Aires. The two men hit it off immediately. Alheshan was impressed with Taabes's yearning to return to his native land. Taabes was now extremely adept at talking about his origins (with some truth involved when he was talking of life in Alexandria).

Taabes inferred from Alheshan's remarks that he was hopeful that the Ba'ath ("Rebirth") party would take over the government of Syria. He was decidedly cool to the faltering United Arab Republic and the domination of Nasser. Taabes pretended to be sympathetic with Alheshan's views but expressed his doubts that he would be welcome back in his "old country." The editor was so convinced of Taabes's sincerity that he offered to provide introductions to his powerful friends in Damascus as soon as Taabes decided to return there.

While expanding his contacts to the point where he was regularly invited to the most important social and embassy functions, Taabes made his most significant contact: General Amin el-Hafez, who was Syrian military attaché in Argentina and one of the strong men of the rising Ba'ath party. Their introduction had been arranged by Alheshan. When Taabes seconded the general's belief in the Ba'ath movement, the handsome, graying Hafez challenged him to return and do something about it. From then on, whenever they met, the general would ask, "Well, when are you going to Syria?"

In August, Taabes was ready to do just that. Alheshan was as good as his word. He gave his friend some impressive letters of introduction, including one to Alheshan's own son.

Taabes went first to Zurich, where he was ordered by Salinger to return to

Tel Aviv for further training. This meant a switch back to the identity of the real Elie Cohen—and a brief reunion with Nadia and Sophie.

This final visit to Israel was chiefly to sharpen Cohen's mastery of the technical aspects of the spying business. He learned how to use special inks and how to hide small objects, such as microfilms, in his clothes and in his apartment. He also perfected his skill at radio transmission.

At this point Cohen learned what for many years was one of the most closely kept secrets of Israeli spying techniques. It had been conceived by the legendary mastermind of the secret services, Nachum Bernstein, who first initiated its use with the American OSS. It had been the custom of agents in trouble to notify headquarters by misspelling the third word in a transmitted message. In time, Bernstein worried that the misspelling would be detected by the enemy as a signal. So he came up with an eminently simple alternative. In all normal transmissions the third word is always misspelled. If the agent is captured and ordered to send a message under duress, he spells the third word correctly.

By coincidence, the period that Cohen was in Israel was marked by political upheavals in Syria. The union with Egypt, never popular with most Syrians, was ended by a Syrian revolt. Its leader was a man ostensibly in Nasser's camp, Brigadier Abdel Karim Nahalawi. Although designated by Nasser as deputy governor of the province of Syria, he correctly judged that Syrians regarded themselves as the second-class partners in Nasser's grand first step in his Pan-Arabic design.

Nahalawi's coup took place on September 28. As deputy governor, he overthrew his own superior, Marshal Abdul Hakim Amer, Nasser's representative as governor. By this time the Syrians could point to a list of grievances—Egyptian commanders over Syrian army units, the transfer of Syrian fighting planes to Egypt, and even Egyptians usurping top posts in the Syrian civil service.

The ouster of the Egyptians played into Elie Cohen's hands in two ways. First, it meant the departure from Syria of hundreds of Egyptian officers and agents, any one of whom might possibly have recognized Cohen from his notoriety in Egypt during the days of the Lavon affair. Second, it brought to the brink of power the Ba'ath party, which had been suppressed during the Egyptian hegemony. In Buenos Aires, Cohen had sensed the ascendancy of the Ba'ath group, an amalgam of socialist ideas in a highly nationalistic framework, and had more or less thrown his lot in with them.

At the end of December 1961 Elie again bade good-bye to Nadia, explaining that he was off on another business trip in Europe. This time his interim destination was Munich for a meeting with Salinger. Again there was the discarding of everything Israeli and the reacquisition of everything Argentinian. He flew to Zurich, where he secured a Syrian visa and passage on the steamship *Astoria*, leaving Genoa for Beirut the first week in January. His most important new acquisition was a modern electric mixer—a useful kitchen appliance to be sure, but in this case one with a powerful miniature transmitter concealed in the base.

The *Astoria* passenger list consisted mainly of wealthy Middle Eastern

businessmen returning to their various countries. Cohen, once again Kamal Amin Taabes, was drawn to an elegantly dressed and self-assured passenger. He was Sheikh Majd el-Ard, a member of the Syrian ruling class, the landed gentry threatened by the possibility of a Ba'ath take-over. He took an immediate liking to Taabes and offered his help and his hospitality en route to Damascus, including a drive to Damascus in his new Peugeot. This meant an easy passage through Lebanese and Syrian customs. The sheikh was as good as his word. With ample *baksheesh* even a spy with a transmitter in his suitcase could go smoothly through the checkpoints. Taabes politely declined el-Ard's offer of hospitality at his villa. He felt it would be better, he explained, to stay at a hotel. The sheikh then insisted that it should be a hotel where he, el-Ard, was known. Taabes was ensconced in the Hotel Semiramis, where a friend of Sheikh el-Ard was assured special treatment.

At last, on January 10, Kamal Amin Taabes reached Damascus, where he would live and die for Israel.

Taabes's reaction to Syria was similar to Lotz's reaction to Egypt. He somehow felt that everyone was listening and watching. But most observers tend to feel that Damascus is a far more uncomfortable city than Cairo. For one thing, it is less cosmopolitan. Foreigners, even those from other Arab countries, are more noticeable and meet with more hostility. Political instability, characterized by repeated coups d'etat, has made Damascus a city where no one knows who will be the person to fear tomorrow.

Taabes's first need was a permanent-residence permit. Here, once again, he called on his friend el-Ard. Predictably this was accomplished with a minimum of official investigation. Next came the search for a suitable flat. Taabes, with the sheikh's help, inspected dozens of them, none acceptable. The basis for the rejection was not always the inadequacy of the living quarters themselves. Taabes had located the headquarters of the Syrian army's General Staff. If possible he wanted a flat close by.

The sheikh, meanwhile, all unknowingly, was offering the spy valuable information on Syrian security. "You know, there are more secret agents than soldiers. Never speak your mind to anyone without knowing whom you are dealing with. They're simply everywhere." Obviously, el-Ard was not taking his own advice.

And, indeed, every political party protected itself and penetrated its opponents with a horde of agents. Information, both official and gossip, was traded in the coffee houses of Damascus, where the men spent hours on end playing *shesh besh*, the ancient game that Westerners call backgammon.

Taabes finally located a suitable dwelling, not with the help of el-Ard but by exploiting another contact, the son of Abdullah Alheshan, the editor in Buenos Aires. The son's first name was Kamal, and he was delighted to meet the good friend of his father. Taabes had to explain to the younger Alheshan that he needed an apartment that could also serve as an office for the export-import business he hoped to set up. After several days' search Taabes found what he was looking for—a fourth-floor flat that was almost ideal. The building had a forest of television antennas on the roof. One more antenna would not be noticed, even if it was for a transmitter beaming messages to

Tel Aviv. In every other way the flat was completely adequate; in good taste, even rich, but not ostentatious. And the window looked directly onto the headquarters of the Syrian army.

Taabes reverted to Elie Cohen, the intelligence agent, as soon as he was safely behind the closed door of his flat. In the center of the living room a large electric light with an ornamental shade hung from the ceiling. He discovered that he could remove the brass fitting that was against the plaster and secrete the transmitter above the ceiling. As for a receiver, he needed only to buy a commercially available radio. On February 12, 1962, his equipment installed, he tapped out his first message, in code, of course. Happily he told Mossad headquarters in Tel Aviv that he was ready to go to work and that he was located next to Syrian army headquarters. The radio transmission and reception was perfect. Cohen's superiors in Tel Aviv were impressed, as well they should have been.

For the next few months Taabes divided his time between two activities. First, he carefully observed the comings and goings of the officers in the staff headquarters, alert for any change from the usual eight-to-six routine, especially noting the comparatively few rooms that remained lighted at night. Second, Taabes, with young Alheshan's help, made many new friends, particularly among the business people of Damascus.

His plan, as he explained to many Damascans, was to develop an export trade in Syrian furniture and art objects. He was a believable figure to the Syrians. They liked him and were impressed. He not only was involved in an enterprise that promised much-needed trade for Syria, but he seemed quietly devoted to the future of his country. For the moment, despite his professed sympathy for the Ba'ath party when he was in Argentina, he remained nonpolitical. Although the party's take-over seemed a probability, he did not dare identify himself with it completely, in case of any other eventuality.

Early in March, Cohen had a chance to convey his first information to Israel, much earlier than he had expected. Radio Damascus announced that Syrian forces had routed "Zionist warships" on the Sea of Galilee. Cohen became aware of an increased number of military vehicles on the street and more lights burning late in the General Staff headquarters. Without knowing what actually had happened (he had no access to official information from Israel), Cohen took note of a surge of bellicose statements in the controlled Syrian press.

What actually had happened was that the Syrians had fired on fishing boats on the Sea of Galilee and then on an Israeli patrol boat rushing to their aid. Two members of the patrol boat crew were injured. Cohen, of course, had to act without knowledge of the facts, but the tension in Syria was sufficient to justify a message to Tel Aviv. His first official operational transmission was to make the Israelis aware of the step-up of military activity in Syria.

His information was welcome. Shortly afterward the Israelis took notice of tanks and troops moving into the Golan Heights. Israeli positions around the Sea of Galilee were strengthened.

On March 16, Syrian guns opened fire on more Israeli fishing boats, and a bloody battle ensued. The Israeli forces, beefed up partly as a result of Cohen's warning, responded by storming the Syrian positions. The so-called battle of Nukeib, named for the strongest Syrian outpost, was eventually won by Israel as the Syrian ramparts were overcome. The Nukeib fortifications were wiped out, but not without relatively serious losses by the Israelis— eight soldiers killed and one missing.

Cohen noted the predictable Syrian claims on the radio and in newspapers of a "glorious victory." He suspected correctly that this was somewhat short of the truth, but the truth was unexpectedly confirmed for him.

"The Israelis won at Nukeib." Kamal Taabes could hardly believe his ears. The information was being volunteered to him in his own apartment by Lieutenant Maazi Zahreddin, nephew of Abdel Karim Zahreddin, chief of staff of the Syrian army. The young lieutenant had come to meet Taabes as someone worldly and admirable. The meeting had been arranged by Kamal Alheshan. Maazi enlarged on his information: "Their air force is first class, whereas ours is weak and, what's more, badly trained by Israeli standards."

Cautiously, Taabes led him on. Had he ever seen the Nukeib area? Certainly, Zahreddin confirmed. Taabes laughed; he couldn't believe Jews were good fighters. "Jewish soldiers carrying weapons? That I'd love to see, even from a distance."

Zahreddin rose to the bait. When things had quieted down he would take Taabes on a tour of the front. But, he warned, "this place is crawling with Zionist spies."

It seemed that Taabes's feast of information was not to end. Zahreddin told Taabes that Colonel Nahalawi, the strong man who had masterminded the break with Egypt, was dissatisfied with the government—it was too weak. "I'm sure the colonel won't hesitate to bring about changes in the government in the very near future."

In a matter of hours Israeli intelligence knew everything that Taabes had learned that night. His information had a direct effect on the decisions of the Israeli government. The government was convinced that the Syrian weakness made an attack unlikely and was able to withdraw some of its forces from the Syrian border.

In the midst of further Syrian turmoil, Elie Cohen pursued his two interests. His cover activity, the setting up of an export business, was moving well. He persuaded Damascus businessmen that he had a market for the ornate *shesh besh* tables that were produced originally for local coffeehouses. His "European agent" was none other than Salinger, the chief of Mossad in Europe. Salinger, for his part, provided that enterprising Syrian, Kamal Amin Taabes, with a guarantee of European purchases.

Cohen's intelligence work was made more complicated by a Syrian coup d'etat on March 28. As expected, Colonel Nahalawi engineered the overthrow of the civil government. Within days, however, an anti-Nahalawi group, resentful of his seizure of power and his break with Egypt, staged a countercoup. Nahalawi and his aides fled in defeat. But what was important

to Elie Cohen was that throughout the successive turnovers, General Zahreddin remained on the job, apparently respected as a patriot above the battle. There was therefore no letup in the flow of information from the General's nephew, Maazi, now the best friend of Kamal Taabes. His uncle, it seemed, was desperately seeking responsible civilian leadership to assume power in the virtually leaderless country. All of this was carefully transmitted to Tel Aviv. Cohen, in three months, had become the most successful spy in Israel's history.

In May, Maazi Zahreddin took Taabes on the promised trip to the Golan Heights. It was a heartrending experience for a Jew whose longing for Israel was overwhelming. From the mountains he looked down on his homeland, the sparkling Sea of Galilee, the industrious kibbutzim, the trim farming cooperatives on which the farmers tilled the fertile soil of northern Israel.

But, first things first. Taabes focused his attention on the military emplacements. He was alarmed and surprised to see at least eighty Russian-made 122-millimeter mortars capable of raining their deadly fire on more than a hundred square miles of the upper Galilee plain. After an extended tour he and Maazi stopped in a coffeehouse in Kursi, close to the Sea of Galilee. They fell into conversation with an old man. He insisted, even over Maazi's objections, that the Syrians had taken a beating at Nukeib.

"What's the use of it all?" the old man said.

Cohen felt the same way, although he argued just the opposite. That night he sent a long message to Israel, describing in detail the military layout of the Golan Heights.

After six successful months in Damascus, Cohen was ordered home. To the Syrians, Taabes was going to Europe to expand his sales of Syrian furniture and art, and in fact he did just that with the help of Salinger. He then returned to Israel for a tearful reunion with Nadia and his little daughter, Sophie. The final stop was for a briefing from his intelligence superior, Yitzhak.

Yitzhak explained that the government of Israel was especially concerned about Syrian designs on the Israeli project to carry water via pipeline and aqueduct from Galilee to the Negev in the south. There were indications that the Syrians would attempt to divert the sources of the Jordan above Galilee so that the sea would be deprived of its inlet, even though this would be a violation of international law.

"Your most urgent task is to get any information you can on this plan," Yitzhak told Cohen. The spy also learned a new cipher, dissuaded Yitzhak from orders that he move his transmitter from the ceiling as too vulnerable a location (Cohen considered it ideal), and was provided with a new transmitter in case the existing one should fail.

Back in Damascus in July 1962, Taabes continued to widen his circle of acquaintances among prominent Syrians. One of these was George Seif, who, at thirty-two, was the bright young man of the Syrian Ministry of Propaganda and Information, head of the radio and press section. Seif proved to be an invaluable contact. For one thing, through Seif, Taabes was reintroduced to his old friend from Buenos Aires, General Hafez, the former military

attaché in Argentina who was back home and working hard for the success of the Ba'ath party. The general immediately took Taabes into his inner circle of confidants. "Let my home be yours," Hafez told Taabes.

Seif became Taabes's closest friend. Almost casually he informed the Israeli spy that a Syrian delegation had visited the Soviet Union to ask for help in the project to divert the Jordan headwaters. Moscow, it seems, was interested but had offered nothing concrete. This bit of information was quickly in the hands of the Israelis.

Through Seif and other new acquaintances, Taabes found himself involved in a hilarious sideshow, reminiscent of the famous movie *The Apartment*. That comedy concerned an underling in a large corporate headquarters who was more or less obliged to make his apartment available to his bosses for their illicit escapades. Taabes found himself precisely in that role, turning over his flat to various top-ranking officers whom he had met through Seif. They brought along their girl friends, secure in the knowledge that in Taabes's apartment, their wives would never find them out. But they also talked shop. Colonel Salim Hatoum was one of the regular visitors who came for the purpose of some amorous divertissement, but with a few drinks (provided by Taabes, who carefully remained sober) he often spoke his mind. He was contemptuous of the civil authorities for their timidity before Israel. Then, to prove his point, he detailed in precise terms exactly the strength of every branch of the Syrian armed forces. Taabes did not miss a word.

Later, following precisely the plot of *The Apartment*, Taabes, aware of the obligation he was imposing on Seif and Hatoum, made the flat available to them when he was not present. Hatoum was so off his guard that in February 1963 he advised his friend Taabes of an impending coup d'etat.

When this event occurred on March 8, Hatoum was one of the prime movers. The Syrian shock troops that he commanded made the assault on the army command headquarters right under Taabes's window and took control of the Damascus radio station. Within hours Hatoum was on the phone to Taabes. He wanted to borrow the apartment for a victory celebration with a Turkish girl friend. Furthermore, he told Taabes, the military leaders had entrusted the country's future to the Ba'ath party. This meant that General Hafez was near the pinnacle of power.

The general was appointed minister of the interior. His responsibilities included counterespionage—that is, tracking down spies in Syria. Taabes sent him a bouquet of flowers and wished him well.

The take-over by the new Ba'ath-dominated government cost Taabes one contact, General Zahreddin. As army chief of staff, he had generally been above politics, but he was not acceptable to the Ba'ath leaders. His nephew, Maazi, however, remained Taabes's close friend, along with George Seif, and the flow of information continued. Sometimes it seemed as if the Israeli spy were a magnet for vital intelligence.

The extent of Elie Cohen's knowledge of Syrian military affairs is best illustrated by an anecdote related by Ben Dan in *The Spy from Israel*. The Israelis had observed four MIG-19 fighter planes that regularly patrolled and overflew Israel along the Golan border. One day the flights stopped. The

Israelis queried Cohen as to whether this was a policy change. He was immediately able to transmit the whole story: "Four MIG-19s based Damascus International Airport grounded. One pilot was removed for political deviation. Second pilot ill. Third pilot injured in car accident."

In other words, it was the coincidental loss of three or four pilots that put an end to the sorties, not a high-level change in strategy or tactics. That Cohen should know these details is an astounding example of the exhaustiveness with which a brilliant agent pursued his task.

The best was yet to come. Taabes's friend George Seif, whose stature had risen under a new minister of information and culture, Sami el-Jundi, came up with a startling idea. He invited Taabes to broadcast a regular five-minute commentary to Syrians abroad, particularly in South America. In addition to the obvious purpose of building sympathy for the new Ba'ath regime among Syrians overseas, the proposed program had a secondary purpose—the raising of money. The Ba'ath leadership was critically short of funds. A former South American resident, like Taabes, was deemed especially qualified to call on his former compatriots for financial assistance.

The timing—the summer of 1963—was propitious because Taabes had told his friends that he was going to visit Europe and South America to seek new outlets for his export business. He could also, he suggested, try to raise funds for the Ba'ath party. His real destination, however, was Israel, for a briefing session and a visit with his family.

There was one final development that capped the ascendancy of Elie Cohen as Kamal Amin Taabes. His old friend General Hafez rose to be the kingpin of the Ba'ath regime and assumed the titles president of the National Council of the Revolutionary Command, military governor, commander in chief, and president of the Ba'ath. When Cohen wrote to Hafez to congratulate him, the spy was promptly invited to an official reception, where he was photographed shaking hands with Syria's new strong man.

Early in August he set out on his trip, leaving keys to his apartment for the benefit of George Seif, Colonel Hatoum, and a Colonel Dalli, a friend of Hatoum. He was not worried about their finding the transmitter. They were interested only in the bed.

Elie Cohen arrived back in Israel shortly after the arrival of his second child, another daughter, which, despite his longing for a son, he accepted with great celebration. (His leaves, it seemed, were ideally spaced for conception.)

With considerable reservations from his Mossad superiors, Cohen was allowed to accept the offer to be a propaganda broadcaster for Damascus radio. Yitzhak was afraid his prominence might provoke a more exhaustive investigation of his background, exposing the fabrications that formed the cover story. Elie was more sanguine; he felt his position in Syria was sufficiently secure and that the broadcasts represented a special opportunity for inserting specific words that would convey information to the Israelis, who would monitor the commentaries. Reluctantly, Mossad went along with the idea.

For no particular reason except that he had told his friends in Syria as much, Cohen had to go to Buenos Aires. One of his first visits there was to

the elder Alheshan, the editor, whose son had written that Taabes would soon be in Argentina. Taabes gave two parties and raised a modest sum of money for the Ba'ath organization—only $9,000 but enough to confirm his stated intentions before he left Syria. He then contributed $1,000 of his own (actually from the taxpayers of Israel) and purchased a $1,000 mink coat for the wife of General Hafez.

Cohen returned to Syria charged by his Israeli superiors with learning as much as possible about Syrian plans to divert water from the Baniyas River, which fed into the Jordan, which in turn fed into the Sea of Galilee. Cohen was able, through Colonel Hatoum, to meet the engineers for the project and learned that the Syrians planned to build a canal from the Baniyas to the Yarmuk River, thus depriving the Jordan of most of its flow. Through their man in Damascus, the Israelis soon knew every detail of the plans.

Directly affecting Israel's efforts to protect its water supply was the Syrian decision to recruit terrorist-commando units to strike at the Galilee-Negev irrigation systems, among other things. Ben Dar points out that in March 1964 Hatoum actually showed his friend Taabes a plan of the irrigation network and carefully pointed out every location where facilities would be blown up by the terrorists. Obviously, thanks to Cohen, the Israelis were ready. Every attempt of the saboteurs failed.

Ben Dar notes that on three separate occasions between February and October 1964, Cohen was escorted by Maazi Zahreddin to the Golan Heights to observe the fortifications. What was perhaps most distressing was that the building of fortifications was largely under the direction of technicians from the Soviet Union and that the weapons were almost entirely Soviet-made. Soviet tanks had been delivered by the hundreds, along with MIG-21 fighter planes. Cohen also got detailed descriptions of the Syrian plans to cut off the northern part of the Galilee region in the event of hostilities.

In November 1964, Elie Cohen went home to Israel again by the usual circuitous route and, like clockwork, arrived after the birth of his third child. This time, at last, it was a boy. The parents named him Shaul. Elie was beside himself with happiness. Only toward the end of his three-week visit did he seem nervous and depressed. He told Nadia this would be his last trip abroad. Sadly, he was right.

In late November there was another skirmish on the Golan Heights after the Syrians had again opened fire on the Israeli kibbutzim. As usual, the Syrian forces, even with their new Russian armaments, were routed. Cohen's information had obviously helped to bring this about.

Despite their continuous fear of Syrian attack, the Israelis had developed a certain contempt for their perennial enemy. It had long been the custom of the Israelis to plant eucalyptus trees along many roads to shield the movement of military units. In 1977 a veteran of the Syrian front during that period told the authors that the Syrians decided to disguise their Golan emplacements in the same way—by surrounding them with trees—but that the Syrians had missed the point completely. "How did you knock out the Syrian emplacements so quickly?" the authors asked him. "It was easy," he laughed. "We just blasted every cluster of eucalyptus trees." The Syrians, of

course, were not really stupid, although it helped the morale of the Israelis to imagine they were.

By January the close friendship of Taabes and the Ba'ath President Hafez was such that Taabes's friends hinted he was due for a cabinet appointment. A few weeks earlier Hafez had entrusted Taabes with an important mission—to visit the former president of Syria, Sallah el-Bitar, who was in exile in Jericho. The Ba'ath regime wanted to get Bitar's support to give it the face of legitimacy. Taabes did not succeed, but he and the former president parted friends.

What Taabes did not realize was that Hafez was becoming increasingly angry at the way the innermost secrets of his government were somehow being revealed in Israel.

Early on the morning of January 21, 1965, Elie Cohen was sending a transmission to Tel Aviv advising that Hafez was planning an expanded Palestinian Commando Brigade for sabotage in Israel. He had just completed the transmission and was waiting for confirmation. The transmitter was still in his hand when, without warning, his door was smashed open. There stood Colonel Ahmed Sweidani, chief of intelligence and counterespionage.

"Caught in the act, you damned spy."

Cohen was arrested in Syria just one month before Lotz was seized in Egypt. By the time each of them was caught, his work was largely completed. Each had supplied a prodigious amount of detailed information to his government. The agonies that they had to endure came when they ended their work.

For the remainder of the day of his capture, Cohen was neither tortured nor even pressured. His apartment was searched, and additional evidence of his espionage activities was turned up—the second transmitter, films he had taken on the Golan Heights, his correspondence with Salinger.

In the evening Colonel Sweidani ordered Cohen to transmit a false message to Tel Aviv, to the effect that the Syrian army was on full alert. When the message was received by the Israelis, it plunged the headquarters into gloom. Cohen had spelled the third word correctly.

There was another twist in the cases of both Cohen and Lotz. The Syrians first assumed that Cohen was not a Jew but a Syrian traitor, a tribute to the effectiveness of his skill in sustaining a consistent mastery of language and mannerisms and his complex cover story. Likewise, the Egyptians, to the end, accepted Lotz's claim that he was not a Jew, but a former German officer working for Israel. Were it not for the painful fact of Lotz's long prison term, the situation could be called ludicrous. In the midst of Lotz's trial the prosecution produced a German weekly magazine, *Der Stern*, that had investigated his background and published an accurate account of his life—revealing that he was not a former German officer but a Jew who had lived in Palestine since 1933 and that he had served with the British army and the Israeli army.

Confronted with the truth, the Egyptian military court, incredibly, chose

to reject it and to believe the defendant's own story. Why the Egyptians acted in such an unlikely manner is a question only for speculation. Two possible explanations are suggested by Lotz himself in his biography. One is that the Egyptian intelligence chiefs could not suffer the humiliation of admitting they had been outwitted by an Israeli. Such an admission could have caused numerous heads to roll (although some were rolling already) and possibly even threatened the Nasser regime. The only public scapegoat was the hapless General Ghorab, who was arrested and imprisoned. The other victims of Lotz's skill suffered their punishments in secret. The second possibility is that, according to Lotz, relations with West Germany were strained (partly under growing pressure from the Soviet Union and East Germany) and the Egyptians found it in their interest to produce a reason for widening the breach. And the fact that Lotz was not circumcised helped to sustain their self-deception.

The large number of German technical experts residing in Egypt to build sophisticated military missiles and aircraft had long been a source of alarm to Israel. Some were threatened, and a few were killed by explosive envelopes mailed by Israeli agents. Among the ten charges against Lotz were six accusing him of various forms of espionage. To all of these he pleaded guilty. To the four charges involving the threats and letter-bombs, he pleaded innocent. In his own account of his work, he insists he was not involved in violence, as his not-guilty plea indicated. In other accounts of Lotz's work, such as the recent book *The Plumbat Affair* by Elaine Davenport, Paul Eddy and Peter Gillman, he is alleged to have participated in the violent anti-German campaign in Egypt.

Even Lotz was surprised when he was not sentenced to death but to life imprisonment. Waltraud was found not guilty of espionage and sabotage but guilty of a minor charge of abetting her husband. She was sentenced to three years.

One common denominator in the relentless and often ruthless interrogation of Lotz and Cohen was the insistence in both cases that each name his accomplices. Neither the Egyptians nor the Syrians could believe that so much espionage could have been accomplished by one man working alone. In neither case were there any accomplices, unless, by stretching the term, Waltraud Lotz could have been considered an accomplice of her husband.

Both, as far as can be determined, were eventually uncovered through interception of their radio transmissions. Both perhaps became casual and even careless as they piled success upon success. Cohen, at one point, is believed to have sent a transmission when there was a power failure in Damascus. His battery-powered signal must have attracted attention in a city where almost all other transmissions depended on the local electric power service.

As Lotz had humiliated counterintelligence in Egypt, Cohen had made fools of the Syrian authorities right to the top. Syrian indignation ran especially high because Kamel Amin Taabes had been so effective in deceiving them. He had played the role of a loyal Syrian patriot with unbelievable finesse. Consequently, when he was exposed and arrested, Syrian wrath

knew no bounds and Cohen was brutally tortured. Electric shocks were administered to his face and his genital organs. His nails were pulled out one by one. But he never broke. Meanwhile his Syrian friends, Sheikh Majd el-Ard, George Seif, and Maazi Zahreddin were arrested. Colonel Hatoum had made sure of this—they knew too much about the colonel's borrowing of Taabes's apartment.

Despite his phenomenal ability as a spy, there was something about the gentleness in Cohen's character, the sincerity of his family life, and his sheer courage in his lonely task that touched the conscience of the world. Pleas to spare his life came from Pope Paul VI, John Diefenbaker, the former prime minister of Canada; Antoine Pinay and Edgar Faure, both former French premiers; Queen Elizabeth of the Belgians; Cardinal Felcius of Buenos Aires, and the International Red Cross. Former Belgian premier Camille Huysmans offered to go to Damascus to plead with President Hafez for Cohen's life.

Considering, however, that Syrians often executed spies, that Cohen had been so devastatingly successful, that Cohen had embarrassed and humiliated the president of Syria, and that the special military court included colonels Dalli and Hatoum (the latter hiding his own dark secrets about his relationship with Cohen), the outcome was certain. He was sentenced to death and was hanged in Martyrs' Square in Damascus, on May 19, 1965.

Lotz was released in a prisoner exchange with Israel in January 1968. He and Waltraud had endured a harrowing three years in separate prisons. They returned to Israel and an extravagant welcome. Waltraud's health, however, had been severely undermined by her long imprisonment, and she died in 1971.

On June 5, 1967, Israel, anticipating attacks from Egypt and Syria, launched a preemptive strike by land and air against both countries. Within the first ninety minutes, more than half of the Egyptian air force had been destroyed on the ground by cannon-firing Israeli fighter planes. Gun emplacements on the Golan Heights were bombed into rubble. The Israelis won a total victory in just six days. Most of the credit must go to the superb intelligence that had pinpointed almost every major Egyptian and Syrian military installation. A large part of this information was gathered only because of the courage of the imprisoned Lotz and the martyred Cohen. Seldom had one nation owed so much to two men.

13

The Missile Boats that Vanished in the Night

BY THE EARLY 1960s Israel's defense planners had begun to project a navy built around a nucleus of small, fast missile boats. So thorough was the commitment to this strategy that any interference in its realization was viewed as a threat to the state's survival. And yet interference was precisely the course chosen by France's Charles de Gaulle.

The Cherbourg shipyard of French industrial tycoon Felix Amiot was, in 1967, building twelve missile boats under a contract with the State of Israel. But the fast friendship between Israel and France that had existed in 1956, when they had a common foe, Egypt, had gradually soured in the ensuing years. As might be expected, the pressure of oil politics played its part. The Arabs did not take kindly to France's supplying arms to Israel, and de Gaulle seemed increasingly concerned about the alienation of the oil states. The blitzkrieg victory of Israel in the Six-Day War of June 1967 ended the once close association between the Jewish state and its principal arms supplier. Immediately after the war an angry de Gaulle imposed a total embargo on arms shipments to the Israelis. The missile boats, however, were excepted because they were being constructed under a binding contract, and work on them was allowed to continue.

By December 1968 five of the boats had been delivered to their home base in Haifa. Then, on December 28, an Israeli commando unit staged a lightning raid on the airport in Beirut, retaliating for the Arab destruction of an El-Al plane at the Athens airport. The commandos destroyed thirteen planes, mainly Arab-owned but two of them French. There were no human casualties, not even a minor injury.

This was too much for the imperious de Gaulle, who was trying to mend

225

his relationship with the Arab states. He extended the arms embargo to cover all shipments to Israel, even shipments fulfilling existing contracts. This included the seven remaining missile boats, which would be the backbone of the Israeli navy. Given de Gaulle's stubbornness and the determination of Israel to acquire the boats, the situation was somewhat akin to the immovable object and the irresistible force.

While France presumably had the right to sell or not to sell arms to whomever it pleased, the missile boats in many ways presented a unique situation. The very fact that they were under construction in France was happenstance. Originally, they were to have been built in Kiel, Germany, to a design of the famous Lurssen naval architectural organization. The engines, likewise, were of German design. The original agreement had been made by Chancellor Konrad Adenauer and Ben-Gurion and had been secretly arranged, for Germany, too, was fearful of offending Arab oil states. Although the agreements had been negotiated in 1962, actual construction had not been started when a *New York Times* story made known the contract in December 1964. Adenauer was said to have been personally sympathetic to the Israelis, but Arab fury and the political realities forced him to halt the project in Germany. Since France was the chief supplier of arms for Israel, a move to a French yard was politically feasible.

Felix Amiot was happy to oblige. He was an industrialist of immense power and prestige who had worked with Lurssen designers before, and his shipyard in Cherbourg was in need of work. The transfer of the project was arranged. Admiral Mordechai Limon, former commander in chief of the Israeli navy, was then living in Paris as chief agent for Israel's European arms procurement. The Israeli government put the responsibility for seeing to the finishing of the boats in his capable hands.

Israel's dependence on missile boats was unique. Because of Israel's geographical and economic situation, the missile boats provided the most defense for the least effort.

As used—and to some extent conceived—by Israel, the missile boat represents a breakthrough in the history of naval warfare. Such was the opinion of Admiral Shlomo Erell, retired commandant of Israeli naval forces. In the early twentieth century, Erell told us, navies were dominated by big ships with big guns. It follows naturally that there would be a corresponding effort devoted to making these behemoths more vulnerable.

"The first breakthrough was the torpedo," he explained. "Suddenly it was realized that a small boat, which was expendable, could carry a lethal weapon capable of killing a battleship. You could, theoretically, throw hundreds of these small boats at a battle fleet.

"The answer to the torpedo boat was the torpedo-boat destroyer. Today, what we call a destroyer was originally called a torpedo-boat destroyer. This was simply a vessel slightly larger than a torpedo boat, with guns. The idea was that the destroyer was not vulnerable: it was too small and too fast to be hit by a torpedo.

"Then it was realized that if this destroyer is a torpedo-boat killer, why shouldn't it carry torpedoes itself? So they put the two into one. These were

the original fleet destroyers. Their mission was to screen and go ahead of the fleet, launch a torpedo attack on the enemy fleet, and defend against torpedo attacks by the enemy destroyers. In World War I, the famous battle of Jutland was a classic example of this kind of warfare. It was this way until the beginning of World War II.

"The destroyer, however, became larger and larger because they added more missions to it—antisubmarine and escort duties. It became so large that the navies went back to PT boats to accomplish what had originally been the destroyer's mission.

"Another revolution involved the appearance of the surface-to-surface missile. Again, this made possible the use of a small boat, expendable but carrying a lethal weapon and theoretically able to destroy a carrier or a cruiser, with a much greater hit probability than the torpedo boat.

"The reaction of most navies was that they wanted a missile-boat destroyer as a match to the missile boat. They started building 150- or 200-ton gunboats, sort of glorified PT boats, too small and too fast to be targets of missiles. They would be both missile boats and missile-boat destroyers.

"This, in a nutshell, is the origin of the concept of the Israeli missile boats. They differ from the Soviet missile boats tremendously. The Soviet boats are not much more than floating missile launchers. They have relatively poor seaworthy qualities, small range of operation, very few weapons, and no electronic equipment other than what is necessary for the missiles themselves. They are equipped with two to four huge missiles with large warheads. They cannot fight anyone; they are directed or guided by shore headquarters. All they have to do is reach their position, launch their missiles, then try to go home, much like the PT boats of World War II."

The boats conceived and built for the Israelis were quite different. "Our boats are much more versatile, more independent, their range of operations is much greater. They can stay at sea for longer periods, they are seaworthy, they can defend themselves from submarines and aircraft, they can fight a surface action with guns or missiles as the situation requires. They have much more independence in the sense of having their own detection and control equipment—very much the same as any large warship. A modern destroyer doesn't have much more."

The firm of Lurssen was first approached in March 1963 and spent two years perfecting the missile-boat design. Concurrently, the Israelis were developing their innovative Gabriel surface-to-surface missile. By developing the boat and its missile simultaneously, the Israelis were able to adapt one to the other in the midst of rapidly advancing weapons technology.

Admiral Erell, in criticizing the French for de Gaulle's later impoundment, repeatedly pointed out that the work was under a privately arranged contract with a private shipyard using a hull of joint German-Israeli design, with German-designed diesel engines. Most important, there were no weapons involved in the Cherbourg contract.

Seemingly assured of a steady delivery of missile boats throughout the middle 1960s, Israel was beginning to hope for superiority over the Mediterranean navies of its enemies, although, as Erell pointed out, the Israeli

advantage would be only qualitative. Hence, every new missile boat had an importance that transcended the usual value of such a relatively small weapons system.

From the mid-1950s, Egypt had begun to accumulate second-line naval vessels from the Soviet Union—Skory-class destroyers, a few submarines, and a few relatively unsophisticated missile boats. Aligned against them were Israel's World War II surplus destroyers and frigates, not a very formidable force in view of the Egyptian buildup.

In the late 1950s the balance began to shift more decisively toward Israel's foes with the arrival of the relatively advanced Soviet Komar and Osa type of missile boats, which were acquired by both Egypt and Syria. The Russians built them by hundreds, and while the boats may have lacked sophistication as independent fighting units, the missiles they carried were the most advanced in the world.

For Israel, it was absolutely essential to develop weapons capable of challenging the proliferating Soviet-built boats. This concern in itself made Israel unique. Most of the countries of the Western world had come to rely on the vast power of the United States Navy for their security. They were not planning elaborate naval defenses of their own. Israel, with its peculiar vulnerability, did not have that option. It was impossible to hide behind a naval defense that envisioned protection across thousands of miles of ocean. Israel's ability to react had to be scaled in terms of minutes or hours, not days or weeks.

When he had been commander in chief, Admiral Erell had discussed the problem of quick response with the naval staffs of Western Europe, but most of them saw the answer in American power. Yet, while they conceded the growing menace of the Russian missile-boat fleet, none saw the possibilities in a unilateral or limited multilateral arrangement to provide the kind of Mediterranean response Israel needed. They put their faith in the North Atlantic Treaty Organization (NATO).

Israel's decision to build its own missile boats was the inevitable outcome of its frustration in seeking help elsewhere. "We had nowhere else to go," Admiral Erell told us.

The arrangement with the Cherbourg shipyard stayed on schedule through 1968, although none of the boats was delivered in time to participate in the Six-Day War of June 1967. The first keel had been laid in late 1965, and the first launching was in April 1967; but this boat was not battle-ready until December of that year. Another was on line in January 1968, and a third, in March. By November, five were commissioned and in use.

That Israeli raid on the Beirut airport in December 1968 had damaged the ego of Charles de Gaulle as well as those thirteen aircraft. The president of France was impetuous as well as powerful. When the total impoundment was ordered, the Israelis were not even officially notified that their boats were trapped in the Cherbourg harbor. There was simply an order from de Gaulle to the Cherbourg customs office: No Israeli missile boats were to be allowed to put out to sea.

As usual, Israeli intelligence was on the job. The information about de

Gaulle's action reached the crews in Cherbourg before the order took effect. The sixth boat left, legally cleared, on December 31. The seventh was made seaworthy as soon as possible. Captain Moshe Tabak, who had been senior officer at the Cherbourg project, took command. Although de Gaulle's impoundment was officially in effect, it had not been implemented. Tabak and a skeleton crew left unmolested on January 1. They had insufficient fuel, and no money to buy any. Tabak's crew joined the sixth boat at Gibraltar, where some fuel was purchased for both. A second stop was made at Palermo, where intelligence operatives were waiting. Fuel and provisions were supplied. The two boats arrived in Haifa on January 9, 1969.

Although Israel was grateful for the arrival of two more boats, the whole balance of her naval power depended on acquiring the remaining five. Seven-twelfths of a missile-boat navy was not enough.

At this point the ire of the French, perhaps of de Gaulle himself, played into the Israelis' hands. The Ministry of Defense at Tel Aviv was informed by French naval authorities that each of the remaining boats would no longer be welcome at the Cherbourg naval berthing facilities once each was completed. Upon launching, the boats were to be berthed at available space along commercial piers. As a result, the boats were forced to make use of an old ferryboat dock. Likewise, the Israeli sailors could no longer live in the naval barracks that had been provided by the French. Forced into civil facilities, the crews and officers found themselves free of the tight military surveillance that was routine in the naval area of Cherbourg.

Admiral Limon was another of those military statesmen who seem to dominate the Israeli armed forces. Born in Poland, his family took him to Palestine when he was eight years old. As a teen-ager, he joined the Pal-Yam, the seagoing version of the land-based Palmach secret strike force. When World War II broke out, Limon joined the British merchant marine. He was on two ships that were torpedoed. By the war's end, although only twenty-one years of age, he was a hardened veteran. His adventures became legendary when he commanded the decrepit refugees' ships that challenged the British blockade of Palestine. Once, when a ship of his under pursuit by a British patrol boat was disabled by a line fouled in its propeller, Limon himself dove under the ship to disentangle the line. In 1950, Limon was made commander in chief of the Israeli navy.

As if he had not yet moved far enough professionally, the restless Limon resigned in 1954 to enroll in Columbia University, where he acquired a master's degree in business administration. His skills in sophisticated warfare and high finance, together with a natural bent toward diplomacy, made him ideally suited for the heavy responsibility placed on him a few years later by his government—as director, supervisor, and broker of arms purchases in Western Europe and the United States.

The embargo was more than enough frustration for Limon; the impoundment of the missile boats was intolerable. He returned to Tel Aviv to discuss the situation with Moshe Dayan, who was then defense minister. They agreed that somehow the boats would be freed, and the Israeli cabinet backed them up.

The result was vintage Israeli. A vast and complex intelligence maneuver was conceived and carried out. The cabinet had ruled out any seizure of the boats by force in some kind of hijacking operation. Instead, a carefully planned deception, if it worked, would enable the boats to be spirited out of the harbor while the French were not looking.

Considering the circumstances, such an operation would seem to be all but impossible. Cherbourg Harbor, one of the busiest in Europe, was under constant surveillance. It was in part man-made, with a two-mile seawall protecting it from the open sea to the north, a project that had begun with Louis XVI in 1776 but had not been completed until the twentieth century. Of the two passages through the wall, the western channel, some sixty feet deep, was the one generally used. The eastern channel, only about fifteen feet deep in some places, was obviously unsuited for any but small craft, and its currents were so treacherous that it was seldom used even by them.

After the departure of the sixth and seventh boats, the construction work continued, but the new boats, finished at the rate of one every two months, were launched only into captivity in the French-guarded harbor. Meanwhile, the Israelis were perfecting their elaborate plan.

Once again, as so often in Jewish history, it was a Christian with a strong sympathy for the Jewish people who became a key figure in a crisis. In the fall of 1969, with only one more boat to be launched, Limon, with guidance from Israeli intelligence, was working on details of the proposed escape. He called on Mila Brenner, president of a huge maritime fruit-shipping company. Brenner was married to the niece of Chaim Weizmann and hence was a man of social, as well as economic, stature. Limon knew that Brenner had an old friend in Norway, Ole Martin Siem, who was also a shipping magnate and was known to be a friend of Israel. One of the Norwegian's interests was the vast North Sea oil-drilling project. Brenner persuaded Siem to seek to purchase the missile boats as small craft for shuttling equipment back and forth to the drilling rigs. The price was $2 million per boat.

Anyone with knowledge of naval architecture would have immediately realized that the missile boats were vastly overpowered, overpriced, and misdesigned for such a mission—were in fact singularly ill-suited for ordinary maneuvering on the stormy waters of the North Sea. Nevertheless, working through a Panamanian company created for the purpose, Siem approached Amiot to make a deal for the five boats. There is good reason to believe that Amiot, with his long experience as a shipbuilder, must have seen through the ruse. But it offered him a means of finishing the ships, getting paid for them, and working himself out of a difficult situation. The French government, advised of Siem's offer, agreed to accept the deal, if Limon would submit a letter to the Foreign Office relinquishing Israeli claims on the boats. Limon quickly complied. Siem's agreement was only to enable Amiot to finish the boats. He did not agree to get involved in getting them away from Cherbourg. That would be up to the Israelis.

Despite the ease of the arrangements for the "sale" of the boats to Norway, the Israelis, including Limon, knew the situation was highly uncertain.

Sooner or later someone would realize there was something irregular in the whole transaction.

Operation Noah's Ark, as the Israelis called it, really got under way when, in early November, seamen began trickling into Cherbourg. Israeli intelligence had played a hand in their selection. There had been skeleton crews for testing the boats since the construction started—about twenty men in all. Now eighty more seamen were needed to provide a total of twenty men per boat.

To continue the ruse, it was preferable that the crewmen at least appear to be Norwegian. Israel was actually able to provide a few blond, blue-eyed Jews. Since it was impossible to provide a full complement of apparent Nordics, the next priority was given to Jews who had lived in the former French North African colonies and whose spoken French was without the accent or nuance of a foreigner.

The prospective crew members arrived, by careful calculation, at different times, by different modes of transportation, and from different directions. Many came with their families, another means of diverting suspicion. None of them knew why they were there, other than to wait for orders. The Israeli authorities knew full well that one loose-tongued sailor could tip off the French and cause the whole project to collapse.

One of the strange aspects of the secrecy was the silence of the Cherbourg newspapers. It is generally believed that they knew what was going on but were also aware that the shipyards were the city's main form of livelihood and that if the secret were exposed, the construction work would be halted and hundreds of the townspeople would be thrown out of work.

In Cherbourg the escape operation was under the direction of Captain Moshe Tabak, who had commanded the seventh boat when it had escaped the previous January, just before the embargo was enforced. He had been stationed at Cherbourg since the construction began as one of the officers charged with testing the boats, and his continued presence therefore did not attract any suspicion.

The eleventh boat slid down the ways in November 1969. That left one to go, but its launching was not scheduled until December 15. The normal time for fitting out a newly launched hull was several months. Every additional day, however, added to the Israelis' fears that the deception, the whole Norwegian flimflam, would be uncovered.

Cherbourg was now crowded with "Norwegian" sailors whose presence was obvious despite their efforts to remain inconspicuous. A few local romances even blossomed between some lonely sailors and the town girls.

In early December, Tabak decided that the ships would attempt to escape on Christmas Eve. This was the latest date he deemed safe. In addition, he assumed that the French, who are inclined to shut down all serious activities for Christmas, would be least alert at that time. Nor would they expect Norwegians—also Christians—to be any less absorbed in the holiday.

The final boat presented a special problem. It was far from finished. And yet it was inconceivable to take it on an ocean trip without the test of a final

shakedown. Its superstructure was not completed, and on December 24 it still would lack radar. Nevertheless, Tabak decided to test it briefly in its unfinished state. On December 20, with Tabak in command, it was taken out. Conditions were far from ideal—there was a dense fog—but any further delay was out of the question. The boat turned out to have a leak in one fuel tank that could have proved disastrous had it not been discovered before the final departure.

The next day, December 21, was a Sunday. Despite the yard's normally being shut down on Sundays, Tabak demanded that the tank be welded immediately. The yard foreman obliged, perhaps ordered to do so by Amiot, the man who almost certainly was aware of the desperate game the Israelis were playing.

The crews were not informed of their mission until less than two days before the departure hour, set for 10 P.M. on December 24. Some of the crews had been out on test runs; the French had permitted this as part of the preparation for the sale of the boats to the Norwegians. Now many seamen had a touchy personal problem. Each had to tell his family (if he had brought one to Cherbourg) that he would be leaving permanently for a trip to an unknown destination on December 24. The Israeli government would see that all dependents were returned to their homelands.

The necessity of stealing out of Cherbourg Harbor was hazardous enough, but getting all the way to Haifa, more than three thousand miles away, presented far greater problems. The boats, cruising at medium speed, had a range of only about fifteen hundred miles, although they did somewhat better at slow speeds. Clandestine refueling would be essential at least twice. There were also unknown dangers. Once the absence of the craft was noticed, would the French seek to intercept them? In the Mediterranean, would the Egyptian navy attack them?

The refueling problem was solved with the help of a freighter of Liberian registry, with a German crew, secretly under the orders of Israeli intelligence. She was the *Scheersberg*, a small vessel but one capable of handling a refueling operation on the high seas. Her captain was given orders to meet the missile boats off Cape Finisterre on Spain's northwest coast, on the morning of December 25. A similar refueling was arranged with small boats off the coast of Sicily for December 27.

As far as the French were concerned, the preparations in Cherbourg Harbor were for the sale to Martin Siem and his Norwegian company. The arrangement having been officially accepted, the French were off their guard. In addition, the boats, having been ordered away from French naval facilities, were subject to far less surveillance at the old ferry pier to which they had been assigned.

December 24 seemed to the crews to arrive too soon. Preparations had been made so quickly, especially for the last two boats, that to leave seemed almost reckless. But it was more reckless to stay; any day, any hour, the flimsy plot could be exposed.

If there was any optimism among the crews, it was dispelled on the morning of December 24 when storm clouds rolled in from the west. By noon a

heavy sea was building beyond the harbor breakwater. In the early afternoon a fine drizzle began to blow in, thickening quickly to a heavy, swirling
rain. The wind began to whip up whitecaps even within the protected harbor. By early evening the wind's force went over forty knots, far beyond gale
force. At 9 P.M. it measured fifty knots. The waves in the open sea were now
mountainous.

Some of the Israelis wondered if God were testing their fortitude. The
Christmas Eve departure time seemed in every way to be ideal in the sense
that it would catch the French off guard. But standing on the open decks of
their boats, the cold rain whipping across their faces, the sailors had little
stomach for departure on such a night of fury.

Tabak sadly accepted the fact that setting forth in such weather would be
a gamble beyond the risk of prudent men. With crestfallen spirits, he
watched the scheduled departure time pass.

For four hours the crews stood by as the boats heaved at their lines in the
choppy harbor. Such weather reports as they could pick up on their radios
offered only the mildest grounds for hope. The height of the storm, according to the forecasters, would pass by at about 2 A.M.

At almost exactly that hour, the wind shifted suddenly from northwest to
southwest. Tabak felt sure this meant a change was coming. At twenty minutes after two the wind velocity dropped dramatically.

"There's still a hell of a sea out there," said Tabak to one of his lieuten-
ants, "but let's go."

Twenty engines—four in every boat—were started. The roar was such
that many of the Israelis feared it would attract the attention of the French
authorities. Tabak had taken the precaution of advising them that the boats
would be leaving from time to time on test runs, which were permitted when
certified as such. A fivefold increase in engine rumble, was, however, a different matter. It seemed impossible that the authorities would not be suspicious.

Perhaps it being the early hours of Christmas morning made the difference, but no one interfered. Tensely, the sailors cast off the lines, one by one,
as the little fleet was bounced around in the turbulent water. The lead boat
was piloted by Ezra Kedem, known as the Shark, a wily seaman who had
piloted the first missile boat on its legal journey to Haifa before the embargo
closed in.

The last boat, although its leaky fuel tank had been repaired, was still
without radar or navigational gear. It simply had to keep up with its fellows,
relying only on visibility and its compass.

As the lines were cast off, the boats, in single file, headed not for the safe,
wide, and deep west passage through the breakwater but the narrow, shallow, and seldom-used east gap. Tabak, Kedem, and the other officers had
agreed that the risk of the east passage was justified by the element of surprise in choosing such a course. No one would have expected any vessels to
use the east passage during a heavy storm, but the highly maneuverable
boats passed their first test.

Once out into the English Channel, the little fleet turned westward, head-

ing for the Atlantic. The crews felt an immense wave of relief when they had made their escape into the open sea, but their adventures were not yet over.

How and when the French discovered the boats were gone is a matter of dispute. Obviously Felix Amiot knew all about it; he was, in fact, on the shore with Mordechai Limon to oversee the operation. But apparently the French government became aware of what had happened through a British newspaperman.*

On December 12, just thirteen days before the great escape, there had been a ceremonial launching of France's second nuclear submarine, *Le Terrible*. Among the reporters present was a French correspondent of the London *Daily Telegraph*. Incidental to his coverage of the submarine story, he noticed the missile boats tied up to the adjacent ferry slip. Returning to Cherbourg on December 26 (perhaps because he had heard rumors of the missile-boat disappearance), he noticed they had, indeed, vanished. As soon as the *Daily Telegraph* ran the story, it was picked up both by the Associated Press and United Press International and was soon all over the world. The French government was an international laughingstock.

Limon, who had driven quickly back to Paris in order to spend the holiday with his family, was plagued with telephone calls. He referred all the reporters to the French Foreign Office. Eisenberg and Landau, in *The Mossad*, describe Foreign Minister Maurice Schumann as telling his staff, "I have been humiliated." President Georges Pompidou, who had succeeded de Gaulle the previous April, was reported to be furious.

The possibility of intercepting the boats was discussed and then dismissed. It would have been difficult as well as of questionable legality. The most serious problem from the French viewpoint was the affair's effect on relations with the Arab countries. Having convinced their present and potential oil suppliers that they were no longer furnishing Israel with arms, the French now appeared to be either dishonest or incredibly inept. Two high officials of the Ministry of Defense were punished.

Meanwhile, the boats had weathered the heavy seas only by dint of excellent seamanship. The pounding and lurching took its toll even among these seasoned sailors and seasickness was rampant.

By noon of Christmas day the seas had quieted somewhat as the little fleet sailed into the Bay of Biscay. On Christmas night some of the crewmen even managed a few hours of restless sleep.

Just as dawn was breaking over the coast of Spain on December 26, the *Scheersberg* hove into sight. It was not a moment too soon. All of the boats were dangerously low on fuel, one of them even down to an hour's supply. Battling the waves had consumed fuel at an exceptional rate.

The boats were first detected as they turned eastward toward Gibraltar.

---

*At least one American newspaper correspondent who was in France at this time believes that the French navy, to the highest levels of authority, and perhaps some members of the French cabinet knew of the escape plan and simply permitted it to be carried out.

French Mirage fighters circled above them but apparently only to keep them in sight.

The boats' only actual danger was unknown to the crews at the time: Nasser of Egypt and Muammar el-Qaddafi of Libya had decided to dispatch a submarine to sink them. Nasser was aware that the boats carried no armor and were practically sitting ducks. Fortunately, the Israelis anticipated this move, for when the submarine emerged from its Egyptian harbor, it encountered a sizable Israeli naval force and prudently decided to return to its base. Russian destroyers also joined in the surveillance of the missile boats in the vicinity of Cyprus but made no effort to interfere with their passage.

Somewhere east of Cyprus, to the joy of the five crews, Israeli jets appeared on the horizon and buzzed the boats in a kind of "welcome home" gesture.

In France, the government had to back, and fill in, its reports to the public. After the first news stories broke, the Foreign Office simply stated that the boats had left for Norway as planned, even though they knew full well that the scheduled delivery to Martin Siem was still many weeks away. When the little fleet was sighted heading for Gibraltar on December 26, Schumann had to concede that the Israelis had pulled off a masterful trick.

Admiral Limon was ordered out of France, ending his seven-year stint as principal procurer of arms for Israel in Europe. Amiot was accused by the press (but not by the government) of involvement in the plot. An immensely powerful man in France's industrial complex and a man through the years who had served his country well, Amiot made no apologies. He had a valid contract to build ships, first for Israel and then for the Norwegian firm. He had abided by the contract, and security was not his problem. In the strictly legal sense, he was right.

Until the boats were safely in Haifa Harbor, the cabinet of Prime Minister Golda Meir offered the same story as the French officials: the boats, so far as was known, were on route to Norway under the command of their "owner."

The triumphal entry into Haifa Harbor was made on December 31, just short of a week after the flight from Cherbourg. The French cabinet's insistence that the boats were headed for Norway had been recognized as a diplomatic lie for several days. Boats heading south from France seldom reach Norway, and the stories of the sightings were printed and broadcast all over the world. Israelis turned out at the Haifa waterfront by the thousands to watch as the five boats, engines throbbing, entered the harbor in the late afternoon sunlight. Defense Minister Moshe Dayan headed the official welcoming party. As the weary crews stepped ashore, Ezra Kedem was called on to speak. His remarks were brief. He asked only that the crew members be allowed to go home and get some sleep.

More than four years later, the missile boats received their baptism of fire in the Yom Kippur War. The Israelis called the boats *sa'ar* (storm) boats. The boats' design and capabilities were advanced, but their principal weapon, the

Gabriel missile, developed in Israel, was unique. On a wartime footing, each carried a crew of six officers and thirty-four sailors.

There were other weapons, of course—two 40-millimeter antiaircraft guns, depth charges, and a variety of conventional light weapons. These were enhanced with highly sophisticated computerized electronic gear for tracking hostile ships and aircraft and for tracking and even disrupting the paths of approaching missiles.

Israel understandably kept the facts about the boats' capabilities as secret as possible. The essential question was how well the sa'ar boats would do against the Soviet-designed Osa and Komar missile boats, with which Egypt and Syria had armed themselves.

The twelve boats built in Cherbourg had constituted the entire Israeli missile-boat armada until 1973, far fewer vessels than the combined Egyptian-Syrian forces had available. In February 1973 the first Israeli-built boat was launched from a shipyard in Haifa, and a second followed a few months later. Israel now had the capability to build its own fleet. Thus, there were fourteen ready for battle on October 6, 1973, when the Yom Kippur War broke out. Several foreign observers called them the "best missile boats in the world." On the first day of the war, the boats proved they were deserving of the praise.

With the Syrians attacking through the Golan Heights and the the Egyptian troops pouring across the Suez Canal into the Sinai, the Israelis assumed that an assault along the Mediterranean coast by the Syrian or Egyptian navy was inevitable. The Israeli missile fleet was given a direct and simple order: Proceed toward the main Syrian port of Latakia and intercept the Syrian Mediterranean fleet—in the harobr, if possible.

The Israelis waited until dark, and then five boats, four of the Cherbourg type and one of the newer home-built versions, headed northward from Haifa. At 10 P.M., they encountered a Syrian destroyer five miles southwest of Latakia. Choosing not to waste the expensive Gabriel missile on the ship, all five boats opened with cannon fire. Apparently taken by surprise, the destroyer was disabled and fled after a few minutes of battle, taking on water rapidly. About ninety minutes later, the quintet of missile boats spotted a Syrian minesweeper accompanied by two Soviet-built Komar-type boats.

This time the Syrians were not surprised, for simultaneously the opposing missile batteries opened fire. Every Gabriel found its mark; none of the Syrian Styx missiles did. All three Syrian ships were sunk. A third Komar approached the scene, but its captain took one look at the havoc wrought by the Gabriels and turned to flee. The vessel was blown up by Israeli cannon flre. In less than two hours, five Syrian warships had been destroyed; the Israeli boats did not have so much as a scratch.

While Israel understandably guards the secrets of its remarkable Gabriel missile and the missile-intercepting capabilities of its sa'ar boats, certain facts are fairly obvious. The Gabriel has a highly sophisticated guidance system that enables the missile to seek out the enemy target. It is fairly certain that the Syrian navy had no comparable weapon.

As to the missile boats' effectiveness in disrupting enemy missile systems,

it is only possible to make an educated guess. Apparently, the Syrian Styx (Russian-designed) missiles are guided by radar, and the Israelis, by interrupting the frequency, can throw them off course. But to do this quickly enough obviously required computer calculations. There seems no other way the Syrian missiles could have completely missed their targets while the Gabriels of the Israelis scored repeated bull's-eyes.

The missile story, however, is not without its human aspects. During the battle with the Syrian boats, the guidance-disruption system of one of the Israeli boats apparently at one point did not function. The Syrian projectile did not change course but headed for its target. Only the quick and courageous reflexes of a sailor—who happened to be the ship's cook—saved the day. Putting down his ladle, he manned his machine gun and blasted the Syrian missile out of the sky, saving not only himself and his mates but the record of the Israelis, who finished the engagement without losing a boat or a man.

Some go so far as to claim that the Gabriel missiles, not the boats, are the real reason for Israel's naval success. The missiles, created by Israel in what may be its supreme indigenous effort, were (after many painful trial and error experiments) so impressive as to become an export industry. Numerous countries purchased the Gabriel and consider it the most effective ship-to-ship missile built in the Western world. But the Gabriel would have been far less effective in a lesser craft than the maneuverable and efficient high-speed boat that served as its platform.

In the eighteen days of the Yom Kippur War, Israel's missile boats sank forty Egyptian and Syrian warships. In doing so, the Israelis made a mockery of their enemies' vow to blockade Israel's Mediterranean ports. Egyptian missile boats venturing out of the port of Damietta were obliterated as soon as they reached the open sea. By controlling the sea-lanes, Israel made it possible for eighty vital supply ships to reach its ports and sustain Israel during the course of the war.

All this was accomplished mainly with fourteen boats, half of them available only because they evaded impoundment in France. This is why, when the question is raised as to how Israel has survived, that brilliantly executed escape from Cherbourg becomes a watershed in the history of the Jewish homeland.

14

Closing in on Terrorists: The Wrath of God

THE WAVE OF TERRORISM that has plagued the world since the late 1960s has stirred both fear and revulsion as well as curiosity as to the nature of terrorists. Attempts to characterize these wanton killers as Marxist ideologues driven by a distorted sense of justice do not, in the last analysis, hold up. In the end, one is forced to the frightening conclusion that many terrorists are simply psychopathic killers dressed in convenient ideological clothing. On the surface it is the bond of radical Marxism that forms the basis of cooperation between Germany's Baader-Meinhof Gang, Italy's Red Brigades, the Japanese Red Army, the Irish Republican Army, and, in the Middle East, the radical faction of the Palestine Liberation Organization (PLO) and the extremist Popular Front for the Liberation of Palestine (PFLP). The conventional Marxist and organized Communist political forces in Western Europe have largely dissociated themselves from the excesses of the terrorists. To a considerable extent, terrorism is motivated by a self-generating cause; that is to say, many kidnappings, hijackings, and extortions are carried out for the sole purpose of forcing the release of terrorists imprisoned for earlier crimes.

Perhaps the ugliest aspect of the whole terrorism picture is the indisputable fact that terrorists are in varying degrees encouraged, financed, supplied, and trained by the Soviet Union. For example, the king of terrorists, Ilich Ramirez Sanchez, better known as Carlos, learned his trade at Patrice Lumumba University in Moscow. Apparently he proved to be too unruly and irresponsible even for the Russians to stomach, but his Moscow tutors must bear a heavy responsibility for the innocents slaughtered by this malevolent Venezuelan.

For reasons that are not always altogether clear, since 1948, and especially since 1967, terrorists have found common cause in their hatred for the State of Israel. That Palestinians should make a target of the Jewish state because they have been wrenched (they believe) from their own territory is not surprising, and to a large segment of world opinion, their incursions are morally justified. That they should find emotional and actual support from the worldwide terrorist club is a situation that evolves from a complex set of circumstances. Israel is a capitalist parliamentary democracy of the Western pattern and thus inimical to the Marxist philosophy. But this seems scarcely sufficient reason for the passionate crusade against Israel and Zionists everywhere on the part of transnational and international terrorists. The implacable hatred of the Jews by the terrorists is instilled mainly by the Soviet Union. The Soviets have their own, nonideological reasons for encouraging ideological terrorism. Their concern is primarily economic and military. They want control of the Middle East, and Israel stands firm as a bastion of Western democratic influence and the staunchest ally of the United States, the ultimate adversary of the Soviet. Israel flanks the crossroads of three continents, a base from which to thwart Soviet military designs in this coveted part of the world.

To a great extent, terrorism against Israel, as against the nations of Western Europe, is the result of political and military frustration. In Europe, Communists have met persistent defeat at the ballot box. In Israel the Arabs have been four times defeated on the battlefields of Palestine. The European ultraradicals and the sullen, discouraged Palestinians had to try to win by stealth what they could not win by conventional political or military means.

The number of actual terrorists is relatively small—perhaps three thousand in all of Western Europe and about the same number in the states surrounding Israel, although the line between terrorist and Palestinian guerrilla is not sharply drawn. The goal of the terrorist is best defined by the word *destabilization*. By frightening innocent people in their daily lives, by kidnaping important political leaders or industrialists, by hijacking airliners, the terrorists hope to put such a burden on the normal functioning of society that it will begin to crumble in fear and turmoil. Governments will thus be destabilized, and—the terrorists hope—the ensuing turmoil will result in social collapse and a take-over by radicals.

Israel is a special case and especially vulnerable. In 1948, when the surrounding Arab nations assumed they would be able to smash the newly founded state by conventional military means, terrorism was not a central part of the Arabs' strategy. But by late 1948, like the Canaanites before Joshua, the enemies of Israel seemed powerless and demoralized. Again, in 1956, the Arab states watched Israeli forces sweep across the Sinai almost at will, to be turned back only by the political intercession of the United States and the Soviet Union through the United Nations. In 1967, with the benefit of accumulated Soviet arms and years of preparation, Arab hopes were high and Palestinians foresaw a return to their homeland. Instead, with a light-

ning preemptive strike, the Israelis won the most decisive victory of all, a triumph that owed most of its success to astoundingly accurate military intelligence.

The humiliation of the Arabs in the Six-Day War created a bitter mixture of despair and determination among the Palestinians. Dreams of victory on the battlefield gave way to a tactic of necessity—warfare by stealth. And such is the nature of the terrorism that the cauldron of hate in Palestine produced a brew that appealed to radicals, anarchists, nihilists, and psychopaths in many countries. The Soviet Union was quick to exploit the movement on a worldwide basis.

In October 1977 we interviewed the late Amihai Paglin, the chief adviser on terrorism to Prime Minister Menachem Begin. There was no doubt in his mind that the Soviets were committed to the support of international terrorism, including conducting training in Russia and elsewhere. Further, they were masterminding terrorist operations in the Middle East, Western Europe, and Latin America.

"It would be unrealistic," Paglin told us, "to assume that the Russians would train, fund, and supply arms to any group without knowing what use would be made of their training and equipment. Israeli intelligence has evidence that the Soviets are operating at least four terrorist or, if you prefer, guerrilla, training camps in Russia. At these camps near Odessa, Baku, Simferopol, and Tashkent, the 'students' are taught the use of small arms, explosives, and sophisticated technology in the art of terrorism."

In confirmation of Paglin's statement, the authors acquired from another source a "diploma" issued to a Palestinian, dated April 13, 1976, on which the Soviet Union credits the student with completion of an advanced course in military tactics, qualifying him as a staff officer. The student received his training at a base in the North Schwerin region of East Germany. Similar training facilities under Soviet control are in Cuba, South Yemen, North Korea, and Bulgaria.

We also interviewed a high official in Israeli military intelligence (we shall call him Colonel Gabi, although that is not his real name) involved with both internal and external terrorism. His records list twelve hundred terrorist acts within Israel in the years from 1965 to 1977.

The terrorists assaulting Israel—in fact, terrorists everywhere—fall into two main categories. International terrorists are those involved in many countries but under the direction and control of the state; this would include those agents under direct orders from the Soviet Union's KGB or those under control of various Arab states. Transnational terrorists are those who operate through independent organizations beyond the control of any government, although often with the sanction of existing states such as Iraq, Syria, Libya, and probably the Soviet Union. These organizations would include the Baader-Meinhof Gang, the Japanese Red Army, and the Red Brigades. Although most of the members of these groups are, respectively, German, Japanese, and Italian, they are outlaws in their own countries as well as in most of the world.

According to Colonel Gabi, Israel maintains a vast computerized dossier

on nearly two thousand terrorists of both the transnational and international type. The information contains biographies, descriptions, aliases, and the *modus operandi* of each terrorist. The information is gathered in conventional ways, but persistence yields a vast store of knowledge. One of the chief sources of information is exhaustive interviewing of every terrorist taken prisoner. There is an art in conducting such interviews, because many facts are gleaned from the combining of presumably inconsequential bits of information—such as pleasantries and asides that in themselves seem of no importance but, when assembled, like a jigsaw puzzle, reveal an important fact. This kind of interview—for example, asking a prisoner about his wife and children–often catches the subject off guard, and he reveals some snippet of information that forms part of a larger picture.

Paid informers, double-agents, and other agents of espionage and counter-espionage provide a great deal of information to the Israeli intelligence service. As a result of secret penetration into the ranks of terrorists, plus the exhaustive gleaning of information from prisoners, Colonel Gabi estimates that at least 20 percent of the incursions against Israel have been anticipated and aborted before they could be carried out.

According to other Israeli sources, the most active group of external terrorists attacking Israel are members of Dr. George Habash's PFLP. Its training camp in South Yemen is staffed by Soviet officers, and the military equipment is supplied by the Kremlin. The "students" include not only Arabs but Europeans, many of them dissidents from aristocratic families. Habash, a Marxist and a Christian Arab, specializes in the hijacking of civilian airlines and in the taking of hostages.

Colonel Gabi laughs sardonically at those who are convinced that the "moderate" PLO is somehow more moderate than Habash's PFLP. He points out that Yasser Arafat's PLO was responsible for the massacre of the Israeli athletes at the Munich Olympic Games. The Soviet Union supplies arms to the PLO, and the PLO's own spokesmen do not deny this. Zehdi Terzi, the PLO observer at the United Nations, has admitted this on American television. They do not admit, however, that the Soviet Union also supplies sophisticated training for PLO terrorists. Agents of the PLO conducted the bloodiest terrorist raid in Israel's history on March 11, 1978. Eleven of them equipped with Soviet-made arms landed on the Mediterranean coast below Haifa. First they killed a woman photographer who, thinking they were travelers, was kind enough to give them directions. They then commandeered a bus loaded with Israelis. When Israeli army units arrived, the ensuing shootout left thirty-five Israelis and nine terrorists dead.

The terrorist trail consistently leads back to the Soviet Union. Both Israeli and American sources agree that this involvement goes back to the late 1960s. That apparently was when the Soviets began systematically to fund, train, and supply arms to a multinational group of terrorists. In addition to the training in terrorist tactics, the Soviets indoctrinate the "students" in the science of dialectical materialism, which is presented as a philosophical undergirding of movements for "national liberation." The exploitation of the masses by the capitalist powers is cited as an intolerable condition that

must not be allowed to continue. And, the trainee is told, since the exploiters maintain their control by force, they can only be deposed by the use of counterforce.

Until the Soviet Union became actively involved in sponsoring terrorism, such tactics did not fit into the conventional Marxist doctrine. As early as 1873 Karl Marx expressed his disagreement with anarchists in their employment of random violence. Terror for terror's sake, he wrote, was not in the interest of the working class. Later, in Czarist Russia, Lenin approved of some of the anarchists' revolutionary aims but deplored their tactics. He continued to criticize what he considered to be acts of senseless violence. After the revolution, the theory evolved that terrorism should not be employed unless it served a politically useful function. After the Israeli victory in the Six-Day War in 1967, the Soviets apparently felt that Marx's reservations about terrorism no longer applied.

There was, as might be expected, a cynical self-interest in this change in direction. The PLO's interests were easily exploitable as a means toward Soviet economic control of the Middle East. By this time the Kremlin was aware that sometime in the 1980s it would no longer be able to subsist on its own oil and would be forced to import large quantities from the oil fields now controlled by Arabs and Iranians.

This economic motive, with Marxism as its facade, was almost certainly behind the decision to underwrite international terrorism and especially the liberation campaign of the Palestinians. Terror directed against Israel fit well into this strategy. This dictated the semicovert alliance with Yasser Arafat's PLO and Habash's PFLP. The intention was to so harass Israel that its society and its government would crumble and ultimately collapse. According to American intelligence sources, this has become an actual goal of the Chief Intelligence Directorate (known by its Russian acronym, GRU) of the Soviet General Staff.

The Soviet Politburo understands that any direct military attack on the oil fields of the Arab states would probably precipitate a Western military response. On the other hand, a revolutionary movement that had as one of its aims the expulsion of Western imperialism from the Middle East could expect support from the Soviet Union.

For the Soviets, however, the future is not so simple as the mere overthrow of the West. The Soviet Union is still dependent on the West despite its long-term goal of expunging capitalism from the world. With the exception of their armaments industry, the technology of the Soviets is second rate when compared to capitalist achievement. Know-how can be purchased, but it must be paid for with convertible currency. The Soviets lack funds for these imports and have thus resorted to massive loans from the West. Their burden of indebtedness to the West is growing. This is one of the reasons the goal of overthrowing capitalism has been put on the back burner.

On the front burner is the new stewpot of destabilization by terrorism. The new hope is that violence will trigger states to resort to counterviolence and the resulting oppression will turn the worker against "the system."

The switch to a policy of supporting terrorism must have involved a

searching of conscience among the members of the Soviet Politburo. Acts of violence against unarmed citizens of foreign countries were not part of their historical experience. There was not such compunction, however, when the victim was a Soviet traitor (or someone viewed as such) living abroad. The assassination of Leon Trotsky in Mexico by Ramon Mercader, an agent of the NKVD, is an example of the flexibility of Communist morality on this issue.

It may be that this moral dilemma was resolved by a decision to train a multinational group of idealistic, semiautonomous free-lance terrorists. The groups would cooperate and assist each other in their struggle against conservative or reactionary governments but would avoid, as far as possible, contact with the KGB or the GRU. Public knowledge of this relationship would not enhance the Soviets' image in civilized society.

In the summer of 1968, the intelligence service in Cuba, Direction General de Inteligencia (DGI), which operates a training camp near Havana, was placed under the supervision of Soviet Colonel Victor Simonov, who is probably a member of the GRU.

Part of the story of cooperation between Cuban and Soviet intelligence services was revealed by Jeraldo Perazo Amerchazurra, a Cuban intelligence agent who defected to the West in December 1971. He confirmed that the DGI was completely subservient to the KGB.

The intricate network of terrorism is best understood through its most successful practitioners. Since the late 1960s two terrorists have become legendary through the daring, success, and ruthlessness of their activities. Following are the stories of Ali Hassan Salameh, known as the Red Prince, and Ilich Ramirez Sanchez, known as Carlos. They present a strong contrast in motivation. Salameh seems to have been destined for terrorism by heritage. Carlos, in contrast, is the degenerate son of a rich dilettante Marxist and seems to have ventured into terrorism more for the satisfaction of some obscure bloodlust than for ideology.

Sheikh Salameh, the father of Ali Hassan Salameh, was a trusted follower of the notorious Grand Mufti of Jerusalem, Haj Amin el-Husseini. In the uprisings from 1936 to 1939, the elder Salameh was a Palestinian Arab leader, fighting in the name of the Grand Mufti. The incursions against the Jewish settlements demanded the full mobilization of every Arab, as the Grand Mufti saw it. Arabs who showed the slightest sign of hesitancy, of willingness to compromise with the Jews, were murdered.

With the outbreak of World War II, the Grand Mufti threw his lot in with the Nazis, hoping that the German armies could drive the British out of the Middle East. In the early 1940s, Sheikh Salameh joined the Germans and anti-British Arabs in attempting to push British forces out of Iraq. When the British prevailed, Salameh and his cohorts were rescued by the Germans and flown to Berlin.

In October 1944 the Germans parachuted Ali Hassan's father into Palestine so that he could organize terrorist opposition against British army outposts and Jewish settlements. He was moderately successful in harassing his enemies and eluded British efforts to capture him. It was not until four

years later, in 1948, that Salameh was killed when Haganah agents planted a bomb at his headquarters at Ramla.

His widow and their five-year-old son, Ali Hassan, fled from Ramla to the town of Nablus on the West Bank, then under Jordanian occupation. The area was overflowing with refugees, but the widow of Sheikh Salameh and her son were given special care.

During his miserable existence as a refugee, young Ali Hassan listened to the tales of his father's exploits over and over. The other refugees instilled in him the compulsion to avenge his father's death. An honorable man, he was told, believes in *gom*, Arabic for "blood revenge." His hatred of the Israelis was fueled by their very success in turning the desert into productive fields while his fellow Arabs lived in misery.

Revenge became an obsession as Salameh grew toward manhood. He was anxious to join the holy war against the Zionists. In the mid-1960s, when he was about seventeen, his opportunity arrived with a PLO officer who came seeking recruits for Yasser Arafat's guerrillas and terrorists. The son of Sheikh Salameh, the martyred Palestinian, was welcomed into the ranks. Arafat sent his new protégé to Egypt, where Salameh was trained in the arts of underground warfare, terror, and survival.

The education of a terrorist includes sustaining an outward appearance of respectability. Salameh had been an excellent student in secondary school, graduating with honors. After his secret training in Egypt he was awarded a full scholarship to the engineering school at the American University in Beirut.

While he was in Beirut, he met a young woman who had the credentials to seal an excellent marriage. She was Nashrawan Sherif, granddaughter of the idol of Salameh's father, the Grand Mufti. She was wealthy and intelligent. When she met Salameh, she was studying for a degree in French literature. Their union added a measure of status to the ambitious Salameh.

Although Arafat's record proves he has no distaste for terrorism, at this time he was building his international reputation as the leader of a "moderate" organization. Arafat, however, had rivals. There was no pretense of moderation in the PFLP of Habash and his military chief and fellow physician, Waddieh Haddad. Their unabashed lust for Israeli blood was more attractive to many young Palestinians than Arafat's moderation, even if such moderation was actually a facade for gaining worldwide acceptance. Arafat had to challenge the growing power of the PFLP by setting up an intelligence-terrorist organization within Al-Fatah, the fighting force of the PLO. Salameh was appointed chief of planning for the new unit of the PLO.

Meanwhile, the ambitious Arafat was attempting to expand his control in two new directions. Sometime in the late 1960s he made contact with the Soviet Union's KGB. As David B. Tinnin reveals in his book *The Hit Team*, the PLO and the KGB had a secret liaison post in Cyprus. The Mossad learned this after it broke the Soviet code. Arafat was meeting with a KGB officer and a GRU representative in the embassy in Nicosia.

Arafat's other new effort was toward the coalescing of the Palestinians of Jordan (where they constitute more than half of the population) into a state within King Hussein's domain. The power of the Palestinians and their expressed hostility toward the king convinced Hussein that they were a menace to the monarchy. In September 1970 he decided to drive their military units out of Jordan. Bedouin troops intensely loyal to Hussein shelled the refugees' camps and the bivouacs of the Palestinians and drove them out of Jordan.

The embittered hard core of the PLO fighters was outraged at this war of Arabs against Arabs. The PLO's terrorist organization now had a name, derived from the month of its defeat—Black September. Salameh was appointed chief of intelligence.

Revenge on King Hussein was Black September's first priority. Shortly after the September massacre, Hussein appointed a new prime minister, Wasfi Tel. To Arafat, the appointment meant that the king was taking a hard line against the Palestinians. While Hussein himself was the ultimate enemy in Jordan, Tel was his faithful servant. As such, the PLO decided he must be liquidated as a first step toward vengeance.

In November, the Arab League was to meet in Cairo. Hussein had at first intended to represent his country but, for reasons he never revealed, decided to send Wasfi Tel in his place. What made Hussein change his mind, other than the obvious awareness of the bitter hatred of Black September? One contention, never substantiated, is that Israeli intelligence had notified Hussein that he would be walking into a trap.

On November 28, 1971, the Arab League held what seemed to be an uneventful luncheon in an uneventful place—the Sheraton Hotel in Cairo. When the meeting drew to an end, Wasfi Tel and his bodyguards walked briskly through the lobby toward Tel's car, waiting just outside. As he approached the main door, two men who had been standing unobtrusively near the door suddenly stepped forward and fired five shots, every one of them striking Wasfi Tel. He died instantly. One of the assailants knelt over his body and lapped up the dead man's blood.

The gunmen were quickly apprehended by the bodyguards and the police. For reasons understandable only to those in the arcanum of Arab politics, the murderers were almost immediately released.

Salameh was hailed by Arafat for the success of his first major terrorist mission. Emboldened by this exploit, Black September planned a series of terrorist exploits, all bold, all ruthless, but not all successful.

The terrorists were aware that in Great Britain, no one is allowed to carry firearms, including bodyguards of embassy personnel. Under these conditions, assailants that do not play by the rules are relatively safe from retribution. Hence, in late December 1971 there was no one prepared to shoot back when, on a busy London street, the car carrying the Jordanian ambassador to Britain was sprayed with machine-gun bullets. Miraculously, not a single bullet struck a human being. The assailant, an Algerian named Frazeh Khelfa, was quickly arrested. He was, however, suspected of terrorist activities in France, and the British were only too glad to let the French

have him. The French, in turn, shipped him to Algeria, where he was supposedly wanted for more serious problems. Apparently, he was not punished.

Salameh, meanwhile, moved to Europe. Black September, under his leadership, had become a large and disciplined organization. Salameh had grown into a handsome and charming young man. In the midst of danger, he loved the sensual life. His life-style was that of a polished and somewhat mysterious gentleman who dined at the most elegant restaurants and took his women to the most luxurious hotels.

In February 1971 this courtly Palestinian and his team blew up oil-storage depots in Rotterdam and Hamburg. Presumably these depots were chosen because the oil in the tanks was Iranian crude that had been shipped through Israel via the Elath-Ashkelon pipeline. In West Germany, Salameh masterminded the bombing of a factory in Bonn that was shipping electric motors to Israel. Near Bonn, five Palestinians were executed, apparently by Salameh's men, for some undetermined failure to carry out orders or some breach of discipline.

As Black September's exploits became more threatening, so did the determination of the Israeli intelligence services to destroy the organization. The Israelis were most successful in intercepting Palestinian terrorist missions on the West Bank. The Black September failures were so frequent that its leadership concluded Israeli counterspies had infiltrated their ranks. By 1977 the Jewish state could claim that better than 20 percent of the terrorist missions were aborted through inside knowledge.

As early as 1972, so many Palestinian prisoners were being held in Israel that the vicious circle of terrorism was under way; that is, one of the principal motives of subsequent terrorist activities was to extort the release of those who had been captured. Hijacking airplanes was the preferred method of Black September, and because El Al planes were closely guarded, the European airlines were easier game.

On May 8, 1972, four terrorists commandeered a Belgian Sabena jet on a flight from Vienna to Tel Aviv. After the plane landed at Lod Airport near Tel Aviv, the terrorists demanded freedom for hundreds of their imprisoned Arab brothers in exchange for the lives of the passengers and crew.

The PLO probably made a serious mistake by misreading the character of Defense Minister Moshe Dayan as described in their intelligence files (it is a fair assumption that Salameh had such a document). Dayan was raised among Arabs, and many of his colleagues contend, half seriously, that he "thinks like an Arab." In any event, Dayan seemed to be able to penetrate the mental processes of the terrorists and decided to take full command of a rescue effort.

At first he agreed to the outlaws' demands. The Black September operatives were gleeful, thinking they had scored an easy victory. The Israelis, they concluded, would protect innocent lives rather than stand by their "Jewish intransigence."

They were wrong. Dayan was playing a game in which the odds in favor of victory were somewhat better than the odds against disaster. On another

707 on the airfield, out of sight of the hostage Sabena jet, a group of Israeli commandos was carefully rehearsing a lightning assault on the Sabena plane. This involved breaking into the plane and disarming the terrorists within seconds. The most difficult part of the assault, obviously, was getting the commandos close enough to attack it.

While this deadly run-through was being practiced, Dayan, in traditional Arab fashion, was haggling over the terms of the release. Finally, an "agreement" was reached under which the Arab prisoners held in Israel would be exchanged for the hostages. The hijackers were jubilant. Their imprisoned comrades would soon be out of the clutches of the Israelis.

At the appointed hour, vanloads of Arab prisoners were brought to the apron beside the plane. But before the actual exchange could take place, the airport authorities informed the terrorists that the plane would have to be refueled and prepared for takeoff. The hijackers agreed.

In a moment a gasoline truck rumbled up toward the plane, drawing to a stop almost under it. Suddenly "mechanics" in white uniforms piled out of the truck. Immediately, they stormed the plane, where sharpshooters opened fire on the terrorists. The terrorists fired back. In the confusion a Dutch girl passenger stood up in her seat and was killed in the crossfire. But in seconds two male Arab terrorists had been killed and two women, Theresa Hassaseh and Rita Tannouse, were captured.

Ali Hassan Salameh had suffered his first serious defeat. Unfortunately, neither the PLO nor the PFLP was deterred in the slightest by this setback. It was as if they had factored a certain number of failures into their strategy.

Only a few weeks later, in late May 1972, a conference of terrorists was held at the Badawi refugee camp near Tripoli in Lebanon. The PFLP was host to the élite of international outlaws. In addition to the PFLP's top brigands, the delegates also represented the PLO, the Baader-Meinhof Gang, the Japanese Red Army, the Irish Republican Army, and the terrorist liberation fronts of Iraq and Turkey; so reports David Tinnin in *The Hit Team*. The meeting seemed to be under the leadership of Waddieh Haddad, the chief badman of the PFLP. Salameh was probably there, but this is not certain.

The conclave also produced a fateful integration of the Japanese Red Army into the fellowship of terrorists. The Japanese attendees were the honored guests of the Iraqi contingent. They had met in 1970 at a terrorist training center in North Korea.

The various contingents pledged solidarity and offered the Japanese Red Army the use of training dens in Aden, Lebanon, and Libya. The Japanese, however, did not even wait for further training to immerse themselves in the cauldron of Middle East terror. It is possible that one of the most gruesome terrorist acts of the century was fashioned at this meeting.

On May 30, 1972, three polite and well-dressed Japanese youths boarded an Air France jet in Rome, bound for Lod Airport in Israel. Because of the occasional laxity of most security precautions, their luggage was not carefully checked at Rome's Leonardo da Vinci Airport. On the arrival of the

flight at Lod, the passengers were taken by bus to the crowded arrival lounge.

As soon as the Japanese had claimed their baggage, they stood together and began opening the suitcases. Then, as if emerging from a football huddle, they turned around and the unsuspecting crowd was suddenly caught in the blazing hell of hand-grenade explosions and machine-gun bullets.

When it was over, twenty-six people were dead—many of them blown to bits—and eighty were wounded, some of them horribly. More than half of the victims were Puerto Rican visitors, joyfully arriving for their first pilgrimage to the Holy Land. Two of the terrorists were also dead, and the third was captured.

The Lod Airport massacre raises the issue of why the collective terrorist organizations sanctioned the wanton murder of people who, by nationality or inclination, did not represent enemies to the causes espoused by the terrorists. The probable answer is that Arafat and other Arab leaders, in their obsession with the destruction of Israel, recognized that tourism is one of the Jewish state's most important industries. An assault on innocent tourists in the airport through which a majority of them arrive would frighten away prospective visitors, thus further harming Israel's struggling economy.

Koto Okamoto, the only survivor among the Japanese killers, shed little light on the Japanese Red Army's tactical motives. He admitted, however, that he had been trained by the PFLP in Lebanon and that he believed the slaughter of innocent people is justified in preparing the world for its inevitable domination by the Red Army and like organizations. The bourgeoisie, he said, must be crushed by any means. Okamoto was sentenced to life imprisonment.

There was a degree of "friendly" competition between the terrorist squads of the PFLP under Haddad and the PLO under Salameh. The PFLP's chief in Europe was Mohammed Boudia, who operated from Paris. Boudia, like his non-Arab successor, Carlos, and like Salameh, was charming and adept at using his sexual prowess to recruit young women into the organization. Boudia, however, was reluctant to engage in overt acts of violence in Europe, for fear of jeopardizing his covert operations.

Salameh had no such reservations and went on to the most ruthless and world-shaking operation of them all—the massacre of the Israeli athletes at Munich. It is often forgotten that this meticulously planned and cold-blooded outrage was a product of the PLO, the organization that calls itself "moderate."

Where, when, and how the Olympic assault was planned is, of course, not known and probably never will be. It depended, however, on a suicide mission, for the Black September assassins knew that they probably had at best an even chance to survive the assault. Tinnan believes that Salameh began to consider the possibility of the Munich onslaught sometime in the early summer of 1972. To carry it out, however, he needed not just covert spies and killers but the active support of legitimate Arab governments. In short, the rulers of Syria, Algeria, Libya, Egypt, and possibly Saudi Arabia knew it was going to happen.

On September 5, 1972, an innocent knock on the door of the apartment

housing twenty-two Israeli athletes in Munich was answered by Moshe Weinberg, the rugged coach of the Israeli wrestling team. Opening the door was Weinberg's first—and last—mistake. When he realized something was wrong and tried to push the door shut again, the terrorists blasted holes in the door with Soviet AK-47 rifles, killing Weinberg instantly. The athletes, suddenly aware of danger, leaped from their beds. Ten escaped out another door or out the windows. A weight-lifter, Joseph Romano, attempted to fight the assassins off; they shot him down with a hail of bullets. Nine Israelis were taken hostage.

Their captors were Salameh's men. The PLO had desecrated the first summer Olympics in Germany since the infamous 1936 games, which Hitler had turned into a propaganda show for the Third Reich. The government and people of West Germany were desperate to present for the world an Olympiad that was truly symbolic of international brotherhood, a pageant to erase the travesty of Hitler's distortion. It was not to be. The Jews, Hitler's scapegoats in 1936, were victimized again in 1972.

The Arabs demanded the release of two hundred Arab prisoners of the Israelis. The hostages would be released when the prisoners were set free in an as-yet-unnamed Arab city. The deadline to agree to the conditions was noon.

In Jerusalem a grim Israeli cabinet under Golda Meir refused to agree to the prisoner release. In Bonn, Chancellor Willy Brandt offered an alternate proposal—a large ransom to the terrorists in return for release of the hostages. Salameh's men flatly turned down the German proposal but agreed to extend the deadline to 3 P.M. Then the German interior minister, Hans-Dietrich Genscher, told the Arabs that the Israeli government was on the verge of accepting the prisoner-release proposal and asked for an extension to 5 P.M. A plan was proposed—and accepted by the Arabs—whereby the captive Israelis would be flown to Cairo for the exchange. The journey would begin with the captives being taken by bus to a helicopter landing site and thence to an airport at Fürstenfeldbruck, fifteen miles north of Munich. Actually, the plan was intended as a trap for the Arabs: they would be shot by German sharpshooters as they transferred from the helicopters to the waiting Lufthansa plane.

The plan failed totally. There were more Arabs than the Germans realized, and the first shots fired missed, giving the terrorists time to kill all nine Israelis in the two helicopters. After the captives had been murdered, hand grenades were tossed into the planes, incinerating the athletes.

The Israelis had never become involved in counterterrorism outside of Israel itself. In this instance, however, the fury of the young nation over the murder of its athletes stirred the demand for retaliation. Golda Meir, who had opposed any such vengeful activity, could no longer resist the clamor that the wrath of God be brought down upon the terrorists. The antiterrorist unit of the Mossad that was set up to operate outside of Israel was called just that—the Wrath of God. The main target was Ali Hassan Salameh.

There was a kind of rivalry between Salameh's Black September terrorists and the agents of the PFLP. When the Israelis sent agents into Europe to

track down Salemeh, they were also seeking Mohammed Boudia his assistant and, later, successor, the most famous terrorist of them all—Carlos, "the Jackal." At this writing, Carlos is still alive and at large.

Boudia, a professional actor and theatrical director, got his start as a revolutionary during the war for independence from France in his native Algeria. He went to France ostensibly as an actor but actually as an Algerian terrorist. His most spectacular exploit was a raid on an oil depot in Marseilles. Some months later, however, he was arrested and sentenced to three years in prison. Released in 1962, his Marxist leanings led him into the company of the PFLP underground.

Like Salameh and Carlos, Boudia seemed able to charm women into his bed, and from between the sheets he enlisted many female terrorists. One of them, the beautiful Evelyne Barges, he dispatched in early 1971 to Tel Aviv, as one of the agents to participate in the blowing up of the opulent Tel Aviv waterfront hotels. Barges, however, was intercepted by Israeli Shin Bet operatives. Because she was carrying explosives, she was charged, convicted, and sentenced to fourteen years in prison. In her interrogation she implicated Boudia. The Israelis, who had already had Boudia under surveillance from time to time, at least knew for certain who they were looking for in Europe.

Boudia still had more mischief ahead in his career before the Israelis were to catch up with him. On August 4, 1972, Boudia led a raid on a huge oil refinery in Trieste, setting fire to four large storage tanks. One of his cohorts, an Italian woman, was the only one arrested. Shortly after this, with Carlos, he drew up a plan for assassinating a long list of prominent Jews in Britain, including playwright John Osborne and the world-famous violinist Yehudi Menuhin. But Boudia backed off from the plan. He may have begun to play it safe. The arrest of Evelyne Barges and other agents he had sent to Israel probably made him wonder whether the Mossad had managed to plant an informer in his midst. The Mossad, of course, to this day reveals nothing, but the circumstantial evidence indicates that it had infiltrated his organization. The Mossad, or its offshoot, the Wrath of God, seemed to be closing in.

In October 1972, just one month after the Munich massacre, Khodr Kannou was shot outside his Paris apartment. He was a Syrian journalist who had often been seen with Boudia and was probably associated with the PFLP. His killers were not caught.

A few days later, Wael Abu Zwaiter, a known representative of the PLO, was assassinated in Rome. Again, no one was arrested. In December, in Paris, Mahmud Hamchari, who was probably associated with both the PLO and the PFLP, was blown to bits in his apartment by an explosive charge in his telephone. Hamchari was in bed with a girl friend when the phone rang. When he lifted the receiver, the charge was detonated. The woman, amazingly, was unhurt. In January 1973 a PLO agent, Bashir Abu Khair, was killed when a bomb exploded in his flat in Nicosia, Cyprus. In April, Basil al-Kubaisi, a PFLP agent, was shot in Paris.

In June the Wrath of God—or so it is assumed—finally caught up with

Boudia. Boudia had parked his car in a Paris suburb, and when he returned to it, a bomb behind the seat was triggered as he took his place behind the wheel. That was the end of the European chief of the PFLP.

With Boudia's death, the mantle of the world's most feared terrorist was shared by his successor, Carlos, representing the PFLP, and Ali Hassan Salameh, the Red Prince of the PLO's Black September.

Carlos is certainly the best known of these international brigands. He is also more of an enigma than Salameh. While the Arab was born into a life of terrorism by being the son of a murdered terrorist, Carlos came from a comfortably wealthy Venezuelan family. He also represents the most solid link between the Soviet Union and international terrorism.

Carlos's father, Altagracia Ramirez, a wealthy lawyer in Caracas, was an intellectual Marxist whose life was rather routinely capitalistic. He not only practiced law successfully, as a specialist in real estate, but he acquired a lot of property and became a millionaire. He had three sons and called each after one of the names of his hero, Vladimir Ilich Lenin. Ilich, the oldest, slipped easily into the crusade against the degenerate capitalists of Latin America. He is quoted by his biographer, Colin Smith (*Carlos: Portrait of a Terrorist*), as deciding even in his middle teen years that "bullets are the only thing that make sense."

Ilich was not too much of a Marxist to turn down his father's offer to send him to London, along with his two younger brothers, Lenin and Vladimir. (The elder Ramirez was estranged from his wife, and so, persuading her to take their sons to England may have been a convenient way of removing her from Caracas.) The three boys attended English grammar schools, but their real awakening was to the free and easy social life in London, extremely tempting to teen-agers reared in the closely supervised family life of Venezuela.

After they had been in London a year, Ramirez visited his three sons. He had a puritanical streak that was offended by the loose life of London and decided that his sons needed an atmosphere with more discipline. His international Marxist connections were strong enough to get Ilich and Lenin accepted at the Patrice Lumumba Friendship University in Moscow. Ilich was then just nineteen.

Ramirez's oldest son had an aptitude for languages and quickly learned Russian, but he could not accept the strict discipline of the university. His father sent him and Lenin plenty of money. Ilich soon had the reputation of a young man more interested in women and Scotch whiskey than in work. His life-style seemed to fit in better with that of the many Arab students than with the less colorful Soviets. Many of the Arabs were in sympathy with, if not actively members of, the PFLP.

The course of Ilich's life after his first year at Patrice Lumumba University is mysterious. Sometime in late 1968 he left Moscow, returned to London, and then disappeared. He did not surface again until he returned to Moscow in February 1970. It seems probable that his departure and return would not have been possible without official Soviet sanction. One speculative report, detailed by Ovid Demaris in *New York Magazine* on November 1,

1977, is that Ilich was sent to Camp Mantanzas in Havana, Cuba, to study guerrilla tactics under Antonio Dages Bouvier, who was later the only terrorist to escape when the Israelis freed the hostages in Entebbe, Uganda, on July 4, 1976. The camp was under the direction of Soviet Colonel Victor Simonov. After leaving Cuba, Ilich is believed to have gone to the Middle East to meet George Habash.

Ilich returned to Moscow in 1970 and resumed his studies at Lumumba University. This time his deportment was even worse than before his hiatus. Accused of drunkenness, cutting classes, and habitual disorderliness, both of the Ramirez brothers were dismissed.

What is not known is whether the dismissal was real or part of a Soviet plot to deliver the now well-trained Ilich to the PFLP. It is known that in August 1970 he arrived at a PFLP training base near Ajlun, Jordan, highly recommended by Dr. Haddad. Thenceforth, Ilich was known as Carlos. The PFLP sent him to a training unit in the midst of a United Nations Arab refugee camp near Amman. (The Palestinians often conducted terrorist and guerrilla training in the midst of refugee camps in order to hide behind the skirts of women and children. If the Israelis attacked, they were immediately accused of wanton disregard of innocent lives.)

In the fall of 1971, Carlos was sent to London as a lieutenant to Mohammed Boudia. Now twenty-two, Carlos was a pudgy, weak-faced man whose overall appearance was somewhat degenerate. Degenerate he was—obsessed with women, a heavy drinker, and a dedicated planner of terrorist plots for Boudia, although, thus far, he was not actively involved himself. He was a key man in contacts with other groups, such as the Japanese Red Army, the Red Brigades, and the Baader-Meinhof Gang.

When the Wrath of God agents of the Mossad killed Boudia in June 1973, Carlos became the head of the PFLP in Europe and the world's most feared terrorist. In memory of his fallen chief, the European unit was called Commando Boudia.

Carlos's first major operation after he took over was one he carried out himself on December 30, 1973, although not with complete success. Whereas Boudia had shunned PFLP activities in London, Carlos had no such reticence. Joseph Edward Sieff, president of the Marks and Spencer chain of stores in England, was a Zionist leader and a friend of Menachem Begin, the former leader of the militant Irgun in Israel and an advocate (at that time) of an Israeli take-over of the land captured on the West Bank of the Jordan in the Six-Day War.

The PFLP wanted Sieff eliminated, possibly as the first of many prominent British Jews. Carlos, armed with a Browning automatic pistol, knocked on the door of Sieff's town house and immediately thrust it at the butler who opened the door. He ordered the servant to take him to Sieff, who was standing before the basin in his bathroom. Prodded by Carlos, the butler asked Sieff to open the door. He did and was shot full in the face by Carlos. When the attack was reported in the news media, the PFLP in Beirut took full credit for it. But amazingly, Sieff did not die; in fact, he made a nearly full

recovery. The bullet had shattered his jaw and stopped short of his spine. But Carlos had spread fear among London's Zionist community.

Carlos was probably also involved in a January 1974 attack on an Israeli bank in London, when a small bomb was thrown through the door. No one was seriously hurt.

Carlos's uncanny appeal to women (many men would wonder why they were attracted to this pudgy, baby-faced man) enabled him to set up safe houses in both London and Paris in the apartments of his various girl friends. Here he stashed weapons and made his plans.

In August 1974, bombs were set off in front of three Jewish-owned Parisian newspaper offices. In September, Carlos went after a bigger target. The French had captured one of the kingpins of the Japanese Red Army. In an effort to free him, Carlos planned a complex operation—the capture of the French embassy in The Hague. It was carried out by three machine-gun-toting members of the Japanese Red Army. When the French would not accede to the terrorists' demands, Carlos, back in Paris, threw a hand grenade into a shopping mall, Le Drugstore. Two people were killed and thirty maimed, some horribly. In the end, Carlos won. The Red Army leader was released, and a ransom was paid to the terrorists.

It was on December 21, 1975, that Carlos and his Commando Boudia group pulled off the greatest coup of all—the capture of eleven OPEC oil ministers in their headquarters in Vienna. It proved to be a piece of showmanship (and a bloody one) directed at the "moderate" Arab states whom the PFLP suspected of changing to a "soft" policy toward Israel. Carlos himself controlled and dominated the whole operation. He cold-bloodedly shot one functionary himself. Altogether seven died in the shootout. The ministers supposedly agreed to a manifesto that set them in unrelenting opposition to the survival of Israel. Carlos, standing guard over the ministers and a total of some forty hostages for two days, reminded them, "I am the great Carlos."

Carlos is still alive somewhere—probably in Libya, protected by Colonel Muammar el-Qaddafi, the most radical and intransigent of the Arab leaders. Certainly the Mossad is looking for Carlos as they did so unsuccessfully for that other master terrorist, Ali Hassan Salameh.

The Wrath of God—or the Hit Team, as Tinnin calls them in his book of the same name—mounted a massive operation all over Europe to track down the man who had perpetrated the infamous Munich Olympic massacre. But they made what has been publicized as a terrible mistake. The trail to Salameh led to Norway and finally to a small town called Lillehammer. There a man with a striking resemblance to Salameh was working as a waiter. On July 21, 1973, while he was walking home from a movie with his pregnant wife, he was gunned down by Wrath of God agents. He was not Salameh but Ahmed Bouchiki. Even worse, the Israelis who committed the murder were captured by Norwegian authorities, tried, and sent to prison. The mistake was acutely distressing to the Israeli government, which endured criticism from all over the world. Five years later, however, the Oslo newspaper *Verd-*

ens Gang reported that Bouchiki was, in fact, a secret agent of the PLO. This has never been confirmed. Nevertheless, the blunder in Norway put an end to the Wrath of God.

The regular agents of the Mossad, however, never gave up their search for Salameh. In late 1978 they tracked him down in Beirut. Studying his movements for weeks, they conceived a means of destroying him. On January 22, 1979, Salameh drove his Chevrolet station wagon away from his apartment on a quiet side street in Beirut. As he passed a Volkswagen parked at the curb, there was a mammoth explosion. The Volkswagen had been loaded with explosives that were triggered by a tiny transmitter that an agent had fastened under the fender of Salameh's car. Salameh and four bodyguards were killed instantly. The author of the Lod Airport massacre and the murderer of the Israeli athletes was dead at last.

15

The Great Mirage Blueprint Switch

THE WORLD was astounded by the success of Israel's armed forces in the Six-Day War of June 1967. While all branches of the service had fought with remarkable courage and efficiency, the achievements of Israel's air force in the first ninety minutes of battle were the most devastating. Through excellent Israeli intelligence (some of it from spies such as Wolfgang Lotz), the pilots knew where to find every airstrip in Egypt, Syria, and Iraq, and some 80 percent of the enemy planes were destroyed before they could leave the ground.

And yet, within weeks after the convincing Israeli victory, while its friends still toasted the lightning conquest, the government of Israel and the officers of its air force were worried. France had imposed an embargo on any shipments of arms to Israel (the same embargo that tied up the missile boats in Cherbourg), which included spare aircraft parts—and the Israeli air force consisted mainly of French-built planes. Without the spare parts the planes could not long be kept battle-ready, and Israel would soon be vulnerable.

When the Six-Day War started on the morning of June 4, 1967, the Israeli air force had 196 operational combat planes at its disposal, among them 92 Dassault Mirage III-E fighter bombers and 82 Mystere fighters. The Arabs, in contrast, had a combined aerial arsenal of 682 combat planes, 431 of them Egyptian.

While the intelligence enabled the Israelis to find the Arab planes, a switch in weapons made the task of destruction easier. The Israeli planes had been equipped with sophisticated air-to-air and air-to-ground missiles, effective for long-range combat but oversophisticated for the task at hand. The missiles were replaced with relatively simple aerial cannons that fired explosive shells. Whereas one plane might carry two to four missiles, it

255

could carry hundreds of rounds of cannon ammunition. The Israelis destroyed on the ground some three hundred Egyptian aircraft, including all thirty Soviet-built Tu-16 long-range bombers and the bulk of the MIG fighters.

With all this success, however, the Israelis could not overlook their own loss of nineteen planes, or 10 percent of their air force. Proportionately, this was a higher loss than they were to suffer in the less successful Yom Kippur War six years later. The French planes still in service had to be kept flying if Israel was to survive future attacks—at least until she could buy from another country or develop her own, home-built aircraft. Both alternatives appeared far in the future.

The managing director of Israel Aircraft Industries, Adolph ("Al") Schwimmer, an American expatriate, realized the full extent of the problem that his adopted country faced. Without spare parts from France it would be just a matter of time before the entire air force would be grounded and the Jewish state would be without its first line of defense.

Al Schwimmer was well equipped to solve the problem. Born in 1920 and raised in Bridgeport, Connecticut, Schwimmer became fascinated with the mysteries of the internal-combustion engine in his early teens and spent a large part of his spare time tinkering with Model-T Fords. When Charles A. Lindbergh flew solo from New York to Paris in 1927, Schwimmer joined a whole new generation of American youth that became addicted to the art of flying.

In high school he realized that his parents would not be able to send him to college. The Great Depression had taken its toll on his father's soft-drink business.

Schwimmer was understandably attracted to the nearby Sikorsky aircraft plant, adjacent to the airport at Stratford, Connecticut. He got a semiskilled job there and learned a lot about both the engines and the frames of Sikorsky airplanes. In the late 1930s he landed a better job at the Glenn L. Martin plant near Baltimore. Martin was building the B-26 bomber, the famous Marauder of World War II. By 1940 Schwimmer had gotten his pilot's license and had acquired a broad and sophisticated knowledge of aircraft and engine construction and maintenance. On the eve of the Pearl Harbor attack, he was hired by the flight-test department of Lockheed Aircraft at Burbank, California. Once the war had started, the opportunities for those with a thorough knowledge of aircraft and flying took a quantum leap. Schwimmer took full advantage of the situation. The Air Transport Command (ATC) which had the responsibility for hiring civilian pilots and crews to fly military personnel, high-priority cargo, and the planes themselves to the war zones, awarded a contract to Trans World Airlines (TWA) in 1942. Schwimmer was hired as a pilot, awarded a simulated rank of captain, and flew all over the world for the ATC. His odyssey included flights to Africa, to the Middle East, and over the "hump" from Burma to China. During one flight, he made his first visit to Palestine. The struggling, industrious Jewish settlements made a lasting impression on him.

Many participants in a war feel a sense of the loss of purpose when the hostilities end, and Schwimmer was no exception. He accepted TWA's offer to remain as a flight engineer, but the excitement of fighting for a just cause was absent. By this time, the American Jewish community was becoming aware of the extent of the Holocaust and the plight of Jewish refugees in Europe. Schwimmer, at that point not a Zionist, began to grow interested in helping his brethren in Palestine. He sought out the Jewish Palestinian underground, which then operated out of the Hotel Fourteen, a residential hotel at 14 East Sixtieth Street in New York City.

Almost by accident, the Fourteen had become a center of secret Zionist activity. The owners, Ruby Barnett and his wife, Fannie, had purchased it in 1944 in a federal bankruptcy sale. Many of their guests were little old ladies who for years had considered the hotel their part- or full-time home. Fannie was well known in the Jewish Agency. She had worked for the Zionist movement since childhood and had served as Chaim Weizmann's secretary on his visit to the United States during World War II.

One of Ben-Gurion's Jewish agency emissaries to the United States in 1945 was a dark-haired Palestinian Jew, Reuben Zaslini. His mission was to acquire arms for the Haganah and to find ships to transport Jewish refugees illegally into Palestine. He operated out of a small suite in the Hotel Fourteen, and Fannie acted as his secretary. While in 1945 it was difficult for Zaslini to get the cooperation of the American Jewish community in helping the Haganah, by the year 1947 things had completely changed.

A stocky, former British army major, Shlomo Rabinovitch, occupied the office at the hotel. And he was flooded with inquiries from people who wanted to volunteer for the cause.

One day a rugged young man walked in. He said his name was Adolph Schwimmer and he was a flight engineer for TWA on the Cairo to Washington run.

"I just wonder whether I can help," he said in a dry New England accent.

Careful questioning revealed that Schwimmer had no ideological zeal. Still he wanted to help the Zionists and felt that his knowledge of airplanes might be useful in the struggle to establish a Jewish state.

Rabinovitch felt that since Schwimmer was an unknown quantity, it would be necessary to test the extent of his commitment. Rabinovitch jotted down the pilot's name and invited him to return at his convenience.

Schwimmer was not discouraged by this initial brush-off. During the summer and fall of 1947, he continued to drop in at Rabinovitch's office.

What Schwimmer did not realize was that during this period his credentials and his character were being carefully investigated. The graduates of Nachum Bernstein's school for spies were known as the Shoo-Shoo Boys, from a Hebrew slang expression for a secret agent. One of their assignments was to conduct background checks of Jewish and gentile volunteers. When they visited Schwimmer's hometown of Bridgeport, they asked a lot of ques-

tions of his neighbors and verified everything he had told them about himself. There was no evidence whatsoever that Schwimmer was any kind of a spy or double agent.

As the dialogue between Schwimmer and Rabinovitch progressed, the latter's doubts seemed gradually to diminish, and he showed signs of accepting Schwimmer's conviction that the new state could build its own air transport system. Still, Rabinovitch seemed to have some reservations, and Schwimmer was growing impatient.

The deadlock was finally broken when Rabinovitch was replaced by a Zionist from Palestine who was more enthusiastic about Schwimmer's plans. The newcomer, Yehuda Arazi, agreed that planes were needed to transport immigrants and cargo. And even though the British had attempted to cut off both immigration and supplies to Palestine, Arazi believed an American embargo and British restrictions could be breached.

The two men reached an agreement. Schwimmer was given the job of acquiring planes for the future state. Enough money was provided by Nachum Bernstein.

Over the next year, Schwimmer purchased surplus American planes, including three Lockheed Constellations for the astounding price of $15,000 apiece. Not only did he buy them but, confronted with heavy repair and maintenance costs, hired some of his old comrades from TWA as mechanics. They acquired ten C-46 transports and three B-17s as well and, in time, used various ruses to spirit them to Palestine.

By the time the War for Independence had started, Schwimmer was the obvious choice as chief of maintenance for the Israeli air force. His service, however, was interrupted when he and several of his comrades had to return to the United States to face a federal indictment for violation of the arms embargo. Their lawyer was Nachum Bernstein. He amazed the courts with proof that he had gotten permission from the State Department to export the airplanes even before the first one left the United States. Bernstein had made his case on the need for the planes to evacuate Israelis from danger areas when the Arabs commenced their expected attack. Schwimmer and all but one of the defendants were either acquitted or given suspended sentences. The exception was Charles Winters, who was sentenced to eighteen months in prison. Ironically, Winters was the only non-Jew in the group.

When the War for Independence had been won, Schwimmer, back in Israel, was asked to set up a maintenance organization for the new commercial flag carrier, El-Al. Subsequently, Schwimmer participated in the establishment of Bedek Aviation, Ltd., to maintain planes at the fast-growing Lod Airport near Tel Aviv. He returned to the United States to buy tools and jigs for repairing parts.

Bedek continued to grow, and by 1954, when the worldwide conversion from piston to jet engines was taking place, Bedek had the only equipment in Israel capable of testing the jets. The company was contracted to overhaul and maintain jets for the Israeli air force.

Bedek began to receive international recognition for its work in aircraft maintenance. In August 1955 the company was certified in the United

States by the Federal Aviation Agency, and similarly received approval from the Air Registration Board of Great Britain. Engine-overhaul agreements were signed with nearly all the major engine manufacturers, including Hispano-Suisa, Turbomeca, Rolls-Royce, Pratt and Whitney, Wright Aeronautical, and General Electric. Years later, following the 1967 war, this acknowledged expertise in rebuilding jet engines was to be an important factor contributing to Israeli survival.

In the meantime, Al Schwimmer had a dream that was based on reality. In a time of crisis, Israel could not depend solely on overseas sources for aircraft. True, the French assistance in 1956 was invaluable, but how long would the honeymoon last? The state had to plan for the future. Israel would have to practice the art of the impossible and build its own airplanes.

At that time, Bedek did not have either the design capability or funds to start from scratch. The alternative was to assemble under license a plane that could be useful to the Israeli air force. The decision was made that initially twelve French Fouga CM-170 Mysteres would be assembled in Israel from imported components. After accomplishing that, Bedek would start building a Fouga, using locally manufactured parts.

The Fouga was basically a jet trainer that could be quickly modified for ground interdiction missions. It carried two 75-millimeter machine guns and bomb racks that could be replaced by air-to-ground rockets. It was capable of speeds in excess of 400 miles per hour, had a range of 570 miles, and could be used against enemy armor or troop concentrations. Altogether, the Fouga was less than ideal, but the Israelis believed that in a crisis they would need everything that could fly. To improve its battle capability, the air force, based on its experience in the 1956 war, required over a hundred modifications of the plane's structure and armor.

The first Israeli-assembled Fouga took to the air on July 7, 1960. Among the notables present at the ceremonies was David Ben-Gurion. The old man promptly renamed Schwimmer's company the Israel Aircraft Industry, known as IAI. Shimon Peres was also in the reviewing stands. In a sense, he had been the political godfather of the project, having shepherded Schwimmer's dream through the Knesset and cut through yards of red tape.

One of the major problems in preparing for the ceremonies had been Al Schwimmer, whose reluctance to speak in public was only matched by his refusal to learn Hebrew. His address was first written for him in English and translated into Hebrew, and then the Hebrew was transcribed into the Latin alphabet. After reading this transliterated script, as Sherman recalls in *Lightning in the Skies,* the American was roundly complimented on his excellent command of the Hebrew language.

The Israeli-modified Fouga Mystere planes proved their worth during the Six-Day War. But when the war was over, France's embargo on spare parts for the planes imperiled Israel's existence. For economic and political reasons, Paris had previously contracted with IAI to manufacture some parts for the Mirage III. These components could also be used as spare parts for the Israeli planes. But Israel's crucial need was parts for the French planes' jet engines and the engine mounts.

Schwimmer's self-imposed charter was clear. Either procure the needed parts by whatever means or acquire the detailed engineering drawings for the machine tools that would enable IAI to manufacture the jet engine components.

How Schwimmer got the drawings is a story that has never been told accurately until now, although an imperfect version of part of the story appeared in the August 30, 1976 edition of *New York Magazine.* Called "How Israel Got Blueprints for France's Hottest Fighter," it was written by Paul Erdman and was allegedly based on an interview with Alfred Frauenknecht while he and Erdman were in a Basel prison.

In 1975, when an Israeli fighter plane, the Kfir (for "lion cub"), was unveiled to the public, *Newsweek* wrote that "much of the credit for the Kfir belongs to a Swiss engineer named Alfred Frauenknecht. When French President Charles de Gaulle embargoed shipments of the Mirage fighter planes to Israel in 1967, the pro-Israel Frauenknecht filched the plans for the Mirage 5 and relayed them to Israel. The Kfir was then developed and manufactured by Israel Aircraft Industries (IAI). . . . He was on hand in Lydda to see his lion cub take to the skies." Other tributes to the Kfir's performance came from *Ordnance* magazine and *U.S. Armed Forces* magazine.

Although the Kfir was an outgrowth of the Mirage, the basic engineering and design was an Israeli achievement. The Kfir was not, however, the first plane designed in Israel. A highly successful Arava STOL (for "short takeoff and landing") plane had been designed and was test flown in 1971. A French aviation writer, Didi Epelbaum, wrote in 1972, "Concerning technological capabilities, Israel is, in some fields, on the first level."*

Despite the approaching home-grown successes, in 1967 the Mirages remained the backbone of Israel's air defense, and Schwimmer had to keep them in the air. His first attempt to acquire the spare parts was through open commercial channels. The Swiss government was building the Mirages under a licensing agreement with the French Dassault armament firm. A diesel engine company, Sulzer of Winterthur, was awarded the contract for the plane's jet engines. Originally the plan was to construct 100 planes, but because of cost overruns, the order was canceled after 55 planes were built. Sulzer, however, had completed most of the parts for the engines, the bulk of which were of no use to the Swiss and were, in addition, taking up valuable warehouse space. Schwimmer was aware of Sulzer's surplus inventory, and in December 1967, six months after the end of the Six-Day War, he arranged for the first tender for their purchase at a Paris meeting of all the users of the Mirage III.

The meeting had been called to exchange technical information on ways to better the plane's performance. In this way it was felt that all users could benefit. Air force officers and representatives of manufacturers from Switzerland, France, and Austria were there. Schwimmer and Colonel Nehemiah Kain, an Israeli military attaché stationed in Rome, were two of the Israeli

---

*Quoted in *Lightning in the Skies,* by Arnold Sherman. The source is not given.

delegates. Sulzer's chief engineer, Alfred Frauenknecht, represented his company. It was clear to the participants that Israel was capable of making a major contribution to the conference, since it was the only country that had used the plane in combat.

There was no reason, however, why Israel should share its expertise with the French. Fifty Mirage planes that Israel had paid for were still on French soil. As the meeting progressed, Frauenknecht felt a growing sense of frustration. The French were willing, even anxious, to benefit from the knowledge gained as a result of the Mirage's performance but refused even to consider lifting the embargo in return for a report on the Israeli experience. The Israelis kept their counsel.

Although at the start of the meeting the Israelis could not have suspected it, Frauenknecht was to play a historic role in helping them acquire their sorely needed engine parts. Before World War II he, like many other German-speaking Swiss citizens, had felt some allegiance to Germany. As the conflict heightened, Frauenknecht became aware of the thousands of Jews crossing the Swiss border, seeking asylum. While some of them were allowed into Switzerland, most were sent back to Germany and the gas ovens.

Until this wrenching war experience, Frauenknecht, a Roman Catholic, had never been concerned with the "Jewish problem." After that, however, he became emotionally involved with the survival of the Jewish state and its citizens. A visit to Dachau hardened his resolve. The Israeli delegates to the meeting, Schwimmer and Kain, would soon give Frauenknecht an opportunity to play a major role in Israel's future.

Shortly after the users' conference in Paris, Schwimmer and Kain met with the Swiss engineer. They outlined the nucleus of a commercial transaction to buy the surplus engine parts that could be presented to the Swiss government for approval.

But first, there was a question of at least one serious technical flaw in the Mirage that, if not corrected, could cause the airplane to crash. In his interview with Paul Erdman of *New York Magazine,* Frauenknecht elaborated on the Israeli findings: "During the Six-Day War they had determined that the Mirage had a major defect. There was only one fuel-feed system in the aircraft, a mechanical system. In hot weather and under stress in war, when the turnaround time was very short, this system would fail and the plane would crash. The Israelis engineered a simple alternate emergency pneumatic system that would be automatically activated if the mechanical system failed."

Frauenknecht said that the Israelis "offered us—and only us Swiss—the design and tooling plans for that alternate system. So we could build them into the Swiss Mirages. . . . The Israelis suggested that much more such information was available, including suggestions regarding the tactical employment of the aircraft in wartime."

A month later, the Israelis made the Swiss government a purchase offer. The essence of the offer was to purchase jet engine parts from Sulzer's surplus inventory. A down payment of 150 million Swiss francs was suggested. As a sweetener, the Israelis also agreed to share with the Swiss their tech-

nical and combat experience in flying the Mirage. The tender was promptly rejected.

Yet another meeting with Frauenknecht was arranged. The date was April 11, 1968, at the Ambassador Hotel in Zurich. According to Frauenknecht's account, as reported by Erdman, the Swiss engineer "still thought that we could, somehow, arrange things quite correctly—through a direct arrangement with my company. My suggestion to Herr Bader (Schwimmer) and Herr Kain was that perhaps more incentive was needed. For instance, it might help if they placed a large order for turbines, generators, pumps—all products of Sulzer. Perhaps if such an order of say 100 million Swiss francs was added to the down payment of 150 million Swiss francs on the Mirage parts . . . then things could be worked out."

Frauenknecht's optimism was based on the knowledge that the deal would be highly profitable for his company. Sulzer had already been paid by the Swiss government for the spare parts. But since they would never be used, and thus not missed, why not sell them to the Israelis?

The Israelis quickly agreed to this new proposal, and then and there, Frauenknecht "picked up the phone and called the *generaldirecktor* of Sulzer, Herr Doktor Schmid."

That evening at seven, Schwimmer and Kain met with Schmid at a hotel, the Baur au Lac. It was not possible to accept the Israeli offer, the Herr Doktor told them. Since the de Gaulle embargo, his company's licensing agreement with Dassault precluded Sulzer from entering into any business arrangement involving the Mirage. Schmid expressed his regrets. It would have been a highly profitable transaction for his company, but the Swiss government could not afford to antagonize the French. A letter confirming this conversation was sent to Colonel Kain at the Israeli embassy in Rome and a carbon copy to Frauenknecht.

Having exhausted legal means, there now seemed to be no alternative but clandestine ones. Operatives at Mossad headquarters in Israel were already discussing various options. Lacking other feasible alternatives, the Mossad agents contacted their friend, Frauenknecht. This time the impasse was broken. Their plan, a masterpiece of simple deception, was, according to Frauenknecht, his brainchild. Israeli participants in the affair, interviewed both in Israel and in the United States, would neither confirm nor deny his claim. A typical comment was "If that is what he said, then it must be so."

In any event, when the dapper Swiss engineer again met with his Israeli co-conspirators, he explained that he was prepared to deliver the complete plans for the Mirage engines, including the drawings for the machine tools that would enable IAI to manufacture the plane's components.*

---

*Two published versions of the Frauenknecht affair provide interesting and generally accurate details, but some errors. Schwimmer told us that the Erdman piece in *New York Magazine* was mistaken in reporting that he and Kain disguised their identities; both were well known and disguise would thus have been pointless. In *The Mossad,* by Dennis Eisenberg, Uri Dan, and Eli Landau, the authors indicate plans for the entire Mirage plane were sought when actually only engine and machine-tool blueprints were involved.

Exactly how he planned to accomplish this risky task he would not reveal. The Israelis would simply have to trust him.

Schwimmer's primary and urgent need was for the machine-tool blueprints to fabricate jet engine parts. The plan was for these drawings to be included in the first delivery. The other drawings would be a welcome bonus.

The magnitude of Frauenknecht's undertaking is illustrated by the sheer volume of the blueprints. For the machine tools alone there were over forty-five thousand drawings. They were estimated to weigh two tons and would have filled a railroad freight car.

Frauenknecht wanted to be paid for the drawings, but in installments only as they were delivered. His price was $200,000, even though he knew the Israelis were willing to pay more. The money was simply insurance for his wife's financial security in case anything should go wrong. He regarded the venture mainly as an atonement for the suffering his government had inflicted on the Jews during World War II by denying them sanctuary.

The Israelis quickly agreed to Frauenknecht's terms. They had no idea how he was planning to steal the drawings, but in their terminology, he was a "serious and sober person." And so, they trusted him.

Still, they had one other question. Where did he plan to deposit the funds that he was to receive? There was a good reason for this query. In spite of the legal and traditional confidentiality of the Swiss banks, if word got out that a Swiss engineer was depositing large sums of money, he would automatically be suspected of wrongdoing, and the Swiss government might conceivably expropriate it. The Jews knew the Nazis had done just that with private bank accounts.

With quiet indignation, Frauenknecht informed his inquisitors that these things did not happen in Switzerland. He trusted the integrity of his government, and he would deposit the monies in a Swiss bank. Frauenknecht was to be proved wrong.

Frauenknecht's plan was an ingenious one. It hinged on the fact that Sulzer, like most large industrial firms, lacked adequate filing space for blueprints no longer in use. The cost of maintaining dead storage for the Mirage prints alone was 100,000 Swiss francs a year. Frauenknecht, always the loyal employee, came up with a practical suggestion. If the blueprints were microfilmed, the drawings could then be destroyed because in case of an emergency, the information could always be retrieved from the negatives. It was understood that the microfilming would be under the direct supervision of the Swiss military and that only one copy of the plans would be made.

Once a week, on a Thursday, approximately fifty kilos (about 110 pounds) of the photographed blueprints would be packed in unmarked cartons and placed in an unmarked Volkswagen van destined for the city incinerator. The driver of the van just happened to be Frauenknecht's cousin, who was employed as a bus driver by the municipal transport authority. Thursday was his day off, and this was a good opportunity for him to make some extra money. To make sure the blueprints reached their destination and were properly destroyed, Frauenknecht accompanied each shipment.

On the way to the incinerator a switch operation took place.

Under Swiss law, the federal patent office in Bern is required to keep blueprint patent applications for fifty years. The applications are then declared surplus and sold for scrap. Frauenknecht, posing as a scrap-paper merchant, became a constant buyer of the unwanted material. In the meantime, his cousin had rented a garage on the route from the Sulzer plant to the incinerator. The co-conspirators purchased their own van and ordered exact copies of the unmarked cartons that Sulzer was using to house the blueprints on their way to the city incinerator.

Every Thursday the cousins would leave the Sulzer plant in their unmarked van with the Mirage blueprints. On the way to their destination they would stop briefly in their rented garage and replace their precious cargo with the blueprints obtained from the Swiss patent office. The switch took less than five minutes.

Fifteen minutes later, the Frauenknechts arrived at the incinerator. They signed in and backed the van up to the chute leading to the furnace. In the presence of an inspector the cartons were opened, and he duly noted their contents—blueprints. The city inspector then witnessed the destruction of these "sensitive military documents" and signed the necessary affidavits, certifying that they had been received and destroyed.

Saturdays were reserved for preparing for the weekly Thursday switch and the actual delivery of the purloined documents to an Israeli agent. Early in the morning, the cousins would enter the rented garage and pack empty cartons with Swiss patent blueprints in preparation for the following week's substitution. The other cartons in the garage, containing the secret Mirage plans, were then loaded into the van and the cousins would drive off in the direction of the Swiss-German border. Their destination was the scenic city of Kaiseraugst, overlooking the Rhine. It is a favorite tourist spot, and thus, the presence of the two strangers would not be especially noticed.

The cousins had made the fifty-mile trip to Kaiseraugst several times in rehearsal for this operation. On Saturday, October 5, 1968, they drove to a warehouse outside of Kaiseraugst owned by a Swiss transport firm, Rotzinger and Company. They carefully unlocked the door to the deserted building, drove the van inside, and unloaded their precious cargo.

At noon, the Frauenknechts went to Hirschen, a popular local pub. As they were drinking their glasses of beer, an Israeli agent, Hans Strecker, entered and sat down at a table across the room. If the delivery had occurred without incident, Frauenknecht would simply nod his head and the cousins would pay their bill and leave.

It is believed that Hans Strecker was not employed by the Mossad but was working for Israeli military intelligence (AMAN) and that he was controlled by Colonel Kain, stationed in Rome. In any event, for a year, he had been processing Rotzinger's trucks between Switzerland and West Germany. Strecker was a familiar figure to the customs guards on both sides of the border. He was a gregarious fellow who did not hesitate to buy beer for new friends.

After Strecker received the covert signal across the beer hall from Frauenknecht, he drove to the deserted warehouse. There he loaded the

plans in the trunk of his black Mercedes and drove across the Rhine to West Germany. The trunk was never opened by the border guards. They were his friends.

Strecker traveled through the Black Forest northeastward on the road to Stuttgart. South of the city, an Italian-registered twin-engine Cessna was waiting on the tarmac of a small airfield for private planes. The Cessna flew over the Alps to Brindisi, an Italian port city on the southern Adriatic. There the blueprints were transshipped to a waiting El-Al plane that took off immediately for Lod Airport in Israel. An armored truck made the short run to a well-guarded building nestled in the IAI complex, where every week new plans for the machine tools were examined and the Israeli mechanics began their top-secret task.

In the meantime, an experiment was being conducted in the IAI hangars. The Israeli air force was taking delivery of the American Phantom F-4 plane from the United States. The "package" included spare General Electric G-79 jet engines. In order to keep the Mirage plans flying while jet-engine replacement parts were being fabricated, the Mirage engines were replaced by the larger General Electric jets. An American consultant commented, "It was a tight fit."

The Mirage blueprints continued to arrive in Israel, and Frauenknecht's bank account in Switzerland became larger as he received periodic funds from the Israelis.

There are, at least, two versions of how this covert operation ended.

Erdman reported in *New York Magazine* that Frauenknecht made his last delivery on Saturday, September 20, 1969. The author claims that the Israeli agent, Hans Strecker, was observed during the loading process in the Rotzinger company warehouse by his employer, Karl Rotzinger. Since Strecker had no legitimate reason to visit the warehouse on Saturday, Rotzinger's suspicions were aroused. As soon as Strecker left, Karl and his brother Hans entered the building and found a large carton containing blueprints stamped "property of the Swiss Military Department." They immediately notified the Swiss police, and Strecker fled the scene.

An Israeli intelligence source has offered a slightly different version of this event. It claimed that an Israeli operative had warned Frauenknecht that the Swiss authorities had him under surveillance. The agent suggested that he cease his activities and consider fleeing the country.

To the agent's surprise, Frauenknecht insisted on completing the delivery. He reasoned that even if the authorities were aware that he was spiriting classified documents out of the country, his government would scarcely want to jeopardize its relations with the French by a public disclosure of their lax security measures. Unfortunately, Frauenknecht was wrong.

Three days after Rotzinger had notified the police, Frauenknecht was arrested and held in "investigative custody." There is no habeas corpus in Switzerland. His trial on the charges of industrial espionage and violating Swiss military security began on April 23, 1971. Four days later he was sentenced to four and a half years at hard labor, and the $200,000 that he had been paid by Israeli intelligence was confiscated.

He was not abandoned by his Jewish friends. During his stay in prison

his wife received an allowance of about $600 a month. Shortly after his release from prison in 1975, Alfred Frauenknecht and his wife, Elizabeth, were invited to visit Israel. Israeli intelligence arranged for the president of the Dan hotel chain, Xiel Federman, to invite the Frauenknechts and to pay for their trip. The occasion was the public unveiling of the Kfir fighter bomber, the descendant of the Mirage. As the Kfir took to the skies, Frauenknecht may have felt with some degree of pride that his country's debt to the survivors of the Holocaust was now at least partially paid.

The Israelis continue to honor their obligations to the Swiss engineer. An Israeli source told the authors, "He and his wife live a quiet, comfortable life in the Swiss village of Aardorf, near Winterthur. Their financial needs are met by consulting jobs that we manage to arrange for him."

16

The 1973 Yom Kippur Failure

THE WELL-DESERVED REPUTATION of Israel's covert services suffered a serious setback in the Yom Kippur War of 1973. By their uncertainty as to when—or if—the attack was coming, the intelligence agencies contributed to their country's losses of men, matériel, and prestige.

This failure was not caused by their inability to gather information but rather by a degree of Jewish chauvinism that permeated the General Staff and blinded government leaders to the realities of the Arab military preparations and the enemy's ability to achieve its objectives. Hundreds of intelligence reports flowed in, indicating the Arabs were preparing for war. But the reports were discounted; the leadership was convinced the Egyptian and Syrian armies were engaged in maneuvers.

By mid-September 1973, Israeli military intelligence and the Mossad received what should have been heeded as alarming news of Egyptian and Syrian troop movements. There was no lack of information being funneled to the office of the prime minister. Furthermore, since the end of the Six-Day War, there had been close and fraternal cooperation between the American and Israeli intelligence services. The CIA and the Defense Intelligence Agency (DIA) met on a regular basis with their Israeli counterparts.

It had not been difficult to follow the movements of Egyptian and Syrian armor on Israel's Sinai and Golan borders since the cease-fire that ended the 1967 war. American photo reconnaissance satellites had been making their periodic passes over the Egyptian and Syrian fronts. As the computerized pictures arrived from space, they were delivered to Israeli intelligence. While this was going on, high-flying Israeli planes were photographing troop movements thirty-five miles deep in enemy territory. This intelligence was supplemented by on-the-ground reports from Mossad agents in Syria and Egypt and indirectly from agents in Europe.

According to Dan Ofry, in *The Yom Kippur War,* from all of these sources it is clear that the Israelis "knew exactly the size and armaments of the military units brought forward to the Suez Canal, and how many Syrian rocket batteries, armored brigades and artillery units had been positioned near the cease-fire lines." Still, in spite of all this evidence, Israeli chief of military intelligence, General Eliyahu Zeira, concluded that "it is unlikely that Sadat would risk war."

Israeli chief of staff, General David Elazar, concurred with this evaluation: "It is true the Egyptian and Syrian troops are nearing the front lines in an aggressive formation, but that does not mean that they are really preparing for war. Egypt is merely holding large-scale military maneuvers, while in the case of Syria, their military command is nervous. . . . There is no need to mobilize. Nothing will come of the whole thing."

Prime Minister Golda Meir and Defense Minister Moshe Dayan both accepted this analysis. It was in harmony with Dayan's "concept." He was convinced that neither Egypt nor Syria would attack without overwhelming air supremacy. And since both their air forces were outclassed by the Israeli air force, they would be committing military suicide if they attacked. There would be no war.

In hindsight, this misreading of Arab intentions is difficult to understand without a review of Israeli attitudes since 1967, for other historical figures have also refused to believe their own intelligence agents when the information was at variance with their own concept of coming events.

For instance, as early as 1935, Joseph Stalin had predicted the invasion of the Soviet Union by German and Japanese forces. The dictator was convinced that Western imperialism was plotting his downfall and that the fascist powers would be unleashed on Mother Russia. The Nazi-Soviet nonaggression pact of 1939 was a play for time on both sides, while toasts of friendship were exchanged. Stalin was convinced that Germany would not be able to move east until the West, including England, was subdued. This Stalin believed in spite of intelligence reports to the contrary from agents in Paris, Geneva, and Tokyo. "Let us not," he patiently explained to his comrades, "provoke the Germans by a premature mobilization. We will quietly continue to prepare for war and wait while the fascists and imperialists bleed each other to death."

The Soviets' evaluation errors in 1941 and Israel's in 1973 both stemmed from a series of misconceptions of the current political and military realities. In each case the countries were brought to the brink of disaster by the refusal of their leaders to take seriously the reports of their own agents.

The causes of Israel's intelligence failures in 1973 may be traced to its army's brilliant success in the Six-Day War of 1967 and the world acclaim that followed. Moshe Dayan's picture was on the cover of *Newsweek,* and the Israeli army and its intelligence services were proclaimed to be among the best in the world. And in general, this media analysis was accurate. The difficulty, however, was that after the 1967 war, the Israeli generals began to believe their own press notices.

A grateful country showered its conquering army with an unending har-

vest of praise. Lavish cocktail parties were organized to exhibit a constant stream of newly recognized heroes. The country was in a state of euphoria, and the army, reflecting the mood of the people, relaxed its vigilance. The lessons of the Six-Day War became the textbook for the next encounter. King David's warriors became a race of Israeli supermen. Another David, Prime Minister Ben-Gurion, complained, "The problem is that our generals consider themselves generals."

The Jews in Israel wanted to know how they had won the war in six days. What tactics, they asked the generals, did we use? The generals were anxious to oblige, and in radio interviews, they answered the questions. The curiosity of the Israeli public was amply satisifed.

The problem, however, was that so was the curiosity of the Egyptians. They were listening and recording the answers as they prepared for the next round. Hour after hour a despondent Nasser listened to a recorded translation of the Israeli tapes. The Egyptian leader still could not understand how the Jews had defeated his armies in so short a time. Perhaps, he apparently thought, this detailed description of Israeli military tactics would provide the answers; if so, the Jews were digging their graves by talking too much.

The Egyptians were digesting the lessons of the 1967 war. The newly appointed chief of staff, General Abdul Monein Riadh, and his colleague, General Ahmed Ismail Ali, agreed that Israeli supremacy, both in the air and in mobile armored warfare, could not be reversed in the foreseeable future. Still, they insisted that ways could be found to neutralize these Israeli advantages. And as the Israelis learned to their sorrow in 1973, the Egyptians were right.

By September 1968, the Egyptians were ready to renew their offensive. The Soviets had resupplied Cairo and Damascus with a wide assortment of sophisticated military hardware, together with Russian "technicians" to teach the Arabs to operate the equipment. The Israeli General Staff's inability to recognize that the Egyptian army was developing new military options proved to be an intelligence failure of the first magnitude.

The Arab states' answer was the so-called War of Attrition, which began on March 8, 1969, with a massive Egyptian bombardment across the Suez Canal directed at the Israeli fortifications on the east bank known as the Bar Lev Line. The line, which by that time had been largely completed, consisted of thirty fortified positions, at average intervals of about three hundred feet. The Israelis had also constructed, along the east bank of the canal, a twenty-to-thirty-foot-high sand rampart with a forty-five-degree slope facing the waterway. Even though this structure was lightly manned, it was still designed to absorb an Egyptian first strike while the Israelis mobilized.

The Egyptian decision to renew hostilities was part of a larger plan that was to lead to the 1973 war. General Riadh later explained to the military historian Trevor N. Dupuy his immediate objectives. They were to destroy the Bar Lev Line fortifications, to prevent the Israelis from reconstructing fortifications after they were destroyed, to make life intolerable for the

Israeli forces on the east bank of the canal, to inspire an offensive spirit in Egyptian troops, and to carry out practice canal-crossing operations.

The rationale behind this Egyptian offensive was that static warfare negated Israeli supremacy in armored mobility. Egypt, with its larger population, could afford to take casualties. Israel could not. And so, for eighty days, the Bar Lev Line was subject to an almost constant bombardment.

Initially, the Israeli Defense Forces responded with alacrity. But Israel could not match in numbers the guns or the ammunition available to the Egyptians. In any saturation shelling there are bound to be casualties, and as Cairo predicted, Israel felt keenly the loss of Jewish lives.

Both sides conducted surprise raids on enemy forces across the canal. The Egyptian purpose was not only to inflict casualties but to test the Israeli military reaction to the raids. They were looking for a pattern of response. The Israelis, on the other hand, tried to destroy Egyptian installations, in order to reduce Egypt's capacity to inflict damage.

Israeli forces had still another objective. Their military intelligence needed to know more about the sophisticated Russian equipment being used by the Egyptian military. American intelligence, with whom the Israelis maintained close contact, was also interested in learning more about Soviet weaponry.

The electronic equipment in the cockpit of the Israeli Mysteres and the F-4 Phantom jets alerts the pilot of the planes when their aircraft is being tracked by enemy radar. The Israelis discovered that a Russian-built advanced low-level radar, the P-12 system, had a range of 188 miles and was dangerously effective against Israeli planes.

The Israeli high command considered a series of options to cope with this hazard. The Israelis already had aerial photographs of the Soviet-built radar. It was housed in a trailer-type cab, but other than confirming its size and approximate weight, the photographs revealed little more.

The Israelis decided there was no substitute for learning about the radar at first hand. A select cadre of commandos began training for a precisely executed manuever that combined unique tactics with excellent intelligence. The result would draw the admiration of the world.

The radar and its trailer housing weighed seventy tons, but the essential radar components constituted only a small part of the total weight. Fortunately for the Israelis, the United States had, just six weeks before, delivered to Israel a fleet of new Sikorsky "Big Bird" helicopters, each with a lifting capacity of three to four tons.

Late in the evening of December 25, 1969, three of the big copters flew over the Sinai low enough to escape detection by Egyptian radar and headed for Ras Gharib, a cape on the Gulf of Suez, site of the highly secret P-12 radar. The commandos quickly overran the station, killing or capturing the defending and operating forces. Within an hour, the cab was ripped apart, the essential parts of the Soviet radar was disassembled, and the operating manuals gathered up. Before leaving, the Israelis blew up a ground-to-air missile that had been coupled to the radar. Prefabricated steel-wire slings

attached to the underbellies of the Israeli helicopters carried the purloined radar sections when the three big birds, under an umbrella of an Israeli fighter escort, flew to an air base deep in the Sinai. Shortly after the copters had safely landed, a team of American radar experts arrived at the Israeli air base. In cooperation with their Israeli counterparts, the radar sections were delivered to a well-guarded hangar, lined up in neat rows, and photographed from every conceivable angle.

Then, as the Israeli and American experts slowly disassembled the radar's components, draftsmen recorded the equipment's complicated circuitry. Finally, the secrets of this tracking device's efficiency were known. Both Jerusalem and Washington were then able to develop countermeasures to neutralize this type of Soviet radar.

It should be noted here that while the initial Egyptian and Syrian successes in the Yom Kippur War stemmed in part from an Israeli intelligence failure, the long-term Israeli skill in intelligence-gathering has engendered unusually close cooperation with the United States. Pentagon officers have often expressed their indebtedness to the Jewish state.

One such officer is Major General George F. Keegan, former chief of United States Air Force Intelligence. In June 1978, at a symposium on the Middle East, sponsored by *Foreign Policy Perspectives*, General Keegan said: "Today the ability of the U.S. Air Force in particular, and the army in general, to defend whatever position it has in NATO owes more to the Israeli intelligence input than it does to any other single source of intelligence, be it technology intercept, or what have you. . . . I could not have procured the intelligence on the Soviet air forces, their combat capabilities, their new weapons, their jamming and their electronics and their SAMs [surface-to-air-missiles] with five CIAs."

General Keegan was referring to a long series of Israeli intelligence reports over a period of years, flowing from Tel Aviv to Washington. A few examples should be noted here:

• The Soviet MIG-21 was one of the most sophisticated fighter planes in the world. The Soviets, using extreme precaution, introduced this plane into the Mideast in 1961. They trained the Egyptian, Syrian, and Iraqi pilots to fly the aircraft, but security and maintenance of the equipment remained the responsibility of the Soviets.

Mossad established contact with an Iraqi MIG-21 pilot, Munir Redfa, whose family of Maronite Christians felt endangered by Muslim fundamentalism. With some degree of hesitation, Redfa agreed to meet with the Israelis. After several months it was agreed that the Iraqi pilot would fly his MIG-21 to Israel. In return his family would be given safe passage out of Iraq and receive a new identity and would be paid £500,000.

A direct flight from Baghdad to Tel Aviv, over enemy territory, would have required aerial refueling and thus was considered too dangerous. On the other hand, Redfa's air base near Mosul in northern Iraq was within a few minutes' flying time from the Turkish border. And this is where the

CIA came in, for it had a secret air base in Turkey. Redfa crossed the Iraqi border and flew to the American base. There Redfa refueled and made his way over the Mediterranean to Israel.

• Since the end of World War II, the American military has obviously been forced to plan for a possible conflict with the Soviets. This planning has been helped immeasurably by the experience of the Israelis in fighting Soviet-trained troops. Using Israeli military intelligence, it has been possible for the Pentagon to construct a battlefield model that reflects Soviet combat doctrine.

• Israel has furnished Washington with captured Soviet air-to-ground and ground-to-air missiles and with Soviet antitank weapons. In addition, from the same source, the Pentagon received Soviet 122- and 130-millimeter artillery pieces, with ammunition for evaluation and testing.

• Within days of the destruction of the Egyptian air force on the ground during the 1967 war by Israeli aerial cannon, a retired U.S. Marine Air Force colonel was given detailed photochrome slides of the action, which were made available to the Pentagon.

• In 1973, American military intelligence knew of the existence of the advanced Soviet T-72 tank. It did not, however, have details of its operating capacity. The Israelis filled this void when they captured undamaged T-72 tanks and armored personnel carriers on the Syrian front. Upon examination, it was discovered that both vehicles were equipped with a special type of air filter. The Soviets were prepared to defend themselves from the effects of gas warfare.

The War of Attrition was escalated when the Israeli air force went into action. This was done to put pressure on the Egyptians to maintain a cease-fire. In his autobiography Dayan reports that on June 15, 1969, following a four-month period in which 29 Israelis were killed and 120 wounded, "I sought and received the approval of the Ministerial Defense Committee to order our air force to attack Egyptian forts, gun emplacements, and SAM-2 missile batteries in the northern canal sector. Four days later our aircraft went into action and bombed and strafed military targets from Kantara to Port Said at the northern end of the canal, for five hours. We shot down five enemy planes and lost two of our own. At the end of July, following the air-to-air encounters in which 12 Egyptian planes were brought down, the commander of the Egyptian air force was fired."

These successes were shortly followed by a raid of the Israeli forces across the Gulf of Suez during which "observation and guard posts, army camps, radar installations and a score of military vehicles were destroyed along the way." Even though more than a hundred Egyptian soldiers were killed in this action, Nasser learned about it only after the mission was completed and the Israelis were returning to their bases. Still, the Egyptian forces persisted in shelling the Bar Lev Line fortifications, and Jewish casualties continued to grow.

The Israelis responded with a series of air attacks on army bases deep inside Egypt. During the months of January, February, and March 1970, the Israeli air force roamed freely over the skies of Egypt and bombed at will

twenty military targets. Egyptian morale crumbled as Israeli planes were sighted flying unchallenged over the Land of the Pyramids.

Nasser was on the horns of a dilemma. One certain way to stop this carnage was to proclaim a cease-fire and to enter into peace negotiations with the enemy. This he refused to consider, and yet his military could not stop the Israeli air incursions. Toward the end of January 1970, he flew to Moscow and pleaded for not only more military hardware but for Soviet troops. Without Soviet help, the stability of his regime was threatened. Nasser's visit to the Soviet Union was well publicized, and Israeli intelligence was alerted. The Soviets, it seemed, were sympathetic.

More Soviet missile units and their operating crews were sent to Egypt. Detailed information to this effect was forwarded to Israeli military intelligence in Tel Aviv. An Israeli military intelligence officer in Washington then contacted his American counterpart at the CIA and presented the alarming news: Soviet troops were in Egypt.

Dayan reported, "On April 1, they [the Soviets] were joined by three squadrons of fighter planes with their Russian crews. Russian pilots defended the skies of Cairo, Alexandria, and Aswan; Russian troops operated the more sophisticated SAM-3 batteries and the entire antiaircraft defense system throughout Egypt was handed over to the Soviet command." Again Israeli intelligence operatives promptly reported this new development to their headquarters in Tel Aviv and to their colleagues in the CIA.

This Israeli intelligence was greeted in Washington with alarm. The Americans were afraid that the war could get out of control and that their forces might become involved. The Israelis were also concerned. They had no desire to become engaged in a battle with Soviet pilots, yet if the Soviets attacked, the Israeli air force would have to defend itself.

Early in March, Israeli photoreconnaissance planes revealed that the Soviets were building a new SAM-3 missile (low-altitude) antiaircraft defense system in Egypt. Directional radio intercepts confirmed that the system was manned by Soviet personnel. By June 1970, a total of fifty-five SAM-3 batteries were in operation.

The Soviet Union expanded its military involvement. On a mission over the Red Sea coast on April 18, Israeli aircraft encountered several MIG-21 intercepters with Egyptian markings. The enemy pilots, however, communicated with each other in their native tongue—Russian.

At this point Israel was anxious to avoid a confrontation with the Soviets, and thus, the General Staff temporarily suspended deep penetration raids. Through undisclosed diplomatic channels, the Israeli Foreign Office informed both Egypt and the Soviet Union that this unilateral moratorium would remain in effect only so long as the enemy missile system was not moved within nineteen miles of the west side of the canal. The Soviets did not heed the Israeli warning, and two months later new missile batteries were installed within sixteen miles of the canal. The effectiveness of the revitalized Egyptian air-defense system was demonstrated during July. In that month, twenty Israeli planes were destroyed. At the same time, Soviet pilots began to extend their areas of operations, and on July 25, 1970, Soviet

fighters attempted to intercept Israeli aircraft near the canal. They were not successful.

This Soviet boldness was intolerable to Israel. Five days later, July 30, 1970, the Israeli air force set up a classical trap for the intruders. Anticipating Soviet interception, a squadron of Israeli Phantom aircraft set out to attack a radar station on the Egyptian side of the Gulf of Suez. What the Soviets evidently did not observe was another squadron of Israeli Mirage planes flying cover for their colleagues.

Out of the blue, sixteen Soviet-piloted MIG-21s appeared and engaged the Israeli Phantoms. In a matter of minutes four MIGs were shot down and a fifth damaged by the high-flying Mirages. The ambush had been successful. The balance of the Soviet-piloted planes withdrew from this unequal conflict, and the Israeli planes returned to their bases without damage.

The War of Attrition continued to grind out casualties on both sides. By August 1970, the Israelis reported the death, on all fronts, of five hundred soldiers. Some two thousand had been wounded. Cairo's precise casualty figures are not available. The Israeli estimate of fifteen thousand Egyptians killed is considered by Depuy to be "at least three times too high." Still, Nasser had paid a high price for this aggression. The cities of the west bank of the Suez Canal had been evacuated to protect their civilian populations from the punishing Israeli raids. Tens of thousands of new Egyptian refugees poured into the streets and alleys of Cairo.

Finally, an American-sponsored cease-fire took effect on August 8, 1970, and with it a still-unexplained lapse of American military intelligence. The key provision of the agreement, negotiated by President Nixon's national security adviser, Henry Kissinger, provided for a total military freeze within an area thirty-one miles wide on each side of the canal. It should have been easy for the United States to observe whether this proviso was violated. There may have been political reasons why the United States Air Force did not continuously monitor the movement of Egyptian armor and missiles while flying over Israeli airspace. But an orbiting photoreconnaissance satellite could have yielded the same basic information.

Two days after the agreement was signed, a puzzled Henry Kissinger spoke to the State Department's director of intelligence and research, Ray Cline. He had received a report from Jerusalem that Egypt, in violation of the agreement, had moved ground-to-air missiles eastward toward the banks of the canal. He asked Cline to look into the Israeli claim. Cline's response was unequivocal: "If the Israelis state that the Egyptians have moved their missiles forward, you can believe them. After all, they have an excellent intelligence-gathering system. By means of radio intercepts and aerial photography they can monitor Russian-Egyptian military activity on the east bank [of the Canal]."

It appears strange that American photo satellites had not discovered this treaty violation. Cline explained, "Most people do not understand that in spite of our excellent photo satellites that can detect military movement above ground, these instruments fly in a predetermined orbit. They cannot monitor all areas of potential danger. For some reason that I do not under-

stand, the satellites were not at that time policing the Sinai peninsula, and thus, Kissinger did not have from American intelligence any confirmation of the Israeli claim."

Within two weeks after the American satellite's orbit was reprogrammed to fly over the Sinai, the Israeli claim that the Egyptians had moved their missiles closer to the canal was accepted by Kissinger. Israel viewed this acknowledged treaty violation with great concern and protested to Washington. Kissinger, however, considered his negotiated cease-fire to be a brilliant diplomatic achievement and was reluctant to admit publicly that its terms had been violated. He seemed more anxious to get on with his primary goal, détente with the Soviet Union.

Gamal Abdel Nasser died of a heart attack in September 1970. His successor, Vice-President Anwar el-Sadat, appeared at first to be a leader with a more moderate stance toward Israel than the bellicose Nasser. The hopes of both Israel and the United States were quickly dashed. Sadat spoke in moderate terms, but his peace proposals, essentially unacceptable to Israel, insisted for the most part on total withdrawal from the territories captured in 1967.

In May 1971 Sadat entered into a comprehensive treaty with the Soviet Union that guaranteed Egypt a lavish supply of arms and the backing of Soviet diplomatic muscle. Thenceforth, the situation deteriorated into hardened positions and finally to the decision of Egypt and Syria to attack on October 6, 1973, catching Israel off guard.

Major General Abraham ("Bren") Adan, a veteran defender of the Jewish enclave since the days before independence, was a tank commander in the Sinai during the Yom Kippur War. He explained to us that in both the 1956 and 1967 wars the Israelis were able to destroy Egyptian armor by engaging in highly mobile flanking maneuvers coupled with strong air-to-ground support. Israel had been able to win over enemies who fought with as much as a three-to-one advantage in military hardware. In the case of Egypt, in both 1956 and 1967 its antitank missiles were not a serious threat to Israeli armor.

By 1973 all this had changed. The Egyptians again had three-to-one advantage in hardware. But, as Adan explained, Israel had lost a great deal of mobility because of the obsolescence of its personnel carriers. "Many of our vehicles were thirty years old. In contrast, Cairo was well equipped with much newer American-built vehicles.

This, however, was not the limit of Israel's lack of preparation. "Our planes and tanks, to which we gave priority, were up to date," said Adan, but "our second-echelon soldiers, who were responsible for supply and evacuation, did not even have rifles, and most of our fighting forces lacked automatic weapons. There was also a shortage of ammunition and night-vision equipment."

When the war started, the Israelis encountered a series of rude surprises. Israeli intelligence had disclosed that both the Egyptian and Syrian armies were equipped with antitank missiles. The range of effectiveness of these weapons was known. The wire-directed antitank weapon, which works like a

wire-guided model airplane, has a range of 3,000 meters; and its junior brother, the RPG-7, a rocket that is fired from the shoulder, is operational to 350 to 400 meters. In contrast, the Israeli antitank missiles had a range of 150 to 180 meters.

At the end of the first day of the Yom Kippur War, the Egyptians destroyed about 180 Israeli tanks out of a force of 300. Many of the casualties resulted from antitank missile fire.

Since Israeli military intelligence knew of the existence of these weapons, what, if any, countermeasures had been taken to plan for the defense of Israeli armor? In essence, none. The fault, which is common in planning military tactics, is relying on the experiences of previous wars in developing strategy. Adan explained: "We had met the missiles in 1956 and 1967. And those times, when we were on the attack, when we were maneuvering, we had all the advantages of surprises and missiles did not cause too many problems. One of the conclusions of the 1967 war was that Arab antitank weapons could not stand against us. We believed that the tank itself is the best antitank weapon."

But this was not 1967. It was clear to Adan and others during the first day of the war that the new antitank missiles represented a threat to Israeli armor and, by extension, to the Jewish state. Again, was Israeli military intelligence at fault? Said Adan, "We did not know in detail the Egyptian tactical plans for the use of the missiles. But we had enough information, if it had been carefully analyzed, to have made a difference. We knew that their tanks would advance on a broad zone supported by infantry. What we did not know, however, was that the infantry, including second-echelon rear units, carried a massive supply of antitank missiles."

As the surprised, ill-equipped Israeli tank force lumbered into battle without infantry or artillery support, it encountered well-prepared ambushes. The terrain of the Suez peninsula is very swampy. The avenues of approach are limited, and so, it was a simple matter for Egyptian infantry, equipped with antitank missiles, to lie in wait for Israeli armor to pass and be destroyed.

Adan recalled, "As our strong points along the canal were being overrun, the defenders called for help. Because of mistakes, two-thirds of our tanks were at the rear instead of being deployed forward. Automatically our tanks divided into small groups and sped to the rescue. Remember, we were moving without infantry and little artillery. As our armor traveled on small, concentrated avenues of approach, we were taken piecemeal by the Egyptians. The second wave of Israeli tanks, two armored brigades, appeared, and they too were ambushed and suffered heavy losses."

But this was not the limit of the problems faced by Israel's armored divisions. The tank commanders had been furnished topographical maps of the Sinai that showed the location of the deadly swamps. And yet, the first night about fifty tanks became entrapped in the marshes with the same result. The tactical mistakes of the Israelis were repeated again on the third night, when another fifty of the tanks under Major General Ariel Sharon were lost to Egyptian fire in the same fashion.

Was Israeli military intelligence responsible for these disasters? Adan told us that "the problems were caused only in part by lack of intelligence. A more valid reason was our misuse of available intelligence data. This was due to overconfidence on the part of our high command." The nightmare of confusion during the first few days was exacerbated when the Egyptians successfully jammed Israeli radio communications. The result was that contact between Israeli forces was disrupted, leading to the unnecessary loss of lives and equipment. In retrospect, there was no excuse for this happening. Enemy jamming was to be expected, and as Adan acknowledges, "We were trained to counter this type of interference, but for the first few days we were unsuccessful."

Radio jamming is effective only when the frequency used remains constant. One common approach to overcome enemy jamming, which the Israelis belatedly used, is to keep changing frequencies on a predetermined schedule. Obviously this requires a high degree of coordination between the sender and the receiver. But it worked, and communications were reestablished between the Israeli high command and their units in the field. In the meantime, infantry and artillery joined the armored divisions and the Israelis swung into their conventional attack formations.

Sharon is one of Israel's most talented and colorful tank commanders. He has been compared to the late American General George Patton, who had a tendency to ignore orders from his military superiors. To both men, the best defense was a good offense.

By the end of the third day of the war, Sharon's forces were within three miles of the canal. It was then he discovered a gap between the Egyptian Second Army to the north and the Third Army. The general immediately reported this intelligence to southern command headquarters and requested permission to plan, and organize his corps for, a crossing.

On October 16, ten days after one hundred thousand Egyptian soldiers had crossed the canal, Israeli forces stood on the banks of the Suez. By the next night Adan's and Sharon's tanks were crossing the canal in spite of withering Egyptian fire. The casualties were high on both sides.

Soon Sharon's tanks joined Israeli paratroopers and the general announced to headquarters, "The invasion of Africa has begun." Indeed, Israel had won, but at a terrible price in casualties and self-esteem. And the terrible price could be traced in great measure to the failure of intelligence in a state still transfixed over its easy blitzkrieg victory of six years earlier. If the earlier Lavon affair was also a failure, it was one based on political rivalry and overzealousness. The 1973 failure stemmed from so many years of success. Even today, Israel's collective psyche has not recovered from it.

After they crossed the canal, the Israelis began to neutralize the belt of deadly Soviet antiaircraft missiles. Most of the installations were destroyed, but the Israelis managed to capture intact several SA-6 missile batteries. This was an important military intelligence breakthrough. This relatively simple, but highly effective, weapon was unknown, both to the Israelis and to the Western powers. After the Americans had studied the missile, a high-ranking Pentagon official was quoted in the December 3, 1973, issue of *Avi-*

ation Week as saying that "the SA-6 carries out its mission excellently. The U.S. is an entire decade behind Russia in this field. In my opinion over the next four years we shall need 100 million dollars to build an antiaircraft missile, which can reach the current accomplishments of the SA-6."

When the Syrians, simultaneously with the Egyptians, opened their offensive on the Golan, the Israeli tank forces were outnumbered: their 177 tanks faced an initial invading force of 500 Syrian tanks, which were joined after midnight by an additional 300. The next day the Syrian tanks penetrated the lines of the outnumbered Israeli forces, and the entire southern sector of the Golan command collapsed. But reinforcements first intended for the Sinai were brought up. By the third day, the tide of battle had changed. The Israeli air force and reserve units had stopped the Syrian advance, and the Syrians retreated. They had lost their appetite for combat.

Israel had soundly beaten the enemy on both fronts. In the north it was within artillery range of Damascus. And in the south the Egyptian Third Army on the west bank of the Suez was surrounded.

With what appeared at that time to be unseemly haste, Kissinger, acting through the United Nations, imposed a cease-fire. He warned the Israelis not to destroy the Egyptian Third Army. And he insisted that food and water be supplied to Sadat's beleaguered forces.

It is now clear that Kissinger had learned that the Soviets were sending nuclear weapons to Egypt. In May 1977, Bob Woodward reported in the *Washington Post* that since 1970 a navy spy unit, operating from an office building in Alexandria, Virginia, controlled a group of undercover agents abroad. As many as seventy-five spies were under contract to monitor ports abroad, looking for Soviet vessels and shipments of nuclear weapons. They used commercial and business cover for their intelligence-gathering operations. And it was their reports that alerted Kissinger to the introduction of Soviet nuclear weapons to Egypt.

Kissinger still had another reason to insist that Sadat's Third Army not be destroyed. He believed, as did Sadat himself, that if this happened Sadat would be overthrown. The American Secretary of State was his only hope. Only Kissinger had the power to force Jerusalem to spare Cairo, and Sadat personally, this ultimate humiliation. The Egyptian accepted the quid pro quo: his army would be spared in return for future American-Egyptian cooperation. He accepted even though the Soviet Union had trained his armies. The Soviets had supplied Egypt with massive quantities of sophisticated arms. The Soviet Union had been his political champion. But the war was lost. With American help he could save his armies and regain the Sinai without risking another military defeat. Hence, Sadat was willing to rid Cairo of Moscow's influence and cast his lot with Washington.

17

The Spy at the Nuclear Dawn

IT IS PROBABLE that Israel possesses nuclear weapons or at least the ability to produce them. The direct evidence of this is understandably hard to find, but the circumstantial evidence is abundant. Furthermore, the Jewish state did not acquire this ability by stealing plans from another nation or by infiltrating the inner councils of the nuclear powers. Israel's success is based on early curiosity, especially that of a scientist-spy named Joseph Blumenfeld, who as early as 1935, in a visit to the Soviet Union, foresaw the dawn of the nuclear age, thereby becoming a kind of nuclear Prometheus of Israel.

The first verified splitting of an atomic nucleus took place in December 1938 and was revealed to the world at the Washington Conference on Nuclear Physics in January 1939. It was not until December 1942, on the squash court at the University of Chicago, that Enrico Fermi and Leo Szilard produced the first controlled nuclear chain reaction, a harbinger of both nuclear weapons and nuclear-generated electric power.

In 1935 only a few scientists and possibly a handful of political leaders were aware of the awesome power waiting to be unleashed. One of these scientists was Chaim Weizmann, a world-famous chemist as well as the leader of the Zionist movement. Another was Blumenfeld, a geochemist and Weizmann's brother-in-law. Both men had been born in Russia; Weizmann had grown up in England and was a British citizen, while Blumenfeld lived most of his life in France. One political leader who may have been prescient enough to foresee the potential of nuclear power was Joseph Stalin, the dictator of the Soviet Union.

Most of the world's nuclear physicists and Stalin, through his scientific advisers, were aware of a historic paper published in 1934 by Leo Szilard, which had attracted virtually no attention among the general public.

The remarkably gifted Szilard, a Hungarian expatriate and a Jew, based his thesis on the discoveries made since 1910 about the nature of matter. Ernest Rutherford, a New Zealander who worked successively at McGill University in Montreal and later at the Cavendish Laboratory at Cambridge University in England, is generally credited with "discovering" the atomic nucleus in 1911—which is to say he determined that the atom was a positively charged nucleus surrounded by negatively charged electrons.

In 1932, James Chadwick, a student of Rutherford, made a further discovery: he showed that the nucleus consisted not only of positively charged protons but also of neutrons. A neutron is of the same mass as the proton but is electrically neutral. Because the neutron had no charge a stream of them fired into a nucleus would penetrate more easily, releasing energy and perhaps unidentified subnuclear particles.

Extrapolating from Chadwick's discovery, Szilard in his 1934 paper (which, in effect, was a patent application) postulated that a neutron fired from an outside source into a nucleus might liberate other neutrons, which in turn would penetrate other nuclei, and so on, creating a chain reaction. Each separation of a neutron would release a cataclysmic amount of energy from the binding force within the nucleus, as postulated by Albert Einstein in his equation $E = mc^2$.

This was such an astounding concept that Szilard had a hard time getting anyone to take it seriously. When he suggested it to the great Rutherford, he was (as he later told fellow Hungarian physicist Edward Teller) "thrown out of Rutherford's office."

As every high school physics student now knows, Szilard was right, although seven years were to pass before Fermi, working with Szilard, proved it. The United States government officially recognized Szilard's amazing foresight by granting him a patent on the chain reaction. Considering the magnitude of the achievement, today's researcher or inventor might wince to know that Szilard sold his patent to the government for a paltry $20,000.

In his paper, Szilard had suggested that the chain reaction might be achieved with at least three heavy elements—uranium, thorium, and beryllium. Anyone who took the chain reaction theory seriously would be concerned about the availability of these metals.

There is no firm evidence that Rutherford, after brushing off Szilard, commented on the Hungarian's outlandish concept. Yet, circumstantially it seems probable that he would at least have mentioned it to two outstanding scientists with whom he was closely associated. One was Peter L. Kapitza, a brilliant Russian-born physicist with whom Rutherford exchanged scientific talk and gossip almost every day. The other was his close friend Weizmann, the chemist and world Zionist leader.

About this time three dissimilar men made pilgrimages to the Soviet Union. One was Kaptiza, who left presumably for a scientific conference in his native land. But Kapitza never returned, and the reasons for his absorption into Russia have never been firmly established. Apparently he was simply kidnapped by the Soviet state and told he must apply his talents to

the Communist society. Rutherford was bitter about Kapitza's disappearance but consoled himself with the opinion that "a scientist can work anywhere if he has the means." Reluctantly he shipped to his former colleague all the elaborate laboratory equipment he had had built for Kapitza at Cambridge. Thenceforth, the Russian became one of the most creative members of the Soviet Union's expanding scientific team. Unwittingly, Rutherford had contributed to Soviet nuclear research.

The second man to visit the Soviet Union was Frédéric Joliot-Curie, an eminent nuclear physicist married to a fellow physicist, Irène Curie. She was the daughter of Marie Curie, the Polish scientist who discovered radium. Joliot-Curie, probably through his friendship with the pro-Soviet writer Romain Rolland, was permitted an interview with Joseph Stalin. It is possible that Joliot-Curie discussed the potential of nuclear energy with Stalin and persuaded the Soviet dictator of the importance of finding uranium deposits in Russia.

But from the standpoint of the future state of Israel, the most important visitor to the Soviet Union was Joseph Blumenfeld. His background left him uniquely qualified to lay the groundwork for Israel's eventual involvement in nuclear development.

Blumenfeld's achievements might have been largely unnoticed had not the authors been given the unpublished records of Boris Guriel's interviews with him. From 1948 to 1952 Guriel was director of the Political Department of the Israeli Foriegn Office, an agency charged with gathering political and, in some cases, scientific intelligence.

Guriel, acting in his intelligence capacity, first interviewed Blumenfeld in the latter's Paris office on the rue de Promy in March 1949. They met again in March 1953, and Blumenfeld elaborated further on his unusual visit to the Soviet Union nearly two decades earlier.

To understand Blumenfeld's contribution it is necessary to begin in 1929, when Chaim Weizmann created the Jewish Agency as a shadow government for the prospective state of Israel. The agency, to achieve its political objectives, required information on which to base its decisions and therefore developed its own intelligence arm. Blumenfeld, as Weizmann's friend and brother-in-law, was not in the strictest sense a spy, but he was anxious to learn what he could about geology and rare metals in the Soviet Union. His visit was made possible by his friendship with Joliot-Curie, who was widely revered in Russia.

Guriel described Blumenfeld as "of medium height, fair complexion, glasses, swift movements; full command of Russian, French, English, German (no Hebrew at all). Very friendly with surrounding people, somewhat enigmatic; very modest in behavior; equal dealing with people of various standing (from chamber maids to ministers and presidents); outspoken in conversation; somewhat didactic habits."

In the memoirs of Vera Weizmann, published in 1967, Blumenfeld is described as "a unique, irreplaceable character, whose kindness, advice and sympathy were always at the service of his numerous friends. . . . He worked for many years with the brilliant French chemist Professor Ur-

bain. . . . And for several years, up to his retirement, was managing director of the Société des Terres Rares. He came to Israel after the formation of the state to promote excavations of rare metals in the Negev."

Blumenfeld told Guriel, "For a long time I had cherished an idea to go to the Soviet Union, to learn about the new unknown phenomenon which had sprung from my 1910 Paris emigré acquaintance—Vladimir Ilich Lenin."

There were other reasons for his trip: "As a man of applied science [chemistry] I was keen to get direct knowledge of Soviet Russian scientific exploits profusely propagated by Communists in Europe." He also believed he could learn more about Kapitza's mysterious disappearance, since he was acquainted with some of the leading Soviet nuclear scientists, including Abram Yoffe, Igor Tamm, and Yakov Zeldovitch. He had also become friendly with Soviet industrial executives, including Gleb. Krzhanovsky (an old crony of Lenin) and Samuel Weizmann, brother of Chaim Weizmann.

Another of Blumenfeld's interests was the state of German-Soviet relations, which had taken strange twists and turns in the era between the wars. As early as 1920, Victor Kopp, a Trotsky collaborator, covertly approached German armament firms about production for the Soviets. In 1921 Germany was offering financial aid to the Soviets, the common bond being the joint belief that Poland should be eliminated, a goal the two nations achieved during their brief entente at the outbreak of World War II. In March 1921 the Germany military agreed to help finance the building of airplanes by the Albatross and Junkers works. In return the new Soviet Union helped to train German aviators and tank crews. The countries jointly developed poison gas in the Soviet Union, and Soviet officers were trained in Berlin. As late as 1928, Major General Werner von Blomberg visited the Soviet Union to review joint military maneuvers. The allies toasted each other and fixed their military sights on Poland.

By the time Joseph Blumenfeld visited the Soviet Union in 1935, military cooperation between the two countries had been discontinued by Hitler's orders, despite the preference for it by the German high command. For several years rumors had persisted that the generals of the Reichswehr and the Red Army were engaged in a conspiracy directed against their respective political leaders. Blumenfeld had learned of this a year earlier from Eduard Beneš, the president of Czechoslovakia who had heard "reliable" rumors from Berlin. By 1935 the Stalin purge trials had started, which convinced Blumenfeld that Beneš's reports were accurate.

Joliot-Curie provided Blumenfeld with a letter of introduction and a message for Soviet scientists. Although peripherally interested in Soviet politics, Blumenfeld's prime concern was the progress of science in the fledgling Communist state. His first stop was the Leningrad Physico-Technical Institute, headed by Abram Yoffe, the father of Soviet physics.

And it was in Yoffe's laboratory that Blumenfeld solved the mystery of the missing Peter Kapitza. The former British resident was working with Yoffe in the well-guarded atomic nuclear laboratory. They were studying neutron release from radioactive uranium ore. Blumenfeld inquired of Ka-

pitza as to "whether he was bound to remain, for the time being, in Russia."

"Kapitza's reply sounded quite ambiguous," he told Guriel in recollecting the meeting. "The USSR was short of scientific personnel to guide the rapid development of Soviet industrialization and to direct the path of scientists in their quest for useful discoveries. Kapitza believed Russia's science was imperfect and in an infantile state; this was so despite a tremendous effort by the old Czarist school of physicists and chemists."

Blumenfeld observed no direct governmental interference with the work of Soviet scientists. He did, however, "perceive some hints as to the tempo of scientific work. There seemed to be indirect government pressure to get the experiments done quickly. Everyone was in a hurry."

The meddling from above, Blumenfeld guessed, "was associated with Russia's admiration for German science. The Russians would praise Roentgen but not Rutherford, Max Planck and not Becquerel, and even Otto Hahn's name was heard more than Poincaré's."

The only exception to this German bias was Frédéric Joliot-Curie. While Joliot-Curie was without question a great physicist, he was also a friend of Communism, which probably accounted for his special standing in the Soviet Union.

Blumenfeld left Leningrad convinced that Soviet scientists were aware of Szilard's postulation of energy from the atomic nucleus. He felt they were pursuing the possibility of creating nuclear energy from radium.

The visiting scientist went on to Moscow, where he soon was welcomed by a then little-known protégé of Stalin, Georgi M. Malenkov (after Stalin's death, he was briefly to be the most powerful man in the Soviet Union). Apparently Malenkov was so impressed with Blumenfeld that he went out of his way to arrange a meeting with Stalin himself.

The dictator proved to be an engaging and genial host. He and his Jewish guest sat in overstuffed leather chairs in Stalin's study in the Kremlin. Stalin showed not only an interest but a surprising knowledge of Blumenfeld's field—rare metals, particularly cerium, thorium, and uranium. He wanted to know about the work of Blumenfeld and other scientists in Western Europe "and our contacts in overseas countries, first of all in the United States and then in South America. He was also keen to know of our efforts to get raw materials (uranium oxide) from French possessions in Africa."

Blumenfeld later recalled that "when Stalin was asking me about raw material sources, he mentioned in an odd way the supply of uranium ore in France and the availability of the metal in Czechoslovakia." Considering that this was only 1935, the Russian dictator seemed remarkably well informed about the frontiers of science. Either he knew of Szilard's work, or his own scientists had briefed him on its implications.

In the fall of 1979 the authors showed the transcript of Blumenfeld's conversations with Guriel, including the former's report on his talk with Stalin, to Edward Teller, one of the world's renowned nuclear physicists. After reading with care the names of the Russian scientists working on

nuclear fission in 1935 and the apparent appreciation of Stalin for the value of uranium, Teller said, "I am not surprised that the Russian scientists were working on nuclear fission that early. They were all extremely capable men. I have read many of their scientific papers. But what does surprise me is that a political figure like Stalin was aware of the importance of uranium deposits. If, at that time, I would have asked Franklin Roosevelt what uranium is used for, he would probably have replied 'I don't know. Is it used in toothpaste?' "

After discussing science with Blumenfeld, Stalin turned to political affairs. "He made some derisive remarks about the new [Hitler] regime in Germany. He spoke about the German historical *Drang nach Osten* and about the looming German-Japanese pincer movement against Russia. He never uttered 'USSR,' but instead emphasized 'Russia.' "

Stalin was interested in Blumenfeld's background. "Are you Jewish?" The quick affirmative answer did not appear to displease Stalin. Blumenfeld explained he had left Russia in 1905 and settled in France.

Now Blumenfeld had a request. He wanted permission to travel to Siberia by way of the Trans-Siberian Railway. He told Stalin he sought to learn more about the Russian mining industry in southern Siberia. And, coincidentally, while he was in that region he wanted to see the countryside where his mother's parents had spent long years as political exiles in czarist Russia.

What Blumenfeld did not tell Stalin was that he was anxious to see with his own eyes the extent of the vast uranium deposits in that part of Siberia. But he also gained Stalin's confidence by surprising him with evidence of the activities of an infamous traitor, Yevno Azev. "I told him," Blumenfeld said, "that I was actually a messenger of revolutionaries and was entrusted to bring proven evidence of Yevno Azev's misdeeds as an agent-provocateur." From the transcript of the interview it is not clear to whom the evidence was presented. Azev was the son of a poor Jewish tailor who became a leader of the Social Revolutionary party's dread terror-fighting section while, at the same time, acting as an informer for the czarist police. He took money from both sides, deceiving and cheating both. (His activities are described in Bertram Wolfe's *Three Who Made a Revolution*.) Blumenfeld's gesture apparently convinced Stalin of his political reliability, and the dictator granted his guest permission to visit the Novosibirsk region.

Blumenfeld had one more card to play. He had known Lenin quite well, and Stalin was aware of this. "Is it true," Stalin finally asked, "that you met Lenin in Paris several times?" Blumenfeld responded with a brief recounting of some of his impressions of the founder of the Soviet state. "You should give us a written recollection of your encounters with Lenin," said Stalin as he rose for a final handshake with his guest.

Blumenfeld found the discussion of Lenin more amusing for what he dared not say, rather than for what he had told Stalin. Blumenfeld recalled his departure from the meeting with Stalin: "Descending the steps leading from Stalin's office, I could hardly control myself from laughing. I recol-

lected that when meeting Lenin in Paris in 1910 I was living on the fourth story of a house on the rue Oudry, and Trotsky was living for a while in the same house, so that when Lenin used to whistle me down to walk with him to a public library, Trotsky, when hearing Lenin's whistle, sometimes was peeping out from his window shouting hello to Lenin, and Lenin would grimace back, making a wry face.

"In recalling my meetings with Lenin twenty-five years later for Stalin, I had to hold back and not tell the whole story. Trotsky's name was anathema to Stalin. Even hearing Trotsky's name mentioned might result in Stalin's accusing the person whom mentioned it of Trotskyism—a most severe crime in Soviet Russia."

With a laissez-passer approved by Stalin himself, Blumenfeld boarded a train with an immediate destination of Novosibirsk on the Trans-Siberian Railroad in southwest Siberia. As he sat in the crowded compartment, peering through the soot-covered windows and the clouds of smoke from the belching engine, his thoughts drifted back to an old friend, Moissey Novomeysky, from whom Blumenfeld had learned that there were vast uranium-ore deposits in the Altai Mountains, southeast of Novosibirsk.

Novomeysky was born and had grown up in southwest Siberia, where he became a highly respected mining engineer. In 1908 he had taken a trip to Palestine to undertake a study of the feasibility of utilizing the minerals in the Dead Sea region. In 1920, having become a Zionist, he immigrated to Palestine and began actively to promote the mining of potash from the Dead Sea. Finally, in 1926, the British government granted a mining concession to a consortium headed by Novomeysky, called the Jordan Exploration Company. Blumenfeld had become one of the shareholders.

The two friends met frequently when Novomeysky came to Paris. For Blumenfeld their friendship was more than a common interest in the mining of rare metals, for Novomeysky had converted his Paris friend to the cause of Zionism.

As the train rumbled across the steppes of Siberia, Blumenfeld took account of his life thus far. "It was Novomeysky who was responsible for my affiliation with Zionism," he thought, "and he urged me to take an interest in Zionism not as a *Weltanschauung* but as a sort of pilot plant to apply to my lifelong chemical and technological vocation—my career in rare earth metallurgy, of extracting metals from their ores. It was Novomeysky who moved me in spirit and body to the Negev of Palestine around the Dead Sea wilderness."

The train's brakes shuddered and interrupted Blumenfeld's thoughts. He had arrived at Novosibirsk.

It was almost a forbidden city to foreigners. Already, in 1935, plans were under way to build a large center for scientific research nearby. The reason for the selection of Novosibirsk was apparently because it was an ideal place to enforce security. (The selection of Los Alamos as a World War II site to develop the nuclear bomb was made for similar reasons.)

Blumenfeld, however, with his top-level credentials from Stalin himself,

found the local officials at his service. First he was taken on a tour of coal mines outside the city and then on a one-hundred-mile drive to the foot of the Altai Mountains and the vast uranium deposits there.

Novomeysky's report was correct: Russia had within her boundaries the raw material needed to enter the nuclear age. To Blumenfeld, who took Szilard's forecast seriously, the promise and peril of this condition was obvious.

The unassuming Blumenfeld, even as a guest of Stalin, had pulled off an intelligence coup of the first magnitude. Combining his knowledge of what was happening at the Leningrad Physico-Technical Institute with the activities at the uranium deposits, he concluded that the scientists were probing the secrets of the nucleus with the intention of making a bomb.

As background to this, he recalled Stalin's almost paranoid fear of the threat from both east and west. This tended to round out the picture of the feverish search for weapons that would ensure security.

An obvious question at this point in our narrative is why the Soviets, among the leaders in nuclear research, did not manage to build a nuclear bomb during World War II, since they had the scientists and the uranium. The answer is twofold. First, the nucleus of the atom was not actually split until December 1938 by Otto Hahn and Fritz Strassman at the Max Planck Institute in Berlin. Until this historic breakthrough, the theory positing nuclear fission had been just that: a theory, and not experimentally proven. Second, the enrichment of uranium oxide to weapons-grade uranium required a tremendous capital investment and a prodigious amount of electrical energy. In 1939 the Soviets, desperately preparing for war, had neither the resources nor the time to explore the nuclear option further.

At the beginning of this chapter, we discussed the world's assumption that Israel has both the raw materials and the scientific capability to produce a fissionable weapon. No one knows whether Israel also possesses the more formidable and efficient fusion weapon—the hydrogen bomb.

Onee thing is certain. The groundwork laid by Blumenfeld, including that historic trip to the Soviet Union, was crucial to Israel's awareness of the power in the atom and its effort to become a nuclear power. That is why, in 1949, Ben-Gurion paid tribute to Blumenfeld as the man who could deliver his people into the atomic age.

There are some gaps in the Israeli nuclear record, as compared with other countries. For example, there is no firm evidence that the Jewish state has ever conducted any nuclear tests. When a nuclear or thermonuclear explosion occurs above ground, radioactive debris is spewed into the atmosphere and carried over vast distances, where it is monitored by scientists of the United States and several other countries.

Since the Limited Test-Ban Treaty of 1963, however, only underground testing has been permitted. In underground testing, radiation does not contaminate the upper air mass and thus cannot be detected. Even seismic shock waves can be muffled by exploding the nuclear device in an oversized underground cavern, limiting its detection area to a radius of a few hundred miles.

Then how do we know that Israel has nuclear and possibly thermonuclear capability? In seeking an answer to the question, we must examine the priorities of the State of Israel at its birth. When the armistice with the Arab belligerents was signed on the island of Rhodes in 1949, the leaders of Israel were obviously obsessed with finding the means for the young state to survive. The peace treaty called for in the text of the agreement never materialized. The determination to destroy the new state could not be expunged from Arab minds.

Ben-Gurion looked across his borders and made a calculation; there were six hundred thousand Jews in Israel and 30 million Arabs in the states surrounding them. The odds spoke for themselves.

The survival of Jews for so many years was in itself miraculous to the prime minister. For Israel's continued existence he placed his faith in intelligence, using the word in both its broad and narrow meanings. He may have prayed for divine guidance, but he turned to productivity and science, including the wonder of nuclear fission.

In the fall of 1949, when Israel was still smarting from the campaign Great Britain had waged unsuccessfully against creation of the Jewish state, Ben-Gurion quipped sarcastically to Blumenfeld, "Our newborn state may become a champion of atomic potentiality surrounded by Arab enemies commanded by Bevin British."

There were some residual benefits from the British mandate. A Professor Piccard, who had been in charge of geological resources under the British mandate, accepted Ben-Gurion's invitation to head Israel's Institute of Geology after independence. Piccard soon convinced his prime minister that phosphates in the Negev could yield the uranium necessary for developing nuclear power.

But Blumenfeld was the key factor in the entire endeavor. Eliezer Kaplan, Ben-Gurion's friend and the state's first minister of finance, emphasized to the prime minister that Blumenfeld possessed rare scientific talents. Ben-Gurion was instrumental in the founding, in 1949, of the Israel Mining Company, a conglomerate that supervised the search for, and the extraction of, copper, iron, manganese, and kaolin in the Negev. Blumenfeld was appointed managing director.

"My main interest," Blumenfeld later told Guriel, "was focused on phosphoric acid—the phosphates of the Negev—as a most valuable fertilizer of the soil. At least of equal importance was that the uranium, when enriched, could be used to produce energy for peaceful purposes and as a deterrent in preventing war."

Ben-Gurion, who served as his own defense minister, assigned Major General Shlomo Shamir, a Haganah leader, as a link between the army and the potash project. Commander Shlomo Gur of the army's scientific corps supervised the Negev operations. Scientists of the Sieff Research Institute provided technical assistance.

Progress was painfully slow. The phosphates were of poor quality, and various means were tried to enrich them, with limited success.

To support the fieldwork, a chemical laboratory was set up in Haifa. After

much trial and error, the laboratory developed a system to extract the impurities from the Negev's low-grade uranium. Once this was accomplished, there was still the problem of producing weapons-grade uranium, which is to say uranium high in the isotope U-235. The United States had solved this problem with the gigantic gaseous diffusion plant in Oak Ridge, which successfully but expensively extracted U-235 from ordinary U-238. The capital cost of such a plant, plus its tremendous energy demands, were far beyond the means of Israel.

Instead, Israel's scientists turned to a system that had proved inadequate in the United States. In 1941 Dr. Jesse Beams had proposed a relatively economical method of separating U-235 from U-238 by using an ultracentrifuge. Beams, a slight, amiable physicist, was a world-renowned authority on the ultracentrifuge and his laboratory at the University of Virginia was a mecca for scientists working in this field. The centrifuge, whirling at fantastic speed, would separate the heavier atoms of uranium from their lighter atomic cousins. During World War II, the centrifuge method was found to be technically unfeasible for the Manhattan Project, which finally settled on the gaseous diffusion system.

In 1951 the Israelis overcame some of the weaknesses in Beam's centrifuge system and were thus able to use this process to produce weapons-grade uranium. This amounted to a major technical breakthrough. The other country that matched Israel's achievements with the ultracentrifuge was West Germany. In 1961 German scientists designed a machine of the same capability as the Israelis, but the design and details were kept secret at the request of the United States government. Since then, the Israelis have obtained patents on an even less costly technique, and it is now possible for even developing nations to produce the bomb—provided they have the raw material.

Getting the raw material was the other urgent problem faced by Israel. The cost of extracting uranium from potash was prohibitive. The government leaders decided it would be essential to obtain uranium oxide, or "yellow cake," from beyond Israel's borders.

This required covert—but not necessarily illegal—action. Many suppliers were willing to exchange uranium for Israeli nuclear technology or even cash. The only restriction on this type of barter was that it was not to be publicized. A few friendly intelligence agencies knew what was going on, but they held their counsel. Sympathetic governments turned a blind eye while their suppliers clandestinely exported uranium to Israel. In case of disclosure the "guilty" government's Foreign Office could plead ignorance or suggest that the embargoed cargo must have been stolen by the crafty agents of the Mossad.

Fortunately for Israel, Blumenfeld had maintained close personal and scientific contacts in the European community. His prestige as founder and director of the Société des Terres Rares served him well here. Many of his former colleagues were keenly interested in Israel's outstanding successes in potash exploitation. They also noted that this small country was one of the new producers and exporters of heavy water, used in some types of nuclear reactors.

Israel's effective work in these two fields was apparent to Blumenfeld's colleagues in France and Belgium. In France, Blumenfeld's scientific ties laid a foundation for the fruitful cooperation that led to the construction of an "experimental" nuclear reactor in the Negev, at the biblical site of Dimona, south of Beersheba. It was a joint French-Israeli project.

It is possible that Israel's first source of overseas uranium arrived from the Belgian Congo (now Zaire). It is a fact that in 1951 Blumenfeld received a delegation from the Belgian Congo Société Générale des Minérals. The society's experts offered to cooperate with Israel in exploiting the resources of the Negev (presumably in their own interest as well as Israel's). The arrangements may have resulted in the Belgians selling Israel uranium oxide, which they had in abundance in the Congo.

In the meantime, Chaim Weizmann, Israel's first president, was working with Blumenfeld in other projects to lay a nuclear groundwork. In 1948, Weizmann dispatched six of his country's most promising scientists to study nuclear physics in Britain, the United States, Switzerland, the Netherlands, and, most important, France. These young physicists soon acquired both the specifics of nuclear technology and an overview of its state in the Western world. This knowledge was to become a valuable asset, especially when combined with Israel's home-grown technical prowess.

France was the country most willing to cooperate. The French opened their secret nuclear laboratories to the Jewish scientists and even permitted them to witness French nuclear bomb tests. Much of this intimacy stemmed from the earlier contacts made by the French-speaking Blumenfeld.

To a large extent, after this period, Blumenfeld's accomplishments are clouded over by other events. There may be an obvious reason for this. It seems probable that he was drawn into the realm of more secret intelligence work in nuclear development. He confided to Guriel in 1952, "I began to take an interest in the operations of the established intelligence agencies. I read Somerset Maugham's thrilling novels of Ashenden's war exploits in Switzerland. Some of my business and scientific co-workers, I discovered, were French intelligence operators. They and other foreign agents formed invisible threads, trapping knowledge in their web for their government to digest.

"If war is an extension of diplomacy by other means, intelligence and covert acts can function as an intermediary step between the two and thus preserve the peace.

"Lawrence of Arabia insured British dominance of the Middle East by leading Arabs in their fight against the Turks for independence. Livingstone of Africa played a similar role in black Africa for the crown. Both appear as intelligence operators of the highest renown.

"I asked myself, why should not a scientist, especially one in the field of applied science, be active in the world of intelligence?

"Boris, you already know my answer to this question. Before 1948 I gathered information for the endangered Jews of Western Europe and since then for the State of Israel.

"You were of great help to me, and your experience in intelligence some-

what balanced my ignorance. I must say that your intelligence outfit was very helpful in finding ways to a certain Israeli-French [nuclear] entente."

Guriel's transcript of his conversations with Blumenfeld ends there, but in 1979 the former intelligence chief told the authors, "If Israel has joined the other countries in the possession of a nuclear capability, it was Blumenfeld who actually furnished the skills and tools to introduce Israel into the atomic age."

By the early 1950s Israel was reviewing its nuclear options. The basic question was whether to develop the uranium bomb, the plutonium version, or both. The uranium bomb, made with fissionable U-235, was the simpler of the two. The odds were overwhelming that it would work without testing, as the United States had shown when it dropped the bomb on Hiroshima on August 6, 1945. A plutonium bomb was the type tested in the world's first nuclear explosion over Alamogordo, New Mexico, on July 16, 1945, and dropped over Nagasaki on August 9.

Fissionable uranium (U-235) is an isotope that constitutes only 0.7 percent of natural uranium. The United States extracted the U-235 with its multibillion-dollar gaseous diffusion system, a process far too vast and costly for Israel. But the centrifuge developed by Israel reduced the cost to a small fraction of the American investment.

Plutonium is a man-made element; it does not exist in nature. It is a by-product of the controlled uranium fission that takes place in a nuclear generating plant. This controlled reaction, however, requires a mixture of natural uranium with its fissionable isotope, U-235, although the U-235 is not required in the amounts needed for a nuclear bomb.

The available evidence indicates that Israel decided to pursue the path of plutonium fission. This was in large part the result of a cooperative arrangement with France.

Plutonium is obtained by extracting it from the fuel rods of a nuclear reactor, and through 1956, Israel possessed no such reactor. The Sinai campaign, however, strengthened the bonds of friendship between Israel and France. Their nuclear cooperation, which had begun in 1953, was accelerated for several years after 1956, and each contributed to the other's technology.

In total secrecy, Paris and Jerusalem agreed in 1957 that Israel would build an experimental twenty-four-megawatt reactor at Dimona. The reactor, according to an account in *The Plumbat Affair*, was modeled after France's El-3 reactor at Brest, on the tip of Brittany. France supplied most of the equipment for the Israeli reactor. It was shipped through a bogus company set up by the French Commissariat à l'Énergie Atomique. The crates were labeled "textile machinery." Paris also agreed to furnish a start-up supply of uranium fuel.

The Dimona reactor used locally produced heavy water as a moderator. The design was similar to the Canadian "Candu" reactor, which India later used to produce plutonium. India separated the man-made element, plutoni-

um, from the fuel rods through a chemical process. This plutonium was used to explode India's first nuclear device.

In a small country it is hard to keep a secret. Ben-Gurion was continually asked what was going on at Dimona, and his answer always was that "it is a textile factory." This answer did not fool many Israelis. The tight security around the area was in itself indicative that something other than a textile factory was in operation. And yet the Israeli populace and the press did not force the issue. The struggle to survive has taught the citizens of the Jewish state that for their own sake some things should not be discussed.

There were, however, crosscurrents of opinion within Israel itself. The Israeli Atomic Energy Commission was distressed by the decision to build the Dimona reactor. The commission's name is somewhat of a misnomer because its responsibility was limited strictly to atoms for nonmilitary purposes. It was involved with the Atoms for Peace program that had been initiated in 1955 by President Eisenhower. Under this program the United States had presented Israel and several other countries with small research reactors. The American-built reactor was installed in Israel at Nahal Sorek. It operated, and still does, under agreed safeguards and is too small to produce militarily significant amounts of plutonium. It remains under control of the International Atomic Energy Commission. Among the reactor's accomplishments are the creation of radioactive trace elements for use in diagnostic medicine.

When plans to build the large Dimona reactor were announced to the commission, it was faced with a moral dilemma. It believed the Middle East should be kept free of nuclear weapons. If Israel developed a nuclear bomb, it could be a provocation for the Arabs to do the same. If Israel abstained from military nuclear development, the Arabs would abstain—or would they?

The upshot was that, except for the chairman, all the members of the commission resigned in protest. The chairman, Dr. Ernst Bergmann, was perhaps more aware of what had been going on in secret nuclear development in Israel and hence was not so surprised by the decision to build the Dimona reactor. He was an internationally known organic chemist who had fled Germany and settled in the United States. After the formation of the Jewish state in 1948, he had been persuaded by his old friend and fellow chemist, Chaim Weizmann, to live and work in Israel.

Probably Bergmann knew of Blumenfeld's earlier work on uranium enrichment. Covert uranium research is believed to have continued after independence, under the direction of the army. Apparently Bergmann alone among the members of the Israeli Atomic Energy Commission was aware of this.

When the authors interviewed Bergmann in his Jerusalem apartment during the Yom Kippur War in 1973, he had just returned from West Germany. Although he has never confirmed it and the government has kept such matters secret, it is probable that Bergmann played a role in the exchange of nuclear technology with West Germany, which began in the late 1950s. At about that time, according to Barbara Rogers and Zdenek Cervenka in *The Nuclear Axis*, Bonn "sponsored research projects and fi-

nanced installations like the 6-million-volt Tandem-Van de Graaf accelerator which enabled Israel to set up a department of experimental nuclear physics at the Weizmann Institute in Rehovot."

Another area of cooperation may have been the gaseous centrifuge for uranium enrichment. Germany had been working on this even before World War II. Professor Hans Martin's Nazi-sponsored work at Kiel University was given top priority. After the war the German work surfaced again through the experiments of Professor W. Groth, under the sponsorship of the Emergency Association for German Science.

There was a certain amount of hypocrisy, even subterfuge, in the way the research was carried out. According to Rogers and Cervenka, it was sponsored by industrial firms that were descendants of some of the industries that had underwritten Hitler. Moreover, the research was ostensibly unlawful under the American occupation, but secretly it was carried out with the approval and even the active cooperation of the American occupation authorities.

There is documentary evidence that as early as 1953 Germany had refined the ultracentrifuge for the purpose of uranium-isotope separation. And apparently the United States, while cooperating in some German nuclear research, tried to prevent Germany from exporting its expertise. Rogers and Cervenka quote the German magazine *Der Spiegel* of January 31, 1977, to the effect that Germany tried to sell ultracentrifuges to Brazil for $80 million in 1953. The United States, then the occupying power, blocked the deal. But on the evidence, it seems clear that the Germans had made the ultracentrifuge a practical device.

There is room for speculation that Israel, at this time, was contributing to West German technology. The vast contribution that Germany made in money and information to Israel would suggest that Israel had something to offer in return, possibly some details on its own breakthrough with the ultracentrifuge.

The cooperation with West Germany became more important to Israel when, by 1960, de Gaulle began to have second thoughts about France's involvement with the Jewish state. Specifically he was concerned about his nation's financing and supplying the Dimona reactor. The French role had been kept secret, but inevitably, the press was beginning to ask questions.

In late 1960 de Gaulle decided to attempt a clean break with Israel. He informed Ben-Gurion that France would no longer supply equipment, funds, or technical personnel to complete the Dimona reactor. Ben-Gurion was so distressed that he took the next plane to Paris to make a personal appeal to de Gaulle. The president of France must have been impressed, because he backed down slightly. Equipment already on order would be delivered, but there would be no more funds or official help.

This slight concession by de Gaulle still left Israel in great difficulty. There was a shortage of domestic funds for the reactor. Ben-Gurion told his finance minister, Levi Eshkol, to find the money somehow. Eshkol responded that it simply was not available. Eventually the reactor was completed but through a large infusion of private funds to supplement the public contribution.

In the waning days of the Eisenhower administration, the president was apparently unhappy over the implications of the Dimona project. On December 9, Secretary of State Christian Herter called on the Israeli ambassador to, in effect, ask what was up at Dimona. Ambassador Avraham Harmon said he would seek full information from his government.

In response, Prime Minister Ben-Gurion gave Herter "categoric assurances" that Israel had no plans to develop nuclear weapons. "The French have also assured us," Ben-Gurion said, "that their assistance is premised on Israel's atomic energy program being solely for peaceful purposes."

These assurances did not satisfy Eisenhower. On January 3, 1961, the Americans served notice that they wanted Israel to declare by midnight that Dimona would be dismantled. The American demand amounted to an ultimatum, and Ben-Gurion would have no part of it. He told the American ambassador he would not comply. The impasse was broken when the Eisenhower administration was succeeded by that of the newly elected John F. Kennedy on January 20. In May, Ben-Gurion went to Washington, where he had a friendly meeting with Kennedy. A system under which American scientists could inspect the Dimona reactor was agreed upon.

Despite the agreement, however, Ben-Gurion seemed to resent the pressure on Israel from the United States. He told the Knesset that the reactor would be open to trainees from other countries. He pointed out that Israel's reactor would be similar to the one that the Canadian government was helping to construct in India—without harassment from any other country.

Senator J. William Fulbright wanted to know when inspections would start. On May 22, 1961, he wrote to acting Secretary of State Chester Bowles, pressing him on the point. On June 5, Bowles responded that according to Ben-Gurion, "Israel is concentrating on the development of cheap atomic power, particularly for use in the desalinization of sea water. The Prime Minister also indicated that visits by impartial scientists to the Israeli reactor might be arranged in the future."

The fact is that the agreement on inspection was made immediately prior to the change from the Eisenhower to the Kennedy administration and the new president did not follow up on his predecessor's demand.

The reactor was completed in 1964, at which point a new decision was forced on the Israeli government and, in effect, was solved by a unilateral decision by Defense Minister Moshe Dayan in 1967. The issue was whether to build a plant to separate the plutonium from the spent uranium fuel in the reactor.

Prior to Ben-Gurion's resignation in June 1963, the prime minister and his deputy minister of defense, Shimon Peres, were in favor of building the separation plant. Other leading members of the cabinet were opposed, including Golda Meir, Yigal Allon, and Ben-Gurion's designated successor, Levi Eshkol. The covert debate continued until, as *Time* magazine reported later (April 12, 1976), "The Israeli equivalent of the U.S. National Security Council vetoed the separation plant in early 1968."

The veto, however, was meaningless because Dayan had taken matters into his own hands. He had, according to *Time*, "in the wake of the Six-Day War secretly ordered the start of construction on a separation plant.

. . . Eshkol and his advisors felt they could only rubber stamp a project already under way."

The cost of Israel's separation plant and the source of the money to build it are not known. India, however, built a separation plant without outside assistance for an estimated 7.5 million, according to *Midstream* (November 1976).

All of these developments provide abundant circumstantial evidence for the existence of Israeli nuclear weapons, but the statement of Moshe Dayan seems to limit the reasons even for doubt. Without claiming or acknowledging that the nuclear option exists, Dayan said, according to the *Jerusalem Post* international edition of December 7, 1976, "The option is no secret and I don't think things should be covered up." He disagreed with the defense establishment leaders who want to buy additional thousands and thousands of tanks. "The official figures show that Israel today has thousands of tanks. England has only 1,000 and so does France. The idea that Israel has to have 10,000 tanks is destructive." He argued further that the financial burden and the difficulty of manning such a massive force of armor was beyond the capability of a small state.

Israel's possession of the bomb, however, could serve as a deterrent to Arab aggression, Dayan reasoned. "Should the Arabs decide one day to throw against us the thousands of tanks and missiles they are accumulating, we'll be able to tell them, 'We can destroy you, too.' "

In all probability, Dayan's warning described an existing condition. As early as October 1973 American intelligence concluded that Israel possessed nuclear weapons, although this apparently was not reported publicly until four years later by Russell Warren Howe, writing in the *Baltimore Sun* of October 30, 1977. Howe wrote that a 1973 overflight of an American S-51 Blackbird carrying infrared cameras and sensors revealed that Israel was installing nuclear warheads on her home-produced Jericho missiles. The Jericho has a range of two-hundred to three-hundred miles, which means it can strike Baghdad, Damascus, or Cairo.

Also in 1977, the *Jerusalem Post* reported that a CIA statement that was somewhat more circumstantial had been made public. It was a document actually written shortly after the May 1974 detonation of a nuclear device in India. It is a matter of conjecture whether the report was released "by mistake," as the CIA claimed, or was leaked purposely.

"We believe," the statement said, "that Israel already has produced nuclear weapons. Our judgment is based on Israeli acquisition of large quantities of uranium, partly by clandestine means; the ambiguous nature of Israeli efforts in the field of uranium enrichment; and Israel's large investment in a costly missile system designed to accommodate nuclear warheads.

"We do not expect the Israelis to provide confirmation of wide-spread suspicions of their capability either by nuclear testing or by threat of use, short of a grave threat to the nation's existence."

The CIA was correct in its expectations. Israel denied the report in toto. There was a bit of obfuscation, however, by Aviezer Pazner at a press conference in the Israeli embassy in Washington. "There is no proof whatsoev-

er," he said. "I can only report to you that Israel will not be the first country in the Middle East to introduce nuclear arms into the region."

Another CIA assessment released "by mistake" was based on a 1976 statement. Carl Duckett, a high CIA official, speaking off the record to a group of aerospace officials, told them Israel had "ten to twenty" nuclear bombs. When CIA Director George Bush was confronted with the Duckett statement, he apologized for it and said it should not have been made, but he did not deny its accuracy. Shortly afterward Duckett retired from the CIA for "reasons of health."

Because it is assumed—for good reason—that Israel possesses nuclear weapons, there has been fascinating speculation on how such a small country acquired the necessary quantity of enriched uranium. It was needed in large amounts for the Dimona reactor, to make plutonium, or for use in a uranium bomb.

That Israel was somehow cornering nuclear material was first discovered in 1965, according to Howard Kohn and Barbara Newman in an article entitled "How Israel Got the Nuclear Bomb," published in *Rolling Stone* on December 1, 1977. According to the authors, a special branch of Mossad was entrusted with the task of acquiring uranium from foreign sources and transporting it to a military base in the Negev.

This seems like a large order, and it was. Yet, according to Kohn and Newman, from 1955 to 1965 Mossad managed to spirit away somewhere between two-hundred and four-hundred pounds of enriched uranium. (Approximately twenty-two pounds are needed to make a small nuclear weapon.)

The uranium was not acquired in some exotic corner of the world, but from a nuclear plant in Apollo, Pennsylvania, just thirty miles northeast of Pittsburgh, according to the *Rolling Stone* article. The acquisition circumstantially points a finger at the president of the Apollo plant, Zalman Shapiro, a frequent visitor to Israel and a man with close connections to the Israeli Ministry of Defense.

During a routine inspection of the plant in 1965, Atomic Energy Commission (AEC) officials found that a substantial amount of enriched uranium was missing. On the basis of the first inventory discrepancy, the AEC probably had little reason to be alarmed. Other plants had "lost" uranium, which in fact had been accidentally buried with nuclear waste. But apparently Shapiro's Israeli connections aroused more than the usual concern at the AEC over the nuclear inventory shortage. Was he covertly exporting it to the Jewish state?

A further check revealed the shortage to be a considerable 194 pounds, far larger than any discrepancy discovered in other facilities up to that time.

The AEC was now highly suspicious. Inspectors were sent back to the plant on October 31. This time the shortage was a disturbing 382 pounds. The mystery deepened when it was learned that in 1964 a suspicious fire in the plant's office had destroyed scores of documents.

The situation obviously called for a full-scale investigation. The Congressional Joint Committee on Atomic Energy met on February 14, 1966, in a

closed session with representatives of the AEC. The upshot was an official request to the Justice Department to initiate an investigation to determine whether the missing uranium had been stolen. Nine days later the Justice Department responded in a letter to the committee with the rather surprising conclusion that "no thievery" had taken place.

But the CIA was not satisfied with this judgment. The intelligence agency was convinced that there had been thievery and that Shapiro was abetting an Israeli smuggling ring. CIA Director Richard Helms reported this to President Lyndon Johnson.

Amazingly, the president or someone in his administration apparently told Helms to quash the investigation. Further, Helms was told not to inform other federal agencies of the situation.

One fairly obvious conclusion that can be drawn from this seeming cover-up of nuclear theft is that, in fact, the CIA in the 1950s was actively assisting Israel to acquire nuclear materials and technology. This is the belief of Tad Szulc, a former *New York Times* reporter and an expert on the CIA. He believes this involvement with Israel necessitated President Johnson's aborting the investigation.

Surveillance of the situation was continued without ever bringing about a full-fledged investigation. It was still going on when Gerald Ford became president in 1974. In 1975 the FBI informed Ford that the missing uranium had been stolen. Ford directed Attorney General Edward Levi to press the issue; but Levi decided the available evidence was not admissible in court, and he declined to seek any indictments.

Probably no one will ever know the real reasons why the theft of uranium, if in fact there was such, was never prosecuted. The tangled web of international intrigue may have meant that an indictment would have been damaging, or at least embarrassing, to the United States.

There is, however, one particularly intriguing question. Did one man, Zalman Shapiro, working alone, pull off this international caper? Were there no American accomplices? The case against Shaprio himself remains unproved.

Also consigned to mystery is Shapiro's connection with the Mossad. The situation is not clarified by the disagreement between the Nuclear Regulatory Commission (successor to the regulatory branch of the AEC) and the CIA's 1966 conclusions. The commission claimed the CIA's assessments were based on "circumstantial evidence and much color."

There is less doubt about another incident on the road toward Israel's becoming a nuclear power. As a result of the Arab boycott of countries doing business with Israel after the 1967 war, many nations and firms that wished to trade with the Jewish state had to do so in secret or through carefully disguised front organizations. In 1968 the Mossad seemed to have hijacked an additional supply of uranium from the French. In fact, however, the operation was carried out with France's cooperation. The French were willing to surrender uranium in return for Israeli scientific secrets and a substantial amount of money.*

*This entire episode is well chronicled in *The Plumbat Affair*, by Davenport, Eddy, and Gillman.

Plans for this uranium "heist" were under way as early as 1967. Into it went all the originality and sound principles of espionage and intelligence that Mossad had acquired over the years. One of these was to seek out carefully individuals of potential use to the agency in future operations. In the case of the Mossad, the details of every contact, the situations, the character, the personality, the work, the sympathies of every person ever contacted by a Mossad agent were organized and stored in a computer. On the basis of computer retrieval, the Mossad discerned that a Belgian company, Société Générale de Belgique, had the largest stockpile of uranium in the world. The uranium had been mined in the Belgian Congo before the Belgians withdrew from their colony, which later became Zaire. The Belgian company was looking for uranium customers, but fearing the Arabs, it could not sell to Israel.

Belgium was a member of the European Economic Community (EEC). The responsibility for importing and controlling the movement of fissionable material within the community was delegated to an EEC agency, Euratom. Any request to ship uranium out of the European community was referred to the EEC's executive committee. The authority was, and is, wary of exercising its discretionary power. The Israeli government was fully aware that even so much as an inquiry on the possibility of buying uranium would stir up a storm. Covert action was therefore the better part of valor.

In Wiesbaden, West Germany, a small chemical company, Asmara Chemie, founded in 1952, had built up a substantial business in creams, soaps, and lotions for United States military bases and for industrial customers. Later the firm expanded into the manufacture of decontaminants—foams and creams to protect human skin against chemical and radioactive burns.

Sometime in 1967 Israel invited Herbert Schulzen, the head of Asmara, to visit the Jewish state. He was given the warmest Israeli hsopitality and taken on a tour of the Weizmann Institute. Shortly thereafter, Israel ordered three-hundred decontamination kits from Asmara. Relations between the Israelis and Schulzen were obviously very cozy.

In March 1968 Asmara placed an order with the Société Générale des Minérals in Brussels for two hundred tons of uranium oxide. The Belgian firm had two questions. First, were the funds—several million dollars—available? A bank in Zurich confirmed that more than enough was already on deposit there. How was the uranium oxide to be used? Schulzen's answer was that his firm was entering the field of petrochemicals and that the uranium was needed as a catalyst.

Then a legal hitch developed—or was contrived to develop. Schulzen wanted the uranium oxide to be treated by a plant in Morocco and then to be shipped back to his plant in Wiesbaden. That, at least, is what he told Denis Dewez, deputy chief of the uranium division of the Société. This raised a problem. Euratom would not approve the movement of uranium outside the EEC.

Enter an old friend of Schulzen, one Francesco Sertorio, the head of a Milan company that sold dyes for use in the textile industry. He had no knowledge of uranium processing, nor equipment to accomplish it. But he happened to be desperately in need of money, and Schulzen was ready with

that as well as with technical assistance. All Sertorio had to do was to agree to accept the uranium shipment to Milan. When he had done so, Dewez of the Société was able to get clearance from Euratom. The uranium oxide was to be transported by sea from Antwerp to Genoa.

A small freighter was chartered for the shipment. It was called the *Scheersberg A* and was acquired in Rotterdam through a newly formed corporation, Biscayne Traders. In fact, Biscayne Traders was a front for the Mossad.

On Sunday, November 17, 1968, the *Scheersberg A*, with two hundred tons of uranium oxide in its hold, sailed from Antwerp. It never arrived in Genoa. When it next appeared, it was in the Turkish port of İskenderun and its hold was empty.

Somewhere along the route, or so it seems, the cargo had been transferred on the open sea to another vessel. Eventually it apparently found its way to the Dimona reactor. The Mossad had done its job.

Israel became a nuclear power not through luck or a few spectacular capers, such as the *Scheersberg A* adventure, although luck and daring did play an important role. Essentially the success sprang from the seeds sown at the dawn of the nuclear age by men such as Joseph Blumenfeld and husbanded by indigenous scientists and technicians before and after the founding of the state.

Although questioning whether Israel is a nuclear power may seem a little coy in view of the accumulated information, the fact is that positive evidence is still lacking. No one has ever detected what would be the absolute proof—the test of a bomb by Israel.

What is less in doubt is the step-by-step movement toward nuclear capability on the part of Israel's enemies. The days of the Jewish state's partnership with Western Europe in nuclear ventures have faded away as the industrial nations become sycophants of the Arab oil powers. The capability is now being handed over to Arab nations by West Germany, France, and Italy.

The most culpable of these is France. As of 1980, the French government had gone a long way toward creating the Arab world's first nuclear power. A succession of deals with Iraq was initiated in 1975 by French Premier Jacques Chirac and President Saddam Hussein of Iraq. France agreed to provide Iraq with a seventy-megawatt reactor and seven pounds of uranium 93 percent enriched and to design and help staff a nuclear research and training center. In return, Iraq agreed to sell France 10 million tons of oil per year. Iraq would buy from France $1.6 billion worth of missiles, tanks, helicopters, and warplanes.

Later, Iraq negotiated a backup agreement with Brazil for uranium and nuclear technology, which the latter had acquired in an earlier arrangement with the West Germans—who were not consulted on the Iraq deal.

France's effort to deliver what it had promised to Iraq was hindered by repeated sabotage and terrorism. Within France itself there was bitter objection to what many French citizens considered a dangerous course. Israel was

furious, but there was also resentment in the rival factions that make up the arcanum of Middle East politics. In July 1978, Palestinian terrorists attacked the Iraqi embassy in Paris, killing a French policeman. In June 1980, a senior Iraqi scientist involved with the proposed Iraqi reactor was murdered in his Paris hotel.

But the most mysterious and amazing event was the destruction, on April 5, 1979, of the core of the Iraq-bound reactor in a warehouse near Toulon. This sabotage, which delayed the reactor delivery by at least a year, has generally been attributed to Israel, possibly with the help of antinuclear elements in France.

The persistence of violence and sabotage caused the French government to reconsider the pact with Iraq. Premier Raymond Barre in July 1979 asked the Iraqis to consider a downgraded version of the reactor that would use low-grade uranium rather than weapons-grade. But the Iraquis stood their ground, demanding from Barre a duplicate of the destroyed core for their Osiris-type reactor, with a cutoff of oil as the alternative. Once again, oil won. The original agreement would be honored. Meanwhile, Saddam Hussein negotiated an agreement with Italy for additional technical help. Italy imports a fifth of its oil from Iraq.

On July 14, 1980, Prime Minister Menachem Begin warned France that it was following a dangerous course. Deputy Prime Minister Yigael Yadin sounded a more ominous warning, to the effect that Israel would take measures against the French-Iraq agreement.

There is reason to believe that tiny Israel, faced with the possibility of being confronted by nuclear weapons in the hands of so volatile an enemy as Iraq, will do everything within its power to prevent such a catastrophe. The brilliant history of Israeli intelligence, plus Israel's proven ability at sabotage and lightning preemptive strikes, would indicate that this chapter is far from ended. The Jews, especially those in Israel, can look back as far as Moses for lessons in how to survive.

Bibliography

Acheson, Dean. *Present at the Creation: My Years at the State Department.* New York: Norton, 1969.

Allon, Yigal. *Shield of David: The Story of Israel's Armed Forces.* New York: Random House, 1970.

Alroy, Gil Carl. *Behind the Middle East Conflict: The Real Impasse Between Arab and Jew.* New York: Putnam, 1975.

Avriel, Ehud. *Open the Gates.* New York: Atheneum, 1975.

Barron, John. *KGB: The Secret Works of Soviet Secret Agents.* New York: Bantam, 1974.

Bar-Zohar, Michael. *Ben-Gurion, the Armed Prophet.* Englewood Cliffs, N.J.: Prentice-Hall, 1966.

_____. *Spies in the Promised Land: Iser Harel and the Israeli Secret Service.* Boston: Houghton Mifflin, 1972.

_____. *Ben-Gurion: A Biography.* New York: Delacorte, 1977.

Begin, Menachem. *The Revolt.* Jerusalem: Steimatzky's Agency, 1977.

Ben-Hanan, Elie. *Our Man in Damascus: Eli Cohn.* New York: Crown, 1969.

Ben-Meir, Alon. *Israel: The Challenge of the Fourth Decade.* New York: Cyrco Press, 1978.

Ben-Porat, Yeshayahu. *Kippur.* Tel Aviv: Special Edition Publ., 1973.

Brecher, Michael. *The Foreign Policy System of Israel—Settings, Images, Process.* New Haven: Yale University Press, 1972.

Caroz, Yaacov. *The Arab Secret Services.* London: Corgi Books, 1978.

Christman, Henry M., *The State Papers of Levi Eshkol.* New York: Funk and Wagnalls, 1969.

Cline, Ray S. *Secrets, Spies and Scholars: Blueprint of the Essential CIA.* Washington, D.C.: Acropolis Books, 1976.

Collins, Larry, and Lapierre, Dominique. *O Jerusalem!* New York: Simon and Schuster, 1972.

Cooper, Chester L. *The Lion's Last Roar: Suez, 1956.* New York: Harper and Row, 1978.

Corti, Egon Caesar. *The Rise of the House of Rothschild.* Trans. by Brian Lunn and Beatrix Lunn. New York: Blue Ribbon Books, 1928.

Dan, Ben. *The Spy from Israel.* London: Vallentine, Mitchell, 1969.

Dan, Uri. *Sharon's Bridgehead.* Israel: E.L. Special Edition, 1975.

Davenport, Elaine; Eddy, Paul; and Gillman, Peter. *The Plumbat Affair.* Philadelphia: Lippincott, 1978.

Dayan, Moshe. *The Sinai Campaign.* New York: Schocken Books, 1967.

_____. *Moshe Dayan: The Story of My Life.* New York: Morrow, 1976.

Derogy, Jacques, and Carmel, Hesi. *The Untold History of Israel.* New York: Grove Press, 1979.

Dimont, Max I. *Jews, God, and History.* New York: New American Library, 1962.

Donovan, Robert J. *Conflict and Crisis: The Presidency of Harry S. Truman, 1945-1948.* New York: Norton, 1977.

Depuy, Trevor. *Elusive Victory: The Arab-Israeli Wars, 1947-1974.* New York: Harper and Row, 1978.

Eban, Abba. *Voice of Israel.* New York: Horizon Press, 1957.

_____. *Abba Eban: An Autobiography.* New York: Random House, 1977.

Eisenberg, Dennis; Dan, Uri; and Landau, Eli. *The Mossad.* New York: Paddington Press, 1978.

Eisenhower, Milton. *The President Is Calling.* Garden City, N.Y.: Doubleday, 1974.

El-Ad, Avri. *Decline of Honor.* Chicago: Regnery, 1976.

Eliav, Arie L. *The Voyage of the Ulua.* New York: Funk and Wagnalls, 1969.

Engle, Anita. *The Nili Spies.* London: Hogarth Press, 1959.

Fein, Leonard J. *Israel, Politics and People.* Boston: Little, Brown, 1967.

Foreign Relations of the United States, 1950. Volume II: *The United Nations: The Western Hemisphere.* Washington, D.C.: U.S. Printing Office, 1976.

Foreign Relations of the United States, 1948 Volume V: *The Near East, South Asia, and Africa.* Washington D.C.: U.S. Government Printing Office, 1976.

Frank, Gerold. *The Deed.* New York: Berkley, 1963.

Freedman, Robert O. *Soviet Policy Toward the Middle East Since 1970.* New York: Praeger, 1975.

Freulich, Roman. *Soldiers in Judea: Stories and Vignettes of the Jewish Legion.* New York: Herzl Press, 1964.

Gervasi, Frank. *The Case for Israel.* New York: Viking Press, 1967.

_____. *Thunder over the Mediterranean.* New York: David McKay, 1975.

_____. *The Life and Times of Menachem Begin: Rebel to Statesman.* New York: Putnam, 1979.

Golan, Aviezer. *Operation Susannah.* New York: Harper and Row, 1978.

Golan, Matti. *The Secret Conversations of Henry Kissinger.* New York: Quadrangle, 1976.

Goldberg, Hirsh M. *The Jewish Connection.* New York: Stein and Day, 1976.

Gur, Shlomo. *The Jordan Rift Valley: A Challenge for Development.* Tel Aviv: University Press, 1970.

Harel, Isser. *The House on Garibaldi Street.* New York: Bantam, 1975.

Harkabi, Y. *Palestinians and Israel.* Jerusalem: Keter, 1974.

Herzog, Chaim. *The War of Atonement: October 1973.* Boston: Little, Brown, 1975.

Joseph, Dov. *The Faithful City: The Siege of Jerusalem.* New York: Simon and Schuster, 1960.

Kagan, Benjamin. *The Secret Battle for Israel.* Cleveland: World, 1966.

Kalb, Marvin, and Kalb, Bernard. *Kissinger.* Boston: Little, Brown, 1974.

Katz, Samuel. *Days of Fire.* Garden City, N.Y.: Doubleday, 1968.

Kimche, David, and Bawly, Dan. *The Six-Day War: Prologue and Aftermath.* New York: Stein and Day, 1968.

Kimche, Jon. *There Could Have Been Peace.* New York: Dial Press, 1973.

Klüger, Ruth, and Mann, Peggy. *The Last Escape.* New York: Pinnacle, 1973.

Kurzman, Dan. *Genesis 1948: The First Arab-Israeli War.* New York: New American Library, 1970.

_____. *The Bravest Battle: The Twenty-eight Days of the Warsaw Ghetto Uprising.* New York: Putnam, 1976.

Laqueur, Walter, ed. *The Israeli-Arab Reader: A Documentary History of the Middle East Conflict.* New York: Citadel Press, 1969.

Larteguy, Jean. *The Walls of Israel.* New York: Evans, 1968.

Lotz, Wolfgang. *The Champagne Spy.* New York: St. Martin's Press, 1972.

Lucas, Noah. *The Modern History of Israel.* New York: Praeger, 1975.

McDonald, James G. *My Mission in Israel, 1948–1951.* New York: Simon and Schuster, 1951.

Meir, Golda. *My Life.* New York: Putnam, 1975.

Meridor, Yaacov. *Long Is the Road to Freedom.* Tujunga, Calif.: Barak, 1961.

Miller, Merle. *Plain Speaking: An Oral Biography of Harry S. Truman.* New York: Berkley, 1974.

Mosley, Leonard. *Dulles: A Biography of Eleanor, Allen and John Foster Dulles and Their Family Network.* New York: Dial Press/James Wade, 1978.

Ofry, Dan. *The Yom Kippur War.* Tel Aviv: Zohar, 1974.

Parmet, Herbert S. *Eisenhower and the American Crusades.* New York: Macmillan, 1972.

Patterson, J. H. *With the Judeans in the Palestine Campaign.* New York: Macmillan, 1922.

Peres, Shimon. *David's Sling.* London: Weidenfeld and Nicolson, 1970.

Prittie, Terence. *Eshkol: The Man and the Nation.* New York: Pitman, 1969.

Rabin, Yitzhak. *The Rabin Memoirs.* Boston: Little, Brown, 1979.

Rogers, Barbara, and Cervenka, Zdenek. *The Nuclear Axis.* New York: Times Books, 1978.

Rosenfeld, Alvin. *The Plot to Destroy Israel.* New York: Putnam, 1977.

Roth, Cecil. *History of the Jews.* New York: Schocken, 1961.

Sachar, Howard Morley. *The Course of Modern Jewish History.* New York: Delta, 1977.

_____. *A History of Israel from the Rise of Zionism to Our Time.* New York: Knopf, 1979.

Schechtman, Joseph B. *The United States and the Jewish State Movement, The Crucial Decade: 1939–1949.* New York: Herzl Press Thomas Yoseloff, 1966.

Schiff, Zeev. *A History of the Israeli Army (1870–1974).* Trans. and ed. by Raphael Rothstein. San Francisco: Straight Arrow, 1974.

Sherman, Arnold. *Lightning in the Skies.* London: Stone, 1973.

Shirer, William L. *The Rise and Fall of the Third Reich.* Greenwich, Conn.: Fawcett, 1959.

Slater, Leonard. *The Pledge.* New York: Simon and Schuster, 1970.

Smith, Colin. *Carlos: Portrait of a Terrorist.* New York: Holt, Rinehart and Winston, 1976.

Stevenson, William. *90 Minutes at Entebbe.* With material from Uri Dan. New York: Bantam, 1976.

Tadmor, Joshua. *The Silent Warriors.* Trans. by Raphael Rothstein. Toronto: Macmillan, 1969.

Tekoah, Yosef. *In the Face of the Nations: Israel's Struggle for Peace.* New York: Simon and Schuster, 1976.

Tinnin, David B., with Dag Christensen. *The Hit Team.* Boston: Little, Brown, 1976.

Tully, Andrew. *CIA, the Inside Story.* Greenwich, Conn.: Fawcett, 1962.

Weizman, Ezer. *On Eagles' Wings.* New York: Macmillian, 1976.

Index

304